Chicago Top 40 Charts
1960-1969

Chicago Top 40 Charts
1960-1969

Compiled by Ron Smith

Writers Club Press
San Jose New York Lincoln Shanghai

Chicago Top 40 Charts 1960-1969

All Rights Reserved © 2001 by Ronald P. Smith

No part of this book may be reproduced or transmitted in any form or by any means, graphic, electronic, or mechanical, including photocopying, recording, taping, or by any information storage retrieval system, without the permission in writing from the publisher.

Writers Club Press
an imprint of iUniverse.com, Inc.

For information address:
iUniverse.com, Inc.
5220 S 16th, Ste. 200
Lincoln, NE 68512
www.iuniverse.com

ISBN: 0-595-19614-4

Printed in the United States of America

Dedication

To my cousin, Michael Hoffman, who has probably forgotten more about music and charts than I'll ever know. Mike, I'm glad you danced.

Contents

Dedication v
Acknowledgements ix
Introduction xi
Methodology 1
Alphabetical Listing By Artist 3
Alphabetical Listing By Title 130
Yearly Top 40 Charts 227
Top 40 Songs of the 60s 246
1964 Rhythm and Blues Charts 248
About the Author 251

ACKNOWLEDGEMENTS

Thank you to those who inspired or helped in compiling this book: Dick Biondi, John Charleson, Dave Douglas, Tommy Edwards, Scott Fischer, Bill Ganson, Barbara Jastrab, Randy Lane, Jack Miller, Lorna Ozmon, Art Roberts, Kurt Scholle, Jim Smith, Bill Stedman and especially to J.R. Dykema who was my sounding board and error-catcher. A special thanks to the person who inspires every book of this type, Joel Whitburn.

INTRODUCTION

We Americans love to rank things. Whether it's the top television programs or movies at the box office, we have a burning desire to know when something is "number one."

Music is no exception. Music charts have been around as long as recorded music and radio programs from *Your Hit Parade* to *American Top 40* have capitalized on the idea of counting down the day's top hits.

It is said that the first printed radio survey of the current top tunes was the WIND Top 21 in Chicago. Whether that's true is irrelevant. Because of it, Chicagoans got into the habit of picking up a list of the latest hits at their local record stores. Later, station WJJD produced a survey. And when ABC bought WLS, "The Prairie Farmer Station" in 1960 and switched it to the fledgling "top 40" format, it soon followed with the "Silver Dollar Survey" of Chicago's top 40 tunes.

For over 30 years, WLS (and its FM successor, WYTZ) kept the surveys going each week. And with its 50,000 watt clear channel signal and enormous respect in the industry, to be listed on WLS' survey was perhaps more of an honor than to appear on the national *Billboard* Hot 100.

Chicago Top 40 Charts 1960-1969 is the first volume in a series that documents those songs that dominated the Midwestern airwaves during that decade— considered by many to be top 40's "golden age." Many of the songs listed did not appear at all on the national charts. Others, including local acts, fared much better in Chicago than in the rest of the country. It's fascinating to see the evolution of rock music unfold through those thin paper listings given away at local record shops. Most of those shops are gone now, replaced by giant chains. And even WLS has become a talk radio station (though just as successful). But the fascination with that music continues.

Chicago Top 40 Charts 1960-1969 contains an alphabetical listing by title and by artist of every tune listed on the WLS Silver Dollar Surveys during those years. It also lists the top 40 songs of each year and for the entire decade, as well as a supplemental listing of songs on the station's Rhythm-and-Blues chart of 1964.

Will there be a second volume of this book, covering the 1970s? I'm working on compiling the data now and the success of this book should ensure its release.

METHODOLOGY

This book is a compilation of the Silver Dollar Surveys published by WLS Radio in Chicago from its beginning on October 14, 1960 until the final survey of the decade on December 29, 1969.

The methodology is rather straightforward— **Debut** is the date the song first appears on the charts. **Peak** is the date it first reaches its highest position. **Pos** is the highest position reached on the charts and **Wks** is the number of weeks it appears on the charts.

It is in **Wks** that some problems arise. On some occasions, special charts took the place of part or all of the normal 40 positions on the Silver Dollar Survey. Songs that appeared on the charts before and after the special survey are given credit for the missing week. Songs debuting after the special survey are not credited for the previous week, even when their debut position is rather high. Songs that drop off the chart after a special survey are not credited for the missing week. During any missing weeks, all other songs not appearing are considered "frozen" at their previous position.

At times, "two-sided hits" appeared on the charts. Both the "A" and "B" sides of a record would be listed. Any time both sides were listed, the "B" side also received credit for the position reached and that week on the chart. However, often the "B" side was only listed during part of the record's run on the chart. Only the weeks a "B" side was actually listed is credited. Therefore, while the Beatles' "I Don't Want To Spoil The Party" receives the same chart credit as its "A" side, "Eight Days A Week", because both songs were listed every week; "The Inner Light" receives credit for six less weeks and one lower position than its "A" side, "Lady Madonna", because it was only listed one-third of the time. In the artist listing, "B" sides are preceded by a slash and listed under their "A" sides.

Artists often recorded under different variations of their names. Name variations are indented under the original artist name. Totally different groups or names are listed separately, with a notation to "also see" the other artist.

Finally, the effective dates of the charts changed frequently (for example, the second survey is dated October 15, 1960, indicating a switch from "Week Ending" to "Week Of". Later this change is reversed).

ALPHABETICAL LISTING BY ARTIST

Artist / Title	Debut	Peak	Pos	Wks
Accents				
New Girl	7/17/64	8/14/64	28	5
Acklin, Barbara				
Love Makes A Woman	8/12/68	9/9/68	19	5
Ad Libs				
The Boy From New York City	1/15/65	2/5/65	14	7
Adams, Johnny				
Reconsider Me	6/30/69	8/4/69	21	7
Adams, Ray				
Violetta	5/26/62	6/16/62	6	6
Adderley, Cannonball				
Mercy, Mercy, Mercy	2/10/67	2/24/67	25	4
Adderly, Tommy				
I Just Don't Understand	9/25/64	10/2/64	21	4
Akens, Jewel				
The Birds And The Bees	1/29/65	3/12/65	7	10
Alaimo, Steve				
I'm Thankful	9/9/61	9/16/61	36	2
Michael—Pt. 1	9/6/63	9/13/63	33	2
Blowin' In The Wind	9/10/65	9/17/65	36	2
Albert, Eddie				
Fall Away	12/11/64	1/1/65	10	5
Alberts, Al				
Heaven Needed An Angel	6/17/61	6/24/61	33	2

Artist / Title	Debut	Peak	Pos	Wks
Alexander, Arthur				
You Better Move On	3/17/62	4/7/62	21	4
Alice Wonder Land				
He's Mine (I Love Him, I Love Him, I Love Him)	9/27/63	10/4/63	22	3
Allan, Davie & the Arrows				
Apache '65	2/26/65	2/26/65	37	2
Blue's Theme	7/7/67	8/11/67	4	7
Allen, Rex				
Don't Go Near The Indians	10/13/62	10/27/62	27	3
Allen, Richie				
Stranger From Durango	10/15/60	11/5/60	14	6
Alley Cats				
Puddin N' Tain (Ask Me Again, I'll Tell You The Same)	1/4/63	2/1/63	13	5
Allisons				
Surfer Street	10/25/63	11/8/63	32	3
Alpert, Herb & the Tijuana Brass				
The Lonely Bull	10/27/62	12/8/62	5	10
The Mexican Shuffle	8/7/64	8/14/64	15	4
Taste Of Honey	10/29/65	12/3/65	3	11
Zorba The Greek	1/7/66	1/28/66	10	5
What Now My Love	3/11/66	3/11/66	35	2
The Work Song	6/24/66	7/1/66	31	2
Flamingo	9/9/66	9/30/66	33	5
Mame	11/18/66	11/25/66	20	5
Mexican Road Race	3/24/67	3/31/67	39	3
Casino Royale	5/5/67	6/2/67	15	6
The Happening	7/14/67	7/28/67	33	3
A Banda	9/15/67	9/29/67	29	3
Carmen	1/29/68	2/5/68	34	2
My Favorite Things	12/23/68	12/23/68	35	3
Alpert, Herb				
This Guy's In Love With You	5/13/68	6/10/68	1	11
To Wait For Love	9/9/68	9/9/68	36	1
Amboy Dukes				
Journey To The Center Of The Mind	7/15/68	8/26/68	5	8
American Breed				
Step Out Of Your Mind	5/26/67	6/30/67	9	8
Bend Me, Shape Me	11/17/67	1/15/68	1	13
Green Light	2/26/68	3/18/68	21	4

Artist	Title	Debut	Peak	Pos	Wks

Ames, Ed
| | My Cup Runneth Over | 2/17/67 | 3/24/67 | 11 | 7 |
| | Who Will Answer | 12/8/67 | 1/8/68 | 9 | 7 |

Anders, Teri
| | All In My Mind | 1/21/61 | 2/11/61 | 29 | 4 |

Anderson, Bill
| | Still | 5/24/63 | 6/14/63 | 6 | 7 |

Andy & the Manhattans
| | Double Mirror Around Shades | 8/28/64 | 8/28/64 | 40 | 1 |

Angello's Angels
| | Spring Cleaning | 4/10/64 | 4/10/64 | 30 | 3 |
| | I Don't Believe It | 7/17/64 | 7/24/64 | 33 | 2 |

Angels
	'Til	11/11/61	12/30/61	17	5
	Cry Baby Cry	3/31/62	4/7/62	37	2
	My Boyfriend's Back	8/2/63	8/9/63	1	9
	I Adore Him	10/11/63	11/8/63	8	7
	/Thank You And Goodnight	10/11/63	10/25/63	13	3
	Wow Wow Wee (He's The Boy For Me)	1/17/64	2/14/64	14	6

Animals
	The House Of The Rising Sun	8/14/64	9/11/64	1	9
	I'm Crying	10/9/64	10/30/64	9	5
	Boom Boom	12/25/64	1/8/65	18	3
	Don't Let Me Be Misunderstood	2/26/65	3/12/65	17	5
	Bring It On Home To Me	5/28/65	6/18/65	21	6
	We Gotta Get Out Of This Place	8/27/65	10/29/65	13	10
	It's My Life	11/26/65	1/7/66	10	9
	Inside- Looking Out	3/25/66	3/25/66	26	3
	Don't Bring Me Down	5/6/66	6/10/66	7	7

Eric Burdon & the Animals
| | See See Rider | 10/7/66 | 11/11/66 | 13 | 7 |
| | Sky Pilot (Part One) | 7/8/68 | 8/5/68 | 19 | 5 |

Anka, Paul
	I Love You In The Same Old Way	10/14/60	10/14/60	28	1
	Summer's Gone	11/5/60	11/5/60	32	1
	The Story Of My Love	2/11/61	2/18/61	29	2
	Tonight My Love, Tonight	4/8/61	5/5/61	12	6
	Dance On Little Girl	6/3/61	7/15/61	13	8
	Kissin' On The Phone	9/2/61	9/23/61	20	5
	Loveland	12/9/61	12/9/61	35	1
	The Fools Hall Of Fame	2/17/62	2/17/62	36	1

Artist	Title	Debut	Peak	Pos	Wks
	Love Me Warm And Tender	3/17/62	3/24/62	20	5
	A Steel Guitar And A Glass Of Wine	6/16/62	6/16/62	30	1
	Every Night (Without You)	9/15/62	9/29/62	22	3
	Eso Beso (That Kiss!)	11/3/62	12/1/62	12	6
	Remember Diana	4/12/63	4/19/63	32	3
	I Can't Get You Out Of My Mind	4/15/68	4/15/68	37	1
	Goodnight My Love	12/16/68	2/3/69	13	9
	In The Still Of The Night	2/24/69	3/10/69	31	5

Annette with the Afterbeats
	Pineapple Princess	10/14/60	10/14/60	16	3
	Talk To Me Baby	12/3/60	12/3/60	32	2
	Dream Boy	3/18/61	3/18/61	36	1

Ann-Margret
	I Just Don't Understand	8/5/61	9/2/61	12	6
	It Do Me So Good	11/25/61	11/25/61	34	1

Anthony & the Sophomores
	Play Those Oldies Mr. D.J.	4/12/63	4/12/63	36	1

Appalachians
	Bony Moronie	3/22/63	3/22/63	36	2

Arbors
	The Letter	2/24/69	4/7/69	21	9

Archies
	Bang-Shang-A-Lang	10/21/68	11/18/68	11	7
	Feelin' So Good (S.k.o.o.b.y-D.o.o)	1/13/69	1/20/69	37	2
	Sugar, Sugar	8/4/69	9/1/69	1	13
	Jingle Jangle	12/1/69	1/5/70	8	9

also see the Cuff Links & the Detergents

Armando
	Tiger Twist	6/16/62	6/23/62	31	2

Armstrong, Louis
	Hello, Dolly!	3/20/64	5/15/64	3	12

also see Ellington, Duke & Louis Armstrong

Arnell, Ginny
	Dumb Head	11/22/63	1/3/64	3	10

Arnold, Eddy
	One Grain Of Sand	10/7/61	10/7/61	39	1
	What's He Doing In My World	6/4/65	6/4/65	39	1
	Make The World Go Away	12/10/65	12/10/65	34	1
	I Want To Go With You	2/18/66	3/4/66	35	3
	The Tip Of My Fingers	8/5/66	8/12/66	31	3

Artist / Title	Debut	Peak	Pos	Wks
Artistics				
Got My Hands On Some Lovin'	9/11/64	9/11/64	38	1
Association				
Along Comes Mary	6/10/66	7/15/66	12	8
Cherish	8/19/66	9/2/66	1	10
No Fair At All	2/3/67	3/3/67	19	7
Windy	5/19/67	6/2/67	1	12
Never My Love	8/18/67	9/29/67	2	12
Everything That Touches You	1/29/68	3/4/68	6	8
Time For Livin'	5/13/68	6/3/68	25	5
Astors				
Candy	8/13/65	8/20/65	28	2
Avalon, Frankie				
The Puppet Song	12/17/60	1/21/61	14	7
Call Me Anytime	3/4/61	3/18/61	29	3
All Of Everything	3/11/61	3/18/61	29	2
You Are Mine	3/31/62	4/21/62	18	5
Babies				
You Made Me Feel Like Someone	7/7/67	7/7/67	33	1
Bacharach, Burt				
Saturday Sunshine	8/9/63	8/9/63	39	1
Bachelors				
Diane	5/8/64	5/29/64	8	7
I Believe	7/10/64	7/31/64	15	4
No Arms Can Ever Hold You	1/22/65	2/19/65	16	6
Marie	7/9/65	7/30/65	23	4
Love Me With All Of Your Heart	4/29/66	5/6/66	31	4
Backus, Gus				
Wooden Heart	7/22/61	8/19/61	4	7
Priscilla	3/3/62	3/3/62	37	1
Baja Marimba Band				
Comin' In The Back Door	1/10/64	1/10/64	34	1
Baker, LaVern				
Bumble Bee	12/3/60	12/31/60	25	6
Saved	4/22/61	5/6/61	30	3
See See Rider	12/15/62	12/29/62	33	3
Baldry, Long John				
Let The Heartaches Begin	12/8/67	12/22/67	27	3

Artist	Title	Debut	Peak	Pos	Wks

Ball, Kenny & his Jazzmen
   Midnight In Moscow — 2/24/62 — 3/10/62 — 2 — 8
   The Green Leaves Of Summer — 7/14/62 — 7/14/62 — 37 — 1

Ballard, Hank & the Midnighters
   Let's Go, Let's Go, Let's Go — 10/15/60 — 11/12/60 — 19 — 6
   The Hoochi Coochi Coo — 1/14/61 — 1/28/61 — 23 — 3

Balloon Farm
   A Question Of Temperature — 2/5/68 — 3/11/68 — 13 — 7

Band
   Up On Cripple Creek — 11/10/69 — 12/15/69 — 11 — 10

Barbarians
   Are You A Boy Or Are You A Girl — 9/10/65 — 9/24/65 — 18 — 4
   Moulty — 2/18/66 — 2/25/66 — 23 — 4

Bare, Bobby
   Sailor Man — 9/16/61 — 9/23/61 — 35 — 2
   Shame On Me — 8/25/62 — 9/22/62 — 15 — 5
   Detroit City — 7/19/63 — 8/9/63 — 3 — 7
   500 Miles Away From Home — 10/11/63 — 11/8/63 — 15 — 6

Bar-Kays
   Soul Finger — 6/30/67 — 7/7/67 — 30 — 3

Barnum, H. B.
   Lost Love — 2/11/61 — 2/18/61 — 36 — 2

Barrett, Hugh
   (There Was A) Fungus Among Us — 6/10/61 — 6/17/61 — 14 — 6

Barretto, Ray
   El Watusi — 5/3/63 — 5/17/63 — 13 — 4

Barry, Joe
   I'm A Fool To Care — 5/6/61 — 5/27/61 — 18 — 5

Barry, John
   Goldfinger — 2/19/65 — 3/26/65 — 4 — 10

Barry, Len
   1-2-3 — 10/22/65 — 11/26/65 — 1 — 9
   Like A Baby — 1/14/66 — 1/14/66 — 35 — 1
   also see the Dovells

Bass, Fontella
   Rescue Me — 10/15/65 — 10/29/65 — 27 — 6
   Recovery — 1/7/66 — 1/14/66 — 25 — 4

Artist / Title	Debut	Peak	Pos	Wks
Bassey, Shirley				
Goldfinger	4/9/65	4/16/65	14	3
B. Bumble & the Stingers				
Bumble Boogie	3/25/61	4/15/61	8	9
Boogie Woogie	7/8/61	7/29/61	18	5
Nut Rocker	3/3/62	3/17/62	3	7
Beach Boys				
Surfin' Safari	9/15/62	9/29/62	5	9
/409	9/29/62	9/29/62	5	7
Ten Little Indians	12/8/62	12/29/62	25	4
Shut Down	5/31/63	6/21/63	3	9
/Surfin' U.S.A.	4/12/63	5/10/63	6	8
Surfer Girl	8/30/63	10/4/63	7	8
/Little Deuce Coupe	9/20/63	10/4/63	7	5
Be True To Your School	11/15/63	12/6/63	7	8
/In My Room	11/15/63	12/6/63	7	7
Fun, Fun, Fun	2/14/64	3/13/64	3	10
I Get Around	5/29/64	7/3/64	1	11
When I Grow Up (To Be A Man)	10/2/64	10/16/64	19	3
Dance, Dance, Dance	11/13/64	12/11/64	10	6
Do You Wanna Dance	3/26/65	4/23/65	5	6
Help Me, Rhonda	5/7/65	5/28/65	2	9
California Girls	7/9/65	8/13/65	3	7
The Little Girl I Once Knew	12/3/65	12/10/65	24	4
Barbara Ann	1/7/66	1/28/66	2	8
Sloop John B	4/1/66	4/15/66	12	6
Wouldn't It Be Nice	8/5/66	9/9/66	7	9
Good Vibrations	10/21/66	11/11/66	1	11
Heroes And Villians	7/28/67	8/25/67	13	7
Wild Honey	10/27/67	11/3/67	31	2
Darlin'	1/29/68	2/5/68	27	3
Friends	4/15/68	4/22/68	37	2
Do It Again	7/29/68	9/16/68	2	11
I Can Hear Music	3/17/69	4/21/69	11	9
Break Away	7/7/69	7/28/69	27	4
also see Wilson, Brian				
Beatles				
Please Please Me	3/8/63	3/15/63	35	2
I Want To Hold Your Hand	1/17/64	1/31/64	1	12
/I Saw Her Standing There	2/21/64	3/6/64	4	7
She Loves You	1/31/64	2/28/64	1	10
Please Please Me	2/21/64	3/20/64	2	7

Artist	Title	Debut	Peak	Pos	Wks
	Twist And Shout	3/6/64	3/13/64	1	8
	Can't Buy Me Love	3/20/64	4/10/64	3	8
	/You Can't Do That	4/17/64	4/17/64	3	4
	Thank You Girl	3/27/64	4/10/64	7	9
	/Do You Want To Know A Secret	4/17/64	4/24/64	7	6
	Love Me Do	4/24/64	5/15/64	1	10
	/P.S. I Love You	5/1/64	5/15/64	1	9
	Sie Liebt Dich (She Loves You)	6/5/64	6/19/64	17	4
	A Hard Day's Night	7/10/64	8/7/64	1	10
	/I Should Have Known Better	7/10/64	7/31/64	1	6
	I'll Cry Instead	7/24/64	8/21/64	19	5
	/I'm Happy Just To Dance With You	7/24/64	8/7/64	20	3
	And I Love Her	8/7/64	8/14/64	21	3
	Ain't She Sweet	8/14/64	8/14/64	39	1
	Match Box	9/11/64	10/16/64	13	7
	/Slow Down	9/11/64	10/2/64	14	5
	I Feel Fine	11/27/64	12/18/64	1	9
	/She's A Woman	11/27/64	12/18/64	1	9
	Eight Days A Week	2/12/65	2/26/65	1	9
	/I Don't Want To Spoil The Party	2/12/65	2/26/65	1	9
	Ticket To Ride	4/16/65	5/7/65	2	8
	/Yes It Is	4/23/65	5/7/65	2	7
	Help!	7/30/65	9/10/65	1	12
	Yesterday	9/3/65	10/15/65	1	11
	Boys	10/22/65	10/29/65	18	5
	We Can Work It Out	12/10/65	12/24/65	1	11
	/Day Tripper	12/24/65	12/24/65	1	9
	Nowhere Man	2/25/66	3/11/66	7	7
	Paperback Writer	6/3/66	6/24/66	2	8
	/Rain	6/10/66	6/24/66	2	7
	Eleanor Rigby	8/12/66	9/2/66	3	8
	/Yellow Submarine	8/12/66	9/23/66	4	6
	Penny Lane	2/24/67	3/10/67	4	8
	/Strawberry Fields Forever	2/24/67	3/10/67	4	7
	All You Need Is Love	7/21/67	8/11/67	8	9
	Hello Goodbye	11/24/67	12/15/67	1	9
	Lady Madonna	3/11/68	4/1/68	1	9
	/The Inner Light	3/11/68	3/25/68	2	3
	Hey Jude	9/2/68	9/16/68	1	11
	/Revolution	9/2/68	9/30/68	2	8
	Get Back	4/28/69	5/12/69	1	11
	Come Together	10/6/69	11/3/69	1	16
	/Something	10/6/69	11/3/69	1	16

also see the Plastic Ono Band

Artist	Title	Debut	Peak	Pos	Wks

Beau Brummels
    Laugh, Laugh   1/29/65   2/26/65   4   9
    Just A Little   5/7/65   6/11/65   6   8
    You Tell Me Why   7/16/65   7/30/65   19   5

Beaumont, Jimmie
    Ev'rybody's Cryin'   12/2/61   12/9/61   27   2
also see the Skyliners

Bee Gees
    New York Mining Disaster, 1941 (Have You Seen My Wife, Mr. Jones)   5/19/67   6/16/67   22   7
    To Love Somebody   8/4/67   8/11/67   31   3
    Holiday   10/27/67   10/27/67   36   1
    (The Lights Went Out In) Massachusetts   11/24/67   12/8/67   21   4
    I've Gotta Get A Message To You   9/8/68   10/21/68   3   10
    I Started A Joke   12/23/68   2/3/69   6   10
    First Of May   4/7/69   4/14/69   32   3
    Tomorrow Tomorrow   6/2/69   6/9/69   36   2

Beecher, Johnny
    Sax Fifth Avenue   3/8/63   3/22/63   22   5

Bell, Archie & the Drells
    Tighten Up   3/25/68   5/13/68   2   10
    I Can't Stop Dancing   8/5/68   8/26/68   11   6
    Do The Choo Choo   9/30/68   10/14/68   25   3
    There's Gonna Be A Showdown   1/6/69   2/3/69   20   6

Bell, Madeline
    I'm Gonna Make You Love Me   2/12/68   2/26/68   36   3

Belmonts
    Tell Me Why   7/1/61   7/1/61   38   1
    Don't Get Around Much Anymore   11/4/61   11/4/61   32   1
    Come On Little Angel   7/7/62   8/11/62   4   8
    Diddle-Dee-Dum (What Happens When Your Love Has Gone)   12/22/62   12/22/62   39   1
    Ann-Marie   4/5/63   4/26/63   16   4
also see Dion

Bendix, Ralph
    Baby Sittin' Boogie   6/9/62   6/23/62   8   5

Bennett, Pete
    Fever   11/25/61   12/2/61   25   2

Bennett, Tony
    I Wanna Be Around   1/19/63   2/15/63   14   7

Artist	Title	Debut	Peak	Pos	Wks
	The Good Life	5/31/63	5/31/63	35	1
	/Spring In Manhattan	5/17/63	5/17/63	37	1
	This Is All I Ask	8/16/63	8/30/63	18	4
	Don't Wait Too Long	10/25/63	10/25/63	31	2
	The Little Boy	1/17/64	1/31/64	16	5
	If I Ruled The World	2/26/65	3/26/65	17	6
	Georgia Rose	7/22/66	7/29/66	38	2
Benton, Brook					
	Someday You'll Want Me To Want You	12/3/60	12/31/60	27	6
	/Fools Rush In (Where Angels Fear To Tread)	12/24/60	12/31/60	27	4
	Think Twice	3/11/61	3/18/61	20	3
	The Boll Weevil Song	6/10/61	7/8/61	15	6
	Frankie And Johnny	9/23/61	9/30/61	21	3
	/It's Just A House Without You	10/7/61	10/7/61	23	1
	Revenge	1/6/62	1/6/62	33	1
	Shadrack	2/3/62	2/3/62	37	1
	Hit Record	6/2/62	6/9/62	33	2
	Lie To Me	9/8/62	9/22/62	31	3
	Hotel Happiness	12/1/62	12/1/62	35	1
	I Got What I Wanted	3/22/63	3/29/63	34	2
	My True Confession	6/28/63	6/28/63	26	1
Berry, Chuck					
	Jaguar And Thunderbird	11/19/60	11/19/60	39	1
	Little Star	3/18/61	3/18/61	37	1
	Nadine (Is It You)	3/6/64	3/6/64	24	3
	No Particular Place To Go	6/19/64	7/3/64	18	4
	Promised Land	1/8/65	1/15/65	32	2
Berry, Jan					
	Universal Coward	11/19/65	12/3/65	35	3
also see Jan & Dean					
Big Brother & the Holding Company					
	Piece Of My Heart	9/30/68	11/4/68	16	6
Big Sambo & the House Wreckers					
	The Rains Came	3/10/62	3/17/62	34	2
Bilk, Mr. Acker					
	Stranger On The Shore	4/7/62	5/12/62	1	12
Billy Joe & the Checkmates					
	Percolator (Twist)	2/10/62	3/3/62	25	4
Black's, Bill, Combo					
	Don't Be Cruel	10/14/60	10/29/60	15	5

Artist	Title	Debut	Peak	Pos	Wks
	Blue Tango	12/31/60	1/14/61	27	3
	Hearts Of Stone	3/25/61	4/1/61	29	4
	Ole Buttermilk Sky	7/8/61	7/15/61	33	2
	Movin'	11/4/61	11/11/61	27	2
	Twist-Her	1/13/62	1/27/62	25	3
	So What	9/22/62	10/6/62	32	3
	Do It—Rat Now	5/10/63	5/24/63	20	3
	Monkey-Shine	10/18/63	10/18/63	36	1

Black, Cilla
	Alfie	7/29/66	8/26/66	19	6

Black, Terry
	Unless You Care	10/23/64	11/13/64	22	4

Blades Of Grass
	Happy	7/7/67	7/7/67	39	2

Bland, Billy
	Harmony	10/14/60	10/14/60	37	1

Bland, Bobby
	I Pity The Fool	3/25/61	3/25/61	35	1
	Turn On Your Love Light	12/23/61	1/6/62	29	3
	Yield Not To Temptation	10/13/62	10/13/62	37	1
	Call On Me	2/1/63	2/1/63	40	1
	/That's The Way Love Is	2/22/63	3/1/63	33	2

Blane, Marcie
	Bobby's Girl	10/20/62	11/17/62	1	13
	What Does A Girl Do	2/8/63	3/1/63	12	4

Blenders
	Daughter	6/21/63	7/12/63	12	5

Blood, Sweat & Tears
	You've Made Me So Very Happy	3/10/69	4/7/69	3	10
	Spinning Wheel	6/2/69	7/7/69	2	10
	And When I Die	10/20/69	11/17/69	4	10

Blue-Belles
	I Sold My Heart To The Junkman	4/28/62	5/26/62	8	6

Blue Cheer
	Summertime Blues	3/11/68	4/15/68	5	8

Blue Jays
	Lover's Island	8/5/61	9/9/61	12	8

Artist	Title	Debut	Peak	Pos	Wks

Blues Magoos
| | (We Ain't Got) Nothin' Yet | 12/23/66 | 2/3/67 | 5 | 9 |

Bob & Earl
| | Harlem Shuffle | 2/7/64 | 2/7/64 | 33 | 2 |

Bob B. Soxx & the Blue Jeans
| | Zip-A-Dee-Doo-Dah | 11/10/62 | 12/8/62 | 13 | 7 |
| | Why Do Lovers Break Each Other's Heart | 2/15/63 | 3/1/63 | 22 | 3 |

Bolt, Ben
| | The Mechanical Man | 1/20/67 | 2/10/67 | 23 | 5 |

Bond, Johnny
| | Hot Rod Lincoln | 10/14/60 | 10/14/60 | 7 | 1 |

Bonds, Gary U.S.
	New Orleans	10/15/60	11/19/60	3	10
	Quarter To Three	6/17/61	6/24/61	1	10
	School Is Out	8/12/61	8/26/61	3	5
	School Is In	11/4/61	11/25/61	17	4
	Dear Lady Twist	1/20/62	2/17/62	12	8
	Twist, Twist Senora	4/14/62	4/28/62	14	4
	Seven Day Weekend	7/28/62	8/4/62	32	2

Booker T. & the MG's
	Green Onions	8/25/62	9/22/62	12	6
	Groovin'	9/8/67	9/8/67	40	1
	Soul-Limbo	7/22/68	9/2/68	13	8
	Hang 'Em High	11/18/68	1/13/69	7	13
	Time Is Tight	3/24/69	5/5/69	10	9
	Mrs. Robinson	6/9/69	7/7/69	25	6

Boone, Pat
	Dear John	12/3/60	12/10/60	36	2
	Moody River	5/27/61	7/1/61	2	8
	Big Cold Wind	9/23/61	10/7/61	27	4
	Johnny Will	12/23/61	1/20/62	21	5
	I'll See You In My Dreams	2/10/62	2/24/62	26	3
	Speedy Gonzales	6/23/62	7/28/62	9	7
	Wish You Were Here, Buddy	10/7/66	10/28/66	18	6

Box Tops
	The Letter	8/18/67	9/22/67	1	13
	Neon Rainbow	11/10/67	12/1/67	9	6
	Cry Like A Baby	3/4/68	4/22/68	2	11
	Choo Choo Train	5/27/68	6/10/68	23	4
	I Met Her In Church	9/2/68	9/30/68	23	5

Artist	Title	Debut	Peak	Pos	Wks
	Soul Deep	7/14/69	8/18/69	3	10
	Turn On A Dream	10/20/69	11/10/69	23	5

Boyce, Tommy
	Along Came Linda	3/3/62	3/10/62	27	3
	I'll Remember Carol	9/15/62	10/6/62	9	5

Boyce, Tommy & Bobby Hart
	Out And About	7/21/67	8/4/67	32	3
	I Wonder What She's Doing Tonite	12/15/67	2/5/68	2	11
	Goodbye Baby (I Don't Want To See You Cry)	4/15/68	5/6/68	28	4
	Alice Long (You're Still My Favorite Girlfriend)	7/15/68	8/26/68	6	8

Bradley, Jan
	We Girls	5/12/62	6/2/62	23	4
	Mama Didn't Lie	12/29/62	1/12/63	30	4

Brass Ring
	The Phoenix Love Theme	2/11/66	3/18/66	20	6
	The Dis-Advantages Of You	2/17/67	2/24/67	36	3

Braun, Bob
	Till Death Do Us Part	8/4/62	8/25/62	13	5

Brenda & the Tabulations
	Dry Your Eyes	4/14/67	4/14/67	38	2

Brennan, Walter
	Old Rivers	4/7/62	5/12/62	3	8

Brewer, Teresa
	Anymore	10/14/60	10/14/60	30	1

Brooklyn Bridge
	Worst That Could Happen	12/16/68	1/27/69	3	11
	You'll Never Walk Alone	9/29/69	10/13/69	33	4

also see Maestro, Johnny

Brooks, Donnie
	Doll House	12/10/60	1/14/61	19	7

Brothers Four
	Frogg	5/27/61	6/3/61	29	3
	Try To Remember	10/8/65	10/22/65	22	7

Brown, Crazy World Of Arthur
	Fire	9/2/68	9/23/68	1	10

Brown, James
	Lost Someone	2/3/62	2/17/62	26	3
	Night Train	5/12/62	5/12/62	30	1
	Shout And Shimmy	7/28/62	8/4/62	31	2

Artist / Title	Debut	Peak	Pos	Wks
Prisoner Of Love	5/17/63	5/24/63	27	3
Papa's Got A Brand New Bag Part I	7/23/65	8/13/65	19	5
I Got You (I Feel Good)	11/19/65	12/24/65	21	6
Cold Sweat—Part 2	8/4/67	8/25/67	30	4
There Was A Time	1/15/68	2/19/68	8	7
I Got The Feelin'	3/18/68	4/29/68	6	8
Licking Stick—Licking Stick (Part 1)	5/20/68	7/1/68	15	7
Mother Popcorn (You Got To Have A Mother For Me) Part 1	6/23/69	7/21/69	15	6

Brown, Maxine
Funny	5/6/61	5/6/61	38	1

Browns
Send Me The Pillow You Dream On	12/17/60	12/31/60	29	4

Brubeck, Dave, Quartet
Take Five	6/24/61	7/1/61	32	2
Unsquare Dance	1/13/62	1/13/62	33	1

Bryant, Anita
One Of The Lucky Ones	11/5/60	11/5/60	31	1
A Place Called Happiness	7/1/61	7/1/61	40	1
Step By Step	3/10/62	3/17/62	31	2

Bubble Puppy
Hot Smoke & Sasafrass	2/17/69	3/24/69	6	8

Buchanan & Greenfield
The Invasion	9/11/64	9/11/64	22	1

Buchanan Brothers
Medicine Man (Part I)	5/5/69	6/16/69	5	10
Son Of A Lovin' Man	9/29/69	10/6/69	35	3

Buckinghams
I'll Go Crazy	3/25/66	5/6/66	19	8
I Call Your Name	6/3/66	7/1/66	14	6
I've Been Wrong	8/19/66	9/23/66	13	7
Kind Of A Drag	11/18/66	12/16/66	2	12
Laudy Miss Clawdy	3/3/67	3/10/67	27	5
Don't You Care	3/24/67	4/28/67	1	10
Mercy, Mercy, Mercy	6/16/67	7/28/67	4	9
Hey Baby (They're Playing Our Song)	9/8/67	10/13/67	5	9
Susan	11/24/67	1/15/68	5	11
Back In Love Again	5/27/68	6/3/68	32	3

Bud & Travis
Ballad Of The Alamo	10/29/60	11/5/60	18	5

Artist / Title	Debut	Peak	Pos	Wks
Buffalo Springfield				
For What It's Worth (Stop, Hey What's That Sound)	2/10/67	3/24/67	4	11
also see Crosby, Stills & Nash				
Burke, Solomon				
Just Out Of Reach (Of My Two Open Arms)	10/21/61	12/2/61	6	9
Cry To Me	2/10/62	2/24/62	28	3
Proud Mary	5/5/69	5/19/69	26	3
Burnette, Johnny				
You're Sixteen	11/19/60	12/17/60	5	9
Little Boy Sad	3/4/61	3/18/61	27	3
God, Country And My Baby	11/18/61	11/18/61	36	2
Burton, Joe				
St. Louis Blues	8/2/63	8/2/63	37	1
Busters				
Bust Out	8/9/63	9/13/63	12	7
Butler, Jerry				
He Will Break Your Heart	11/12/60	11/19/60	16	10
Find Another Girl	4/1/61	4/1/61	35	1
I'm A Telling You	9/2/61	9/16/61	29	4
Moon River	11/4/61	11/4/61	35	1
Make It Easy On Yourself	8/11/62	8/11/62	28	2
Never Give You Up	6/10/68	6/17/68	29	2
Hey, Western Union Man	9/30/68	10/28/68	17	6
Only The Strong Survive	3/3/69	4/7/69	8	11
Moody Woman	5/26/69	6/16/69	21	5
What's The Use Of Breaking Up	9/1/69	9/29/69	23	6
Don't Let Love Hang You Up	12/1/69	12/22/69	29	5
Butler, Jerry & Betty Everett				
Let It Be Me	9/11/64	9/18/64	27	2
also see Everett, Betty and the Impressions				
Byliners				
Archie's Melody	1/13/62	1/13/62	38	1
Byrds				
Mr. Tambourine Man	5/28/65	6/18/65	1	9
All I Really Want To Do	6/25/65	7/23/65	11	7
/I'll Feel A Whole Lot Better	6/25/65	7/2/65	30	2
Turn! Turn! Turn! (To Everything There Is A Season)	10/29/65	12/10/65	6	8
Eight Miles High	4/8/66	4/29/66	15	6

Artist	Title	Debut	Peak	Pos	Wks
	Mr. Spaceman	10/7/66	10/14/66	27	3
	So You Want To Be A Rock 'N' Roll Star	2/3/67	2/24/67	20	5
also see Crosby, Stills & Nash					
Bystanders					
	Royal Blue Summer Sunshine Day	6/30/67	7/7/67	35	2
Caiola, Al					
	The Magnificent Seven	11/12/60	1/14/61	3	12
	Bonanza	4/8/61	5/13/61	4	8
	Autumn In Cheyenne	10/14/61	10/14/61	34	1
Callender, Bobby					
	Little Star	3/15/63	3/15/63	39	1
Cameos					
	Canadian Sunset	11/12/60	11/26/60	30	3
Campbell, Glen					
	Turn Around, Look At Me	10/28/61	12/2/61	13	7
	Kentucky Means Paradise	11/17/62	12/8/62	16	5
	By The Time I Get To Phoenix	12/1/67	12/15/67	32	3
	I Wanna Live	4/22/68	6/3/68	19	7
	Dreams Of The Everyday Housewife	7/8/68	7/15/68	28	4
	Gentle On My Mind	10/7/68	10/14/68	26	2
	Wichita Lineman	11/11/68	12/9/68	8	11
	Galveston	3/10/69	4/7/69	5	8
	Where's The Playground Susie	5/12/69	6/2/69	29	4
	True Grit	7/21/69	8/11/69	25	4
	Try A Little Kindness	10/6/69	11/3/69	8	8
Campbell, Jo Ann					
	A Kookie Little Paradise	10/14/60	10/14/60	20	1
	(I'm The Girl On) Wolverton Mountain	8/18/62	8/25/62	25	4
Canned Heat					
	On The Road Again	8/26/68	9/30/68	8	8
	Going Up The Country	12/9/68	1/13/69	6	9
Cannibal & the Headhunters					
	Land Of 1000 Dances	3/12/65	4/9/65	5	7
Cannon, Ace					
	Tuff	1/27/62	2/24/62	18	7
	Blues (Stay Away From Me)	5/19/62	5/26/62	34	2
	Volare	11/24/62	11/24/62	38	1
Cannon, Freddy					
	Muskrat Ramble	3/4/61	3/4/61	34	1

Artist	Title	Debut	Peak	Pos	Wks
	Buzz Buzz A-Diddle-It	6/3/61	6/3/61	32	2
	Transistor Sister	7/22/61	8/19/61	18	6
	For Me And My Gal	10/28/61	11/11/61	24	3
	Palisades Park	5/26/62	6/9/62	2	8
	Patty Baby	5/31/63	5/31/63	30	2
	Everybody Monkey	9/13/63	9/13/63	37	1
	Abigail Beecher	1/31/64	2/28/64	17	6
	Action	8/27/65	9/24/65	4	7
	The Dedication Song	2/25/66	2/25/66	33	1
Capitols					
	Cool Jerk	5/13/66	6/10/66	8	7
Capris					
	There's A Moon Out Tonight	1/28/61	2/18/61	7	7
Caravelles					
	You Don't Have To Be A Baby To Cry	11/1/63	11/22/63	8	6
Cardigans					
	Your Graduation Means Goodbye	6/10/61	7/8/61	8	6
	Your Graduation Means Goodbye	5/31/63	6/21/63	13	5
Carefrees					
	We Love You Beatles	3/6/64	3/20/64	9	5
Cargill, Henson					
	Skip A Rope	12/8/67	1/15/68	7	8
Carlin, George					
	Hippy Dippy Weatherman	3/10/67	4/7/67	17	7
Caron, Don					
	Work Song	8/11/62	9/8/62	26	5
Carr, Cathy					
	Sailor Boy	1/4/63	1/4/63	36	1
Carr, Vikki					
	It Must Be Him	9/22/67	11/10/67	6	10
	With Pen In Hand	6/2/69	6/16/69	31	3
Carroll, Andrea					
	It Hurts To Be Sixteen	9/13/63	9/13/63	39	1
Carroll, Bernadette					
	Party Girl	5/22/64	6/26/64	8	8
Carroll, Cathy					
	Jimmy Love	6/24/61	7/22/61	11	7

Artist / Title	Debut	Peak	Pos	Wks
Carroll, David				
Mexican Joe	10/28/61	11/11/61	29	3
The White Rose Of Athens	3/17/62	3/24/62	29	2
Carter, Calvin				
What'd I Say	1/27/62	2/3/62	35	2
Carter, Clarence				
Looking For A Fox	2/19/68	2/26/68	37	2
Slip Away	7/15/68	8/26/68	13	7
Too Weak To Fight	12/9/68	1/13/69	17	7
Snatching It Back	3/31/69	3/31/69	36	2
Carter, Mel				
When A Boy Falls In Love	6/28/63	7/26/63	13	5
Hold Me, Thrill Me, Kiss Me	7/23/65	8/27/65	4	9
Band Of Gold	4/29/66	6/3/66	21	7
You You You	7/22/66	8/5/66	33	4
Cascades				
Rhythm Of The Rain	1/25/63	2/22/63	2	10
The Last Leaf	4/19/63	5/17/63	14	5
Casey, Al, Combo				
Cookin'	3/24/62	4/14/62	13	5
Jivin' Around	7/28/62	8/11/62	20	4
Surfin' Hootenanny	6/28/63	7/26/63	27	5
Cash, Alvin & the Crawlers				
Twine Time	1/1/65	1/29/65	13	6
The Barracuda	4/9/65	4/16/65	28	3
Cash, Johnny				
Going To Memphis	10/15/60	10/15/60	27	1
Ring Of Fire	6/21/63	7/12/63	10	7
The Matador	11/15/63	11/29/63	17	3
Understand Your Man	3/13/64	4/17/64	18	6
Belshazah	6/19/64	7/3/64	34	3
Orange Blossom Special	3/5/65	3/12/65	23	4
The One On The Right Is On The Left	3/11/66	3/11/66	36	2
Daddy Sang Bass	1/27/69	2/17/69	31	4
A Boy Named Sue	7/14/69	8/11/69	7	10
Get Rhythm	11/3/69	11/24/69	18	6
Cash, Tommy				
Six White Horses	12/22/69	12/29/69	37	3
Casinos				
Then You Can Tell Me Goodbye	1/13/67	3/10/67	8	11

Artist Title	Debut	Peak	Pos	Wks

Castaways
   Liar, Liar   9/24/65   10/22/65   7   9

Castells
   Sacred   6/24/61   7/22/61   6   9
   So This Is Love   4/28/62   6/2/62   9   7
   Oh! What It Seemed To Be   8/11/62   8/18/62   32   2

Castle Sisters
   Goodbye Dad   6/30/62   7/21/62   18   4

Castor, Jimmy
   Hey, Leroy, Your Mama's Callin' You   1/20/67   2/3/67   31   4

Caswell, Johnny
   At The Shore   8/2/63   8/9/63   17   3

Cat Mother & the All Night News Boys
   Good Old Rock 'N Roll   6/30/69   7/28/69   16   6

Cathy Jean & the Roommates
   Please Love Me Forever   3/18/61   4/15/61   4   7
   also see the Roommates

Chad & Jeremy
   Yesterday's Gone   4/17/64   5/22/64   3   9
   A Summer Song   8/28/64   9/18/64   6   7
   Willow Weep For Me   12/18/64   1/1/65   13   6
   If I Loved You   2/19/65   3/12/65   16   5
   What Do You Want With Me   5/7/65   5/7/65   23   3
   Before And After   5/21/65   6/18/65   17   6
   I Don't Want To Lose You Baby   8/6/65   8/20/65   27   3
   September In The Rain   9/10/65   9/24/65   26   3
   Distant Shores   7/15/66   8/12/66   21   6

Chamberlain, Richard
   Theme From Dr. Kildare (Three Stars Will Shine Tonight)   6/16/62   7/14/62   13   6
   All I Have To Do Is Dream   3/1/63   3/15/63   17   5
   Blue Guitar   10/11/63   10/18/63   34   2

Chambers Brothers
   Time Has Come Today   9/16/68   10/7/68   13   6
   I Can't Turn You Loose   11/25/68   12/23/68   16   6

Champs
   Limbo Rock   4/21/62   6/2/62   5   9

Chancellors
   Little Latin Lupe Lu   4/2/65   5/7/65   14   7

Artist	Title	Debut	Peak	Pos	Wks

Chandler, Gene
- Duke Of Earl — 1/27/62 — 2/10/62 — 1 — 9
- Tear For Tear — 10/6/62 — 10/13/62 — 34 — 2
- Man's Temptation — 8/16/63 — 8/16/63 — 37 — 3
- Think Nothing About It — 2/21/64 — 2/28/64 — 32 — 2
- Just Be True — 7/3/64 — 7/17/64 — 24 — 5
- What Now — 1/8/65 — 1/8/65 — 36 — 1
- Nothing Can Stop Me — 5/7/65 — 5/21/65 — 35 — 3

also see the Dukays

Channel, Bruce
- Hey! Baby — 2/10/62 — 3/3/62 — 1 — 10
- Number One Man — 4/21/62 — 5/19/62 — 25 — 5
- Come On Baby — 7/28/62 — 7/28/62 — 34 — 1

Chantays
- Pipeline — 3/15/63 — 4/19/63 — 1 — 9
- Pipeline — 10/14/66 — 10/28/66 — 20 — 4

Chantels
- Look In My Eyes — 9/16/61 — 10/21/61 — 12 — 7
- Well, I Told You — 12/2/61 — 12/9/61 — 29 — 3

Chaplain, Paul & his Emeralds
- Shortnin' Bread — 10/14/60 — 10/14/60 — 1 — 4

Charles, Harry
- My Laura — 8/2/63 — 8/2/63 — 39 — 1

Charles, Jimmy
- The Age For Love — 3/18/61 — 3/18/61 — 38 — 1

Charles, Ray
- Georgia On My Mind — 10/14/60 — 10/14/60 — 14 — 6
- Ruby — 12/24/60 — 12/31/60 — 35 — 3
- Them That Got — 2/25/61 — 3/11/61 — 27 — 3
- One Mint Julep — 4/1/61 — 4/22/61 — 24 — 5
- Hit The Road Jack — 9/16/61 — 10/21/61 — 4 — 8
- Unchain My Heart — 12/16/61 — 1/13/62 — 24 — 5
- Hide 'Nor Hair — 4/14/62 — 4/14/62 — 40 — 1
- I Can't Stop Loving You — 5/12/62 — 5/26/62 — 1 — 10
- You Don't Know Me — 7/28/62 — 8/18/62 — 14 — 5
- You Are My Sunshine — 11/17/62 — 12/1/62 — 21 — 4
- Don't Set Me Free — 3/8/63 — 3/8/63 — 30 — 1
- Take These Chains From My Heart — 4/12/63 — 4/26/63 — 18 — 4
- No One — 6/21/63 — 6/28/63 — 35 — 2
- Busted — 9/13/63 — 10/25/63 — 17 — 7
- That Lucky Old Sun — 12/20/63 — 12/20/63 — 29 — 2

Artist	Title	Debut	Peak	Pos	Wks
	Baby, Don't You Cry	2/28/64	3/6/64	33	2
	Makin' Whoopee	1/15/65	1/22/65	36	3
	Crying Time	1/7/66	1/21/66	33	5
	Together Again	4/8/66	4/15/66	36	3
	Here We Go Again	6/2/67	7/7/67	18	9
	Yesterday	11/10/67	12/1/67	24	4

Charles, Ray, Singers
	Love Me With All Your Heart (Cuando Calienta El Sol)	5/8/64	5/22/64	6	8
	Al-Di-La	7/17/64	7/24/64	29	3
	One More Time	12/18/64	12/25/64	16	2

Charles, Sonny & the Checkmates, Ltd.
	Black Pearl	5/26/69	7/7/69	13	8

Chartbusters
	She's The One	6/26/64	7/31/64	9	7

Checker, Chubby
	The Hucklebuck	10/29/60	11/19/60	6	9
	/Whole Lotta Shakin' Goin' On	10/15/60	10/15/60	33	1
	Pony Time	2/18/61	3/11/61	10	7
	Dance The Mess Around	5/13/61	5/20/61	32	2
	Let's Twist Again	7/15/61	8/12/61	2	8
	The Fly	10/14/61	11/18/61	15	6
	The Twist	12/16/61	1/20/62	2	11
	Slow Twistin'	3/17/62	4/21/62	8	7
	Dancin' Party	7/14/62	8/4/62	23	4
	Limbo Rock	10/6/62	11/3/62	23	5
	Let's Limbo Some More	2/15/63	3/1/63	25	3
	/Twenty Miles	3/22/63	3/29/63	33	2
	Birdland	5/17/63	5/24/63	28	2
	Loddy Lo	11/22/63	12/13/63	14	6
	Hey, Bobba Needle	3/20/64	3/20/64	28	3
	Lazy Elsie Molly	7/3/64	7/17/64	33	3

also see Rydell, Bobby & Chubby Checker

Cher
	Where Do You Go	11/5/65	11/12/65	28	3
	Bang Bang (My Baby Shot Me Down)	3/11/66	4/15/66	3	10
	You Better Sit Down Kids	11/3/67	12/8/67	3	10

also see Sonny & Cher

Chicago Loop
	(When She Needs Good Lovin') She Comes To Me	11/11/66	11/18/66	30	4

Artist	Title	Debut	Peak	Pos	Wks
Chiffons					
	Tonight's The Night	10/14/60	10/14/60	24	1
	He's So Fine	3/8/63	3/22/63	1	10
	One Fine Day	5/24/63	6/14/63	5	7
	A Love So Fine	10/4/63	10/11/63	25	2
	I Have A Boyfriend	12/20/63	1/10/64	21	6
	Sweet Talkin' Guy	5/6/66	6/17/66	18	8
also see the Four Pennies					
Chimes					
	Once In Awhile	1/28/61	2/25/61	6	8
	I'm In The Mood For Love	4/29/61	5/13/61	27	4
Chipmunks					
	Alvin For President	10/14/60	10/14/60	31	1
	The Alvin Twist	3/10/62	3/17/62	28	2
	Eefin Alvin	10/18/63	10/18/63	40	1
Choir					
	It's Cold Outside	6/16/67	6/30/67	25	5
Chordettes					
	Never On Sunday	7/29/61	8/5/61	31	4
	/Faraway Star	10/21/61	10/21/61	34	1
Christie, Dean					
	Heart Breaker	10/27/62	11/17/62	17	4
Christie, Lou					
	Two Faces Have I	4/19/63	5/10/63	1	9
	How Many Teardrops	7/19/63	8/9/63	19	4
	Lightnin' Strikes	1/7/66	2/4/66	1	9
	Outside The Gates Of Heaven	3/4/66	4/15/66	17	8
	Shake Hands And Walk Away Cryin'	4/14/67	4/21/67	30	4
	I'm Gonna Make You Mine	8/25/69	9/29/69	2	10
Christie, Susan					
	I Love Onions	7/1/66	7/22/66	30	5
Church Street Five					
	A Night With Daddy G	1/14/61	2/4/61	7	6
also see Bonds, Gary U.S.					
Clanton, Jimmy					
	Venus In Blue Jeans	9/1/62	9/29/62	2	8
	Darkest Street In Town	12/15/62	1/4/63	15	4
Clark, Claudine					
	Party Lights	6/30/62	8/11/62	10	7

Artist	Title	Debut	Peak	Pos	Wks

Clark, Dave, Five
	Glad All Over	2/14/64	3/27/64	2	11
	Bits And Pieces	4/3/64	5/1/64	5	6
	Do You Love Me	5/8/64	6/12/64	6	8
	Can't You See That She's Mine	6/19/64	7/10/64	2	7
	Because	8/7/64	9/4/64	2	8
	Everybody Knows (I Still Love You)	10/9/64	11/6/64	15	5
	Any Way You Want It	11/27/64	1/1/65	4	10
	Come Home	2/19/65	3/19/65	7	7
	Reelin' And Rockin'	4/23/65	5/21/65	11	7
	I Like It Like That	7/2/65	7/23/65	7	8
	Catch Us If You Can	7/23/65	9/3/65	3	9
	Over And Over	11/12/65	12/10/65	2	9
	At The Scene	1/28/66	2/25/66	13	7
	Try Too Hard	3/25/66	4/15/66	16	7
	Please Tell Me Why	6/10/66	6/17/66	28	3
	Satisfied With You	8/12/66	9/2/66	29	6
	Nineteen Days	10/28/66	12/2/66	21	7
	I've Got To Have A Reason	1/6/67	1/20/67	23	5
	You Got What It Takes	3/31/67	4/21/67	6	7
	You Must Have Been A Beautiful Baby	6/9/67	6/23/67	21	4
	A Little Bit Now	8/11/67	8/11/67	38	1
	Everybody Knows	12/15/67	1/15/68	19	6

Clark, Dee
	Your Friends	3/4/61	3/18/61	31	3
	Raindrops	5/20/61	7/8/61	2	9
	Crossfire Time	11/8/63	11/29/63	26	5

Clark, Lucky
| | So Sick | 4/15/61 | 4/15/61 | 40 | 1 |

Clark, Michael
| | Work Out | 3/1/63 | 4/5/63 | 24 | 4 |

Clark, Petula
	Downtown	12/25/64	1/15/65	1	11
	I Know A Place	3/26/65	4/16/65	2	8
	You'd Better Come Home	7/2/65	7/30/65	17	5
	My Love	1/7/66	2/4/66	8	9
	A Sign Of The Times	3/25/66	4/8/66	25	4
	I Couldn't Live Without Your Love	7/22/66	8/12/66	3	6
	Who Am I	10/28/66	11/11/66	27	4
	Color My World	1/6/67	2/3/67	19	6
	This Is My Song	3/3/67	3/24/67	9	7
	Don't Sleep In The Subway	6/2/67	7/7/67	15	6

Artist	Title	Debut	Peak	Pos	Wks
	The Cat In The Window (The Bird In The Sky)	9/8/67	9/8/67	28	3
	The Other Man's Grass Is Always Greener	12/1/67	12/22/67	22	5
	Kiss Me Goodbye	2/12/68	3/11/68	7	9
	Don't Give Up	7/8/68	8/5/68	31	6

Clark, Roy
	Yesterday, When I Was Young	6/30/69	7/28/69	24	5

Clarke, Tony
	The Entertainer	4/9/65	4/16/65	36	3

Classics
	Till Then	6/14/63	7/19/63	5	7

Classics IV
	Spooky	12/29/67	2/12/68	3	11

Classics IV featuring Dennis Yost
	Stormy	11/4/68	12/23/68	4	11
	Traces	2/17/69	3/17/69	3	9
	Everyday With You Girl	5/12/69	6/23/69	14	9

Classmen
	Do You Want To Dance	3/27/64	3/27/64	33	1

Cleftones
	Heart And Soul	6/17/61	7/15/61	4	7

Cliff, Jimmy
	Wonderful World, Beautiful People	11/24/69	1/5/70	10	10

Clifford, Buzz
	Baby Sittin' Boogie	2/11/61	3/11/61	3	8

Clifford, Mike
	Close To Cathy	9/29/62	10/27/62	5	6
	What To Do With Laurie	12/22/62	1/19/63	10	6
	One Boy Too Late	5/3/63	5/3/63	35	1

Cline, Patsy
	I Fall To Pieces	8/5/61	9/2/61	17	5
	Crazy	11/25/61	12/16/61	23	4
	She's Got You	3/3/62	3/10/62	18	4

Clique
	Sugar On Sunday	9/22/69	10/27/69	16	6
	I'll Hold Out My Hand	11/24/69	12/8/69	28	4

Coasters
	Shoppin' For Clothes	10/15/60	10/29/60	27	2
	Little Egypt (Ying-Yang)	6/17/61	6/17/61	37	1

Artist Title	Debut	Peak	Pos	Wks

Cochran, Hank
    Sally Was A Good Old Girl   8/4/62   8/4/62   38   1

Coeds
    Annabelle Lee   11/18/61   12/2/61   23   3

Colder, Ben
    Don't Go Near The Eskimos   11/17/62   12/8/62   33   3
also see Wooley, Sheb

Cole, Nat "King"
    Take A Fool's Advice   7/22/61   7/29/61   31   2
    Let True Love Begin   10/14/61   10/21/61   30   2
    Ramblin' Rose   8/11/62   9/15/62   3   9
    Dear Lonely Hearts   11/24/62   12/1/62   27   2
    Those Lazy-Hazy-Crazy Days Of Summer   5/17/63   6/7/63   17   4
    That Sunday, That Summer   10/4/63   11/1/63   12   8
    My True Carrie, Love   2/28/64   2/28/64   37   1
    I Don't Want To Be Hurt Anymore   4/24/64   5/8/64   28   3

Colley, Keith
    Enamorado   9/20/63   10/11/63   16   4

Collins, Judy
    Both Sides Now   11/4/68   12/9/68   9   10
    Turn! Turn! Turn!/To Everything There Is A Season   12/1/69   12/15/69   32   3

Como, Perry
    Caterina   4/21/62   5/19/62   9   7
    Dream On Little Dreamer   4/16/65   5/7/65   15   5
    Seattle   4/21/69   6/2/69   27   7

Comstock, Bobby
    Garden Of Eden   11/18/61   12/16/61   10   6

Conley, Arthur
    Sweet Soul Music   4/14/67   6/2/67   7   9
    Shake, Rattle & Roll   6/30/67   6/30/67   37   2
    Funky Street   3/25/68   5/13/68   8   9
    People Sure Act Funny   6/24/68   7/8/68   31   3
    Ob-La-Di, Ob-La-Da   1/13/69   1/20/69   38   2

Conniff, Ray
    Somewhere, My Love   7/1/66   8/12/66   18   8

Conrad, Bob
    Love You   12/16/61   12/16/61   35   3

Artist	Title	Debut	Peak	Pos	Wks
Contours					
	Do You Love Me	8/25/62	9/22/62	5	9
	Shake Sherry	2/1/63	2/1/63	34	2
	Can You Do It	5/8/64	5/8/64	38	1
Cooke, Sam					
	Chain Gang	10/14/60	10/14/60	17	2
	Cupid	7/22/61	8/5/61	28	4
	Twistin' The Night Away	3/3/62	3/31/62	3	9
	Havin' A Party	6/23/62	7/7/62	27	3
	Nothing Can Change This Love	10/20/62	11/3/62	27	3
	Send Me Some Lovin'	2/15/63	2/22/63	36	2
	Another Saturday Night	4/26/63	5/3/63	34	2
	Frankie And Johnny	8/16/63	8/16/63	34	3
	Little Red Rooster	11/1/63	11/8/63	29	4
	Good News	2/14/64	2/21/64	33	3
	Good Times	7/3/64	7/17/64	34	3
	Shake	1/22/65	1/22/65	28	5
	It's Got Whole World Shakin'	5/7/65	5/7/65	38	1
	Sugar Dumpling	8/6/65	8/6/65	39	1
Cookie & his Cupcakes					
	Got You On My Mind	5/3/63	5/17/63	34	3
Cookies					
	Chains	12/1/62	1/4/63	17	6
	Don't Say Nothin' Bad (About My Baby)	3/8/63	4/19/63	5	8
	Will Power	7/26/63	8/2/63	34	2
	Girls Grow Up Faster Than Boys	12/27/63	1/17/64	31	5
Cooper, Johnny					
	Rivalry	1/6/62	1/6/62	38	1
	Bonnie Do	1/4/63	1/25/63	19	5
Cooper, Les					
	Wiggle Wobble	11/3/62	12/1/62	20	6
Corsairs					
	Smokey Places	12/2/61	1/6/62	7	10
	I'll Take You Home	4/14/62	5/5/62	16	5
	Stormy	4/5/63	4/26/63	21	4
Cortez, Dave "Baby"					
	Hurricane	10/29/60	11/19/60	18	5
	Rinky Dink	7/7/62	8/18/62	12	7
	Organ Shout	8/2/63	8/2/63	30	2

Artist	Title	Debut	Peak	Pos	Wks

Cosby, Bill
    Little Ole Man (Uptight-Everything's Alright) — 9/8/67 — 9/29/67 — 3 — 8

Costa, Don
    Never On Sunday — 10/14/60 — 10/14/60 — 6 — 2
    The Misfits — 1/21/61 — 1/28/61 — 36 — 2

Count Five
    Psychotic Reaction — 9/9/66 — 10/28/66 — 8 — 10

Covay, Don
    The Popeye Waddle — 1/19/63 — 1/25/63 — 30 — 2

Cowsills
    The Rain, The Park And Other Things — 9/29/67 — 11/17/67 — 2 — 13
    We Can Fly — 1/8/68 — 2/12/68 — 18 — 6
    In Need Of A Friend — 3/25/68 — 4/1/68 — 27 — 3
    Indian Lake — 6/3/68 — 7/15/68 — 5 — 11
    Poor Baby — 9/9/68 — 9/30/68 — 31 — 4
    Hair — 3/10/69 — 4/28/69 — 1 — 12

Cramer, Floyd
    Last Date — 11/26/60 — 12/24/60 — 10 — 9
    On The Rebound — 4/8/61 — 4/29/61 — 19 — 5
    San Antonio Rose — 7/22/61 — 8/5/61 — 11 — 6
    Chattanooga Choo Choo — 2/10/62 — 2/17/62 — 32 — 3
    Java — 1/25/63 — 2/22/63 — 22 — 5
    Naomi — 4/10/64 — 4/10/64 — 37 — 1

Crawford, Johnny
    Daydreams — 7/29/61 — 8/19/61 — 17 — 6
    Patti Ann — 1/27/62 — 3/10/62 — 9 — 8
    Cindy's Birthday — 5/12/62 — 6/9/62 — 5 — 8
    Your Nose Is Gonna Grow — 8/4/62 — 9/1/62 — 8 — 6
    Rumors — 11/10/62 — 12/1/62 — 9 — 5
    Proud — 1/12/63 — 2/8/63 — 18 — 5

Crazy Elephant
    Gimme Gimme Good Lovin' — 3/17/69 — 4/28/69 — 5 — 10

Cream
    Sunshine Of Your Love — 12/22/67 — 2/5/68 — 8 — 9
    Anyone For Tennis — 5/13/68 — 5/20/68 — 38 — 3
    Sunshine Of Your Love — 7/22/68 — 8/26/68 — 7 — 7
    White Room — 9/23/68 — 10/28/68 — 4 — 10
    Crossroads — 2/3/69 — 3/3/69 — 15 — 6

Creedence Clearwater Revival
    Susie Q (Part One) — 9/9/68 — 10/14/68 — 6 — 9

Artist	Title	Debut	Peak	Pos	Wks
	Proud Mary	1/27/69	3/10/69	3	10
	Bad Moon Rising	5/12/69	6/9/69	1	11
	Green River	7/28/69	9/1/69	4	10
	Fortunate Son	10/27/69	12/8/69	3	12
	/Down On The Corner	11/10/69	12/8/69	3	10
Crescents					
	Pink Dominos	1/31/64	2/7/64	28	4
Crestones					
	She's A Bad Motorcycle	4/3/64	5/1/64	11	5
	I've Had It	6/19/64	7/10/64	21	4
Crewe, Bob, Generation					
	Music To Watch Girls By	1/6/67	2/10/67	12	6
Criss, Gary					
	Our Favorite Melodies	6/9/62	6/16/62	31	3
Critters					
	Mr. Dieingly Sad	8/26/66	9/30/66	13	8
	Don't Let The Rain Fall On Me	8/4/67	8/11/67	29	2
Crockett, G.L.					
	It's A Man Down There	9/10/65	9/17/65	34	2
Crosby, Stills & Nash					
	Marrakesh Express	7/14/69	8/11/69	15	6
	Suite: Judy Blue Eyes	9/22/69	11/3/69	3	11
	also see Buffalo Springfield, the Byrds & the Hollies				
Crow					
	Evil Woman Don't Play Your Games With Me	11/10/69	12/22/69	6	11
Cryan' Shames					
	Sugar And Spice	7/1/66	7/29/66	4	8
	I Wanna Meet You	10/21/66	12/2/66	6	8
	Mr. Unreliable	3/10/67	4/14/67	7	8
	It Could Be We're In Love	7/7/67	8/4/67	1	12
	Up On The Roof	2/26/68	4/1/68	10	7
	Young Birds Fly	5/20/68	6/24/68	15	6
	Greenberg, Glickstein, Charles, David Smith And Jones	9/16/68	10/14/68	11	6
Crystals					
	There's No Other (Like My Baby)	12/16/61	12/30/61	23	5
	Uptown	3/31/62	5/12/62	5	9
	He's A Rebel	9/29/62	10/27/62	2	11
	He's Sure The Boy I Love	1/12/63	2/8/63	7	7
	Da Doo Ron Ron (When He Walked Me Home)	4/26/63	5/17/63	3	8

Artist	Title	Debut	Peak	Pos	Wks
	Then He Kissed Me	8/16/63	8/30/63	5	7
	Little Boy	1/31/64	1/31/64	32	2

Cuba, Joe, Sextet
	"Bang" "Bang"	10/21/66	10/28/66	31	3
	Oh Yeah!	1/20/67	2/3/67	34	4

Cuff Links
	Tracy	9/8/69	10/27/69	2	11
	When Julie Comes Around	12/15/69	12/22/69	34	3

also see the Archies & the Detergents

Cupids
	Brenda	6/21/63	7/5/63	27	4

Curtola, Bobby
	Fortuneteller	6/9/62	7/7/62	6	8

Cymbal, Johnny
	The Water Was Red	3/11/61	4/8/61	12	6
	Bachelor Man	1/25/63	2/8/63	19	3
	Mr. Bass Man	3/8/63	4/5/63	16	6

also see Derek

Cyrkle
	Red Rubber Ball	5/27/66	7/8/66	4	10
	Turn-Down Day	8/26/66	9/16/66	15	7
	Please Don't Ever Leave Me	11/18/66	12/2/66	28	4

Daddy Cool
	Daddy Cool	1/28/61	2/4/61	36	3

Dale, Dick & the Del-Tones
	Let's Go Trippin'	12/2/61	12/30/61	19	5

Dale & Grace
	I'm Leaving It Up To You	9/27/63	10/11/63	2	8
	Stop And Think It Over	1/24/64	2/7/64	13	8
	The Loneliest Night	5/8/64	5/8/64	35	3

Damone, Vic
	You Were Only Fooling (While I Was Falling In Love)	5/14/65	5/28/65	21	4

Dana, Vic
	Little Altar Boy	11/25/61	12/16/61	19	4
	I Will	4/21/62	4/28/62	31	2
	More	9/6/63	9/13/63	14	5
	Shangri-La	5/8/64	6/5/64	9	7
	Love Is All We Need	7/17/64	7/24/64	19	5
	Garden In The Rain	10/2/64	10/16/64	25	3

Artist	Title	Debut	Peak	Pos	Wks
	Red Roses For A Blue Lady	3/12/65	4/9/65	15	5
	Moonlight And Roses (Bring Mem'ries Of You)	8/27/65	8/27/65	36	1
	Aren't We The Lucky Ones	10/20/69	11/17/69	28	6
	If I Never Knew Your Name	12/15/69	2/9/70	7	13

Danny & the Juniors
	Twistin' U.S.A.	10/14/60	11/5/60	8	6

Darian, Fred
	Johnny Willow	9/9/61	10/7/61	14	5

Darin, Bobby
	Somebody To Love	10/14/60	10/14/60	40	1
	Lazy River	2/25/61	3/25/61	9	8
	You Must Have Been A Beautiful Baby	9/16/61	9/30/61	7	6
	Irresistible You	1/6/62	1/27/62	12	6
	What'd I Say (Part 1)	4/14/62	4/28/62	26	4
	Things	7/21/62	8/18/62	10	5
	If A Man Answers	9/29/62	10/13/62	25	3
	You're The Reason I'm Living	1/19/63	3/1/63	6	8
	18 Yellow Roses	5/10/63	6/7/63	11	6
	Treat My Baby Good	9/13/63	10/4/63	20	4
	Be Mad Little Girl	12/13/63	12/13/63	34	2
	Milord	6/5/64	6/19/64	28	3
	The Things In This House	10/16/64	11/6/64	22	3
	If I Were A Carpenter	10/14/66	11/11/66	16	8
	Lovin' You	1/20/67	2/3/67	23	4

Darlin, Florraine
	Long As The Rose Is Red	9/22/62	10/6/62	25	3

Darren, James
	Goodbye Cruel World	10/14/61	11/18/61	1	12
	Her Royal Majesty	2/24/62	3/17/62	6	6
	Conscience	4/28/62	5/19/62	18	4
	Mary's Little Lamb	8/4/62	8/4/62	39	1
	Pin A Medal On Joey	3/15/63	3/15/63	36	1
	Because You're Mine	8/27/65	8/27/65	34	1
	All	12/16/66	1/20/67	19	7

Dartells
	Hot Pastrami	4/26/63	5/17/63	10	5

Darvell, Barry
	Silver Dollar	12/16/61	12/30/61	25	3

David & Jonathan
	Michelle	1/7/66	1/28/66	23	4

Artist	Title	Debut	Peak	Pos	Wks

Davis, Jan
    Fugitive   5/8/64   5/15/64   20   3

Davis Jr., Sammy
    What Kind Of Fool Am I   9/22/62   10/6/62   18   4
    The Shelter Of Your Arms   2/14/64   3/20/64   8   9
    I've Gotta Be Me   1/20/69   2/24/69   4   10

Davis, Skeeter
    The End Of The World   2/8/63   3/8/63   1   11
    I'm Saving My Love   5/10/63   5/17/63   23   3
    I Can't Stay Mad At You   9/27/63   10/25/63   5   9
    He Says The Same Things To Me   2/21/64   2/28/64   29   4

Davis, Spencer, Group
    Gimme Some Lovin'   1/6/67   2/10/67   8   7
    I'm A Man   3/24/67   4/28/67   22   7
    Somebody Help Me   7/7/67   8/4/67   21   6

Davis, Tyrone
    Can I Change My Mind   1/6/69   2/3/69   10   7

Daylighters
    Cool Breeze   9/15/62   10/13/62   17   4

Deal, Bill & the Rhondels
    May I   2/10/69   3/17/69   8   8
    I've Been Hurt   4/14/69   5/19/69   9   9
    What Kind Of Fool Do You Think I Am   8/18/69   9/1/69   17   7

Dean, Jimmy
    Big Bad John   10/7/61   10/28/61   2   11
    To A Sleeping Beauty   2/10/62   3/3/62   7   6
    P.T. 109   4/14/62   5/5/62   10   5
    Little Black Book   9/29/62   10/20/62   18   5

Dean & Jean
    Tra La La La Suzy   10/11/63   10/25/63   12   5
    Hey Jean, Hey Dean   2/28/64   3/6/64   38   2

Dee, Dave; Dozy, Beaky, Mick & Tich
    Zabadak   12/29/67   1/15/68   34   3

Dee, Joey & the Starliters
    Peppermint Twist—Part I   12/16/61   1/6/62   2   9
    Hey, Let's Twist   3/10/62   3/10/62   34   2
    Shout—Part 1   3/24/62   4/14/62   3   6
    What Kind Of Love Is This   8/25/62   9/15/62   9   7

Artist / Title	Debut	Peak	Pos	Wks
Dee, Joey				
I Lost My Baby	11/10/62	11/24/62	28	3
Dance, Dance, Dance	7/19/63	7/26/63	33	2
Dee, Kathy				
If I Never Get To Heaven	12/15/62	12/15/62	34	3
Dee, Ricky				
Workout (Part 1)	7/21/62	7/21/62	36	1
Dee, Tracy				
Teenage Cleopatra	10/11/63	10/25/63	32	3
Gonna Get Along Without You Now	5/15/64	5/29/64	32	3
Deep Purple				
Hush	8/26/68	9/23/68	5	8
Kentucky Woman	11/18/68	12/16/68	25	5
Dekker, Desmond & the Aces				
Israelites	5/19/69	6/30/69	4	10
Delcoes				
Arabia	4/5/63	4/5/63	40	1
Delfonics				
La- La- Means I Love You	2/19/68	3/25/68	6	9
Dells				
The (Bossa Nova) Bird	11/24/62	12/8/62	19	3
There Is	12/22/67	2/12/68	10	9
Wear It On Our Face	4/22/68	4/29/68	32	4
Stay In My Corner	7/1/68	8/5/68	9	9
Always Together	11/4/68	11/18/68	34	3
I Can Sing A Rainbow/Love Is Blue	6/9/69	6/23/69	28	3
Oh, What A Night	8/25/69	9/15/69	31	5
DeLory, Al				
Yesterday	11/19/65	12/10/65	25	4
Del-Vetts				
Last Time Around	6/24/66	7/15/66	26	6
also see the Pride and Joy				
Demensions				
Zing Went The Strings Of My Heart	10/29/60	10/29/60	39	1
Denny, Martin				
A Taste Of Honey	9/15/62	9/22/62	32	3
Derek				
Cinnamon	11/4/68	11/25/68	4	12

Artist	Title	Debut	Peak	Pos	Wks
	Back Door Man	2/24/69	3/10/69	29	3
also see Cymbal, Johnny					

DeShannon, Jackie
	Lonely Girl	12/3/60	12/3/60	37	1
	What The World Needs Now Is Love	6/18/65	7/23/65	4	8
	The Weight	8/19/68	9/23/68	22	6
	Put A Little Love In Your Heart	6/23/69	8/4/69	3	12
	Love Will Find A Way	10/13/69	11/24/69	14	9

Detergents
	Leader Of The Laundromat	12/11/64	12/25/64	7	3
also see the Archies & the Cuff Links					

Devotions
	Rip Van Winkle	2/21/64	3/13/64	12	4

Diamond, Neil
	Cherry, Cherry	9/9/66	10/21/66	2	9
	I Got The Feelin' (Oh No No)	11/4/66	12/9/66	19	8
	You Got To Me	1/27/67	2/24/67	16	7
	Girl, You'll Be A Woman Soon	4/7/67	4/28/67	9	7
	I Thank The Lord For The Night Time	7/28/67	8/25/67	6	8
	Kentucky Woman	10/13/67	11/17/67	16	6
	New Orleans	12/29/67	1/22/68	27	5
	Brooklyn Roads	5/6/68	6/3/68	22	5
	Two-Bit Manchild	6/24/68	8/5/68	24	7
	Brother Love's Travelling Salvation Show	3/3/69	4/21/69	7	10
	Sweet Caroline (Good Times Never Seemed So Good)	6/30/69	8/4/69	8	11
	Holly Holy	10/13/69	11/17/69	2	14

Dick & DeeDee
	The Mountain's High	8/19/61	9/16/61	1	8
	Tell Me	4/21/62	5/26/62	5	7
	Young And In Love	3/8/63	4/26/63	11	8
	Love Is A Once In A Lifetime Thing	6/21/63	6/28/63	39	2
	Turn Around	11/22/63	12/20/63	12	6
	Thou Shalt Not Steal	1/1/65	1/22/65	6	5

Dickens, Little Jimmy
	May The Bird Of Paradise Fly Up Your Nose	10/22/65	11/12/65	32	4

Diddley, Bo
	Gunslinger	1/28/61	2/11/61	30	3
	Bo Diddley	11/18/61	11/25/61	32	2
	You Can't Judge A Book By The Cover	8/4/62	8/18/62	25	4

Artist / Title	Debut	Peak	Pos	Wks
Dinning, Mark				
Top Forty, News, Weather And Sports	3/4/61	3/25/61	13	5
All Of This For Sally	3/24/62	3/24/62	40	1
Dino, Kenny				
Your Ma Said You Cried In Your Sleep Last Night	11/18/61	12/9/61	13	6
Dino, Desi & Billy				
I'm A Fool	7/9/65	7/30/65	4	7
Not The Lovin' Kind	10/1/65	10/15/65	24	5
Please Don't Fight It	12/24/65	12/24/65	31	1
Two In The Afternoon	6/16/67	6/30/67	29	3
Dion				
Lonely Teenager	11/5/60	12/3/60	3	12
Havin' Fun	3/11/61	3/25/61	27	3
Runaround Sue	10/7/61	10/21/61	1	11
The Wanderer	1/6/62	2/10/62	2	10
/The Majestic	12/16/61	1/27/62	10	7
Lovers Who Wander	5/5/62	6/2/62	6	8
Little Diane	7/21/62	8/18/62	5	7
Love Came To Me	11/24/62	12/15/62	3	7
Ruby Baby	1/12/63	2/15/63	2	11
Sandy	3/15/63	4/12/63	9	6
This Little Girl	4/19/63	5/10/63	19	5
Come Go With Me	6/14/63	7/5/63	11	5
Be Careful Of Stones That You Throw	6/28/63	7/19/63	19	5
Donna The Prima Donna	9/13/63	10/4/63	3	7
Drip Drop	11/8/63	11/29/63	3	8
Abraham, Martin And John	11/4/68	12/2/68	1	11
also see the Belmonts				
Dirksen, Senator Everett McKinley				
Gallant Men	12/16/66	12/23/66	24	4
Dixie Cups				
Chapel Of Love	5/8/64	5/29/64	3	8
People Say	7/17/64	8/14/64	10	6
You Should Have Seen The Way He Looked At Me	10/23/64	11/20/64	14	5
Little Bell	1/8/65	1/15/65	25	3
Iko Iko	4/2/65	5/7/65	9	7
Dixiebelles				
(Down At) Papa Joe's	9/20/63	10/11/63	13	5
Southtown, U.S.A.	2/7/64	2/14/64	22	3

Artist Title	Debut	Peak	Pos	Wks

Dodd, Ken
    Tears — 11/12/65 — 12/3/65 — 23 — 6

Dodds, Nella
    Finders Keepers, Losers Weepers — 1/15/65 — 1/29/65 — 34 — 3

Doggett, Bill
    (Let's Do) The Hully Gully Twist — 12/17/60 — 12/31/60 — 31 — 5

Domino, Fats
    Three Nights A Week — 10/14/60 — 10/14/60 — 23 — 2
    My Girl Josephine — 11/5/60 — 12/10/60 — 20 — 7
    What A Price — 2/25/61 — 3/4/61 — 31 — 4
    Shu Rah — 5/6/61 — 5/13/61 — 34 — 2
    It Keeps Rainin' — 6/24/61 — 7/8/61 — 16 — 5
    Let The Four Winds Blow — 8/12/61 — 9/16/61 — 14 — 7
    What A Party — 10/21/61 — 10/28/61 — 30 — 2
    I Hear You Knocking — 12/23/61 — 1/6/62 — 34 — 3
      /Jambalaya (On The Bayou) — 12/9/61 — 12/9/61 — 38 — 1
    You Win Again — 3/10/62 — 3/24/62 — 32 — 3
    There Goes (My Heart Again) — 5/31/63 — 6/14/63 — 35 — 3

Don & Juan
    What's Your Name — 3/3/62 — 3/24/62 — 6 — 6

Donegan, Lonnie & his Skiffle Group
    Does Your Chewing Gum Lose Its Flavor (On The Bedpost Over Night) — 8/26/61 — 9/16/61 — 4 — 6
    Rock Island Line — 10/14/61 — 10/14/61 — 37 — 1

Donner, Ral
    Girl Of My Best Friend — 3/25/61 — 4/15/61 — 2 — 8
    You Don't Know What You've Got (Until You Lose It) — 7/15/61 — 8/12/61 — 3 — 8
    Please Don't Go — 10/7/61 — 11/4/61 — 15 — 6
    She's Everything (I Wanted You To Be) — 12/16/61 — 1/27/62 — 7 — 9
    (What A Sad Way) To Love Someone — 3/17/62 — 4/7/62 — 8 — 5
    Loveless Life — 5/26/62 — 6/9/62 — 28 — 3
    To Love — 11/24/62 — 12/15/62 — 16 — 5
    I Got Burned — 2/22/63 — 3/8/63 — 17 — 4

Donovan
    Catch The Wind — 6/4/65 — 6/18/65 — 20 — 5
    Universal Soldier — 10/15/65 — 10/29/65 — 16 — 4
    Sunshine Superman — 8/5/66 — 8/26/66 — 1 — 10
    Mellow Yellow — 11/11/66 — 12/9/66 — 2 — 10
    Epistle To Dippy — 2/3/67 — 2/24/67 — 21 — 7
    There Is A Mountain — 8/18/67 — 9/8/67 — 22 — 5

Artist	Title	Debut	Peak	Pos	Wks
	Wear Your Love Like Heaven	12/8/67	1/8/68	23	4
	Jennifer Juniper	3/11/68	4/15/68	13	8
	Hurdy Gurdy Man	7/1/68	7/29/68	6	8
	Atlantis	4/28/69	5/19/69	11	6

Doors

Title	Debut	Peak	Pos	Wks
Light My Fire	6/23/67	8/18/67	2	14
People Are Strange	9/15/67	10/13/67	18	6
Hello, I Love You	7/1/68	7/29/68	1	11
Touch Me	12/30/68	2/3/69	1	10

Dorsey, Lee

Title	Debut	Peak	Pos	Wks
Ya Ya	9/23/61	10/21/61	6	7
Do-Re-Mi	1/13/62	2/10/62	22	5
Ride Your Pony	7/30/65	7/30/65	28	1
Working In The Coal Mine	8/19/66	9/2/66	22	7

Douglas, Mike

Title	Debut	Peak	Pos	Wks
The Men In My Little Girl's Life	12/24/65	1/21/66	12	6

Douglas, Ronny

Title	Debut	Peak	Pos	Wks
Run, Run, Run	7/8/61	7/15/61	29	3

Dovale, Debbie

Title	Debut	Peak	Pos	Wks
Hey Lover	10/4/63	10/25/63	11	7

Dove, Ronnie

Title	Debut	Peak	Pos	Wks
Say You	9/11/64	9/25/64	22	3
Right Or Wrong	11/6/64	11/20/64	13	6
Hello Pretty Girl	2/12/65	2/12/65	37	1
One Kiss For Old Times' Sake	3/19/65	4/9/65	10	7
A Little Bit Of Heaven	6/11/65	7/2/65	16	6
I'll Make All Your Dreams Come True	8/27/65	9/10/65	22	6
Kiss Away	11/5/65	11/26/65	18	5
When Liking Turns To Loving	2/4/66	2/25/66	26	5
Let's Start All Over Again	4/15/66	5/13/66	29	5
Happy Summer Days	6/24/66	7/1/66	38	2
I Really Don't Want To Know	9/9/66	9/30/66	24	4
Cry	11/25/66	12/9/66	16	7
One More Mountain To Climb	3/10/67	3/24/67	36	4
My Babe	5/12/67	5/19/67	31	3
I Want To Love You For What You Are	8/18/67	8/25/67	32	2
Mountain Of Love	6/17/68	7/15/68	27	5

Dovells

Title	Debut	Peak	Pos	Wks
Bristol Stomp	9/23/61	10/28/61	4	9
Do The New Continental	3/3/62	3/10/62	25	3
Bristol Twistin' Annie	6/2/62	6/30/62	10	6

Artist	Title	Debut	Peak	Pos	Wks
	Hully Gully Baby	9/8/62	9/29/62	10	5
	You Can't Sit Down	4/26/63	5/24/63	3	10
	Betty In Bermudas	10/4/63	10/4/63	40	1

also see Barry, Len

Dowell, Joe
	Little Red Rented Rowboat	6/30/62	8/4/62	20	6

Downing, Big Al
	The Story Of My Life	4/7/62	4/28/62	15	5

Dr. Feelgood & the Interns
	Doctor Feel-Good	4/21/62	5/12/62	15	5
	Right String But The Wrong Yo-Yo	8/11/62	8/18/62	12	7

Drake, Charlie
	My Boomerang Won't Come Back	2/17/62	3/3/62	17	5

Drake, Pete & his Talking Steel Guitar
	Forever	3/13/64	4/24/64	8	10
	I'm Sorry	7/10/64	7/10/64	26	3

Draper, Rusty
	Night Life	10/25/63	11/8/63	23	3

Dreamers
	Teenage Vows Of Love	12/31/60	1/28/61	11	6

Drew-Vels
	Tell Him	12/13/63	1/17/64	21	6
	Everybody Knows	4/3/64	4/3/64	35	2

Drew, Patti
	Workin' On A Groovy Thing	8/5/68	9/9/68	17	6

Drifters
	Save The Last Dance For Me	10/14/60	10/15/60	2	7
	I Count The Tears	1/14/61	2/4/61	14	5
	Some Kind Of Wonderful	4/8/61	5/13/61	9	6
	Please Stay	6/24/61	7/22/61	23	5
	Sweets For My Sweet	9/30/61	10/21/61	9	6
	Room Full Of Tears	1/6/62	1/13/62	31	2
	When My Little Girl Is Smiling	3/3/62	3/17/62	29	3
	Up On The Roof	12/15/62	1/4/63	5	8
	On Broadway	3/8/63	4/12/63	12	7
	Rat Race	6/14/63	6/28/63	33	3
	I'll Take You Home	9/20/63	10/4/63	26	3
	Vaya Con Dios	2/21/64	2/28/64	24	3
	One Way Love	6/5/64	6/5/64	37	1
	Under The Boardwalk	7/17/64	8/28/64	4	9

Artist / Title	Debut	Peak	Pos	Wks
Saturday Night At The Movies	12/4/64	12/25/64	18	4
At The Club	2/5/65	2/5/65	35	2
I'll Take You Where The Music's Playing	8/13/65	8/27/65	19	3
Still Burning	12/22/67	1/8/68	29	3

also see King, Ben E. and McPhatter, Clyde

D'Rone, Frank
Strawberry Blonde	11/19/60	12/10/60	27	4

Duals
Stick Shift	8/12/61	9/2/61	15	5

Dudley, Dave
Six Days On The Road	7/12/63	7/19/63	14	5

Dukays
Nite Owl	12/23/61	1/13/62	18	5
Please Help	6/2/62	6/9/62	27	2

also see Chandler, Gene

Duke, Patty
Don't Just Stand There	6/25/65	8/13/65	7	9
Say Something Funny	10/29/65	10/29/65	39	1

Duprees
You Belong To Me	7/28/62	9/8/62	4	8
My Own True Love	11/10/62	12/8/62	12	7
Why Don't You Believe Me	9/6/63	9/6/63	37	1
Have You Heard	11/22/63	12/13/63	25	4
(It's No) Sin	2/28/64	2/28/64	38	2

Dutones
The Bird	1/12/63	2/8/63	21	5

Dyke & the Blazers
We Got More Soul	7/7/69	7/7/69	35	2

Dylan, Bob
Subterranean Homesick Blues	4/16/65	4/23/65	34	4
Like A Rolling Stone	8/6/65	8/27/65	7	6
Positively 4th Street	10/1/65	10/22/65	9	6
Rainy Day Women #12 & 35	4/15/66	5/13/66	3	7
I Want You	6/24/66	7/1/66	22	4
Just Like A Woman	9/9/66	9/16/66	37	3
Lay Lady Lay	8/4/69	8/18/69	4	9

Earls
Life Is But A Dream	7/15/61	7/22/61	33	2
Remember Then	11/17/62	12/22/62	14	6
Never	5/3/63	5/10/63	26	2

Artist	Title	Debut	Peak	Pos	Wks
Easybeats					
	Friday On My Mind	5/12/67	5/19/67	25	3
Echoes					
	Baby Blue	4/8/61	5/20/61	4	10
	Bluebirds Over The Mountain	10/6/62	11/17/62	15	7
Eddy, Duane					
	Peter Gunn	10/15/60	11/5/60	10	9
	"Pepe"	1/14/61	1/28/61	12	4
	Theme From Dixie	4/15/61	5/6/61	17	5
	My Blue Heaven	9/30/61	9/30/61	40	1
	(Dance With The) Guitar Man	10/6/62	11/10/62	6	8
	Boss Guitar	2/8/63	2/22/63	26	3
Edsels					
	Rama Lama Ding Dong	5/27/61	6/17/61	9	6
Edwards, Bobby					
	You're The Reason	10/7/61	11/4/61	3	9
	What's The Reason	2/10/62	2/17/62	31	2
Egyptian Combo					
	Gale Winds	10/9/64	10/30/64	16	5
El Clod					
	Tijuana Border	9/15/62	9/22/62	27	2
Electric Indian					
	Keem-O-Sabe	8/4/69	9/1/69	13	7
Electric Prunes					
	I Had Too Much To Dream (Last Night)	12/16/66	2/10/67	6	11
	Get Me To The World On Time	5/5/67	5/5/67	28	2
Elledge, Jimmy					
	Funny How Time Slips Away	1/20/62	2/3/62	23	3
Ellington, Duke & Louis Armstrong					
	Duke's Place	11/11/61	11/11/61	35	1
also see Armstrong, Louis					
Elliot, Mama Cass					
	Dream A Little Dream Of Me	7/15/68	8/19/68	12	8
	Make Your Own Kind Of Music	11/3/69	11/24/69	20	5
also see the Mamas & the Papas and the Mugwumps					
Ellis, Shirley					
	The Nitty Gritty	11/29/63	11/29/63	36	1
	The Name Game	12/25/64	1/15/65	8	7
	The Clapping Song (Clap Pat Clap Slap)	3/26/65	4/9/65	27	3

Artist / Title	Debut	Peak	Pos	Wks
Ellison, Lorraine				
Dig You Baby	1/14/66	1/14/66	36	1
Embers				
Solitaire	9/2/61	9/9/61	36	2
Emotions				
A Story Untold	10/11/63	10/25/63	25	4
English, Barbara				
Ta Ta Tee Ta Ta	5/26/62	6/9/62	34	3
Equals				
Baby, Come Back	9/16/68	10/28/68	15	7
Esquires				
Get On Up	9/22/67	9/29/67	24	3
Essex				
Easier Said Than Done	5/31/63	6/21/63	1	10
A Walkin' Miracle	9/6/63	10/4/63	5	6
She's Got Everything	11/15/63	11/29/63	22	4
Eubanks, Jack				
Searching	11/25/61	12/2/61	17	2
Evans, Barbara				
Charlie Wasn't There	5/20/61	5/27/61	29	2
Evans, Elliott				
Concerto For The X-15	1/20/62	2/10/62	20	4
Evans, Paul				
Hushabye Little Guitar	11/5/60	11/12/60	23	2
Everett, Betty				
You're No Good	11/1/63	11/15/63	17	4
The Shoop Shoop Song (It's In His Kiss)	3/20/64	3/27/64	31	2
There'll Come A Time	2/17/69	2/17/69	36	2
also see Butler, Jerry & Betty Everett				
Everett, Vince				
Such A Night	5/26/62	6/16/62	16	5
Everette, Keith				
Don't You Know	3/4/66	4/15/66	8	9
Everly Brothers				
So Sad (To Watch Good Love Go Bad)	10/14/60	10/15/60	3	3
Like Strangers	11/26/60	12/10/60	16	4
Walk Right Back	2/25/61	3/25/61	1	11
Temptation	6/10/61	7/15/61	2	8

Artist	Title	Debut	Peak	Pos	Wks
	Don't Blame Me	10/14/61	11/4/61	17	4
	Crying In The Rain	1/27/62	3/3/62	5	9
	That's Old Fashioned (That's The Way Love Should Be)	5/26/62	6/9/62	8	7
	I'm Here To Get My Baby Out Of Jail	10/6/62	10/20/62	31	3
	Gone, Gone, Gone	11/13/64	12/4/64	13	5
	Bowling Green	6/9/67	6/16/67	34	3

Every Mothers' Son
	Come On Down To My Boat	5/26/67	7/21/67	2	14

Excellents
	Coney Island Baby	1/4/63	1/4/63	31	1

Exciters
	Tell Him	11/24/62	12/22/62	15	7
	He's Got The Power	4/5/63	4/5/63	35	1

Exports
	Car Hop	8/14/64	9/11/64	9	7

Fabares, Shelley
	Johnny Angel	3/10/62	3/24/62	1	10
	Johnny Loves Me	6/30/62	7/21/62	16	4
	Ronnie, Call Me When You Get A Chance	5/3/63	5/17/63	26	3

Fabian
	You Know You Belong To Someone	1/21/61	1/28/61	37	2

Fabric, Bent
	Alley Cat	8/11/62	9/15/62	6	10

Fabulous Pack
	Wide Trackin'	9/29/67	9/29/67	36	1

Faith, Adam
	It's Alright	1/29/65	2/12/65	11	6

Faithfull, Marianne
	As Tears Go By	11/20/64	12/18/64	11	6
	Come And Stay With Me	3/26/65	4/16/65	19	5
	Summer Nights	9/10/65	10/15/65	10	7

Fame, Georgie
	Yeh, Yeh	3/5/65	3/26/65	16	6
	Get Away	9/9/66	9/30/66	21	5
	The Ballad Of Bonnie And Clyde	2/26/68	4/1/68	9	9

Family
	Face The Autumn	10/13/67	11/17/67	12	7

Artist / Title	Debut	Peak	Pos	Wks
Fantastic Johnny C				
Boogaloo Down Broadway	11/17/67	1/8/68	6	10
Hitch It To The Horse	7/8/68	7/29/68	32	4
Fardon, Don				
(The Lament Of The Cherokee) Indian Reservation	8/19/68	9/23/68	6	8
Feliciano, Jose				
Light My Fire	7/22/68	8/19/68	4	10
Hi-Heel Sneakers	10/7/68	11/4/68	20	6
Fendermen				
Don't You Just Know It	10/14/60	10/14/60	39	1
Ferrante & Teicher				
Exodus	11/26/60	12/24/60	1	15
Love Theme From One Eyed Jacks	4/22/61	4/22/61	31	2
Theme From "Goodbye Again"	7/1/61	7/1/61	36	1
Tonight	10/28/61	11/25/61	9	8
Lisa	6/9/62	6/16/62	28	2
Theme From Lawrence Of Arabia	2/22/63	3/8/63	27	3
Midnight Cowboy	11/17/69	1/12/70	6	12
Field, Sally				
Felicidad	11/10/67	11/17/67	33	3
Fields, Ernie				
The Charleston	6/17/61	7/1/61	12	7
Fiestas				
Broken Heart	8/18/62	8/18/62	39	1
Fifth Dimension				
Go Where You Wanna Go	2/10/67	3/10/67	14	8
Another Day, Another Heartache	5/5/67	5/19/67	23	4
Up-Up And Away	5/26/67	6/16/67	5	6
Paper Cup	10/27/67	11/24/67	26	5
Carpet Man	2/19/68	3/11/68	31	4
Stoned Soul Picnic	6/24/68	7/29/68	7	9
Sweet Blindness	10/21/68	11/18/68	19	5
California Soul	12/30/68	1/20/69	18	6
Aquarius/Let The Sunshine In	3/10/69	3/24/69	1	13
Workin' On A Groovy Thing	7/14/69	8/11/69	11	9
Wedding Bell Blues	9/29/69	11/3/69	2	12
Fifth Estate				
Ding Dong! The Witch Is Dead	5/19/67	6/16/67	13	6

Artist	Title	Debut	Peak	Pos	Wks

Finnegan, Larry
    Dear One — 2/17/62 — 3/10/62 — 4 — 7
    Pretty Suzy Sunshine — 6/16/62 — 6/23/62 — 36 — 2
    The Other Ringo — 12/11/64 — 12/11/64 — 28 — 1

First Edition
    Just Dropped In (To See What Condition My Condition Was In) — 2/5/68 — 3/11/68 — 4 — 8
    But You Know I Love You — 1/20/69 — 3/3/69 — 13 — 8

Kenny Rogers & the First Edition
    Ruby, Don't Take Your Love To Town — 6/16/69 — 7/14/69 — 5 — 9
    Reuben James — 9/15/69 — 10/20/69 — 10 — 9

Fisher, Toni
    West Of The Wall — 5/19/62 — 6/16/62 — 9 — 7

Five Americans
    I See The Light — 1/7/66 — 2/11/66 — 16 — 7
    Evol-Not Love — 4/22/66 — 5/27/66 — 8 — 6
    Western Union — 2/17/67 — 3/24/67 — 10 — 10
    Sound Of Love — 5/19/67 — 6/23/67 — 15 — 7
    Zip Code — 8/4/67 — 9/1/67 — 12 — 7

Five By Five
    Fire — 9/30/68 — 11/4/68 — 5 — 9

Five Du-Tones
    Shake A Tail Feather — 4/5/63 — 4/19/63 — 31 — 4

Five Emprees
    Little Miss Sad — 7/23/65 — 8/27/65 — 3 — 8
    Hey Baby — 11/5/65 — 11/19/65 — 24 — 4

Flaming Ember
    Mind, Body And Soul — 10/20/69 — 11/17/69 — 22 — 6

Flamingos
    Your Other Love — 12/10/60 — 1/14/61 — 22 — 6
    Time Was — 8/12/61 — 8/26/61 — 31 — 3
    I'm No Fool Anymore — 5/26/62 — 5/26/62 — 37 — 2

Flares
    Foot Stomping—Part 1 — 8/26/61 — 9/23/61 — 13 — 8

Flatt, Lester & Earl Scruggs
    The Ballad Of Jed Clampett — 12/29/62 — 1/12/63 — 17 — 5

Fleetwoods
    The Last One To Know — 10/14/60 — 10/14/60 — 19 — 1
    Confidential — 12/10/60 — 12/24/60 — 26 — 3

Artist	Title	Debut	Peak	Pos	Wks
	Tragedy	4/22/61	5/27/61	4	7
	(He's) The Great Impostor	9/30/61	10/28/61	15	5
	Lovers By Night, Strangers By Day	9/29/62	11/10/62	6	9
	Goodnight My Love	5/31/63	7/5/63	15	7

Flint, Shelby
	Angel On My Shoulder	1/21/61	3/4/61	8	9

Flirtations
	Nothing But A Heartache	4/28/69	5/19/69	17	5

Flock
	Can't You See I Still Love You	12/16/66	1/20/67	22	7
	Are You The Kind	2/24/67	3/10/67	23	4
	Take Me Back	7/14/67	8/25/67	12	9

Floyd, Eddie
	I've Never Found A Girl (To Love Me Like You Do)	8/26/68	9/2/68	38	2
	Bring It On Home To Me	10/28/68	11/18/68	24	5

Flying Machine
	Smile A Little Smile For Me	10/13/69	12/1/69	8	12

Fontana, Wayne & the Mindbenders
	Game Of Love	3/12/65	4/2/65	2	8
	It's Just A Little Bit Too Late	6/25/65	7/23/65	20	5

Mindbenders
	A Groovy Kind Of Love	4/8/66	5/20/66	2	10

Fortunes
	You've Got Your Troubles	8/20/65	10/1/65	12	9
	Here It Comes Again	11/26/65	11/26/65	31	1
	This Golden Ring	2/25/66	2/25/66	38	1

Foundations
	Baby, Now That I've Found You	1/8/68	2/19/68	5	9
	Back On My Feet Again	3/18/68	3/25/68	32	2
	Build Me Up Buttercup	1/13/69	2/17/69	3	9

Four Couquettes
	Sparkle And Shine	5/20/61	5/20/61	38	1

Four Jacks & A Jill
	Master Jack	4/22/68	5/27/68	5	8

Four Pennies
	My Block	7/5/63	7/19/63	33	3

also see the Chiffons

Four Preps
	More Money For You And Me	8/19/61	9/9/61	7	7

Artist	Title	Debut	Peak	Pos	Wks
	The Big Draft	4/7/62	4/14/62	31	2
	A Letter To The Beatles	3/27/64	3/27/64	35	1

Four Seasons

	Sherry	8/18/62	9/1/62	1	8
	Big Girls Don't Cry	10/13/62	10/27/62	1	9
	Walk Like A Man	1/19/63	2/15/63	1	10
	Ain't That A Shame	4/19/63	4/26/63	28	4
	Candy Girl	7/5/63	8/2/63	3	10
	/Marlena	8/30/63	8/30/63	17	2
	New Mexican Rose	10/4/63	10/11/63	20	2
	Dawn (Go Away)	1/31/64	2/7/64	2	7
	Stay	3/20/64	5/1/64	13	7
	Ronnie	4/10/64	5/15/64	10	7
	Rag Doll	6/26/64	7/17/64	1	10
	Alone	7/24/64	7/24/64	39	2
	Save It For Me	9/11/64	10/2/64	16	4
	Big Man In Town	12/11/64	12/11/64	22	1
	Bye, Bye Baby (Baby Goodbye)	1/22/65	2/12/65	10	6
	Girl Come Running	6/25/65	7/2/65	36	2
	Let's Hang On	10/22/65	12/3/65	1	13
	Little Boy (In Grown Up Clothes)	1/14/66	1/14/66	37	1
	Working My Way Back To You	2/11/66	3/4/66	12	8
	Opus 17 (Don't You Worry 'Bout Me)	5/20/66	6/17/66	25	5
	I've Got You Under My Skin	9/23/66	10/7/66	22	5
	Tell It To The Rain	12/23/66	1/27/67	21	8
	Beggin'	3/17/67	4/21/67	23	7
	C'mon Marianne	6/9/67	7/21/67	8	10
	Watch The Flowers Grow	10/20/67	11/24/67	9	7
	Will You Love Me Tomorrow	2/19/68	3/11/68	15	6
	Saturday's Father	6/10/68	6/17/68	31	2

Wonder Who?

	Don't Think Twice	11/26/65	12/17/65	8	6

also see Valli, Frankie

Four Tops

	Baby I Need Your Loving	8/28/64	10/2/64	13	7
	Ask The Lonely	2/19/65	2/19/65	29	4
	I Can't Help Myself	5/21/65	6/25/65	1	11
	It's The Same Old Song	7/23/65	8/6/65	6	5
	Something About You	11/19/65	11/19/65	25	3
	Shake Me, Wake Me (When It's Over)	2/25/66	3/11/66	27	3
	Reach Out I'll Be There	9/23/66	11/4/66	2	10
	Standing In The Shadows Of Love	12/16/66	1/20/67	10	8
	Bernadette	3/17/67	4/21/67	20	7

Artist	Title	Debut	Peak	Pos	Wks
	7 Rooms Of Gloom	6/2/67	6/16/67	27	4
	You Keep Running Away	9/22/67	10/20/67	28	5
	Walk Away Renee	2/5/68	2/26/68	10	5
	If I Were A Carpenter	5/6/68	6/10/68	7	8
	Yesterday's Dreams	7/15/68	7/29/68	26	3
	I'm In A Different World	10/14/68	11/11/68	26	5

Four Young Men
	You've Been Torturing Me	2/4/61	2/11/61	27	2

Foxx, Inez
	Mockingbird	8/9/63	8/16/63	27	4

Francis, Connie
	My Heart Has A Mind Of Its Own	10/14/60	10/14/60	3	2
	Many Tears Ago	11/26/60	12/17/60	14	6
	Where The Boys Are	2/4/61	3/25/61	2	11
	Breakin' In A Brand New Broken Heart	5/6/61	5/27/61	6	7
	Together	7/15/61	8/19/61	8	7
	(He's My) Dreamboat	9/30/61	10/21/61	19	5
	When The Boy In Your Arms (Is The Boy In Your Heart)	12/16/61	1/20/62	14	6
	Don't Break The Heart That Loves You	2/24/62	3/17/62	5	7
	Second Hand Love	5/26/62	6/9/62	26	3
	Vacation	8/4/62	8/18/62	27	3
	I Was Such A Fool (To Fall In Love With You)	10/20/62	11/3/62	34	3
	I'm Gonna Be Warm This Winter	1/4/63	1/12/63	28	3
	Follow The Boys	3/29/63	4/12/63	26	4
	If My Pillow Could Talk	5/17/63	6/28/63	28	4
	/You're The Only One	6/21/63	6/28/63	28	2
	Drownin' My Sorrows	8/30/63	9/13/63	27	3
	Your Other Love	10/25/63	11/1/63	33	3
	Blue Winter	3/20/64	3/20/64	27	3
	Be Anything (But Be Mine)	5/22/64	5/22/64	21	4
	Looking For Love	8/14/64	8/21/64	37	2
	Don't Ever Leave Me	11/27/64	11/27/64	28	1
	Whose Heart Are You Breaking Tonight	1/22/65	2/5/65	25	6
	Wishing It Was You	5/21/65	5/21/65	31	4
	Spanish Nights And You	11/25/66	12/2/66	18	5

Franklin, Aretha
	Rock-A-Bye Your Baby With A Dixie Melody	11/11/61	11/18/61	30	2
	Don't Cry, Baby	7/21/62	7/21/62	37	1
	Trouble In Mind	1/12/63	1/19/63	24	3
	Respect	5/5/67	6/2/67	10	8
	Baby I Love You	7/21/67	8/25/67	16	8

Artist	Title	Debut	Peak	Pos	Wks
	A Natural Woman (You Make Me Feel Like)	9/29/67	10/20/67	23	6
	Chain Of Fools	12/1/67	1/22/68	5	10
	(Sweet Sweet Baby) Since You've Been Gone	2/19/68	3/25/68	5	9
	/Ain't No Way	4/8/68	4/29/68	14	5
	Think	5/13/68	6/10/68	11	8
	I Say A Little Prayer	8/12/68	9/16/68	8	8
	/The House That Jack Built	8/12/68	8/26/68	16	5
	See Saw	11/25/68	12/16/68	12	6
	The Weight	2/24/69	2/24/69	34	2
	Share Your Love With Me	8/11/69	8/18/69	33	2
	Eleanor Rigby	11/10/69	11/24/69	23	5

Fred, John & his Playboy Band

	Judy In Disguise (With Glasses)	11/24/67	12/22/67	1	12

Freddie & the Dreamers

	I'm Telling You Now	3/12/65	4/2/65	1	8
	I Understand (Just How You Feel)	4/9/65	4/16/65	24	3
	You Were Made For Me	4/23/65	5/7/65	22	6
	Do The Freddie	5/7/65	5/21/65	9	6
	A Little You	8/13/65	8/20/65	30	2

Freeman, Bobby

	C'mon And Swim (Part 2)	7/31/64	8/28/64	8	7

Freeman, Ernie

	Theme From "The Dark At The Top Of The Stairs"	10/15/60	10/15/60	35	1

Friend & Lover

	Reach Out Of The Darkness	5/6/68	5/27/68	3	8
	If Love Is In Your Heart	8/19/68	8/26/68	36	2

Friends Of Distinction

	Grazing In The Grass	4/7/69	6/9/69	6	13

Frizzell, Lefty

	Saginaw, Michigan	1/31/64	3/13/64	25	5

Frogmen

	Underwater	4/15/61	5/20/61	2	9

Frost, Max & the Troopers

	Shape Of Things To Come	9/16/68	10/14/68	4	7

Fugitives

	Freeway	12/31/60	1/21/61	16	6

Artist	Title	Debut	Peak	Pos	Wks
Fuller, Bobby, Four					
	I Fought The Law	1/7/66	2/11/66	4	9
	Love's Made A Fool Of You	4/8/66	4/15/66	20	3
Galens					
	Baby I Do Love You	11/29/63	11/29/63	35	1
Gallis, Paul					
	Boogie Twist	2/17/62	3/10/62	31	4
Gants					
	Road Runner	9/24/65	10/29/65	10	8
Gardner, Don & Dee Dee Ford					
	I Need Your Loving	7/7/62	7/28/62	27	5
Gari, Frank					
	Utopia	1/21/61	2/11/61	14	6
	Lullaby Of Love	6/3/61	7/1/61	26	5
	Princess	8/26/61	9/9/61	27	3
Garnett, Gale					
	We'll Sing In The Sunshine	9/11/64	10/9/64	7	9
Garrett, Kelly					
	Tommy Makes Girls Cry	8/30/63	9/20/63	23	4
Gary, Phil					
	Bobby Layne	2/18/61	3/4/61	30	4
Gaye, Marvin					
	Stubborn Kind Of Fellow	11/3/62	11/3/62	38	1
	Hitch Hike	2/22/63	3/1/63	36	2
	Pride And Joy	7/26/63	8/2/63	28	3
	Can I Get A Witness	12/13/63	12/20/63	33	3
	How Sweet It Is To Be Loved By You	1/1/65	1/1/65	18	3
	I'll Be Doggone	4/16/65	5/21/65	29	7
	Pretty Little Baby	8/6/65	8/27/65	17	4
	You	1/22/68	1/29/68	36	3
	Chained	9/16/68	10/7/68	32	4
	I Heard It Through The Grapevine	11/18/68	12/9/68	1	13
	Too Busy Thinking About My Baby	4/28/69	6/16/69	7	12
	That's The Way Love Is	9/1/69	10/6/69	6	9
Gaye, Marvin & Tammi Terrell					
	Ain't No Mountain High Enough	6/30/67	7/14/67	25	5
	Your Precious Love	10/6/67	10/20/67	20	5
	If I Could Build My Whole World Around You	12/1/67	1/15/68	11	9
	Ain't Nothing Like The Real Thing	4/29/68	6/3/68	16	6
	You're All I Need To Get By	8/5/68	9/9/68	14	7

Artist	Title	Debut	Peak	Pos	Wks
	Keep On Lovin' Me Honey	10/14/68	10/21/68	34	3
	Good Lovin' Ain't Easy To Come By	2/3/69	2/17/69	22	4
	What You Gave Me	12/15/69	12/22/69	32	2

Gaye, Marvin & Mary Wells
	Once Upon A Time	5/22/64	6/5/64	25	5

also see Wells, Mary

G-Clefs
	I Understand (Just How You Feel)	10/21/61	12/2/61	4	10

Gene & Debbe
	Playboy	3/4/68	3/25/68	28	5

Gene & Wendell
	The Roach	10/14/61	10/28/61	24	3

Gentry, Bobbie
	Ode To Billie Joe	8/4/67	9/1/67	1	11

Gentrys
	Keep On Dancing	10/8/65	11/12/65	1	11

George, Barbara
	I Know (You Don't Love Me No More)	12/2/61	1/27/62	9	10
	You Talk About Love	4/14/62	5/5/62	33	4

Gerry & the Pacemakers
	Don't Let The Sun Catch You Crying	6/12/64	7/17/64	6	9
	How Do You Do It	7/17/64	8/21/64	6	8
	I Like It	10/9/64	10/9/64	22	2
	I'll Be There	1/8/65	1/15/65	25	3
	Ferry Cross The Mersey	2/19/65	3/12/65	1	7
	It's Gonna Be Alright	4/16/65	5/7/65	7	5
	Give All Your Love To Me	8/13/65	9/3/65	12	4
	Girl On A Swing	9/9/66	10/21/66	13	7

Getz, Stan & Charlie Byrd
	Desafinado	10/13/62	10/27/62	21	5

Getz, Stan & Astrud Gilberto
	The Girl From Ipanema	6/12/64	6/26/64	6	7

Gilmer, Jimmy & the Fireballs
	Sugar Shack	9/13/63	10/4/63	1	11
	Daisy Petal Pickin'	12/13/63	1/17/64	9	8
	Ain't Gonna Tell Anybody	3/20/64	4/10/64	19	6

Fireballs
	Long Green	2/10/69	3/17/69	10	7

Artist	Title	Debut	Peak	Pos	Wks

Gilreath, James
Little Band Of Gold — 3/22/63 — 4/26/63 — 9 — 7

Glencoves
Hootenanny — 6/14/63 — 7/12/63 — 14 — 7
Devil's A'waitin' — 11/15/63 — 12/6/63 — 24 — 4

Goldsboro, Bobby
Molly — 12/29/62 — 1/19/63 — 22 — 5
See The Funny Little Clown — 1/10/64 — 2/28/64 — 4 — 10
Whenever He Holds You — 4/10/64 — 5/8/64 — 9 — 7
Me Japanese Boy I Love You — 8/7/64 — 8/28/64 — 26 — 4
Little Things — 2/5/65 — 3/12/65 — 6 — 8
Voodoo Woman — 5/14/65 — 6/18/65 — 22 — 6
If You Wait For Love — 8/27/65 — 8/27/65 — 38 — 1
It's Too Late — 2/25/66 — 3/18/66 — 37 — 4
I Know You Better Than That — 4/29/66 — 5/13/66 — 28 — 4
Goodbye To All You Women — 4/21/67 — 4/21/67 — 40 — 1
Honey — 3/18/68 — 4/8/68 — 1 — 10
Autumn Of My Life — 6/24/68 — 8/5/68 — 11 — 8
The Straight Life — 11/11/68 — 12/2/68 — 27 — 5

Goodees
Condition Red — 12/16/68 — 1/13/69 — 15 — 5

Goodman, Dickie
The Touchables — 2/18/61 — 3/4/61 — 1 — 7
The Touchables In Brooklyn — 5/6/61 — 5/20/61 — 16 — 4
Ben Crazy — 7/7/62 — 7/21/62 — 25 — 3
Batman And His Grandmother — 5/6/66 — 5/27/66 — 9 — 4
Luna Trip — 8/18/69 — 8/18/69 — 34 — 2

Gore, Lesley
It's My Party — 5/3/63 — 5/24/63 — 1 — 8
Judy's Turn To Cry — 7/19/63 — 8/16/63 — 6 — 7
She's A Fool — 10/4/63 — 11/8/63 — 2 — 10
You Don't Own Me — 1/3/64 — 1/24/64 — 1 — 9
That's The Way Boys Are — 3/27/64 — 4/24/64 — 13 — 8
I Don't Wanna Be A Loser — 5/29/64 — 6/5/64 — 35 — 3
Maybe I Know — 8/7/64 — 8/28/64 — 21 — 6
Look Of Love — 1/8/65 — 1/29/65 — 25 — 4
All Of My Life — 4/9/65 — 4/16/65 — 35 — 2
Sunshine, Lollipops And Rainbows — 6/11/65 — 7/23/65 — 13 — 7
My Town, My Guy And Me — 9/24/65 — 9/24/65 — 33 — 1
Young Love — 4/1/66 — 4/8/66 — 38 — 3
California Nights — 3/10/67 — 4/28/67 — 8 — 9

Artist	Title	Debut	Peak	Pos	Wks

Gorme, Eydie
    Blame It On The Bossa Nova — 2/15/63 — 3/22/63 — 4 — 9
    Don't Try To Fight It, Baby — 6/21/63 — 6/21/63 — 25 — 3
    Everybody Go Home — 10/11/63 — 10/11/63 — 22 — 2
  also see Lawrence, Steve & Eydie Gorme

Grace, Buddy
    Mr. Lonely — 10/20/62 — 11/10/62 — 17 — 5

Grant, Earl
    Swingin' Gently — 6/23/62 — 6/23/62 — 38 — 1

Grant, Janie
    Triangle — 5/13/61 — 6/3/61 — 5 — 9

Grass Roots
    Where Were You When I Needed You — 7/22/66 — 7/29/66 — 27 — 3
    Let's Live For Today — 5/19/67 — 6/30/67 — 4 — 11
    Things I Should Have Said — 9/15/67 — 9/15/67 — 34 — 1
    Midnight Confessions — 9/2/68 — 10/7/68 — 2 — 11
    Bella Linda — 12/16/68 — 1/20/69 — 12 — 7
    Lovin' Things — 2/3/69 — 2/24/69 — 25 — 5
    I'd Wait A Million Years — 7/28/69 — 9/8/69 — 5 — 11
    Heaven Knows — 11/17/69 — 12/15/69 — 22 — 8

Gray, Claude
    I'll Just Have A Cup Of Coffee (Then I'll Go) — 4/1/61 — 5/6/61 — 18 — 7

Gray, Dobie
    The "In" Crowd — 1/15/65 — 1/29/65 — 20 — 6

Gray, Maureen
    Dancin' The Strand — 6/16/62 — 6/16/62 — 34 — 1

Grean, Charles Randolph, Sounde
    Quentin's Theme — 6/23/69 — 7/21/69 — 3 — 9

Greaves, R.B.
    Take A Letter Maria — 10/6/69 — 11/24/69 — 6 — 11

Greeley, George
    Love Music — 1/7/61 — 1/21/61 — 30 — 3

Greene, Lorne
    Ringo — 10/30/64 — 12/4/64 — 2 — 8

Gregg, Bobby & his Friends
    The Jam—Part 1 — 3/31/62 — 4/21/62 — 26 — 4

Griffin, Jimmy
    All My Loving — 3/20/64 — 4/17/64 — 14 — 6

Artist / Title	Debut	Peak	Pos	Wks
Guaraldi, Vince, Trio				
Cast Your Fate To The Wind	1/4/63	2/8/63	3	8
Guess Who				
Shakin' All Over	4/2/65	4/16/65	12	8
Hey Ho	8/27/65	8/27/65	39	1
These Eyes	4/14/69	5/19/69	3	10
Laughing	7/7/69	8/11/69	12	8
Gypsies				
Jerk It	6/4/65	6/18/65	33	3
Haley, Bill & his Comets				
(We're Gonna) Rock Around The Clock	6/26/64	6/26/64	35	1
Hall, Dora				
Hello Faithless	12/15/62	12/15/62	39	1
Halos				
"Nag"	9/16/61	9/16/61	37	1
Hamilton IV, George				
Abilene	7/26/63	9/6/63	5	10
Hamilton, Roy				
You Can Have Her	2/25/61	3/18/61	18	5
Let's Go	6/7/63	6/14/63	39	2
Happenings				
See You In September	7/22/66	8/19/66	4	10
Go Away Little Girl	10/7/66	10/21/66	15	4
I Got Rhythm	4/28/67	5/19/67	2	9
My Mammy	7/14/67	8/4/67	16	5
Harnell, Joe				
Fly Me To The Moon-Bossa Nova	1/25/63	2/8/63	12	6
Harper, Willie				
New Kind Of Love	12/23/61	1/6/62	20	5
Harpers Bizarre				
The 59th Street Bridge Song (Feelin' Groovy)	2/24/67	3/31/67	18	8
Anything Goes	9/8/67	9/29/67	18	5
Harpo, Slim				
Rainin' In My Heart	5/27/61	6/17/61	15	5
Baby Scratch My Back	2/18/66	2/25/66	20	4
Harris, Eddie				
Exodus	5/6/61	5/20/61	8	7
Listen Here	8/26/68	9/2/68	34	2

Artist / Title	Debut	Peak	Pos	Wks
Harris, Richard				
MacArthur Park	5/6/68	6/3/68	5	8
Harris, Rolf				
Sun Arise	3/1/63	3/29/63	6	5
Tie Me Kangaroo Down, Sport	6/28/63	7/19/63	4	6
Harry & the Marvels				
The UT	9/2/61	9/9/61	37	2
Hatfield, Bobby				
Only You (And You Alone)	2/10/69	3/24/69	12	9
also see the Righteous Brothers and the Paramours				
Hawkins, Edwin, Singers				
Oh Happy Day	4/21/69	5/26/69	5	9
Head, Roy				
Treat Her Right	9/3/65	10/15/65	14	8
Just A Little Bit	11/26/65	12/3/65	31	2
Apple Of My Eye	12/3/65	12/3/65	38	2
Hebb, Bobby				
Sunny	7/15/66	8/19/66	8	11
Hedgehoppers Anonymous				
It's Good News Week	12/10/65	1/14/66	3	7
Don't Push Me	3/4/66	3/25/66	34	5
Hefti, Neil				
Batman Theme	2/11/66	3/4/66	29	4
Henderson, Joe				
Snap Your Fingers	6/2/62	6/16/62	23	4
You Take One Step	4/24/64	4/24/64	39	1
Hendrix, Jimi, Experience				
Purple Haze	9/22/67	11/10/67	7	9
All Along The Watchtower	10/7/68	10/28/68	25	4
Henry, Clarence "Frogman"				
(I Don't Know Why) But I Do	3/25/61	5/6/61	5	9
You Always Hurt The One You Love	6/10/61	7/1/61	11	5
Herman's Hermits				
I'm Into Something Good	10/23/64	11/20/64	1	12
Can't You Hear My Heartbeat	1/29/65	3/12/65	3	10
Mrs. Brown, You've Got A Lovely Daughter	4/2/65	4/23/65	1	10
Silhouettes	4/23/65	5/21/65	1	10
Wonderful World	5/28/65	6/25/65	3	7
I'm Henry VIII, I Am	6/25/65	7/16/65	2	6

Artist	Title	Debut	Peak	Pos	Wks
	Just A Little Bit Better	9/17/65	10/22/65	2	9
	A Must To Avoid	12/17/65	1/21/66	5	7
	Listen People	1/21/66	2/18/66	3	8
	Leaning On The Lamp Post	4/8/66	5/6/66	9	7
	This Door Swings Both Ways	7/1/66	7/22/66	9	6
	Dandy	9/30/66	10/28/66	6	8
	East West	12/2/66	12/23/66	7	7
	There's A Kind Of Hush	2/3/67	3/3/67	2	10
	Don't Go Out Into The Rain (You're Going To Melt)	6/16/67	6/30/67	22	6
	Museum	8/18/67	8/25/67	28	2
	I Can Take Or Leave Your Loving	12/29/67	2/12/68	22	7
Highwaymen					
	Michael	7/8/61	7/29/61	1	11
	The Gypsy Rover	12/2/61	12/2/61	32	1
	/Cotton Fields	1/27/62	2/24/62	3	7
	I'm On My Way	4/28/62	5/5/62	18	3
	The Bird Man	8/11/62	8/11/62	33	2
Hill, Bunker					
	Hide & Go Seek, Part I	10/6/62	10/6/62	33	1
Hill, Jessie					
	Scoop Scoobie Doobie	10/15/60	10/29/60	31	2
Hill, Wendy					
	Without Your Love	11/4/61	11/11/61	28	3
Hinton, Joe					
	Funny	9/4/64	9/4/64	19	2
Hippies					
	Memory Lane	4/5/63	4/26/63	29	4
Hirt, Al					
	Java	1/10/64	1/17/64	10	7
	Cotton Candy	5/8/64	5/29/64	19	4
	Sugar Lips	7/10/64	7/17/64	27	4
Ho, Don & the Aliis					
	Tiny Bubbles	11/4/66	12/2/66	24	6
Hodges, Eddie					
	I'm Gonna Knock On Your Door	7/15/61	8/19/61	6	7
	(Girls, Girls, Girls) Made To Love	6/30/62	7/21/62	12	6
	New Orleans	7/9/65	8/13/65	8	6
Holiday, Jimmy					
	How Can I Forget	3/1/63	3/15/63	21	4

Artist	Title	Debut	Peak	Pos	Wks
Holiday, Johnny					
	One More Time	11/25/61	11/25/61	40	1
Holidays					
	One Little Kiss	4/22/61	4/22/61	38	1
Holidays					
	I'll Love You Forever	5/27/66	5/27/66	35	1
Holland, Eddie					
	Jamie	1/27/62	2/24/62	24	5
Hollies					
	I'm Alive	8/13/65	8/27/65	28	3
	Look Through Any Window	10/8/65	11/12/65	3	9
	I Can't Let Go	3/4/66	4/15/66	11	8
	Bus Stop	7/8/66	8/12/66	1	11
	Stop Stop Stop	10/21/66	11/25/66	8	8
	On A Carousel	3/3/67	4/28/67	2	11
	Pay You Back With Interest	5/26/67	6/23/67	9	6
	Carrie-Anne	7/14/67	8/18/67	4	9
	Dear Eloise	12/1/67	12/1/67	38	1
	Jennifer Eccles	4/15/68	5/6/68	15	6
	also see Crosby, Stills & Nash				
Holloway, Brenda					
	Every Little Bit Hurts	7/3/64	7/3/64	32	2
	When I'm Gone	4/9/65	4/9/65	39	1
Holman, Eddie					
	Hey There Lonely Girl	12/29/69	2/2/70	3	13
Holmes, Richard "Groove"					
	Misty	7/15/66	7/29/66	34	5
Hombres					
	Let It Out (Let It All Hang Out)	9/15/67	10/20/67	2	10
Hondells					
	Little Honda	9/11/64	10/9/64	13	7
	Sea Cruise	10/22/65	10/29/65	32	2
Honeycombs					
	Have I The Right	9/25/64	10/23/64	1	10
Hooker, John Lee					
	Boom Boom	5/5/62	5/19/62	23	3
Hopkin, Mary					
	Those Were The Days	9/30/68	10/28/68	1	12
	Goodbye	5/5/69	6/2/69	16	6

Artist	Title	Debut	Peak	Pos	Wks

Horton, Johnny
    North To Alaska — 11/26/60 — 12/24/60 — 7 — 8
    They'll Never Take Her Love — 4/15/61 — 4/15/61 — 30 — 1

Houston, David
    Mountain Of Love — 11/8/63 — 11/8/63 — 40 — 1

Howard, Pete
    Mah-Na-Mah-Na — 9/1/69 — 9/15/69 — 34 — 3

Hughes, Jimmy
    Steal Away — 7/24/64 — 8/21/64 — 28 — 5

Human Beinz
    Nobody But Me — 1/8/68 — 2/19/68 — 6 — 9

Humperdinck, Engelbert
    Release Me (And Let Me Love Again) — 5/5/67 — 5/26/67 — 8 — 6
    There Goes My Everything — 7/14/67 — 7/14/67 — 28 — 3
    The Last Waltz — 9/29/67 — 10/20/67 — 18 — 6
    Am I That Easy To Forget — 12/15/67 — 1/15/68 — 14 — 7
    A Man Without Love — 4/29/68 — 6/3/68 — 21 — 7
    Les Bicyclettes De Belsize — 11/25/68 — 12/2/68 — 31 — 2
    The Way It Used To Be — 4/7/69 — 4/14/69 — 31 — 3
    Winter World Of Love — 12/15/69 — 1/26/70 — 13 — 9

Husky, Ferlin
    Wings Of A Dove — 1/21/61 — 2/11/61 — 15 — 8

Hutton, Danny
    Roses And Rainbows — 9/17/65 — 10/22/65 — 10 — 7
    Big Bright Eyes — 1/7/66 — 1/28/66 — 17 — 7
    also see Three Dog Night

Hyland, Brian
    That's How Much — 10/15/60 — 10/15/60 — 36 — 1
    Let Me Belong To You — 7/29/61 — 8/19/61 — 2 — 9
    I'll Never Stop Wanting You — 11/11/61 — 11/25/61 — 25 — 4
    Ginny Come Lately — 3/24/62 — 4/14/62 — 17 — 5
    Sealed With A Kiss — 6/23/62 — 7/21/62 — 1 — 9
    Warmed Over Kisses (Left Over Love) — 9/15/62 — 10/20/62 — 12 — 6
    I May Not Live To See Tomorrow — 12/1/62 — 12/8/62 — 32 — 2
    I'm Afraid To Go Home — 7/12/63 — 8/16/63 — 7 — 6
    The Joker Went Wild — 8/19/66 — 9/16/66 — 8 — 9

Hyman, Dick & his Electric Eclectics
    The Minotaur — 6/16/69 — 6/30/69 — 32 — 3

Artist	Title	Debut	Peak	Pos	Wks

Ian, Janis
    Younger Generation   9/29/67   9/29/67   28   2

Ian & Sylvia
    Four Strong Winds   9/13/63   9/20/63   33   2

Ideals
    The Gorilla   12/20/63   1/17/64   19   6

Ides Of March
    You Wouldn't Listen   5/27/66   6/17/66   7   9
    Roller Coaster   8/26/66   9/16/66   19   6

Ifield, Frank
    I Remember You   8/25/62   9/15/62   8   6
    Lovesick Blues   1/4/63   1/4/63   33   1

Ikettes
    I'm Blue (The Gong-Gong Song)   2/17/62   2/17/62   37   1
    Peaches 'N' Cream   4/9/65   4/16/65   26   3
  also see Turner, Ike & Tina

Illusion
    Did You See Her Eyes   8/4/69   9/1/69   10   7

Impressions
    Gypsy Woman   10/21/61   12/2/61   11   5
    Minstrel And Queen   11/24/62   11/24/62   34   1
    Sad, Sad Girl And Boy   5/24/63   5/31/63   25   3
    It's All Right   9/27/63   11/8/63   17   7
    Talking About My Baby   1/24/64   1/31/64   36   4
    Keep On Pushing   7/24/64   8/7/64   31   3
    Amen   1/8/65   1/15/65   34   2
    Fool For You   10/7/68   10/28/68   31   4
  also see Butler, Jerry

In Crowd
    Questions And Answers   11/25/66   12/2/66   29   3

Ingmann, Jorgen
    Apache   1/28/61   2/25/61   1   10

Ingram, Luther
    My Honey And Me   12/29/69   1/26/70   19   6

Innocence
    There's Got To Be A Word   11/25/66   12/30/66   18   7
    Mairzy Doats   2/17/67   3/10/67   21   5

Artist / Title	Debut	Peak	Pos	Wks
Innocents				
Gee Whiz	11/19/60	12/31/60	18	7
also see Young, Kathy & the Innocents				
Intruders				
Cowboys To Girls	4/8/68	5/20/68	8	8
Irish Rovers				
The Unicorn	3/25/68	4/29/68	7	9
Iron Butterfly				
In-A-Gadda-Da-Vida	9/16/68	10/7/68	22	4
Irwin, Big Dee				
Swinging On A Star	7/5/63	7/5/63	38	1
Isley Brothers				
Twist And Shout	7/7/62	8/4/62	15	5
This Old Heart Of Mine (Is Weak For You)	3/18/66	3/18/66	29	3
It's Your Thing	3/10/69	4/14/69	1	11
I Turned You On	6/16/69	6/30/69	35	3
Ives, Burl				
A Little Bitty Tear	1/27/62	2/10/62	7	6
Funny Way Of Laughin'	4/21/62	5/19/62	19	5
Call Me Mr. In-Between	7/28/62	8/18/62	16	5
True Love Goes On And On	1/17/64	2/28/64	21	7
Pearly Shells	10/30/64	11/13/64	18	4
Iveys				
Maybe Tomorrow	2/24/69	2/24/69	37	1
Jackson, Chuck				
I Don't Want To Cry	3/18/61	3/25/61	28	3
I Wake Up Crying	9/23/61	9/23/61	37	1
Any Day Now (My Wild Beautiful Bird)	4/28/62	5/12/62	31	3
I Keep Forgettin'	9/15/62	9/15/62	37	1
Tell Him I'm Not Home	3/8/63	3/15/63	25	4
Jackson, Deon				
Love Makes The World Go Round	2/11/66	3/11/66	21	6
Jackson, Jerry				
Time	5/20/61	5/20/61	39	1
Jackson, J.J.				
But It's Alright	5/26/69	6/9/69	24	5
Jackson, Stonewall				
Greener Pastures	3/25/61	4/15/61	13	6

Artist	Title	Debut	Peak	Pos	Wks

Jackson, Wanda
	Right Or Wrong	8/19/61	9/2/61	19	4
	In The Middle Of A Heartache	11/4/61	11/25/61	21	5
	If I Cried Every Time You Hurt Me	4/21/62	5/5/62	26	3

Jackson 5
| | I Want You Back | 11/17/69 | 12/15/69 | 2 | 12 |

James, Etta
	Don't Go To Strangers	1/7/61	1/21/61	27	3
	At Last	2/11/61	3/4/61	28	4
	Trust In Me	4/15/61	4/15/61	32	1
	Dream	7/1/61	7/1/61	37	1
	Something's Got A Hold On Me	3/24/62	3/31/62	30	2
	Stop The Wedding	8/11/62	8/11/62	34	3
	Pushover	4/26/63	5/10/63	28	4
	Tell Mama	12/8/67	1/8/68	19	6
	Security	3/25/68	3/25/68	34	2

James, Sonny
| | A Mile And A Quarter | 9/8/62 | 9/8/62 | 38 | 1 |
| | You're The Only World I Know | 1/8/65 | 1/8/65 | 28 | 2 |

James, Tommy & the Shondells
	Hanky Panky	6/3/66	6/17/66	1	9
	Say I Am (What I Am)	7/29/66	8/26/66	2	6
	It's Only Love	10/28/66	11/25/66	11	8
	I Think We're Alone Now	2/3/67	2/24/67	1	10
	Mirage	4/21/67	5/19/67	1	8
	I Like The Way	6/16/67	7/14/67	13	8
	Gettin' Together	8/18/67	9/8/67	13	6
	Out Of The Blue	10/20/67	11/17/67	14	6
	Get Out Now	1/22/68	2/19/68	27	5
	Mony Mony	4/1/68	5/6/68	1	12
	Somebody Cares	7/1/68	8/5/68	14	7
	Do Something To Me	10/7/68	11/11/68	19	6
	Crimson And Clover	12/9/68	1/13/69	1	12
	Sweet Cherry Wine	3/17/69	4/21/69	4	11
	Crystal Blue Persuasion	6/9/69	7/7/69	1	12
	Ball Of Fire	9/22/69	10/20/69	9	9
	She	12/8/69	12/29/69	23	6

Jamies
| | Summertime, Summertime | | 6/9/62 | 7/7/62 | 5 | 6 |

Jan & Dean
| | Heart And Soul | 8/26/61 | 9/16/61 | 6 | 6 |

Artist	Title	Debut	Peak	Pos	Wks
	Tennessee	6/30/62	7/14/62	20	4
	Linda	2/15/63	3/8/63	9	7
	Surf City	6/14/63	7/12/63	1	10
	Honolulu Lulu	9/20/63	10/4/63	6	6
	Drag City	11/29/63	1/10/64	1	10
	Dead Man's Curve	3/27/64	5/8/64	1	13
	/The New Girl In School	3/27/64	5/8/64	1	11
	The Little Old Lady (From Pasadena)	7/3/64	7/24/64	5	9
	Ride The Wild Surf	10/16/64	11/6/64	17	4
	Sidewalk Surfin'	11/20/64	11/27/64	20	4
	Freeway Flyer	3/19/65	3/19/65	30	3
	I Found A Girl	11/12/65	12/3/65	9	7
	Batman	2/11/66	2/25/66	25	3
	Popsicle	5/27/66	7/1/66	20	7

also see Berry, Jan

Jankowski, Horst
	A Walk In The Black Forest	5/21/65	6/18/65	5	9

Jarmels
	A Little Bit Of Soap	8/26/61	9/16/61	20	4

Jay, Morty & the Surferin' Cats
	Saltwater Taffy	10/25/63	11/8/63	26	4

Jay & the Americans
	She Cried	3/24/62	4/21/62	1	9
	Only In America	9/6/63	10/11/63	9	7
	Come A Little Bit Closer	9/25/64	10/23/64	3	10
	Let's Lock The Door (And Throw Away The Key)	1/8/65	1/29/65	4	9
	Think Of The Good Times	5/7/65	5/7/65	34	2
	Cara, Mia	6/18/65	7/16/65	3	8
	Some Enchanted Evening	9/3/65	9/24/65	3	6
	Sunday And Me	11/19/65	12/10/65	10	5
	Crying	5/27/66	5/27/66	26	3
	This Magic Moment	1/6/69	2/17/69	6	9
	Hushabye	6/23/69	6/30/69	38	3
	Walkin' In The Rain	12/22/69	2/2/70	11	9

Jay & the Techniques
	Apples, Peaches, Pumpkin Pie	8/25/67	9/29/67	8	8
	Keep The Ball Rollin'	12/1/67	12/1/67	26	2

Jaye, Jerry
	My Girl Josephine	5/5/67	5/19/67	16	5

Jaynetts
	Sally, Go 'Round The Roses	8/30/63	9/27/63	2	6

Artist	Title	Debut	Peak	Pos	Wks
	Keep An Eye On Her	11/15/63	11/15/63	35	2
	Snowman Snowman	12/20/63	12/27/63	37	2

Jefferson Airplane
	Somebody To Love	4/7/67	5/26/67	1	11
	White Rabbit	6/30/67	7/21/67	6	7
	Ballad Of You & Me & Pooneil	8/25/67	9/15/67	28	4

Jeffrey, Joe, Group
	My Pledge Of Love	6/9/69	7/14/69	11	9

Jelly Beans
	I Wanna Love Him So Bad	6/26/64	8/7/64	6	8
	Baby Be Mine	9/25/64	10/16/64	15	6

Jenkins, Donald & the Delighters
	(Native Girl) Elephant Walk	8/30/63	9/13/63	22	4
	Adios (My Secret Love)	11/29/63	12/6/63	36	2

Jensen, Kris
	Torture	9/15/62	9/29/62	23	3

Jim & Joe
	Fireball Mail	10/11/63	10/25/63	15	4

Jim & Monica
	Slippin' & Slidin'	12/6/63	1/3/64	12	9
	What A Sad Thing That Was	5/15/64	6/12/64	27	5

Jimenez, Jose
	The Astronaut, (Part 1)	8/26/61	9/23/61	5	6

Jive Five
	My True Story	9/16/61	10/7/61	18	5
	Hully Gully Callin' Time	3/31/62	4/28/62	27	4
	I'm A Happy Man	8/6/65	8/27/65	15	4

Jo, Damita
	I'll Save The Last Dance For You	11/12/60	11/19/60	17	4
	If You Go Away	12/16/66	12/23/66	34	2

Jo & Eddie
	There's A Meetin' Tonight	3/27/64	4/10/64	34	3

John, Little Willie
	Sleep	10/14/60	10/29/60	4	6

Johnny & the Debonaires
	The Bonecracker	1/27/62	1/27/62	38	2

Johnson, Marv
	(You've Got To) Move Two Mountains	10/14/60	10/14/60	34	1

Artist / Title	Debut	Peak	Pos	Wks
Jolly, Pete, Trio				
Little Bird	4/5/63	4/5/63	38	2
Jon & Robin & the In Crowd				
Do It Again A Little Bit Slower	6/2/67	7/7/67	7	8
Jones, Davy				
What Are We Going To Do	7/23/65	8/6/65	30	3
also see the Monkees				
Jones, Jack				
Lollipops And Roses	4/7/62	4/14/62	26	2
Wives And Lovers	11/29/63	12/27/63	13	5
The First Night Of The Full Moon	6/19/64	7/3/64	11	8
The Race Is On	3/12/65	4/2/65	17	5
Love Bug	1/7/66	1/7/66	31	1
Lady	3/10/67	4/7/67	33	5
Jones, Joe				
You Talk Too Much	10/14/60	10/14/60	4	3
Jones, Tom				
It's Not Unusual	5/7/65	5/28/65	3	8
Little Lonely One	6/18/65	7/9/65	34	4
What's New Pussycat	7/2/65	7/30/65	2	8
With These Hands	9/10/65	9/24/65	16	4
Green, Green Grass Of Home	1/13/67	2/17/67	11	8
Detroit City	3/10/67	3/31/67	26	6
Funny Familiar Forgotten Feelings	6/16/67	6/30/67	33	4
Delilah	4/1/68	5/6/68	24	6
Day By Day	8/12/68	8/19/68	36	2
Help Yourself	9/9/68	10/14/68	27	6
Love Me Tonight	5/19/69	6/30/69	9	11
I'll Never Fall In Love Again	7/21/69	9/1/69	8	11
Without Love (There Is Nothing)	12/22/69	2/2/70	7	10
Jordan Brothers				
Things I Didn't Say	12/3/60	12/10/60	33	2
Joye, Col. & the Joy Boys				
Today's Teardrops	5/19/62	5/19/62	39	1
Just Us				
I Can't Grow Peaches On A Cherry Tree	4/1/66	4/1/66	36	1
Justis, Bill				
Tamoure	5/10/63	5/31/63	7	6

Artist	Title	Debut	Peak	Pos	Wks

Kaempfert, Bert
    Wonderland By Night — 12/3/60 — 12/31/60 — 1 — 13
    Red Roses For A Blue Lady — 2/26/65 — 3/12/65 — 12 — 4
    Moon Over Naples — 8/6/65 — 8/27/65 — 16 — 4

Kallen, Kitty
    My Coloring Book — 12/15/62 — 1/12/63 — 8 — 6

Kallman, Gunter, Chorus
    Wish Me A Rainbow — 1/6/67 — 1/20/67 — 38 — 4

Kasenetz-Katz Singing Orchestral Circus
    Quick Joey Small (Run Joey Run) — 10/7/68 — 11/11/68 — 14 — 9

K-Doe, Ernie
    Mother-In-Law — 4/1/61 — 5/13/61 — 3 — 9

Keith
    Ain't Gonna Lie — 9/9/66 — 10/21/66 — 14 — 8
    98.6 — 12/9/66 — 1/27/67 — 10 — 10
    Tell It To My Face — 4/7/67 — 4/21/67 — 28 — 3

Kellum, Murry
    Long Tall Texan — 11/29/63 — 1/17/64 — 15 — 9
    Red Ryder — 4/17/64 — 5/8/64 — 25 — 5

Kenner, Chris
    I Like It Like That, Part 1 — 6/24/61 — 7/29/61 — 8 — 8
    Land Of 1000 Dances — 6/14/63 — 7/12/63 — 22 — 5

Kent, Al
    You've Got To Pay The Price — 9/15/67 — 10/6/67 — 32 — 4

Kenton, Stan
    Mama Sang A Song — 10/6/62 — 10/27/62 — 11 — 6

Kevin & Greg
    Boy You Ought To See Her Now — 1/10/64 — 1/17/64 — 37 — 2

Kids Next Door
    Inky Dinky Spider (The Spider Song) — 10/8/65 — 10/22/65 — 28 — 3

Kilgore, Theola
    The Love Of My Man — 5/24/63 — 5/24/63 — 33 — 1
    This Is My Prayer — 10/4/63 — 10/4/63 — 39 — 1

Kim, Andy
    How'd We Ever Get This Way — 5/6/68 — 6/24/68 — 3 — 10
    Baby, I Love You — 6/9/69 — 7/21/69 — 4 — 12
    So Good Together — 10/20/69 — 11/10/69 — 24 — 4

Artist / Title	Debut	Peak	Pos	Wks
Kimberly, Adrian				
The Graduation Song...Pomp And Circumstance	6/17/61	7/1/61	21	3
King, Ben E.				
Spanish Harlem	2/18/61	3/25/61	3	8
Stand By Me	6/10/61	6/24/61	29	3
Amor	8/26/61	9/16/61	18	5
Don't Play That Song (You Lied)	5/26/62	6/16/62	25	4
I (Who Have Nothing)	8/2/63	8/2/63	32	2
also see the Drifters				
King, Carole				
It Might As Well Rain Until September	9/1/62	9/22/62	13	5
King, Claude				
Wolverton Mountain	5/26/62	7/14/62	7	8
The Burning Of Atlanta	10/13/62	10/27/62	26	3
King, Jonathan				
Everyone's Gone To The Moon	9/24/65	11/5/65	10	7
Round Round	5/19/67	6/2/67	23	4
King Curtis & the Noble Knights				
Soul Twist	3/17/62	4/7/62	28	4
Beach Party	8/4/62	8/4/62	35	2
Kingpins				
Ode To Billie Joe	9/29/67	10/20/67	29	4
Kingsmen				
Louie Louie	11/8/63	12/13/63	2	9
Money	4/10/64	4/10/64	35	1
The Climb	6/11/65	6/11/65	38	1
Gamma Goochee	12/24/65	1/7/66	38	3
Killer Joe	4/22/66	5/20/66	20	7
Kingston Trio				
Where Have All The Flowers Gone	3/3/62	3/31/62	8	7
Jane, Jane, Jane	5/5/62	5/26/62	25	4
Greenback Dollar	1/25/63	2/15/63	12	5
Reverend Mr. Black	4/5/63	5/3/63	6	6
Desert Pete	8/2/63	8/16/63	25	3
Kinks				
You Really Got Me	10/16/64	11/13/64	2	8
All Day And All Of The Night	1/15/65	2/19/65	3	8
Tired Of Waiting For You	3/26/65	4/30/65	2	8
Set Me Free	6/25/65	7/9/65	26	4
Who'll Be The Next In Line	8/6/65	8/27/65	14	4

Artist	Title	Debut	Peak	Pos	Wks
	A Well Respected Man	12/17/65	1/28/66	16	7
	Till The End Of The Day	3/25/66	4/15/66	24	5
	Sunny Afternoon	8/5/66	9/9/66	12	7
	Mr. Pleasant	6/16/67	6/30/67	28	4

Kip & Ken
	Trouble With A Woman	8/20/65	9/24/65	9	8

Knickerbockers
	Lies	1/7/66	2/4/66	6	7
	One Track Mind	3/25/66	3/25/66	27	3

Knight, Baker
	Would You Believe	4/29/66	5/6/66	34	3

Knight, Gladys & the Pips
	Every Beat Of My Heart	6/10/61	6/24/61	28	3
	Letter Full Of Tears	1/13/62	2/10/62	21	6
	I Heard It Through The Grapevine	11/24/67	12/29/67	9	8
	The End Of Our Road	2/26/68	3/11/68	25	3
	The Nitty Gritty	7/21/69	9/1/69	20	8

Knight, Robert
	Everlasting Love	10/20/67	11/17/67	6	7

Knox, Buddy
	Lovey Dovey	1/21/61	2/18/61	16	6

Kokomo
	Asia Minor	3/11/61	4/8/61	3	9

Kramer, Billy J. & the Dakotas
	Little Children	5/8/64	6/19/64	1	11
	/Bad To Me	5/22/64	6/19/64	1	5
	I'll Keep You Satisfied	7/24/64	8/7/64	16	5
	From A Window	9/11/64	10/9/64	4	8
	It's Gotta Last Forever	2/5/65	2/12/65	35	2

Kuban, Bob & the In-Men
	The Cheater	3/11/66	3/18/66	28	2

La Rolls
	Everybody Knew	2/4/61	2/11/61	37	2

Laine, Frankie
	Don't Make My Baby Blue	6/7/63	6/7/63	27	1
	I'll Take Care Of Your Cares	2/24/67	3/10/67	31	5
	You Gave Me A Mountain	3/3/69	3/31/69	26	5

Artist	Title	Debut	Peak	Pos	Wks

Lance, Major
	The Monkey Time	8/9/63	8/16/63	24	4
	Hey Little Girl	11/8/63	11/8/63	20	4
	Um, Um, Um, Um, Um, Um	1/17/64	2/14/64	21	6
	The Matador	4/17/64	4/17/64	39	1
	Sometimes I Wonder	1/8/65	1/15/65	37	2
	Ain't It A Shame	6/11/65	6/18/65	34	2

Landon, Michael
	Gimme A Little Kiss	7/14/62	7/14/62	34	1

Larks
	The Jerk	1/8/65	1/15/65	33	2

Laurie, Linda
	Jose He Say	6/5/64	6/5/64	26	2

Lawrence, Steve
	Portrait Of My Love	2/18/61	4/1/61	6	9
	In Time	8/5/61	8/5/61	29	1
	Go Away Little Girl	12/1/62	12/22/62	1	10
	Don't Be Afraid, Little Darlin'	3/15/63	4/5/63	13	5
	Poor Little Rich Girl	5/24/63	5/31/63	18	3
	Walking Proud	10/18/63	10/18/63	28	2
	Millions Of Roses	9/10/65	9/24/65	27	3

Lawrence, Steve & Eydie Gorme
	I Want To Stay Here	9/6/63	10/11/63	18	6
	I Can't Stop Talking About You	1/10/64	1/17/64	26	2

also see Gorme, Eydie

Leaders
	Night People	8/27/65	8/27/65	33	1

Leapy Lee
	Little Arrows	11/4/68	12/9/68	18	6

Leaves
	Hey Joe	5/20/66	7/1/66	11	8

Led Zeppelin
	Whole Lotta Love	11/24/69	1/5/70	2	11

Lee, Barry, Show
	I Don't Want To Love You	2/26/68	3/4/68	28	4

Lee, Brenda
	I Want To Be Wanted	10/14/60	10/29/60	7	8
	Emotions	1/28/61	2/11/61	28	4
	You Can Depend On Me	4/22/61	5/6/61	28	4

Artist	Title	Debut	Peak	Pos	Wks
	Dum Dum	7/8/61	8/5/61	16	7
	Fool # 1	10/7/61	11/18/61	7	10
	Break It To Me Gently	1/20/62	2/10/62	14	6
	Everybody Loves Me But You	4/14/62	5/12/62	17	5
	Heart In Hand	7/28/62	8/11/62	19	3
	All Alone Am I	10/20/62	12/1/62	4	9
	Your Used To Be	2/8/63	2/15/63	32	2
	Losing You	4/19/63	5/31/63	9	7
	The Grass Is Greener	10/25/63	11/1/63	28	2
	As Usual	1/10/64	1/31/64	15	6
	Coming On Strong	11/4/66	12/2/66	15	6
	Johnny One Time	3/10/69	3/31/69	31	4

Lee, Curtis
| | Pretty Little Angel Eyes | 8/5/61 | 9/2/61 | 7 | 7 |
| | Under The Moon Of Love | 11/11/61 | 11/18/61 | 29 | 2 |

Lee, Dickey
	Patches	9/22/62	10/13/62	1	7
	I Saw Linda Yesterday	12/15/62	1/4/63	6	8
	Don't Wanna Think About Paula	3/1/63	3/15/63	16	4
	The Day The Sawmill Closed Down	9/13/63	10/4/63	19	4
	Laurie (Strange Things Happen)	6/11/65	7/16/65	8	7

Lee, Jackie
| | The Duck | 12/24/65 | 12/24/65 | 40 | 1 |

Lee, Peggy
| | Is That All There Is | 9/29/69 | 10/20/69 | 16 | 6 |

Lefevre, Raymond
| | Come Softly To Me | 4/8/61 | 4/8/61 | 38 | 1 |

Left Banke
| | Pretty Ballerina | 1/27/67 | 2/17/67 | 16 | 4 |

Lemon Pipers
| | Green Tambourine | 12/1/67 | 1/29/68 | 2 | 12 |
| | Jelly Jungle (Of Orange Marmalade) | 5/13/68 | 6/3/68 | 29 | 4 |

Lester, Ketty
| | Love Letters | 3/17/62 | 4/7/62 | 13 | 5 |
| | But Not For Me | 7/14/62 | 7/14/62 | 27 | 1 |

Lettermen
	The Way You Look Tonight	9/2/61	9/30/61	4	9
	When I Fall In Love	12/9/61	12/16/61	11	8
	Come Back Silly Girl	3/10/62	3/31/62	15	5
	How Is Julie	5/26/62	5/26/62	31	2

Artist	Title	Debut	Peak	Pos	Wks
	Again	11/10/62	11/10/62	39	1
	Theme From "A Summer Place"	6/18/65	7/2/65	25	5
	Goin' Out Of My Head/Can't Take My Eyes Off You	1/8/68	1/29/68	5	8
	Sherry Don't Go	4/15/68	4/29/68	33	3
	Hurt So Bad	7/14/69	8/18/69	2	13
	Shangri-La	11/3/69	11/10/69	36	2
Levine, Hank					
	Image—Part 1	12/2/61	12/2/61	37	1
Lewis, Barbara					
	Hello Stranger	5/17/63	6/14/63	3	6
	Puppy Love	2/21/64	3/27/64	16	7
	Baby, I'm Yours	7/2/65	8/6/65	4	7
	Make Me Your Baby	10/1/65	10/29/65	14	6
Lewis, Bobby					
	Tossin' And Turnin'	7/1/61	7/29/61	3	8
	One Track Mind	9/30/61	10/7/61	21	3
	What A Walk	12/2/61	12/16/61	22	4
	I'm Tossin' And Turnin' Again	8/18/62	8/18/62	38	1
Lewis, Gary & the Playboys					
	This Diamond Ring	1/15/65	2/5/65	1	10
	Count Me In	4/9/65	5/7/65	4	8
	Save Your Heart For Me	7/2/65	7/30/65	3	7
	Everybody Loves A Clown	10/8/65	10/29/65	5	7
	She's Just My Style	12/10/65	1/28/66	7	9
	Sure Gonna Miss Her	3/4/66	3/25/66	12	5
	Green Grass	5/6/66	5/20/66	11	7
	My Heart's Symphony	8/5/66	8/12/66	20	3
	(You Don't Have To) Paint Me A Picture	10/7/66	10/28/66	14	5
	Where Will The Words Come From	12/23/66	2/3/67	15	8
	The Loser (With A Broken Heart)	3/24/67	3/31/67	25	3
	Girls In Love	5/19/67	6/2/67	21	5
	Jill	8/11/67	8/11/67	37	1
	Sealed With A Kiss	7/1/68	8/5/68	5	9
Lewis, Jerry Lee					
	What'd I Say	3/25/61	4/22/61	13	7
Lewis, Ramsey					
	The "In" Crowd	8/6/65	9/17/65	2	10
	Hang On Sloopy	11/19/65	12/3/65	19	5
	A Hard Day's Night	1/28/66	2/4/66	30	2
	Wade In The Water	8/5/66	8/12/66	26	3

also see Young-Holt Trio & Unlimited

Artist	Title	Debut	Peak	Pos	Wks

Lincoln, X.
    Heartaches And Happiness — 2/8/63 — 2/8/63 — 40 — 1

Lind, Bob
    Elusive Butterfly — 2/11/66 — 3/11/66 — 5 — 8

Little Anthony & the Imperials
    Please Say You Want Me — 3/25/61 — 3/25/61 — 32 — 1
    Hurt So Bad — 3/5/65 — 3/12/65 — 26 — 5
    Take Me Back — 7/16/65 — 7/23/65 — 25 — 3
    I Miss You So — 10/15/65 — 10/22/65 — 29 — 4
    Out Of Sight, Out Of Mind — 7/28/69 — 9/8/69 — 15 — 8
    The Ten Commandments Of Love — 10/13/69 — 11/24/69 — 28 — 7

Little Billy
    The Dance Is Over — 9/8/62 — 9/15/62 — 33 — 2

Little Boy Blues
    The Great Train Robbery — 1/20/67 — 1/27/67 — 33 — 3

Little Caesar & the Romans
    Those Oldies But Goodies (Remind Me Of You) — 6/3/61 — 7/1/61 — 9 — 6
    Memories Of Oldies But Goodies — 10/14/61 — 10/14/61 — 39 — 1

Little Eva
    The Loco-Motion — 7/21/62 — 8/25/62 — 2 — 9
    Keep Your Hands Off My Baby — 11/10/62 — 11/17/62 — 30 — 2
    Let's Turkey Trot — 2/8/63 — 2/22/63 — 35 — 3
    Old Smokey Locomotion — 5/31/63 — 5/31/63 — 26 — 1

Little Joey & the Flips
    Bongo Stomp — 6/16/62 — 7/7/62 — 17 — 5

Little Richard
    Annie Is Back — 6/26/64 — 7/3/64 — 36 — 2

Little Sisters
    Going To Boston — 1/12/63 — 1/19/63 — 36 — 2

Livers
    Beatle Time — 3/27/64 — 4/17/64 — 28 — 4

Lolita
    Sailor (Your Home Is The Sea) — 10/29/60 — 11/12/60 — 5 — 10

London, Julie
    I'm Coming Back To You — 10/18/63 — 10/25/63 — 34 — 2

Long, Shorty
    Here Comes The Judge — 6/3/68 — 6/24/68 — 11 — 5

Artist	Title	Debut	Peak	Pos	Wks

Lopez, Trini
    If I Had A Hammer   8/9/63   9/13/63   7   8
    Kansas City   12/20/63   1/10/64   31   4
    What Have I Got Of My Own   6/5/64   7/17/64   5   8
    Michael   8/28/64   8/28/64   30   3
    Lemon Tree   1/29/65   2/12/65   27   4
    Sinner Man   10/15/65   11/26/65   14   8
    I'm Comin' Home, Cindy   4/8/66   4/8/66   26   3

Lord Didd
    Gunga Didn't   3/3/62   3/3/62   36   1

Los Bravos
    Black Is Black   8/26/66   9/30/66   4   9

Los Indios Tabajaras
    Maria Elena   10/18/63   11/15/63   2   9

Love
    My Little Red Book   5/20/66   7/1/66   18   8
    7 And 7 Is   8/19/66   9/9/66   28   5

Love, Darlene
    (Today I Met) The Boy I'm Gonna Marry   5/3/63   5/17/63   19   4
    Wait Til My Bobby Gets Home   7/5/63   8/2/63   13   5
    A Fine Fine Boy   10/11/63   11/1/63   18   5

Love, Ronnie
    Chills And Fever   12/17/60   1/14/61   5   9

Love Generation
    Montage From How Sweet It Is (I Know That You Know)   7/22/68   7/22/68   39   2

Lovin' Spoonful
    Do You Believe In Magic   8/27/65   9/10/65   12   7
    You Didn't Have To Be So Nice   12/10/65   1/14/66   11   8
    Daydream   3/4/66   4/1/66   3   6
    Did You Ever Have To Make Up Your Mind   4/29/66   6/3/66   3   8
    Summer In The City   7/8/66   7/29/66   1   9
    Rain On The Roof   10/14/66   11/18/66   9   7
    Nashville Cats   12/9/66   1/6/67   14   6
    Darling Be Home Soon   2/10/67   3/10/67   18   7
    Six O'Clock   4/28/67   5/12/67   17   7
    She Is Still A Mystery   10/27/67   11/17/67   18   5

Lucas, Matt
    I'm Movin' On   5/24/63   6/21/63   10   6

Artist / Title	Debut	Peak	Pos	Wks
Lulu & the Luvers				
Shout	7/24/64	8/21/64	31	5
Lulu				
To Sir With Love	9/15/67	11/3/67	1	13
Me, The Peaceful Heart	4/1/68	4/1/68	35	2
Luman, Bob				
Let's Think About Living	10/14/60	10/15/60	9	4
Lundberg, Victor				
An Open Letter To My Teenage Son	11/3/67	12/1/67	6	6
Ly-Dells				
Wizard Of Love	10/7/61	10/7/61	32	1
Lyman, Arthur, Group				
Yellow Bird	6/3/61	7/8/61	3	9
Love For Sale	2/15/63	3/8/63	23	5
Lynn, Barbara				
You'll Lose A Good Thing	7/7/62	7/21/62	23	4
Lynne, Gloria				
I Wish You Love	11/29/63	12/20/63	10	7
MacArthur, James				
The In Between Years	12/1/62	12/22/62	9	6
The Ten Commandments Of Love	6/14/63	7/12/63	18	5
Mack, Lonnie				
Memphis	5/31/63	6/28/63	11	7
Wham!	9/13/63	9/27/63	33	3
Maestro, Johnny				
Model Girl	3/4/61	3/18/61	32	3
also see the Brooklyn Bridge				
Magic Lanterns				
Shame, Shame	10/14/68	11/25/68	5	10
Maharis, George				
Teach Me Tonight	5/19/62	6/2/62	18	3
Love Me As I Love You	8/25/62	9/8/62	21	3
Baby Has Gone Bye Bye	12/8/62	12/15/62	26	4
Majestics				
Oasis (Part 2)	10/21/61	10/28/61	28	2
Majors				
A Wonderful Dream	7/28/62	8/25/62	6	6
She's A Troublemaker	11/10/62	11/24/62	13	4

Artist	Title	Debut	Peak	Pos	Wks

Malmkvist, Siw & Umberto Marcato
    Sole Sole Sole — 7/24/64 — 8/7/64 — 21 — 3

Maltby, Richard
    The Rat Race — 11/12/60 — 12/3/60 — 8 — 10
    Manhunt — 3/4/61 — 3/18/61 — 28 — 3

Mamas & the Papas
    California Dreamin' — 1/14/66 — 3/4/66 — 1 — 14
    Monday Monday — 4/8/66 — 5/6/66 — 1 — 9
    I Saw Her Again — 6/24/66 — 7/29/66 — 3 — 8
    Look Through My Window — 10/14/66 — 10/21/66 — 22 — 3
    Words Of Love — 12/2/66 — 1/13/67 — 5 — 10
      /Dancing In The Street — 12/9/66 — 1/13/67 — 5 — 8
    Dedicated To The One I Love — 2/24/67 — 3/31/67 — 3 — 8
    Creeque Alley — 5/5/67 — 5/19/67 — 15 — 4
    Twelve Thirty (Young Girls Are Coming To The Canyon — 8/18/67 — 8/25/67 — 23 — 5
    Glad To Be Unhappy — 10/20/67 — 11/17/67 — 17 — 5
    also see Elliot, Mama Cass & the Mugwumps

Mancini, Henry
    Moon River — 12/9/61 — 12/30/61 — 3 — 15
    Love Theme From Romeo & Juliet — 5/19/69 — 6/16/69 — 1 — 11

Mann, Barry
    Who Put The Bomp (In The Bomp, Bomp, Bomp) — 8/12/61 — 8/26/61 — 4 — 6
    Little Miss U.S.A. — 11/18/61 — 12/9/61 — 19 — 4

Mann, Manfred
    Do Wah Diddy Diddy — 9/11/64 — 9/25/64 — 2 — 10
    Sha La La — 12/4/64 — 1/15/65 — 11 — 8
    Come Tomorrow — 3/19/65 — 3/19/65 — 38 — 3
    Pretty Flamingo — 6/24/66 — 7/8/66 — 15 — 6
    Mighty Quinn (Quinn The Eskimo) — 2/26/68 — 4/15/68 — 7 — 9

Manno, Tommy
    That's For Me To Know — 6/9/62 — 6/30/62 — 26 — 4

Manuel & the Renegades
    Rev Up — 8/16/63 — 9/20/63 — 5 — 7

Marathons
    Peanut Butter — 5/20/61 — 6/17/61 — 19 — 5

Marcels
    Blue Moon — 3/25/61 — 4/1/61 — 1 — 9
    Summertime — 5/27/61 — 6/17/61 — 8 — 5

Artist	Title	Debut	Peak	Pos	Wks
	Heartaches	10/21/61	11/18/61	11	7
	My Melancholy Baby	2/17/62	2/24/62	34	2

March, Little Peggy
	I Will Follow Him	4/5/63	4/26/63	1	7
	I Wish I Were A Princess	6/21/63	6/21/63	27	1
	Hello Heartache, Goodbye Love	9/27/63	9/27/63	31	2
	The Impossible Happened	12/6/63	12/13/63	35	3

Marcy Joe
	Ronnie	5/27/61	6/3/61	31	3

Maresca, Ernie
	Shout! Shout! (Knock Yourself Out)	4/7/62	5/12/62	4	7

Mark II
	Night Theme	10/15/60	10/29/60	29	4

Marketts
	Surfer's Stomp	2/10/62	2/24/62	33	3
	Balboa Blue	6/23/62	7/21/62	11	6
	Out Of Limits	1/24/64	2/28/64	3	8
	Batman Theme	1/28/66	2/25/66	17	6

Mar-Keys
	Last Night	7/22/61	8/5/61	14	6

Marterie, Ralph
	Bacardi	6/3/61	6/3/61	36	1

Martha & the Vandellas
	Come And Get These Memories	4/5/63	5/3/63	11	5
	Heat Wave	8/16/63	9/13/63	20	8
	Quicksand	12/6/63	12/20/63	22	4
	Live Wire	2/28/64	3/6/64	37	2
	In My Lonely Room	5/15/64	5/15/64	35	1
	Dancing In The Street	9/11/64	10/9/64	6	8
	Nowhere To Run	3/19/65	4/16/65	20	6
	My Baby Loves Me	2/4/66	2/4/66	40	1
	I'm Ready For Love	10/28/66	11/25/66	19	8
	Jimmy Mack	3/24/67	4/28/67	11	7
	Love Bug Leave My Heart Alone	9/8/67	9/8/67	31	3
	Honey Chile	12/1/67	12/29/67	20	5

Martin, Bobbi
	Don't Forget I Still Love You	12/18/64	1/29/65	14	7
	I Can't Stop Thinking Of You	5/7/65	5/7/65	36	1

Artist / Title	Debut	Peak	Pos	Wks
Martin, Dean				
From The Bottom Of My Heart (Dammi, Dammi, Dammi)	12/8/62	12/22/62	11	6
Everybody Loves Somebody	7/17/64	8/14/64	1	9
The Door Is Still Open To My Heart	10/16/64	11/6/64	7	5
You're Nobody Till Somebody Loves You	1/8/65	1/15/65	20	3
Send Me The Pillow You Dream On	2/26/65	3/19/65	21	4
(Remember Me) I'm The One Who Loves You	5/21/65	5/21/65	40	1
Houston	8/27/65	8/27/65	40	1
Nobody's Baby Again	10/14/66	10/21/66	39	2
In The Chapel In The Moonlight	7/28/67	7/28/67	40	1
You've Still Got A Place In My Heart	4/15/68	4/15/68	35	3
Martin, Trade				
That Stranger Used To Be My Girl	10/27/62	11/17/62	14	5
Martino, Al				
Little Girl, Little Boy	3/25/61	4/8/61	27	3
I Love You Because	4/19/63	5/17/63	5	6
Painted, Tainted Rose	8/2/63	9/13/63	15	8
Living A Lie	11/22/63	11/29/63	25	2
I Love You More And More Every Day	2/7/64	2/28/64	8	8
Tears And Roses	5/29/64	6/19/64	25	5
Always Together	8/28/64	8/28/64	38	1
My Heart Would Know	1/29/65	2/5/65	28	3
Spanish Eyes	12/10/65	12/31/65	17	6
Daddy's Little Girl	2/17/67	2/24/67	34	4
Mary In The Morning	6/9/67	6/16/67	28	3
Love Is Blue	2/12/68	2/19/68	38	2
I Started Loving You Again	12/29/69	1/5/70	38	2
Marvelettes				
Please Mr. Postman	10/14/61	12/16/61	9	11
Twistin' Postman	2/24/62	2/24/62	39	1
Playboy	5/12/62	5/26/62	17	6
Beechwood 4-5789	9/1/62	9/15/62	28	4
Strange I Know	1/4/63	1/12/63	32	4
Don't Mess With Bill	1/28/66	1/28/66	30	2
The Hunter Gets Captured By The Game	2/24/67	3/3/67	29	3
Masakela, Hugh				
Grazing In The Grass	6/17/68	7/22/68	3	10
Mason, Barbara				
Yes, I'm Ready	6/25/65	7/23/65	19	6

Artist	Title	Debut	Peak	Pos	Wks

Mathews, Tobin & Co.
	Ruby Duby Du	10/15/60	10/29/60	1	8
	Steel Guitar Rag	2/18/61	2/25/61	30	2

Mathis, Johnny
	How To Handle A Woman	12/10/60	12/10/60	39	1
	Should I Wait	7/29/61	8/5/61	26	2
	Gina	9/22/62	11/3/62	3	10
	What Will Mary Say	1/25/63	2/15/63	9	7
	Every Step Of The Way	6/21/63	7/19/63	25	6
	Come Back	10/11/63	10/18/63	32	2
	Bye Bye Barbara	2/21/64	2/21/64	29	2

Matys Brothers
	Who Stole The Keeshka	1/25/63	2/8/63	17	5

Mauds
	Hold On	6/16/67	7/7/67	15	8
	Soul Drippin'	9/9/68	9/30/68	12	5

Mauriat, Paul
	Love Is Blue	1/15/68	2/5/68	1	11

Mayer, Nathaniel & the Fabulous Twilights
	Village Of Love	4/14/62	5/19/62	2	9

McCoys
	Hang On Sloopy	8/20/65	9/24/65	1	10
	Fever	11/12/65	12/10/65	16	6
	Up And Down	2/25/66	2/25/66	34	1
	Come On Let's Go	5/20/66	6/17/66	11	6
	(You Make Me Feel) So Good	7/22/66	7/29/66	35	3

McCurn, George
	When The Wind Blows In Chicago	12/13/63	12/20/63	31	2

McDaniels, Gene
	A Hundred Pounds Of Clay	4/8/61	5/6/61	10	9
	A Tear	8/5/61	8/5/61	37	1
	Tower Of Strength	10/21/61	11/11/61	10	6
	Chip Chip	2/3/62	2/24/62	21	4
	Point Of No Return	9/1/62	9/29/62	21	5
	Spanish Lace	11/24/62	12/1/62	33	2
	Anyone Else	11/29/63	11/29/63	39	1

McGriff, Jimmy
	I've Got A Woman Part 1	10/13/62	10/13/62	38	2

Artist	Title	Debut	Peak	Pos	Wks
McGuire, Barry					
	Child Of Our Times	10/22/65	11/12/65	25	5
also see New Christie Minstrels					
McGuire Sisters					
	Just For Old Time's Sake	4/1/61	5/13/61	10	8
	Tears On My Pillow	8/12/61	8/12/61	35	1
	Just Because	11/11/61	11/11/61	39	1
McKenzie, Scott					
	San Francisco (Be Sure To Wear Flowers In Your Hair)	6/2/67	7/14/67	5	11
McLain, Tommy					
	Sweet Dreams	7/15/66	7/29/66	9	5
McLean, Phil					
	Small Sad Sam	12/9/61	12/30/61	14	5
McNair, Barbara					
	That's All I Want From You	3/25/61	3/25/61	33	1
McPhatter, Clyde					
	Lover Please	3/10/62	3/31/62	13	6
	Little Bitty Pretty One	7/14/62	7/21/62	34	2
also see the Drifters					
Medley, Bill					
	I Can't Make It Alone	5/20/68	5/27/68	37	2
also see the Righteous Brothers and the Paramours					
Megatons					
	Shimmy Shimmy Walk, Part 1	2/10/62	2/24/62	31	3
Mel & Tim					
	Backfield In Motion	11/3/69	11/24/69	13	7
Melody Mates					
	Enchantment	1/14/61	1/28/61	14	4
Melrose Elementary Band					
	Little Blue River	6/5/64	6/12/64	33	2
Mendes, Sergio & Brasil '66					
	The Look Of Love	5/20/68	6/24/68	9	7
	The Fool On The Hill	8/12/68	9/30/68	9	9
	Scarborough Fair	11/18/68	12/16/68	19	7
Mercy					
	Love (Can Make You Happy)	4/21/69	5/19/69	2	10

Artist / Title	Debut	Peak	Pos	Wks
Metcalfe, Ronn				
Twistin' At The Woodchopper's Ball	3/10/62	3/10/62	39	1
Michael & the Messengers				
In The Midnight Hour	3/31/67	5/19/67	5	10
(Just Like) Romeo And Juliet	6/23/67	7/14/67	12	8
Miller, Bobby				
Uncle Willie Time	1/10/64	1/10/64	36	1
Miller, Frankie				
Black Land Farmer	7/15/61	7/29/61	13	6
Miller, Jody				
Queen Of The House	5/7/65	5/14/65	16	4
Home Of The Brave	10/15/65	10/15/65	37	1
Miller, Mitch				
The Longest Day	10/27/62	11/17/62	19	4
Miller, Ned				
From A Jack To A King	12/22/62	1/25/63	7	7
Another Fool Like Me	8/2/63	8/16/63	23	3
Invisible Tears	4/3/64	4/10/64	32	3
Do What You Do Well	1/8/65	1/15/65	26	2
Miller, Roger				
Dang Me	6/5/64	7/17/64	11	9
Chug-A-Lug	9/11/64	10/9/64	5	7
Do-Wacka-Do	12/11/64	1/1/65	17	5
King Of The Road	2/5/65	3/5/65	3	10
Engine Engine #9	5/7/65	5/21/65	6	5
One Dyin' And A Buryin'	7/2/65	7/9/65	28	4
/It Just Happened That Way	7/16/65	7/16/65	31	4
Kansas City Star	9/10/65	9/24/65	36	3
England Swings	11/12/65	12/3/65	15	7
Husbands And Wives	2/25/66	2/25/66	31	2
Little Green Apples	3/4/68	3/4/68	34	1
Mills, Hayley				
Let's Get Together	9/23/61	10/14/61	1	9
Johnny Jingo	3/17/62	4/14/62	18	5
Castaway	3/15/63	3/15/63	31	1
Mimms, Garnet				
Cry Baby	9/20/63	9/27/63	36	3
Mina				
This World We Love In	3/25/61	4/1/61	12	6

Artist	Title	Debut	Peak	Pos	Wks
Miracles					
	I Need A Change	11/26/60	12/3/60	30	2
	Shop Around	12/31/60	1/28/61	2	9
	Everybody's Gotta Pay Some Dues	11/4/61	11/11/61	26	2
	What's So Good About Good-By	2/10/62	2/17/62	34	2
	I'll Try Something New	6/30/62	6/30/62	37	2
	You've Really Got A Hold On Me	1/19/63	2/8/63	28	4
	A Love She Can Count On	5/3/63	5/10/63	33	3
	Mickey's Monkey	8/16/63	9/13/63	16	6
	I Like It Like That	8/7/64	8/21/64	32	4
	Ooo Baby Baby	5/7/65	5/21/65	27	4
	The Tracks Of My Tears	7/23/65	7/30/65	37	2
	Going To A Go-Go	1/21/66	1/28/66	25	4
	(Come 'Round Here) I'm The One You Need	11/25/66	11/25/66	37	2
Smokey Robinson & the Miracles					
	I Second That Emotion	11/10/67	12/15/67	8	10
	If You Can Want	3/4/68	4/8/68	16	6
	Yester Love	6/3/68	6/17/68	32	3
	Special Occasion	9/2/68	9/9/68	34	2
	Baby, Baby Don't Cry	1/6/69	3/10/69	6	12
Mirettes					
	In The Midnight Hour	3/11/68	3/11/68	39	1
Mitchell, Chad, Trio					
	Lizzie Borden	3/17/62	3/24/62	25	2
	The Marvelous Toy	12/20/63	12/27/63	26	2
Mitchell, McKinley					
	The Town I Live In	3/10/62	3/10/62	36	2
	A Bit Of Soul	9/6/63	9/13/63	32	2
Mitchell, Willie					
	20-75	9/18/64	10/16/64	20	4
	Soul Serenade	3/25/68	5/13/68	19	8
Mojo Men					
	Dance With Me	10/15/65	11/5/65	27	4
Monkees					
	Last Train To Clarksville	9/16/66	10/21/66	1	11
	I'm A Believer	12/9/66	12/30/66	1	12
	/(I'm Not Your) Steppin' Stone	12/9/66	12/30/66	1	12
	A Little Bit Me, A Little Bit You	3/24/67	4/14/67	1	8
	Pleasant Valley Sunday	7/14/67	7/28/67	2	10
	/Words	7/14/67	7/28/67	2	10
	Daydream Believer	11/3/67	11/24/67	1	13

Artist	Title	Debut	Peak	Pos	Wks
	Valleri	2/26/68	3/25/68	1	8
	/Tapioca Tundra	3/4/68	3/25/68	1	4
	It's Nice To Be With You	6/3/68	6/24/68	21	4
	/D. W. Washburn	6/3/68	6/3/68	31	1

also see Jones, Davy

Monro, Matt
	My Kind Of Girl	7/8/61	8/5/61	24	6
	Walk Away	12/4/64	12/25/64	19	6

Montanas
	You've Got To Be Loved	1/29/68	3/11/68	11	8
	Run To Me	9/23/68	11/11/68	8	11

Monte, Lou
	Pepino The Italian Mouse	11/17/62	12/8/62	7	8
	Pepino's Friend Pasqual (The Italian Pussy-Cat)	3/29/63	3/29/63	38	1

Montenegro, Hugo
	The Good, The Bad And The Ugly	3/18/68	5/13/68	4	11

Montez, Chris
	Let's Dance	9/1/62	9/29/62	1	9
	Some Kinda Fun	11/17/62	12/15/62	9	7
	Call Me	2/18/66	3/11/66	17	5
	The More I See You	5/27/66	7/8/66	10	8
	There Will Never Be Another You	8/12/66	9/9/66	24	6
	Time After Time	11/4/66	12/2/66	17	6

Moody Blues
	Go Now!	3/5/65	4/9/65	4	10
	Tuesday Afternoon (Forever Afternoon)	8/5/68	9/9/68	12	8

Moore, Bob
	My Three Sons	4/22/61	5/20/61	20	6
	Mexico	8/26/61	10/7/61	1	10
	Kentucky	5/31/63	6/28/63	14	6

Moore, Bobby
	Searching For My Love	7/29/66	8/5/66	25	5

Morgan, Jane
	Bless 'Em All	12/27/63	1/10/64	24	5

Morris, Marlowe, Quintet
	Play The Thing	1/27/62	2/3/62	38	2

Morrison, Van
	Brown Eyed Girl	8/18/67	10/6/67	4	11

also see Them

Artist / Title	Debut	Peak	Pos	Wks
Motherlode				
When I Die	8/18/69	10/6/69	15	9
Mouskouri, Nana				
Wildwood Flower	11/3/62	11/17/62	27	3
Mugwumps				
Jug Band Music	8/26/66	9/16/66	20	5
Searchin'	5/5/67	5/19/67	33	4
also see Elliot, Mama Cass and the Mamas & the Papas				
Murad's, Jerry, Harmonicats				
Cherry Pink And Apple Blossom White	2/18/61	2/25/61	32	2
Murmaids				
Popsicles And Icicles	12/13/63	1/10/64	4	9
Music Explosion				
Little Bit O' Soul	5/12/67	7/7/67	1	13
Music Machine				
Talk Talk	11/11/66	12/2/66	8	6
Mustangs				
The Dartell Stomp	8/7/64	8/21/64	13	6
Napoleon XIV				
They're Coming To Take Me Away, Ha-Haaa!	7/15/66	7/22/66	6	2
Nash, Johnny				
Hold Me Tight	10/14/68	11/18/68	5	8
Cupid	12/22/69	12/29/69	35	3
Nashville Teens				
Tobacco Road	9/25/64	10/23/64	4	8
Google Eye	12/18/64	12/25/64	25	2
Nazz				
Hello It's Me	1/27/69	2/3/69	36	2
Nelson, Nate				
Tell Me Why	11/4/61	11/4/61	40	1
Nelson, Ricky				
You Are The Only One	12/24/60	1/21/61	17	6
Hello Mary Lou	5/13/61	5/27/61	1	10
Nelson, Rick				
Everlovin'	10/7/61	11/11/61	7	7
/A Wonder Like You	11/11/61	11/11/61	7	2
Young World	3/10/62	4/7/62	7	8
Teen Age Idol	8/18/62	9/22/62	16	7

Artist	Title	Debut	Peak	Pos	Wks
	It's Up To You	12/22/62	1/12/63	12	7
	I'm In Love Again	2/8/63	3/8/63	22	4
	/That's All	3/1/63	3/8/63	22	2
	You Don't Love Me Anymore (And I Can Tell)	3/22/63	3/22/63	31	2
	Gypsy Woman	5/24/63	6/28/63	6	8
	/String Along	5/31/63	6/14/63	12	3
	Fools Rush In	11/1/63	11/29/63	13	7
	For You	1/10/64	2/14/64	8	7
	Today's Teardrops	1/17/64	1/24/64	33	2
	Congratulations	4/10/64	4/24/64	32	3

Nelson, Sandy

	Let There Be Drums	11/4/61	12/2/61	1	13
	Drums Are My Beat	2/10/62	3/3/62	21	5
	Drummin' Up A Storm	5/26/62	6/9/62	25	3
	All Night Long	7/14/62	7/21/62	33	2
	Teen Beat '65	10/23/64	11/27/64	15	5

Nelson, Willie

	Half A Man	2/22/63	2/22/63	39	1

Neon Philharmonic

	Morning Girl	4/28/69	6/2/69	2	8

Nettles, Roosevelt

	Mathilda	2/1/63	2/1/63	39	1

Neville, Aaron

	Over You	10/14/60	10/14/60	27	1
	Tell It Like It Is	12/16/66	1/20/67	11	7

New Christy Minstrels

	Green, Green	7/19/63	8/2/63	10	5
	Saturday Night	11/1/63	11/1/63	40	1
	Today	5/8/64	5/22/64	14	5
	Silly Ol' Summertime	8/21/64	8/21/64	39	1

also see McGuire, Barry

New Colony Six

	I Confess	12/17/65	2/4/66	2	10
	I Lie Awake	3/25/66	4/8/66	20	7
	Cadillac	7/1/66	7/22/66	27	5
	Love You So Much	12/16/66	1/27/67	2	10
	You're Gonna Be Mine	3/31/67	4/21/67	8	5
	I'm Just Waiting Anticipating For Her To Show Up	6/23/67	7/21/67	14	8
	Treat Her Groovy	9/29/67	11/3/67	12	7
	I Will Always Think About You	2/12/68	3/25/68	1	11
	Can't You See Me Cry	6/3/68	7/8/68	10	8

Artist	Title	Debut	Peak	Pos	Wks
	Things I'd Like To Say	11/11/68	12/30/68	2	13
	I Could Never Lie To You	4/28/69	5/26/69	7	8
	I Want You To Know	8/11/69	9/22/69	11	9
	Barbara, I Love You	12/8/69	1/12/70	13	8
	also see Rice, Ronnie				

New Vaudeville Band
	Winchester Cathedral	10/28/66	12/9/66	1	12

Newbeats
	Bread And Butter	8/28/64	10/2/64	5	7
	Everything's Alright	11/20/64	12/18/64	13	5
	Break Away (From That Boy)	1/22/65	2/5/65	23	4
	Run, Baby Run (Back Into My Arms)	11/12/65	12/17/65	12	7

Newley, Anthony
	Pop Goes The Weasel	12/16/61	12/30/61	27	3

Newton, Wayne
	Danke Schoen	7/19/63	8/16/63	17	5
	Red Roses For A Blue Lady	3/5/65	4/9/65	15	6
	I'll Be With You In Apple Blossom Time	6/18/65	6/18/65	37	1
	Dreams Of The Everyday Housewife	6/24/68	6/24/68	37	2

Nilsson
	Everybody's Talkin'	9/1/69	10/6/69	5	8

Nimoy, Leonard
	Visit To A Sad Planet	9/15/67	9/29/67	22	3

1910 Fruitgum Co.
	Simon Says	1/29/68	3/11/68	2	11
	1,2,3, Red Light	7/15/68	8/26/68	2	11
	Goody Goody Gumdrops	10/28/68	12/9/68	15	10
	Indian Giver	1/27/69	3/10/69	5	10
	Special Delivery	5/12/69	6/16/69	11	9
	The Train	8/11/69	9/22/69	9	10

Nino & the Ebb Tides
	Juke Box Saturday Night	9/30/61	9/30/61	38	1

Nitty Gritty Dirt Band
	Buy For Me The Rain	4/14/67	5/12/67	21	7

Noble, Nick
	Excuse Me	11/12/60	11/19/60	35	3
	Over Someone's Shoulder	2/25/61	3/4/61	32	2
	They Call Me The Fool	5/13/61	5/27/61	27	3
	My Heart Comes Running Back	5/12/62	5/26/62	33	3

Artist	Title	Debut	Peak	Pos	Wks
	Hello Out There	8/25/62	9/15/62	15	5
	Closer To Heaven	2/8/63	3/1/63	23	4
	Gee Little Girl	5/24/63	5/31/63	22	4
	Sleep Walk	11/22/63	11/22/63	33	1
	Stay With Me	1/10/64	1/31/64	18	5
	Girl With Red Hair	11/5/65	11/12/65	34	2

Nobles, Cliff & Co.
	The Horse	5/27/68	7/1/68	4	10

Norton, Billie Jean
	Angel Hands	2/25/61	2/25/61	37	1

Norton, Jamie
	They're Playing Our Song	12/2/61	12/2/61	34	1
	Only Forever	9/8/62	9/8/62	39	1

Novas
	The Crusher	1/8/65	2/5/65	6	6

Ohio Express
	Beg, Borrow And Steal	11/10/67	11/10/67	31	2
	Yummy Yummy Yummy	4/22/68	5/20/68	1	11
	Down At Lulu's	8/12/68	9/16/68	3	8
	Chewy Chewy	10/21/68	11/25/68	3	10
	Mercy	3/24/69	4/28/69	9	9

O'Jays
	Lipstick Traces (On A Cigarette)	5/28/65	6/18/65	25	4

O'Kaysions
	Girl Watcher	9/2/68	10/7/68	7	9

Oliver
	Good Morning Starshine	5/26/69	6/16/69	3	12
	Jean	8/25/69	10/13/69	3	12
	Sunday Mornin'	12/15/69	12/22/69	37	2

Oliver Cool
	Oliver Cool	11/5/60	11/5/60	33	1

Olympics
	Shimmy Like Kate	10/14/60	10/29/60	14	6
	Dance By The Light Of The Moon	12/24/60	1/28/61	9	9
	Little Pedro	3/25/61	3/25/61	26	1
	The Bounce	5/24/63	5/31/63	19	4

Orbison, Roy
	Blue Angel	10/15/60	11/19/60	11	7
	Running Scared	5/13/61	6/3/61	2	9

Artist	Title	Debut	Peak	Pos	Wks
	Crying	9/16/61	10/7/61	3	7
	/Candy Man	9/9/61	9/23/61	4	4
	Dream Baby (How Long Must I Dream)	3/10/62	3/31/62	10	6
	The Crowd	6/23/62	7/14/62	16	4
	Workin' For The Man	10/20/62	11/3/62	26	3
	In Dreams	3/1/63	3/15/63	14	6
	Falling	6/7/63	7/5/63	6	7
	Mean Woman Blues	9/13/63	10/18/63	4	11
	/Blue Bayou	9/27/63	10/18/63	4	7
	Pretty Paper	12/13/63	12/20/63	16	3
	It's Over	4/24/64	5/29/64	9	8
	Oh, Pretty Woman	8/28/64	9/18/64	1	13
	Goodnight	2/5/65	3/12/65	18	6
	(Say) You're My Girl	7/30/65	8/13/65	18	3
	Ride Away	9/10/65	10/1/65	20	4
	Breakin' Up Is Breakin' My Heart	1/21/66	1/28/66	35	2
	Twinkle Toes	4/22/66	5/6/66	23	5
	Communication Breakdown	12/9/66	12/16/66	25	3
	Cry Softly Lonely One	8/18/67	8/25/67	27	3

Orchestra Del Oro
| | Theme From Lolita | 5/5/62 | 5/5/62 | 40 | 1 |

Originals
| | Gimme A Little Kiss | 12/23/61 | 12/23/61 | 39 | 1 |

Originals
| | Baby, I'm For Real | 10/27/69 | 12/1/69 | 6 | 10 |

Orlando, Tony
| | Halfway To Paradise | 6/3/61 | 6/3/61 | 37 | 1 |
| | Bless You | 9/16/61 | 10/7/61 | 11 | 5 |

Orlons
	The Wah Watusi	6/23/62	7/14/62	4	6
	Don't Hang Up	10/27/62	11/17/62	12	7
	South Street	2/15/63	3/8/63	6	7
	Not Me	5/31/63	7/19/63	22	7
	Cross Fire	9/27/63	10/18/63	23	4
	Shimmy Shimmy	2/21/64	2/21/64	39	1

Outsiders
	Time Won't Let Me	3/25/66	4/22/66	4	8
	Girl In Love	5/13/66	6/17/66	10	7
	Respectable	8/5/66	8/19/66	5	4
	Help Me Girl	11/4/66	12/2/66	19	6

Artist	Title	Debut	Peak	Pos	Wks

Overlanders
    Don't It Make You Feel Good — 10/23/64 — 12/4/64 — 7 — 7

Owens, Buck
    My Heart Skips A Beat — 6/19/64 — 7/3/64 — 24 — 4
    I Don't Care (Just As Long As You Love Me) — 9/18/64 — 10/2/64 — 28 — 2
    I've Got A Tiger By The Tail — 1/22/65 — 2/5/65 — 20 — 5

Packers
    Hole In The Wall — 11/5/65 — 11/12/65 — 36 — 2

Page, Patti
    I Need You — 10/29/60 — 10/29/60 — 17 — 2
    Most People Get Married — 4/28/62 — 4/28/62 — 24 — 2
    The Boys' Night Out — 8/11/62 — 8/11/62 — 35 — 1
    How Much Is That Doggie In The Window — 1/12/63 — 1/12/63 — 40 — 1
    Hush, Hush, Sweet Charlotte — 5/28/65 — 6/11/65 — 13 — 7
    Happy Birthday Sweet Jesus — 12/23/66 — 12/23/66 — 39 — 1

Palmer, Earl
    New Orleans Medley — 8/19/61 — 8/19/61 — 34 — 1

Parade
    Sunshine Girl — 5/12/67 — 5/19/67 — 39 — 3

Paradons
    Diamonds And Pearls — 10/14/60 — 10/14/60 — 36 — 1

Paramours
    That's The Way We Love — 4/15/61 — 4/15/61 — 37 — 1
  also see the Righteous Brothers, Bill Medley and Bobby Hatfield

Paris Sisters
    Be My Boy — 5/6/61 — 5/20/61 — 7 — 7
    I Love How You Love Me — 9/30/61 — 11/18/61 — 2 — 9
    He Knows I Love Him Too Much — 1/27/62 — 2/10/62 — 16 — 7

Parker, Bobby
    Watch Your Step — 7/22/61 — 7/22/61 — 32 — 1

Parker, Little Junior
    Annie Get Your Yo-Yo — 3/24/62 — 3/31/62 — 33 — 2

Parker, Robert
    Barefootin' — 5/27/66 — 5/27/66 — 37 — 1

Parton, Dolly
    Happy Birthday Baby — 10/1/65 — 10/15/65 — 29 — 3

Pastel Six
    The Cinnamon Cinder (It's A Very Nice Dance) — 12/29/62 — 1/12/63 — 18 — 6

Artist / Title	Debut	Peak	Pos	Wks
Patty & the Emblems				
Mixed-Up, Shook-Up Girl	7/3/64	7/24/64	16	5
Patty Cakes				
I Understand Them	5/15/64	6/5/64	14	5
Paul, Les & Mary Ford				
Jura (I Swear I Love You)	6/3/61	6/17/61	28	3
Paul & Paula				
Hey Paula	12/29/62	1/25/63	1	11
Young Lovers	3/8/63	4/12/63	7	7
First Quarrel	5/31/63	5/31/63	37	3
Something Old, Something New	9/6/63	9/6/63	39	1
Pavone, Rita				
Remember Me	6/26/64	7/3/64	23	4
Peaches & Herb				
Close Your Eyes	4/14/67	5/12/67	28	6
Love Is Strange	10/13/67	11/17/67	11	7
Pearlettes				
Duchess Of Earl	4/7/62	4/7/62	39	1
Peek, Paul				
Pin The Tail On The Donkey	4/29/66	4/29/66	40	1
Pentagons				
To Be Loved (Forever)	4/1/61	4/15/61	16	4
I Wonder (If Your Love Will Ever Belong To Me)	10/28/61	11/18/61	18	5
People				
I Love You	5/20/68	7/1/68	2	9
Peppermint Rainbow				
Will You Be Staying After Sunday	3/17/69	4/28/69	14	9
Percells				
What Are Boys Made Of	4/12/63	4/12/63	38	1
Pericoli, Emilio				
Al Di La	6/16/62	7/7/62	3	7
Persuaders				
Drums A Go-Go	8/20/65	8/27/65	21	2
Peter & Gordon				
A World Without Love	5/22/64	6/12/64	1	9
Nobody I Know	7/3/64	7/17/64	4	7
I Don't Want To See You Again	10/2/64	11/6/64	18	5
I Go To Pieces	1/15/65	2/12/65	5	8

Artist	Title	Debut	Peak	Pos	Wks
	True Love Ways	5/7/65	5/21/65	18	6
	To Know You Is To Love You	7/9/65	7/16/65	33	4
	Woman	2/18/66	3/11/66	16	7
	Lady Godiva	11/4/66	11/25/66	5	7
	Knight In Rusty Armor	12/23/66	1/20/67	16	6
	Sunday For Tea	3/31/67	4/14/67	26	4
	The Jokers	6/2/67	6/2/67	37	2
Peter, Paul & Mary					
	Lemon Tree	6/2/62	6/23/62	17	4
	If I Had A Hammer (The Hammer Song)	8/11/62	9/8/62	2	8
	Settle Down (Goin' Down That Highway)	2/1/63	2/15/63	20	3
	Puff The Magic Dragon	3/15/63	4/12/63	6	8
	Blowin' In The Wind	7/5/63	8/30/63	4	10
	Don't Think Twice, It's All Right	10/4/63	10/18/63	16	4
	Stewball	12/13/63	12/13/63	36	1
	Tell It On The Mountain	4/3/64	4/10/64	29	2
	For Lovin' Me	2/5/65	2/12/65	34	3
	I Dig Rock And Roll Music	8/18/67	9/29/67	14	7
	Day Is Done	5/5/69	6/2/69	11	7
	Leaving On A Jet Plane	10/13/69	12/1/69	4	15
Petersen, Paul					
	She Can't Find Her Keys	3/31/62	5/12/62	8	8
	Lollipops And Roses	9/15/62	9/22/62	26	4
	My Dad	12/8/62	1/4/63	4	8
	Amy	4/26/63	4/26/63	39	1
	The Cheer Leader	12/6/63	12/6/63	40	1
	She Rides With Me	2/28/64	2/28/64	33	1
Peterson, Ray					
	Corinna, Corinna	12/17/60	1/7/61	6	8
	Missing You	9/23/61	10/7/61	9	5
Phillips, Esther					
	Release Me	11/3/62	12/1/62	18	6
	And I Love Him	5/7/65	5/7/65	39	1
	Moonglow And Theme From Picnic	8/6/65	8/13/65	32	2
Pickett, Bobby "Boris" & the Crypt-Kickers					
	Monster Mash	9/8/62	10/20/62	1	9
	Monsters' Holiday	12/8/62	12/22/62	8	4
Pickett, Wilson					
	In The Midnight Hour	9/10/65	9/17/65	33	2
	634-5789 (Soulsville, U.S.A.)	4/1/66	4/8/66	35	2
	Land Of 1000 Dances	8/5/66	8/19/66	19	5

Artist	Title	Debut	Peak	Pos	Wks
	Funky Broadway	8/18/67	9/22/67	7	8
	Stag-O-Lee	10/20/67	11/17/67	15	6
	/I'm In Love	12/15/67	12/29/67	18	4
	Jealous Love	2/12/68	2/26/68	25	3
	She's Lookin' Good	4/1/68	5/20/68	11	9
	I'm A Midnight Mover	6/24/68	7/29/68	17	6
	Hey Jude	12/23/68	1/27/69	21	6
	Mini-Skirt Minnie	4/14/69	4/21/69	33	2

Pieces of Eight
	Lonely Drifter	7/7/67	8/25/67	18	10

Pierce, Webb
	The French Riviera	6/19/64	6/26/64	37	2

Pitney, Gene
	(I Wanna) Love My Life Away	1/21/61	2/11/61	8	7
	Louisiana Mama	4/29/61	4/29/61	40	1
	Every Breath I Take	7/22/61	7/29/61	30	2
	Town Without Pity	12/30/61	1/20/62	1	9
	(The Man Who Shot) Liberty Valence	5/19/62	6/2/62	3	8
	Only Love Can Break A Heart	9/15/62	10/20/62	2	9
	Half Heaven—Half Heartache	12/15/62	1/12/63	10	6
	Mecca	3/22/63	4/19/63	6	6
	True Love Never Runs Smooth	7/19/63	8/9/63	11	7
	Twenty Four Hours From Tulsa	11/1/63	12/6/63	2	10
	That Girl Belongs To Yesterday	1/24/64	2/7/64	31	4
	It Hurts To Be In Love	8/28/64	9/25/64	6	9
	I'm Gonna Be Strong	11/13/64	12/25/64	17	7
	I Must Be Seeing Things	3/5/65	3/5/65	25	3
	Last Chance To Turn Around	5/21/65	6/4/65	28	3
	Looking Through The Eyes Of Love	7/30/65	8/20/65	21	4
	Princess In Rags	12/10/65	12/17/65	36	2
	Backstage	4/15/66	5/6/66	10	7
	Just One Smile	12/2/66	1/6/67	10	7
	She's A Heartbreaker	5/20/68	6/24/68	7	9

Pixies Three
	Birthday Party	9/13/63	10/4/63	8	6

Plastic Ono Band
	Give Peace A Chance	7/21/69	8/4/69	17	6

also see the Beatles

Platters
	To Each His Own	10/29/60	12/3/60	12	8

Artist	Title	Debut	Peak	Pos	Wks
	If I Didn't Care	1/21/61	1/28/61	30	3
	I'll Never Smile Again	8/12/61	8/26/61	28	4 |//
Playmates
	Wait For Me	10/14/60	11/5/60	4	10
	Little Miss Stuck-Up	3/18/61	4/8/61	5	7

Poppies
	Lullaby Of Love	3/18/66	3/18/66	34	1

Posey, Sandy
	Born A Woman	7/1/66	8/19/66	14	12
	Single Girl	11/25/66	12/23/66	13	5
	What A Woman In Love Won't Do	3/10/67	3/24/67	31	4
	I Take It Back	7/21/67	8/4/67	23	4

Power Plant
	Can't Happen Without You	10/6/67	10/20/67	33	3

Powers, Joey
	Midnight Mary	11/15/63	1/3/64	4	9

Pozo-Seco Singers
	I Can Make It With You	9/23/66	11/11/66	17	9
	Look What You've Done	1/6/67	1/13/67	35	3

Prado, Perez
	Patricia—Twist	3/17/62	4/7/62	26	4

Premiers
	Farmer John	6/19/64	7/10/64	22	4

Presley, Elvis
	It's Now Or Never	10/14/60	10/14/60	5	2
	Are You Lonesome To-Night	11/19/60	12/3/60	1	12
	Surrender	2/18/61	3/11/61	5	8
	I Feel So Bad	5/27/61	6/10/61	15	4
	Little Sister	9/9/61	9/30/61	6	6
	Can't Help Falling In Love	12/23/61	2/3/62	4	8
	/Rock-A-Hula Baby	12/23/61	1/6/62	10	4
	Good Luck Charm	3/10/62	3/31/62	2	7
	/Anything That's Part Of You	3/10/62	3/17/62	13	2
	Follow That Dream	5/19/62	6/2/62	16	4
	She's Not You	8/11/62	9/8/62	13	5
	King Of The Whole Wide World	9/22/62	10/6/62	23	3
	Return To Sender	10/20/62	12/15/62	2	12
	One Broken Heart For Sale	2/22/63	3/8/63	18	4
	(You're The) Devil In Disguise	7/5/63	8/2/63	5	6

Artist	Title	Debut	Peak	Pos	Wks
	Bossa Nova Baby	10/18/63	11/15/63	13	9
	/Witchcraft	10/25/63	11/15/63	13	4
	Kissin' Cousins	3/6/64	3/20/64	20	5
	What'd I Say	5/22/64	5/29/64	26	5
	Such A Night	8/21/64	8/21/64	38	1
	Ask Me	11/6/64	11/27/64	5	8
	Do The Clam	3/12/65	3/19/65	32	4
	Crying In The Chapel	5/21/65	6/25/65	7	9
	It Feels So Right	6/18/65	7/23/65	22	5
	/(Such An) Easy Question	6/25/65	7/2/65	24	3
	I'm Yours	9/10/65	9/24/65	15	4
	Puppet On A String	11/26/65	12/24/65	27	5
	Tell Me Why	12/24/65	1/7/66	23	3
	Frankie And Johnny	3/25/66	4/8/66	27	5
	Love Letters	7/8/66	7/8/66	22	7
	Spinout	10/7/66	10/21/66	23	4
	If Every Day Was Like Christmas	12/16/66	12/16/66	33	2
	Indescribably Blue	2/3/67	2/17/67	25	4
	Long Legged Girl (With The Short Dress On)	6/2/67	6/2/67	35	2
	Big Boss Man	11/3/67	11/3/67	36	1
	/You Don't Know Me	11/3/67	11/3/67	36	1
	U.S. Male	3/25/68	5/13/68	11	8
	Let Yourself Go	6/17/68	7/8/68	24	4
	If I Can Dream	12/9/68	2/3/69	7	11
	Memories	3/24/69	4/14/69	21	5
	In The Ghetto	5/12/69	6/2/69	4	8
	Clean Up Your Own Backyard	7/21/69	7/28/69	34	3
	Suspicious Minds	9/22/69	10/13/69	1	11
	Don't Cry Daddy	11/24/69	1/12/70	4	11

Preston, Johnny
	Free Me	1/20/62	1/20/62	37	1

Price, Lloyd
	Misty	10/25/63	11/8/63	31	4

Pride & Joy
	Girl	5/5/67	5/12/67	27	4

also see the Del-Vetts

Princeton Five
	Roll Over Beethoven	3/20/64	3/20/64	37	1

Princetons
	Georgiana	1/14/66	2/25/66	10	7

Artist	Title	Debut	Peak	Pos	Wks

Procol Harum
    A Whiter Shade Of Pale   7/14/67   8/4/67   11   6

Puckett, Gary & the Union Gap
    Woman, Woman   12/1/67   12/29/67   3   11
    Young Girl   3/4/68   4/1/68   2   10
    Lady Willpower   6/10/68   7/15/68   4   10
    Over You   9/9/68   10/14/68   1   11
    Don't Give In To Him   3/17/69   4/14/69   6   9
    This Girl Is A Woman Now   8/18/69   9/15/69   3   11

Purify, James & Bobby
    I'm Your Puppet   10/7/66   10/21/66   26   4

Pursell, Bill
    Our Winter Love   3/1/63   3/29/63   3   7

Pyramids
    Penetration   1/24/64   2/21/64   4   8

? & the Mysterians
    96 Tears   9/9/66   10/14/66   1   11
    I Need Somebody   12/9/66   12/23/66   33   3

Radiants
    Shy Guy   11/1/63   11/29/63   19   6

Raindrops
    What A Guy   4/19/63   5/31/63   6   9
    The Kind Of Boy You Can't Forget   8/9/63   9/6/63   4   7
    That Boy John   11/29/63   12/13/63   21   5
    Book Of Love   3/20/64   3/20/64   29   2

Rambeau, Eddie
    Concrete And Clay   5/14/65   5/28/65   16   5

Ramblers
    Father Sebastian   6/19/64   7/10/64   10   6

Ramrods
    (Ghost) Riders In The Sky   2/4/61   2/25/61   18   6
    Don't Fool With Fu Manchu   11/12/65   11/12/65   37   1

Randazzo, Teddy
    Happy Ending   4/22/61   5/13/61   26   4
    Let The Sunshine In   7/8/61   7/22/61   28   3
    Big Wide World   2/1/63   2/15/63   15   4

Ran-Dells
    Martian Hop   8/16/63   9/6/63   2   8

Artist / Title	Debut	Peak	Pos	Wks
Randolph, Boots				
Yakety Sax	3/1/63	3/8/63	25	2
Hey, Mr. Sax Man	4/10/64	4/17/64	36	3
Randy & the Rainbows				
Denise	7/19/63	8/9/63	6	8
Rawls, Lou				
Love Is A Hurtin' Thing	10/14/66	10/21/66	32	5
Your Good Thing (Is About To End)	7/28/69	9/15/69	13	11
Ray, Diane				
Please Don't Talk To The Lifeguard	8/30/63	8/30/63	30	1
Ray, James				
If You Gotta Make Fool Of Somebody	12/30/61	1/13/62	30	3
Itty Bitty Pieces	5/5/62	5/19/62	32	3
Ray, Ricardo				
Nitty Gritty	9/23/68	10/7/68	36	3
Ray & Bob				
Air Travel	7/21/62	7/21/62	40	1
Rays				
Magic Moon (Clair De Lune)	9/2/61	9/23/61	21	4
Razor's Edge				
Let's Call It A Day Girl	8/12/66	9/9/66	21	7
Rebels				
Wild Weekend	1/25/63	3/15/63	3	10
Redding, Otis				
I've Been Loving You Too Long (To Stop Now)	6/18/65	6/18/65	35	1
(Sittin' On) The Dock Of The Bay	1/29/68	3/11/68	2	11
The Happy Song (Dum-Dum)	4/29/68	5/13/68	26	4
Papa's Got A Brand New Bag	12/16/68	1/6/69	25	4
Reed, Jerry				
Goodnight Irene	6/30/62	6/30/62	32	1
Reeves, Del				
Girl On The Billboard	4/9/65	4/23/65	17	4
Reeves, Jim				
Am I Losing You	12/24/60	12/24/60	37	2
Distant Drums	5/27/66	5/27/66	31	1
Reflections				
In The Still Of The Night	1/10/64	1/17/64	16	4

Artist	Title	Debut	Peak	Pos	Wks
	(Just Like) Romeo & Juliet	4/3/64	5/22/64	13	9
	Poor Man's Son	3/19/65	4/2/65	25	3
Regents					
	Barbara-Ann	5/20/61	6/10/61	3	8
	Runaround	8/12/61	8/12/61	37	1
Reid, Clarence					
	Nobody But You Babe	9/1/69	9/22/69	23	4
Remo, Sam					
	Hungry For Love	10/8/65	10/15/65	20	3
Renay, Diane					
	Navy Blue	2/7/64	3/6/64	5	6
	Kiss Me Sailor	4/10/64	4/24/64	18	3
	Growin' Up Too Fast	7/10/64	7/10/64	32	1
Rene & Ray					
	Queen Of My Heart	6/30/62	7/7/62	35	2
Rene & Rene					
	Angelito	8/21/64	8/21/64	40	1
	Chantilly Lace	6/11/65	7/2/65	19	5
	Lo Mucho Que Te Quiero (The More I Love You)	12/2/68	1/20/69	19	8
Reno, Jack					
	Blue	3/8/63	4/5/63	20	5
Reparata & the Delrons					
	Whenever A Teenager Cries	2/19/65	3/12/65	15	6
	Tommy	5/14/65	6/4/65	22	5
Revere, Paul & the Raiders					
	Like, Long Hair	4/1/61	4/15/61	9	6
	Over You	11/13/64	11/27/64	22	3
	Steppin' Out	10/1/65	10/22/65	17	6
	Just Like Me	11/26/65	12/24/65	9	9
	Kicks	3/11/66	4/8/66	1	13
	Hungry	6/17/66	7/22/66	3	11
	The Great Airplane Strike	9/30/66	10/28/66	9	6
	Good Thing	12/9/66	1/6/67	4	7
	Ups And Downs	2/17/67	3/17/67	8	7
	Him Or Me—What's It Gonna Be	4/21/67	5/26/67	4	9
	I Had A Dream	8/18/67	9/8/67	8	6
	Peace Of Mind	11/10/67	12/1/67	22	4
	Too Much Talk	2/5/68	3/11/68	8	8
	Don't Take It So Hard	6/10/68	7/29/68	11	9

Artist	Title	Debut	Peak	Pos	Wks
	Mr. Sun, Mr. Moon	2/24/69	4/14/69	5	11
	Let Me	5/12/69	6/16/69	4	11
Revlons					
	Boy Trouble	11/17/62	12/8/62	27	5
Reynolds, Lawrence					
	Jesus Is A Soul Man	9/15/69	10/13/69	11	7
Ribbons					
	Ain't Gonna Kiss Ya	1/12/63	1/12/63	39	2
Rice, Ronnie					
	Over The Mountain (Across The Sea)	12/2/61	1/13/62	27	6
	Maybe It's Because I Love You	6/30/62	7/7/62	33	2
	Come Back Little Girl	1/12/63	2/8/63	20	6
	I Know	7/26/63	8/2/63	36	2
	also see the New Colony 6				
Rich, Charlie					
	There's Another Place I Can't Go	5/17/63	5/17/63	40	1
	Big Boss Man	12/13/63	12/13/63	38	1
	Mohair Sam	8/20/65	8/27/65	22	2
Richard, Cliff					
	It's All In The Game	2/7/64	3/27/64	7	10
	I Only Have Eyes For You	5/8/64	5/15/64	19	4
Rick & the Keens					
	Peanuts	7/1/61	7/22/61	3	8
Riddle, Nelson					
	Route 66 Theme	7/14/62	7/28/62	26	3
Riddles					
	Sweets For My Sweet	3/24/67	4/21/67	19	6
Righteous Brothers					
	Little Latin Lupe Lu	5/31/63	5/31/63	32	1
	My Babe	10/25/63	10/25/63	39	1
	You've Lost That Lovin' Feelin'	12/25/64	1/22/65	2	10
	Bring Your Love To Me	3/5/65	3/12/65	34	2
	Just Once In My Life	4/23/65	6/4/65	11	8
	Unchained Melody	7/16/65	8/27/65	13	7
	/Hung On You	7/16/65	7/23/65	31	2
	Ebb Tide	12/10/65	12/24/65	18	5
	(You're My) Soul And Inspiration	3/11/66	5/6/66	8	11
	He	6/10/66	6/17/66	29	3
	Melancholy Music Man	5/5/67	5/5/67	29	2
	also see the Paramours, Bill Medley and Bobby Hatfield				

Artist	Title	Debut	Peak	Pos	Wks

Riley, Jeannie C.
| | Harper Valley P.T.A. | 8/19/68 | 9/2/68 | 1 | 6 |

Rip Chords
	Here I Stand	4/26/63	5/24/63	16	5
	Hey Little Cobra	12/27/63	1/31/64	4	9
	Three Window Coupe	5/15/64	6/19/64	10	8

Ritter, Tex
| | I Dreamed Of A Hill-Billy Heaven | 6/24/61 | 7/15/61 | 7 | 7 |

Rivers, Johnny
	Memphis	5/29/64	6/26/64	3	9
	Maybelline	8/14/64	9/18/64	12	6
	Mountain Of Love	11/13/64	12/25/64	5	9
	Midnight Special	2/5/65	2/19/65	23	4
	Seventh Son	6/4/65	7/2/65	11	7
	Where Have All The Flowers Gone	10/15/65	10/29/65	25	5
	Under Your Spell Again	12/24/65	1/7/66	33	3
	Secret Agent Man	3/18/66	4/15/66	2	10
	(I Washed My Hands In) Muddy Water	7/1/66	7/8/66	21	5
	Poor Side Of Town	9/23/66	11/18/66	4	13
	Baby I Need Your Lovin'	2/3/67	3/10/67	5	10
	The Tracks Of My Tears	6/2/67	7/7/67	9	8
	Summer Rain	12/1/67	1/15/68	8	9
	Look To Your Soul	4/15/68	5/13/68	21	5
	Right Relations	11/25/68	12/2/68	36	3

Rivieras
	California Sun	12/20/63	1/24/64	3	10
	Let's Have A Party	4/17/64	6/5/64	4	9
	/Little Donna	4/10/64	6/5/64	4	8
	Rockin' Robin	8/7/64	8/21/64	8	5
	Let's Go To Hawaii	4/16/65	4/23/65	25	2
	Somebody New	9/10/65	9/17/65	32	2

Rivingtons
	Papa-Oom-Mow-Mow	8/11/62	9/1/62	28	4
	Mama-Oom-Mow-Mow	2/8/63	2/15/63	37	2
	The Bird's The Word	4/12/63	4/26/63	31	3

Robbins, Marty
	Don't Worry	2/18/61	3/18/61	1	9
	It's Your World	10/14/61	11/11/61	11	6
	Love Can't Wait	4/28/62	4/28/62	40	1
	Devil Woman	8/18/62	9/1/62	19	4
	Ruby Ann	12/8/62	12/15/62	13	3

Artist / Title	Debut	Peak	Pos	Wks
Robbs				
Race With The Wind	6/10/66	7/1/66	16	5
Roberts, Renee				
I Want To Love You	3/31/62	4/14/62	19	4
Rochell & the Candles				
Once Upon A Time	3/25/61	4/8/61	26	3
Rockingham, David, Trio				
Dawn	9/27/63	11/1/63	16	6
Midnight	3/13/64	3/20/64	19	4
Rocky Fellers				
Killer Joe	5/3/63	5/24/63	22	4
Rodgers, Jimmie				
Woman From Liberia	10/29/60	11/5/60	16	3
No One Will Ever Know	8/4/62	8/11/62	31	4
Rainbow At Midnight	11/10/62	11/24/62	15	4
The World I Used To Know	5/8/64	5/22/64	10	6
It's Over	5/6/66	5/27/66	24	6
Child Of Clay	9/22/67	11/3/67	17	7
Roe, Tommy				
Sheila	7/21/62	8/25/62	1	9
Susie Darlin'	10/6/62	10/27/62	22	4
Everybody	9/27/63	10/18/63	3	6
Come On	1/31/64	2/14/64	28	3
Sweet Pea	6/10/66	8/5/66	9	9
Hooray For Hazel	9/23/66	10/28/66	4	9
It's Now Winter's Day	12/23/66	1/27/67	14	9
Dizzy	2/10/69	3/3/69	1	11
Jack And Jill	9/22/69	10/20/69	24	5
Jam Up And Jelly Tight	11/17/69	1/5/70	5	13
Rogers, Julie				
The Wedding	11/20/64	1/1/65	8	9
Like A Child	2/12/65	2/12/65	38	2
Rogues				
Everyday	1/8/65	1/22/65	22	3
Rollers				
The Continental Walk	4/22/61	4/29/61	33	3
Rolling Stones				
Not Fade Away	4/17/64	5/22/64	19	7
It's All Over Now	8/21/64	9/11/64	16	6

Artist	Title	Debut	Peak	Pos	Wks
	Time Is On My Side	11/6/64	11/27/64	7	7
	Heart Of Stone	1/29/65	2/5/65	11	5
	The Last Time	4/9/65	5/14/65	4	9
	(I Can't Get No) Satisfaction	6/18/65	7/9/65	1	10
	Get Off Of My Cloud	10/8/65	10/29/65	1	9
	As Tears Go By	12/24/65	1/14/66	16	4
	19th Nervous Breakdown	2/18/66	3/25/66	3	8
	Paint It, Black	5/13/66	5/27/66	1	7
	Mother's Little Helper	7/8/66	7/29/66	12	5
	Have You Seen Your Mother, Baby, Standing In The Shadow	9/30/66	10/21/66	8	5
	Ruby Tuesday	1/20/67	2/24/67	2	9
	We Love You	9/8/67	10/13/67	16	7
	/Dandelion	9/15/67	10/13/67	16	6
	Jumpin' Jack Flash	6/17/68	7/1/68	1	11
	Honky Tonk Women	7/14/69	7/28/69	1	11

Roman, Dick
	Theme From A Summer Place	6/9/62	6/23/62	9	5

Romeos
	Precious Memories	4/21/67	4/21/67	37	1

Rondels
	Back Beat No. 1	9/9/61	9/23/61	9	5

Ron-Dels
	If You Really Want Me To, I'll Go	6/18/65	7/2/65	21	4

Ronettes
	Be My Baby	8/30/63	9/20/63	2	8
	Baby, I Love You	1/10/64	1/17/64	20	4
	(The Best Part Of) Breakin' Up	4/3/64	4/24/64	23	4
	Do I Love You	7/31/64	8/21/64	23	4
	Walking In The Rain	11/6/64	11/27/64	17	5

Ronnie & the Hi-Lites
	I Wish That We Were Married	3/24/62	4/14/62	7	6

Ronny & the Daytonas
	G.T.O.	8/28/64	9/18/64	13	5
	Sandy	12/24/65	1/28/66	9	9

Rooftop Singers
	Walk Right In	12/29/62	1/19/63	1	10
	Tom Cat	3/29/63	5/3/63	13	7
	Mama Don't Allow	7/19/63	8/2/63	18	4

Artist	Title	Debut	Peak	Pos	Wks

Roommates
| | Glory Of Love | 4/15/61 | 4/15/61 | 38 | 1 |
| | Band Of Gold | 9/9/61 | 9/23/61 | 24 | 3 |

also see Cathy Jean & the Roommates

Rose, David
| | The Stripper | 6/2/62 | 6/16/62 | 1 | 10 |

Rose Garden
| | Next Plane To London | 10/6/67 | 12/29/67 | 26 | 7 |

Rosie & the Originals
| | Angel Baby | 12/17/60 | 1/7/61 | 4 | 9 |

Ross, Jack
| | Happy Jose (Ching, Ching) | 1/13/62 | 1/20/62 | 25 | 2 |
| | Cinderella | 4/14/62 | 4/14/62 | 34 | 1 |

Ross, Jackie
| | Selfish One | 8/14/64 | 8/28/64 | 33 | 3 |

Rosso, Nini
| | Il Silenzio | 12/3/65 | 12/24/65 | 8 | 5 |

Routers
| | Let's Go (Pony) | 10/13/62 | 11/10/62 | 7 | 8 |
| | Sting Ray | 5/10/63 | 6/7/63 | 6 | 7 |

Royal, Billy Joe
	Down In The Boondocks	7/9/65	8/27/65	5	8
	I Knew You When	10/1/65	10/22/65	20	5
	I've Got To Be Somebody	12/24/65	12/24/65	35	1
	Hush	9/22/67	11/10/67	5	9
	Cherry Hill Park	11/3/69	11/3/69	35	1

Royal Guardsmen
	Snoopy Vs. The Red Baron	12/9/66	12/30/66	2	9
	The Return Of The Red Baron	2/24/67	3/10/67	20	5
	Airplane Song (My Airplane)	6/16/67	6/16/67	36	1
	Snoopy's Christmas	11/24/67	12/15/67	5	6
	Snoopy For President	6/10/68	6/10/68	36	1
	Baby Let's Wait	1/6/69	2/3/69	17	6

Royalettes
| | It's Gonna Take A Miracle | 8/20/65 | 9/3/65 | 15 | 3 |

Royaltones
| | Flamingo Express | 1/7/61 | 1/21/61 | 5 | 8 |

Ruby & the Romantics
| | Our Day Will Come | 2/8/63 | 3/8/63 | 7 | 5 |

Artist	Title	Debut	Peak	Pos	Wks
	My Summer Love	5/24/63	5/31/63	21	2
	Young Wings Can Fly (Higher Than You Know)	10/25/63	11/15/63	24	4

Ruffin, David
	My Whole World Ended (The Moment You Left Me)	2/17/69	3/17/69	15	5

Ruffin, Jimmy
	What Becomes Of The Brokenhearted	9/30/66	11/18/66	11	9
	I've Passed This Way Before	1/13/67	1/27/67	31	4

Rugbys
	You, I	8/25/69	9/29/69	8	8

Rush, Merrilee & the Turnabouts
	Angel Of The Morning	5/20/68	6/17/68	2	9

Russ, Lonnie
	My Wife Can't Cook	12/1/62	12/15/62	36	3

Russo, Charlie
	Preacherman	3/22/63	3/29/63	36	2

Rusty & Doug
	Louisiana Man	5/13/61	6/10/61	6	9

Rydell, Bobby
	Volare	10/14/60	10/14/60	29	1
	Sway	11/19/60	12/10/60	8	6
	Good Time Baby	2/4/61	3/4/61	9	7
	That Old Black Magic	5/20/61	6/10/61	11	6
	/Don't Be Afraid	5/20/61	6/10/61	11	6
	The Fish	7/29/61	8/5/61	18	4
	I Wanna Thank You	11/11/61	12/2/61	14	5
	/The Door To Paradise	11/25/61	12/2/61	14	3
	I've Got Bonnie	3/10/62	3/24/62	17	5
	I'll Never Dance Again	6/16/62	7/21/62	7	8
	The Cha-Cha-Cha	10/13/62	11/3/62	18	5
	Butterfly Baby	2/8/63	2/22/63	17	5
	Wildwood Days	5/10/63	5/31/63	15	6
	Forget Him	11/29/63	2/7/64	5	12
	Make Me Forget	4/17/64	4/17/64	30	2
	A World Without Love	5/22/64	5/29/64	10	5
	I Just Can't Say Goodbye	12/4/64	12/11/64	25	2
	Diana	2/26/65	2/26/65	38	1

Rydell, Bobby & Chubby Checker
	Teach Me To Twist	4/28/62	5/5/62	32	2

also see Checker, Chubby

Artist / Title	Debut	Peak	Pos	Wks
Ryder, Mitch & the Detroit Wheels				
Jenny Take A Ride!	1/7/66	2/4/66	18	7
Little Latin Lupe Lu	3/18/66	3/25/66	28	2
Break Out	6/17/66	6/17/66	35	1
Devil With A Blue Dress On & Good Golly Miss Molly	10/21/66	12/9/66	4	14
Sock It To Me-Baby!	2/10/67	3/3/67	10	7
Too Many Fish In The Sea & Three Little Fishes	5/5/67	5/5/67	33	2
Sadler, S/Sgt. Barry				
The Ballad Of The Green Berets	2/4/66	3/11/66	2	8
The "A" Team	5/13/66	5/13/66	34	1
Safaris				
The Girl With The Story In Her Eyes	10/14/60	10/14/60	32	1
Sagittarius				
My World Fell Down	6/30/67	7/14/67	19	6
Sakamoto, Kyu				
Sukiyaki	5/24/63	5/31/63	1	9
China Nights (Shina No Yoru)	8/16/63	9/13/63	21	5
Sales, Soupy				
White Fang	1/6/62	1/20/62	31	3
Sam & Dave				
Soul Man	9/22/67	11/3/67	13	8
I Thank You	1/22/68	3/11/68	14	8
You Don't Know What You Mean To Me	5/27/68	6/10/68	35	3
Can't You Find Another Way (Of Doing It)	8/5/68	8/5/68	38	2
Sam the Sham & the Pharaohs				
Wooly Bully	4/23/65	6/11/65	1	11
Ju Ju Hand	7/23/65	7/23/65	37	2
Ring Dang Doo	10/1/65	10/22/65	18	5
Lil' Red Riding Hood	6/17/66	8/12/66	4	12
The Hair On My Chinny Chin Chin	10/21/66	11/18/66	18	7
How Do You Catch A Girl	1/20/67	2/10/67	21	5
Oh That's Good, No That's Bad	3/31/67	3/31/67	31	2
Sandpipers				
Guantanamera	8/12/66	9/23/66	7	8
Louie, Louie	10/21/66	11/18/66	21	7
Sands, Evie				
Any Way That You Want Me	10/6/69	10/27/69	23	5
Santamaria, Mongo				
Watermelon Man	4/5/63	4/26/63	20	5

Artist	Title	Debut	Peak	Pos	Wks

Santo & Johnny
    Manhattan Spiritual   5/24/63   6/21/63   20   5

Saridis, Saverio
    Love Is The Sweetest Thing   2/24/62   3/3/62   18   4

Schifrin, Lalo
    Mission-Impossible   2/5/68   2/19/68   31   3

Scott, Clifford
    Lavender Sax   5/22/64   6/5/64   32   3

Scott, Freddie
    Hey, Girl   8/9/63   9/20/63   12   7
    I Got A Woman   11/22/63   11/29/63   23   3
    Where Does Love Go   4/10/64   4/24/64   21   3

Scott, Jack
    Patsy   10/15/60   10/29/60   35   2

Scott, Linda
    I've Told Every Little Star   4/1/61   5/13/61   2   9
    Starlight, Starbright   8/5/61   9/9/61   4   8
    I Don't Know Why   12/9/61   12/30/61   7   7
    Bermuda   2/17/62   2/17/62   38   1
    Count Every Star   5/19/62   6/2/62   21   3
    Never In A Million Years   7/14/62   7/21/62   38   2

Scott, Neil
    Bobby   6/17/61   7/15/61   8   7

Scott, Peggy & Jo Jo Benson
    Lover's Holiday   6/17/68   7/22/68   23   7
    Pickin' Wild Mountain Berries   11/18/68   12/9/68   29   4
    Soulshake   1/27/69   2/17/69   20   4

Sea, Johnny
    Day For Decision   5/27/66   6/10/66   9   3

Searchers
    Needles And Pins   2/28/64   4/3/64   15   6
    Don't Throw Your Love Away   6/26/64   7/24/64   6   6
    Some Day We're Gonna Love Again   9/11/64   10/2/64   19   5
    When You Walk In The Room   11/13/64   11/13/64   28   1
    Love Potion Number Nine   12/18/64   1/8/65   1   10
    What Have They Done To The Rain   2/12/65   2/26/65   29   4
    Bumble Bee   4/2/65   4/2/65   30   2

Secrets
    The Boy Next Door   11/1/63   11/29/63   8   7

Artist	Title	Debut	Peak	Pos	Wks
Sedaka, Neil					
	You Mean Everything To Me	10/14/60	10/14/60	9	2
	Calendar Girl	1/28/61	2/11/61	11	4
	Little Devil	5/27/61	6/10/61	12	6
	Happy Birthday, Sweet Sixteen	11/11/61	12/16/61	5	10
	Breaking Up Is Hard To Do	7/14/62	8/4/62	1	9
	Next Door To An Angel	10/6/62	10/27/62	8	6
	Alice In Wonderland	2/8/63	3/1/63	19	4
	Let's Go Steady Again	5/10/63	5/24/63	26	3
	The World Through A Tear	8/20/65	10/1/65	4	9
	The Answer To My Prayer	1/21/66	2/25/66	19	7
	The Answer Lies Within	7/8/66	7/8/66	40	1
Seeds					
	Pushin' Too Hard	1/6/67	2/17/67	1	9
	Can't Seem To Make You Mine	4/7/67	5/19/67	9	8
Seeger, Pete					
	Little Boxes	2/21/64	3/20/64	25	5
Seekers					
	I'll Never Find Another You	3/12/65	4/23/65	9	11
	A World Of Our Own	6/18/65	7/2/65	23	3
	Georgy Girl	12/23/66	2/3/67	2	11
	Morningtown Ride	2/17/67	3/10/67	29	6
Seger, Bob, System					
	Ramblin' Gamblin' Man	1/20/69	3/3/69	2	9
Senator Bobby					
	Wild Thing	1/6/67	1/6/67	30	2
Sensations					
	Music, Music, Music	8/12/61	8/12/61	30	1
	Let Me In	1/27/62	3/10/62	6	9
Serendipity Singers					
	Don't Let The Rain Come Down (Crooked Little Man)	3/13/64	4/17/64	1	10
	Beans In My Ears	5/29/64	6/5/64	32	5
Sevilles					
	Charlena	2/18/61	3/11/61	24	4
Shades Of Blue					
	Oh How Happy	6/10/66	6/24/66	17	3
Shadows Of Knight					
	Gloria	2/18/66	4/1/66	1	12
	Oh Yeah	5/20/66	6/3/66	13	6

Artist	Title	Debut	Peak	Pos	Wks
	Bad Little Woman	8/26/66	9/9/66	19	6
	I'm Gonna Make You Mine	11/11/66	11/25/66	25	4
	Shake	11/18/68	12/9/68	12	6

Shangri-Las

	Remember (Walkin' In The Sand)	8/28/64	9/11/64	2	6
	Leader Of The Pack	10/16/64	11/6/64	1	8
	Give Him A Great Big Kiss	1/8/65	1/29/65	10	5
	Out In The Streets	4/16/65	4/16/65	37	2
	Give Us Your Blessings	5/21/65	6/11/65	9	7
	I Can Never Go Home Anymore	11/12/65	12/3/65	6	6
	Long Live Our Love	1/21/66	2/11/66	29	5
	He Cried	4/1/66	4/8/66	34	3
	Past, Present And Future	7/1/66	7/1/66	37	1

Shannon

	Abergavenny	7/14/69	8/11/69	20	5

Shannon, Del

	Runaway	4/8/61	4/29/61	1	10
	Hats Off To Larry	7/8/61	7/22/61	2	9
	So Long Baby	10/7/61	11/11/61	14	7
	Hey! Little Girl	12/9/61	1/6/62	19	5
	The Swiss Maid	9/22/62	9/22/62	35	2
	Little Town Flirt	1/12/63	2/15/63	5	9
	Two Kinds Of Teardrops	4/19/63	5/10/63	20	4
	From Me To You	6/21/63	7/12/63	15	6
	Sue's Gotta Be Mine	10/25/63	11/8/63	16	4
	Handy Man	7/10/64	8/14/64	7	9
	Keep Searchin' (We'll Follow The Sun)	12/25/64	1/22/65	4	7
	Stranger In Town	3/5/65	3/5/65	34	3

Shapiro, Helen

	Walkin' Back To Happiness	12/2/61	12/9/61	33	2

Sharp, Dee Dee

	Mashed Potato Time	3/3/62	4/14/62	2	12
	Gravy (For My Mashed Potatoes)	6/23/62	6/23/62	37	1
	Ride!	11/3/62	11/24/62	20	4
	Do The Bird	3/8/63	3/15/63	26	3
	Rock Me In The Cradle Of Love	7/5/63	7/19/63	32	4

Shaw, Sandie

	Girl Don't Come	4/16/65	4/16/65	39	1

Shaw, Timmy

	Gonna Send You Back To Georgia (A City Slick)	2/14/64	2/14/64	31	1

Artist / Title	Debut	Peak	Pos	Wks
Sheep				
Hide & Seek	2/4/66	2/11/66	38	2
Shells				
Baby Oh Baby	12/3/60	12/17/60	33	3
Shep & the Limelites				
Daddy's Home	5/6/61	5/27/61	10	6
Shepherd Sisters				
Don't Mention My Name	3/1/63	3/29/63	7	6
Shepherds				
Come Home, Come Home	10/14/60	10/14/60	22	1
Sherman, Allan				
Hello Muddah, Hello Faddah! (A Letter From Camp)	8/2/63	8/16/63	2	6
I Can't Dance	3/20/64	3/20/64	39	1
Sherman, Bobby				
Little Woman	9/1/69	9/29/69	1	10
La La La (If I Had You)	11/24/69	1/12/70	10	10
Sherrys				
Pop Pop Pop-Pie	9/22/62	10/27/62	6	7
Shirelles				
Will You Love Me Tomorrow	12/31/60	2/4/61	1	12
Dedicated To The One I Love	3/4/61	4/8/61	4	7
Mama Said	5/13/61	6/3/61	10	6
What A Sweet Thing That Was	7/22/61	7/29/61	33	2
Big John	10/21/61	10/28/61	34	2
Baby It's You	1/13/62	2/24/62	5	9
Soldier Boy	3/31/62	5/5/62	1	9
Welcome Home Baby	7/21/62	7/28/62	31	2
Stop The Music	10/6/62	10/13/62	31	2
Everybody Loves A Lover	12/8/62	12/29/62	36	4
Foolish Little Girl	4/19/63	5/24/63	5	8
Don't Say Goodnight And Mean Goodbye	6/21/63	6/28/63	27	5
31 Flavors	11/15/63	11/15/63	38	2
Shirley, Don, Trio				
Water Boy	7/8/61	8/5/61	7	7
Shocking Blue				
Venus	12/1/69	1/5/70	1	12

Artist	Title	Debut	Peak	Pos	Wks

Shondell, Troy
    This Time   8/19/61   9/9/61   1   8
    Na Ne Noe   5/19/62   5/19/62   37   1

Showmen
    It Will Stand   12/30/61   2/17/62   6   9

Sierras
    I'll Believe It When I See It   8/30/63   9/13/63   23   3

Sigler, Bunny
    Let The Good Times Roll & Feel So Good   8/11/67   8/11/67   35   1

Silkie
    You've Got To Hide Your Love Away   10/15/65   10/29/65   15   4

Simmons, "Jumpin'" Gene
    Haunted House   8/7/64   9/25/64   12   8

Simon, Joe
    The Chokin' Kind   3/24/69   5/12/69   10   10

Simon & Garfunkel
    The Sounds Of Silence   12/10/65   1/14/66   1   10
    Homeward Bound   2/4/66   2/25/66   8   7
    I Am A Rock   4/29/66   6/10/66   3   9
    The Dangling Conversation   8/12/66   8/26/66   24   3
    A Hazy Shade Of Winter   11/4/66   12/2/66   14   6
    At The Zoo   3/24/67   4/14/67   16   8
    Fakin' It   8/4/67   8/18/67   23   4
    Scarborough Fair/Canticle   3/11/68   4/1/68   19   4
    Mrs. Robinson   4/29/68   5/27/68   2   11
    The Boxer   3/31/69   5/5/69   1   11
  also see Tico & the Triumphs

Sims Twins
    Soothe Me   10/28/61   11/25/61   12   7

Sinatra, Frank
    Ol' MacDonald   11/19/60   12/3/60   18   6
    Pocketful Of Miracles   12/23/61   1/27/62   20   6
    Softly, As I Leave You   9/11/64   10/2/64   23   4
    It Was A Very Good Year   1/14/66   2/11/66   22   5
    Strangers In The Night   5/13/66   6/10/66   2   10
    Summer Wind   9/9/66   9/30/66   27   5
    That's Life   11/25/66   12/23/66   18   7
    Cycles   10/21/68   11/25/68   13   8
    My Way   3/31/69   4/14/69   28   3

Artist / Title	Debut	Peak	Pos	Wks
Sinatra, Nancy				
These Boots Are Made For Walkin'	1/28/66	2/11/66	2	10
How Does That Grab You, Darlin'	4/15/66	5/13/66	11	6
Friday's Child	7/1/66	7/1/66	34	3
Sugar Town	11/11/66	12/30/66	5	10
Love Eyes	3/31/67	4/14/67	23	5
Lightning's Girl	10/13/67	10/20/67	25	3
Sinatra, Nancy & Frank				
Somethin' Stupid	3/17/67	4/21/67	2	10
Sinatra, Nancy & Lee Hazelwood				
Jackson	6/23/67	7/7/67	26	6
Lady Bird	11/17/67	11/24/67	39	2
Singing Nun (Soeur Sourire)				
Dominique	11/8/63	11/15/63	1	9
Sir Douglas Quintet				
She's About A Mover	4/23/65	6/4/65	14	8
The Tracker	7/30/65	7/30/65	26	1
Mendocino	2/17/69	3/24/69	11	7
Skel, Bobby				
Kiss And Run	12/25/64	1/29/65	6	8
Skyliners				
The Door Is Still Open To My Heart	4/29/61	4/29/61	39	1
The Loser	7/16/65	7/16/65	39	1
also see Beaumont, Jimmie				
Slatkin, Felix				
Theme From The Sundowners	10/29/60	11/5/60	29	3
Slay, Frank				
Flying Circle	12/23/61	1/20/62	13	7
Sledge, Percy				
When A Man Loves A Woman	5/20/66	6/3/66	10	5
Take Time To Know Her	3/18/68	4/29/68	24	7
Sly & the Family Stone				
Dance To The Music	2/19/68	3/18/68	11	8
Everyday People	12/30/68	2/10/69	1	12
/Sing A Simple Song	2/17/69	2/17/69	1	2
Hot Fun In The Summertime	9/8/69	10/20/69	3	10
Small, Millie				
My Boy Lollipop	5/29/64	6/26/64	5	7
Sweet William	8/14/64	8/28/64	32	3

Artist	Title	Debut	Peak	Pos	Wks
Small Faces					
	Itchycoo Park	1/15/68	2/12/68	11	6
Smith					
	Baby It's You	9/22/69	11/10/69	3	12
Smith, Huey (Piano)					
	Pop-Eye	3/24/62	3/31/62	32	2
Smith, Jimmy					
	Walk On The Wild Side—Part 1	6/2/62	6/2/62	28	1
	Got My Mojo Working (Part 1)	4/8/66	4/22/66	32	4
Smith, O. C.					
	Little Green Apples	9/23/68	10/21/68	4	9
	Daddy's Little Man	8/18/69	9/22/69	17	8
Smith, Whistling Jack					
	I Was Kaiser Bill's Batman	4/21/67	5/19/67	13	6
Society Girls					
	S.P.C.L.G.	8/2/63	8/16/63	32	3
Soffici, Piero					
	That's The Way With Love	4/29/61	5/20/61	5	6
Sommers, Joanie					
	Johnny Get Angry	6/23/62	7/28/62	3	8
Sonny & Cher					
	I Got You Babe	7/23/65	8/13/65	1	12
	Just You	8/20/65	9/17/65	19	7
	Baby Don't Go	9/10/65	9/17/65	24	2
	But You're Mine	10/8/65	10/29/65	23	5
	What Now My Love	1/28/66	2/25/66	21	8
	Little Man	10/7/66	10/21/66	19	4
	The Beat Goes On	1/27/67	3/3/67	5	8
	A Beautiful Story	5/5/67	5/5/67	38	2
	It's The Little Things	7/28/67	7/28/67	39	1
Sonny					
	Laugh At Me	8/27/65	9/17/65	12	6
	also see Cher				
Sopwith Camel					
	Hello Hello	1/20/67	1/20/67	28	2
Sorrows					
	Take A Heart	10/29/65	11/19/65	16	6

Artist	Title	Debut	Peak	Pos	Wks
Soul, Jimmy					
	Twistin' Matilda	5/12/62	6/2/62	10	6
	If You Wanna Be Happy	4/12/63	5/3/63	2	9
Soul Sisters					
	I Can't Stand It	3/27/64	3/27/64	32	1
Soul Survivors					
	Expressway To Your Heart	9/22/67	11/17/67	9	10
	Explosion In Your Soul	12/8/67	1/22/68	23	7
Soulful Strings					
	Burning Spear	1/22/68	1/29/68	32	3
Sounds Orchestral					
	Cast Your Fate To The Wind	4/9/65	4/16/65	27	2
South, Joe					
	Games People Play	1/20/69	2/17/69	8	8
	Don't It Make You Want To Go Home	8/25/69	9/29/69	15	8
	Walk A Mile In My Shoes	12/22/69	1/26/70	12	9
Spacemen					
	Man In Orbit	5/13/61	5/27/61	25	3
Spanky & Our Gang					
	Sunday Will Never Be The Same	6/2/67	7/7/67	12	8
	Lazy Day	11/17/67	12/1/67	33	3
	Like To Get To Know You	5/13/68	6/10/68	9	6
Spellman, Benny					
	Lipstick Traces (On A Cigarette)	4/21/62	5/26/62	10	6
Spinners					
	That's What Girls Are Made For	8/5/61	8/5/61	38	2
	I'll Always Love You	7/16/65	7/23/65	29	4
Spiral Starecase					
	More Today Than Yesterday	5/5/69	5/12/69	34	3
Spirit					
	I Got A Line On You	1/20/69	2/24/69	7	8
Springfield, Dusty					
	Stay Awhile	4/17/64	4/17/64	37	2
	Wishin' And Hopin'	7/3/64	8/14/64	2	10
	You Don't Have To Say You Love Me	6/3/66	7/1/66	5	9
	All I See Is You	9/23/66	10/7/66	28	4
	The Look Of Love	10/13/67	11/10/67	9	7

Artist	Title	Debut	Peak	Pos	Wks
	Son-Of-A Preacher Man	11/25/68	1/13/69	4	11
	A Brand New Me	11/10/69	12/15/69	19	8

Springfields
	Silver Threads And Golden Needles	8/11/62	9/15/62	7	7
	Island Of Dreams	3/29/63	4/19/63	14	4

St. Peters, Crispian
	The Pied Piper	6/10/66	7/22/66	2	9
	Changes	9/23/66	10/14/66	25	5

St. Romain, Kirby
	Summer's Comin'	6/7/63	6/21/63	19	4

Stacy, Clyde & the Nitecaps
	You Want Love	10/14/60	11/5/60	12	4

Stafford, Terry
	Suspicion	3/13/64	4/10/64	1	10
	I'll Touch A Star	6/12/64	7/3/64	17	5

Standells
	Dirty Water	4/22/66	6/24/66	6	13
	Sometimes Good Guys Don't Wear White	8/26/66	9/9/66	39	3

Starcher, Buddy
	History Repeats Itself	4/15/66	4/15/66	18	5

Starr, Edwin
	Agent Double-O-Soul	9/10/65	9/17/65	29	3
	Stop Her On Sight (S.O.S.)	3/18/66	3/25/66	35	2
	Twenty-Five Miles	3/3/69	3/31/69	11	9

Starr, Lucille
	The French Song	6/26/64	7/3/64	31	2
	Yours	10/2/64	10/2/64	25	1

Statler Brothers
	Flowers On The Wall	12/3/65	12/24/65	20	5

Statues
	Blue Velvet	10/15/60	10/15/60	37	1

Status Quo
	Pictures Of Matchstick Men	6/3/68	7/8/68	3	10
	Ice In The Sun	9/16/68	9/23/68	34	2

Steam
	Na Na Hey Hey Kiss Him Goodbye	10/27/69	12/1/69	1	13

Steppenwolf
	Born To Be Wild	7/8/68	8/12/68	1	11

Artist	Title	Debut	Peak	Pos	Wks
	Magic Carpet Ride	10/14/68	11/11/68	2	8
	Rock Me	2/17/69	4/7/69	6	11
Stevens, Connie					
	Now That You've Gone	3/26/65	4/23/65	6	5
Stevens, Ray					
	Jeremiah Peabody's Poly Unsaturated Quick Dissolving Fast Acting Pleasant Tasting Green And Purple Pills	9/30/61	9/30/61	36	2
	Ahab, The Arab	7/14/62	7/28/62	6	5
	Santa Claus Is Watching You	12/15/62	12/22/62	19	2
	Harry The Hairy Ape	7/5/63	7/12/63	34	2
	Gitarzan	4/7/69	5/5/69	2	8
	Along Came Jones	6/16/69	7/21/69	16	6
Stewart, Billy					
	I Do Love You	5/7/65	5/7/65	35	2
	Summertime	8/5/66	8/19/66	18	4
	Secret Love	10/14/66	11/4/66	26	5
Stites, Gary					
	Little Tear	11/19/60	12/10/60	25	4
Stompers					
	Quarter To Four Stomp	2/24/62	3/10/62	22	3
Stone Poneys					
	Different Drum	12/15/67	2/12/68	4	11
Stories					
	I Really Love You So	9/16/61	10/7/61	17	6
Storm, Billy					
	El Cid	3/3/62	3/3/62	35	1
Strange, Billy					
	The James Bond Theme	10/2/64	10/23/64	11	5
Strangeloves					
	I Want Candy	6/4/65	7/2/65	4	8
	Cara-Lin	9/10/65	9/24/65	28	5
	Night Time	2/4/66	2/4/66	37	1
Strawberry Alarm Clock					
	Incense And Peppermints	9/29/67	11/10/67	2	11
	Tomorrow	12/22/67	2/19/68	13	9
Streisand, Barbra					
	People	5/8/64	5/22/64	16	8

Artist	Title	Debut	Peak	Pos	Wks
	Second Hand Rose	1/7/66	2/4/66	20	6
	Free Again	10/28/66	11/11/66	24	4

String-A-Longs
	Wheels	12/17/60	1/7/61	8	9

Strong, Nolan
	Mind Over Matter	10/27/62	11/10/62	16	3

Summers, Susan
	Mommy And Daddy Were Twistin'	1/13/62	1/27/62	21	4

Sunny & the Sunglows
	Talk To Me	9/20/63	10/18/63	13	5

Sunny & Sunliners
	Rags To Riches	12/6/63	12/20/63	32	3

Sunglows
	Peanuts (La Cacahuata)	6/11/65	6/18/65	26	2

Sunrays
	I Live For The Sun	8/27/65	9/10/65	28	4
	Andrea	1/14/66	2/4/66	12	6

Supremes
	Let Me Go The Right Way	1/25/63	2/8/63	23	3
	When The Lovelight Starts Shining Through His Eyes	12/6/63	1/10/64	18	7
	Where Did Our Love Go	7/31/64	8/21/64	1	8
	Baby Love	10/16/64	11/20/64	6	9
	Come See About Me	11/20/64	1/1/65	2	10
	Stop! In The Name Of Love	2/19/65	3/19/65	2	9
	Back In My Arms Again	5/7/65	6/4/65	5	8
	Nothing But Heartaches	7/30/65	8/27/65	10	5
	I Hear A Symphony	10/29/65	11/26/65	3	8
	My World Is Empty Without You	1/21/66	2/4/66	17	7
	Love Is Like An Itching In My Heart	4/29/66	5/6/66	25	4
	You Can't Hurry Love	8/12/66	9/30/66	2	10
	You Keep Me Hangin' On	10/28/66	11/25/66	3	8
	Love Is Here And Now You're Gone	1/27/67	2/10/67	9	8
	The Happening	4/7/67	4/28/67	7	6

Diana Ross & the Supremes
	Reflections	8/11/67	9/29/67	4	9
	In And Out Of Love	11/10/67	12/8/67	13	6
	Forever Came Today	3/18/68	4/22/68	19	7
	Some Things You Never Get Used To	6/3/68	7/8/68	18	6
	Love Child	10/14/68	11/11/68	1	14
	I'm Livin' In Shame	1/13/69	2/10/69	11	8

Artist / Title	Debut	Peak	Pos	Wks
The Composer	4/7/69	5/5/69	21	5
No Matter What Sign You Are	5/26/69	6/23/69	20	5
Someday We'll Be Together	11/10/69	12/8/69	1	14

Diana Ross & the Supremes & the Temptations

Title	Debut	Peak	Pos	Wks
I'm Gonna Make You Love Me	12/2/68	1/6/69	1	12
I'll Try Something New	3/17/69	3/31/69	23	3

also see the Temptations

Surfaris

Title	Debut	Peak	Pos	Wks
Wipe Out	7/12/63	8/2/63	1	8
Wipe Out	8/19/66	9/16/66	4	9

Sweet Inspirations

Title	Debut	Peak	Pos	Wks
Sweet Inspiration	3/11/68	4/1/68	13	7

Swinging Blue Jeans

Title	Debut	Peak	Pos	Wks
Hippy Hippy Shake	3/6/64	3/27/64	13	5
Good Golly Miss Molly	5/8/64	5/29/64	21	4

Syndicate Of Sound

Title	Debut	Peak	Pos	Wks
Little Girl	6/10/66	7/1/66	28	4

Taffys

Title	Debut	Peak	Pos	Wks
The Key To My Heart	7/12/63	7/12/63	39	1

Tams

Title	Debut	Peak	Pos	Wks
Untie Me	9/22/62	10/13/62	21	4
What Kind Of Fool (Do You Think I Am)	1/31/64	1/31/64	33	3

Tanega, Norma

Title	Debut	Peak	Pos	Wks
Walkin' My Cat Named Dog	3/18/66	3/18/66	35	2

Taylor, Bobby & the Vancouvers

Title	Debut	Peak	Pos	Wks
Does Your Mama Know About Me	4/29/68	5/20/68	22	4

Taylor, Johnnie

Title	Debut	Peak	Pos	Wks
Who's Making Love	10/28/68	11/25/68	8	9
Testify (I Wonna)	5/19/69	6/2/69	32	3

Taylor, Little Johnny

Title	Debut	Peak	Pos	Wks
Part Time Love	9/27/63	9/27/63	39	1

T-Bones

Title	Debut	Peak	Pos	Wks
No Matter What Shape (Your Stomach's In)	12/17/65	1/21/66	6	10

Tempo, Nino & April Stevens

Title	Debut	Peak	Pos	Wks
Sweet And Lovely	8/25/62	9/1/62	35	2
Deep Purple	10/4/63	11/8/63	1	8
Whispering	1/10/64	1/10/64	17	4
Stardust	3/6/64	3/6/64	28	3

Artist	Title	Debut	Peak	Pos	Wks

Temptations
	The Way You Do The Things You Do	3/13/64	3/27/64	27	3
	The Girl's Alright With Me	8/21/64	8/21/64	36	1
	My Girl	1/29/65	3/5/65	19	7
	It's Growing	5/7/65	5/7/65	32	2
	Since I Lost My Baby	8/6/65	8/13/65	25	2
	My Baby	11/19/65	11/26/65	29	2
	Ain't Too Proud To Beg	7/1/66	7/1/66	36	2
	Beauty Is Only Skin Deep	9/9/66	9/23/66	18	5
	(I Know) I'm Losing You	12/16/66	12/23/66	20	2
	All I Need	6/2/67	6/23/67	33	4
	You're My Everything	8/11/67	9/15/67	20	6
	(Loneliness Made Me Realize) It's You That I Need	10/6/67	10/27/67	28	5
	I Wish It Would Rain	1/15/68	2/19/68	2	8
	I Could Never Love Another (After Loving You)	5/6/68	6/24/68	13	8
	Please Return Your Love To Me	8/5/68	8/19/68	29	5
	Cloud Nine	12/2/68	1/6/69	11	9
	Run Away Child, Running Wild	3/3/69	3/31/69	7	7
	I Can't Get Next To You	8/18/69	10/6/69	2	14

also see Supremes, Diana Ross &, and the Temptations

Tex, Joe
	Hold What You've Got	1/22/65	1/29/65	33	2
	Skinny Legs And All	10/27/67	12/8/67	10	8
	Men Are Gettin' Scarce	2/19/68	3/4/68	24	4
	Keep The One You Got	8/19/68	8/26/68	37	2

Texans
	Green Grass Of Texas	3/11/61	3/18/61	23	3

Thee Midniters
	Whittier Blvd.	7/16/65	8/6/65	20	5

Them
	Mystic Eyes	11/19/65	11/26/65	23	2

also see Morrison, Van

Third Booth
	I Need Love	5/27/68	7/8/68	2	10

Third Rail
	Run, Run, Run	8/4/67	8/25/67	19	6

Thomas, B. J.
	I'm So Lonesome I Could Cry	2/25/66	4/8/66	10	10
	Mama	5/20/66	5/27/66	29	2
	Billy And Sue	7/15/66	8/5/66	31	5

Artist	Title	Debut	Peak	Pos	Wks
	The Eyes Of A New York Woman	8/5/68	9/16/68	19	7
	Hooked On A Feeling	12/2/68	1/20/69	5	12
	It's Only Love	4/14/69	4/21/69	29	4
	Raindrops Keep Fallin' On My Head	11/17/69	12/22/69	2	13
Thomas, Carla					
	Gee Whiz (Look At His Eyes)	2/11/61	2/25/61	19	3
	A Love Of My Own	5/27/61	6/3/61	33	2
Thomas, Gene					
	Sometime	8/19/61	8/19/61	39	1
Thomas, Irma					
	Wish Someone Would Care	5/8/64	5/8/64	36	2
Thomas, Rufus					
	Walking The Dog	11/29/63	11/29/63	30	2
Thompson, Sue					
	Sad Movies (Make Me Cry)	9/30/61	11/4/61	6	8
	Norman	1/13/62	2/3/62	3	7
	Two Of A Kind	4/14/62	4/21/62	29	2
	Have A Good Time	6/30/62	7/14/62	21	4
	James (Hold The Ladder Steady)	10/13/62	10/27/62	29	3
	Paper Tiger	1/22/65	2/19/65	11	6
Three Dog Night					
	Nobody	11/11/68	11/25/68	34	3
	One	5/19/69	6/23/69	1	11
	Easy To Be Hard	8/4/69	9/22/69	1	12
	Eli's Coming	10/20/69	11/17/69	3	9
also see Hutton, Danny					
Three Friends					
	Dedicated (To The Songs I Love)	7/29/61	8/5/61	27	2
Thunder, Johnny					
	Loop De Loop	12/29/62	1/19/63	13	6
Tico & the Triumphs					
	Motorcycle	1/20/62	1/20/62	36	1
also see Simon & Garfunkel					
Tillman, Bertha					
	Oh My Angel	5/5/62	5/19/62	24	3
Tillotson, Johnny					
	Poetry In Motion	10/15/60	11/12/60	1	11
	Jimmy's Girl	2/11/61	3/11/61	4	8
	Without You	9/2/61	9/23/61	8	6

Artist	Title	Debut	Peak	Pos	Wks
	Dreamy Eyes	2/3/62	3/3/62	8	7
	It Keeps Right On A-Hurtin'	5/12/62	6/16/62	10	8
	Send Me The Pillow You Dream On	8/25/62	9/8/62	23	3
	I Can't Help It (If I'm Still In Love With You)	10/20/62	11/17/62	20	4
	Out Of My Mind	3/1/63	3/15/63	15	3
	You Can Never Stop Me Loving You	8/2/63	9/6/63	9	8
	Funny How Time Slips Away	10/25/63	10/25/63	35	1
	Talk Back Trembling Lips	11/22/63	11/29/63	12	6
	Worried Guy	2/28/64	2/28/64	25	2
	I Rise, I Fall	5/22/64	6/19/64	22	5
	Worry	7/31/64	8/14/64	19	5
	She Understands Me	11/13/64	12/11/64	13	6
	Angel	2/12/65	2/26/65	34	3
	Then I'll Count Again	6/18/65	6/25/65	24	2
	Our World	11/26/65	12/3/65	36	2

Tim Tam & the Turn-Ons
	Wait A Minute	2/25/66	3/11/66	26	4

Tino, Babs
	Forgive Me	9/1/62	9/1/62	36	1

Tiny Tim
	Tip-Toe Thru The Tulips With Me	5/27/68	6/10/68	14	3

Tokens
	Tonight I Fell In Love	4/15/61	5/20/61	3	8
	The Lion Sleeps Tonight	11/25/61	12/23/61	1	11
	B'wa Nina (Pretty Girl)	2/24/62	3/10/62	23	4
	I Hear Trumpets Blow	4/1/66	4/29/66	20	6

Toney Jr., Oscar
	For Your Precious Love	6/30/67	7/7/67	36	3

Torme, Mel
	Comin' Home Baby	11/10/62	11/24/62	32	3

Tornadoes
	Telstar	10/27/62	12/1/62	1	11
	Globetrottin'	2/1/63	3/1/63	10	5

Townsend, Ed
	Stay With Me	10/29/60	10/29/60	40	1

Toys
	A Lover's Concerto	9/24/65	11/5/65	2	10
	Attack	1/7/66	1/14/66	24	2

Artist / Title	Debut	Peak	Pos	Wks
Tracy, Norma				
Leroy	1/29/65	1/29/65	35	2
Trade Winds				
New York's A Lonely Town	2/26/65	3/19/65	22	4
Trashmen				
Surfin' Bird	12/20/63	1/10/64	3	8
Bird Dance Beat	2/14/64	3/13/64	14	6
Tremeloes				
Here Comes My Baby	4/7/67	5/12/67	3	9
Silence Is Golden	6/30/67	8/25/67	9	11
Even The Bad Times Are Good	10/27/67	11/10/67	28	3
Suddenly You Love Me	3/4/68	3/25/68	29	4
Troggs				
Wild Thing	6/17/66	7/15/66	1	9
With A Girl Like You	8/5/66	9/9/66	15	7
Love Is All Around	2/12/68	3/25/68	23	7
Trolls				
Every Day And Every Night	8/26/66	9/30/66	10	7
Troy, Doris				
Just One Look	6/28/63	7/12/63	26	3
Tucker, Tommy				
Hi-Heel Sneakers	1/31/64	2/21/64	12	6
Turner, Ike & Tina				
A Fool In Love	10/15/60	11/5/60	27	5
It's Gonna Work Out Fine	8/26/61	9/9/61	30	3
Poor Fool	12/23/61	1/20/62	26	5
also see the Ikettes				
Turner, Sammy				
Love Keeps Calling	2/4/61	2/11/61	38	2
Turner, Spyder				
Stand By Me	2/10/67	2/24/67	31	4
Turner, Titus				
Sound-Off	2/25/61	2/25/61	38	1
Turtles				
It Ain't Me Babe	8/6/65	9/10/65	6	10
Let Me Be	11/19/65	12/3/65	33	3
You Baby	2/18/66	4/1/66	5	11
Grim Reaper Of Love	6/10/66	7/1/66	26	4
Happy Together	2/10/67	3/31/67	1	12

Artist	Title	Debut	Peak	Pos	Wks
	She'd Rather Be With Me	5/19/67	6/9/67	4	8
	You Know What I Mean	8/11/67	9/29/67	9	9
	She's My Girl	11/17/67	11/24/67	13	7
	Sound Asleep	3/4/68	4/1/68	23	5
	The Story Of Rock And Roll	6/10/68	7/1/68	33	4
	Elenore	9/30/68	11/4/68	2	9
	You Showed Me	1/6/69	2/17/69	2	11

Twilighters
	Scratchin'	10/28/61	10/28/61	36	1

Twitty, Conway
	C'est Si Bon (It's So Good)	1/14/61	1/14/61	38	1
	Portrait Of A Fool	3/3/62	3/3/62	32	1

Two Of Clubs
	Walk Tall	2/17/67	4/14/67	9	10

Tymes
	So Much In Love	6/7/63	7/19/63	3	10
	Wonderful! Wonderful!	9/6/63	9/27/63	10	5
	Somewhere	1/10/64	1/17/64	34	3

Underground Sunshine
	Birthday	7/7/69	8/11/69	2	9

Unifics
	Court Of Love	10/21/68	10/28/68	27	3

Uniques
	Not Too Long Ago	3/5/65	4/2/65	24	5

Unit 4+2
	Concrete And Clay	5/21/65	5/28/65	16	3

University Orchestra
	Magic Trumpet	5/7/65	5/7/65	33	1

Untouchables
	You're On Top	9/9/61	9/16/61	35	2

Upchurch, Phil, Combo
	You Can't Sit Down Part 2	6/17/61	7/15/61	11	6

Vale, Jerry
	Have You Looked Into Your Heart	1/15/65	1/29/65	8	6

Valentino, Mark
	The Push And Kick	11/10/62	11/17/62	29	4

Artist / Title	Debut	Peak	Pos	Wks
Valjean				
Theme From Ben Casey	5/5/62	6/2/62	11	6
Till There Was You	9/8/62	9/8/62	34	1
Valli, Frankie				
Can't Take My Eyes Off You	6/2/67	7/14/67	1	13
I Make A Fool Of Myself	8/25/67	9/29/67	10	8
To Give (The Reason I Live)	12/22/67	1/22/68	7	8
also see the Four Seasons				
Van Dyke, Leroy				
Walk On By	11/11/61	12/16/61	4	11
Vanilla Fudge				
You Keep Me Hangin' On	7/29/68	9/2/68	5	8
Take Me For A Little While	10/28/68	11/4/68	38	2
Vanity Fare				
Early In The Morning	11/17/69	12/15/69	16	9
Vaughan, Sarah				
A Lover's Concerto	4/15/66	4/15/66	40	1
Vaughn, Billy				
Berlin Melody	9/30/61	10/7/61	33	2
A Swingin' Safari	7/21/62	8/18/62	7	6
Vee, Bobby				
Devil Or Angel	10/14/60	10/29/60	12	4
Rubber Ball	12/24/60	1/21/61	6	9
Stayin' In	3/4/61	3/25/61	18	6
How Many Tears	6/24/61	6/24/61	31	4
Take Good Care Of My Baby	8/26/61	9/23/61	1	9
Run To Him	11/25/61	12/9/61	2	10
Please Don't Ask About Barbara	3/17/62	3/31/62	28	3
Sharing You	6/9/62	6/23/62	25	3
Punish Her	9/22/62	10/13/62	16	5
The Night Has A Thousand Eyes	12/15/62	1/4/63	2	9
Charms	4/5/63	5/10/63	11	7
Be True To Yourself	6/28/63	7/19/63	12	5
Yesterday And You (Armen's Theme)	11/15/63	11/29/63	18	5
I'll Make You Mine	2/28/64	3/20/64	15	6
Hickory, Dick And Doc	6/12/64	7/17/64	18	6
Come Back When You Grow Up	8/4/67	9/8/67	2	11
Beautiful People	11/10/67	12/8/67	6	8
Maybe Just Today	2/5/68	2/26/68	19	5
My Girl/Hey Girl	4/1/68	5/6/68	6	10

Artist	Title	Debut	Peak	Pos	Wks
	Do What You Gotta Do	8/5/68	8/19/68	37	3
	I'm Into Lookin' For Someone To Love Me	12/9/68	1/6/69	31	5
Vega, Carol					
	Sugar Over You	4/24/64	5/22/64	31	5
Vegas, Bob					
	Playboy	11/11/61	11/11/61	36	1
Vejtables					
	I Still Love You	9/10/65	9/24/65	23	3
Velaires					
	Roll Over Beethoven	8/19/61	8/26/61	29	2
Velvets					
	Tonight (Could Be The Night)	7/1/61	7/22/61	12	6
Ventures					
	Walk— Don't Run	10/14/60	10/14/60	21	1
	Perfidia	11/5/60	12/3/60	11	9
	The 2,000 Pound Bee (Part 2)	1/4/63	2/8/63	8	7
	Skip To M' Limbo	5/3/63	5/17/63	25	3
	Walk— Don't Run '64	7/31/64	8/28/64	15	7
	Hawaii Five-O	3/31/69	5/5/69	16	6
Vera, Billy & Judy Clay					
	Country Girl—City Man	2/26/68	3/4/68	26	4
Vera, Billy					
	With Pen In Hand	6/17/68	7/1/68	35	4
Verne, Larry					
	Mr. Custer	10/14/60	10/14/60	2	3
Vibrations					
	The Watusi	2/4/61	2/25/61	16	6
	Stranded In The Jungle	7/8/61	7/15/61	32	2
	Oh Cindy	1/20/62	1/20/62	38	1
	My Girl Sloopy	4/17/64	5/15/64	28	5
Viceroys					
	Seagrams	1/25/63	2/8/63	27	5
	Liverpool	2/28/64	3/13/64	24	4
Victorians					
	What Makes Little Girls Cry	8/2/63	8/16/63	18	6
Village Stompers					
	Washington Square	10/11/63	11/1/63	1	9

Artist / Title	Debut	Peak	Pos	Wks
Vinton, Bobby				
Roses Are Red (My Love)	6/9/62	6/30/62	1	10
I Love You The Way You Are	7/28/62	8/18/62	3	8
Rain Rain Go Away	9/22/62	10/6/62	19	4
Trouble Is My Middle Name	1/12/63	1/12/63	27	2
Over The Mountain (Across The Sea)	3/29/63	4/26/63	19	5
Blue On Blue	5/31/63	6/21/63	4	9
Blue Velvet	8/30/63	9/13/63	1	9
There! I've Said It Again	11/29/63	1/3/64	1	11
My Heart Belongs To Only You	3/6/64	4/3/64	4	9
Tell Me Why	5/22/64	6/26/64	17	7
Clinging Vine	8/28/64	9/25/64	13	7
Mr. Lonely	11/13/64	12/11/64	2	11
Long Lonely Nights	3/12/65	4/16/65	18	6
L-O-N-E-L-Y	5/21/65	6/4/65	26	4
What Color (Is A Man)	10/15/65	10/15/65	40	1
Satin Pillows	12/24/65	1/14/66	32	5
Dum-De-Da	5/27/66	5/27/66	36	1
Coming Home Soldier	12/23/66	1/20/67	17	6
Please Love Me Forever	10/13/67	11/17/67	5	9
Just As Much As Ever	12/22/67	1/22/68	13	7
Take Good Care Of My Baby	4/1/68	5/6/68	8	7
Halfway To Paradise	7/8/68	8/12/68	15	7
I Love How You Love Me	11/4/68	12/16/68	2	13
To Know You Is To Love You	4/7/69	4/28/69	24	5
The Days Of Sand And Shovels	6/16/69	6/30/69	31	5
Virtues				
Guitar Boogie Shuffle Twist	3/10/62	3/31/62	21	4
Viscounts				
Wabash Blues	12/3/60	1/14/61	8	8
Harlem Nocturne	12/3/65	12/24/65	11	4
Vito & the Salutations				
Unchained Melody	11/1/63	11/15/63	32	3
Vogues				
You're The One	9/24/65	10/29/65	2	9
Five O'Clock World	11/19/65	12/17/65	1	10
Magic Town	2/11/66	3/18/66	11	7
The Land Of Milk And Honey	5/27/66	7/8/66	18	8
That's The Tune	1/13/67	1/20/67	30	3
Turn Around, Look At Me	6/17/68	7/22/68	2	11
My Special Angel	8/26/68	9/30/68	4	10
Till	11/11/68	12/16/68	11	8

Artist	Title	Debut	Peak	Pos	Wks
	No, Not Much	2/3/69	3/17/69	4	10
	Earth Angel (Will You Be Mine)	4/7/69	5/5/69	18	5
	Moments To Remember	6/9/69	7/7/69	21	5
	Green Fields	8/11/69	8/25/69	27	3

Volumes
	I Love You	5/12/62	6/9/62	7	6

Wade, Adam
	Take Good Care Of Her	4/1/61	4/22/61	12	6
	The Writing On The Wall	6/24/61	7/1/61	30	2
	As If I Didn't Know	9/9/61	9/23/61	26	3

Wade, Cory
	Daydreamin'	11/24/62	11/24/62	36	1

Waikakis
	Hawaii Tattoo	12/18/64	1/1/65	12	5

Wailers
	Tall Cool One	4/10/64	5/8/64	4	9

Walker, Gary
	You Don't Love Me	5/6/66	5/20/66	23	4

Walker, Jr. & the All-Stars
	Shotgun	3/5/65	4/9/65	16	8
	Cleo's Back	11/12/65	11/12/65	38	1
	(I'm A) Road Runner	6/10/66	6/10/66	38	1
	Come See About Me	1/15/68	1/22/68	36	2
	What Does It Take (To Win Your Love)	6/2/69	7/21/69	5	11
	These Eyes	12/8/69	12/22/69	28	4

Walker Brothers
	Make It Easy On Yourself	10/22/65	11/19/65	23	8
	My Ship Is Comin' In	2/4/66	2/11/66	36	2
	The Sun Ain't Gonna Shine (Anymore)	4/22/66	5/13/66	19	5

Wallace, Jerry
	There She Goes	12/24/60	1/21/61	22	6
	Shutters And Boards	12/1/62	12/15/62	15	7
	In The Misty Moonlight	7/17/64	8/14/64	11	7

Wammack, Travis
	Scratchy	11/13/64	11/27/64	12	6

Wanderers
	There Is No Greater Love	9/8/62	9/15/62	35	2

Artist / Title	Debut	Peak	Pos	Wks
Wanderley, Walter				
Summer Samba (So Nice)	9/9/66	9/23/66	20	6
Ward, Dale				
Letter From Sherry	12/27/63	2/14/64	7	9
Ward, Robin				
Wonderful Summer	11/8/63	12/6/63	1	10
Warner Brothers				
Please Mr. Sullivan	11/5/65	11/12/65	35	2
Warwick, Dionne				
Don't Make Me Over	12/22/62	1/12/63	25	5
This Empty Place	4/5/63	4/12/63	32	2
Anyone Who Had A Heart	1/10/64	1/31/64	23	6
Walk On By	6/19/64	6/26/64	22	3
/Any Old Time Of The Day	6/19/64	6/19/64	37	1
A House Is Not A Home	8/28/64	8/28/64	39	3
Reach Out For Me	11/27/64	11/27/64	29	1
Message To Michael	4/22/66	5/13/66	25	5
Trains And Boats And Planes	7/15/66	7/29/66	28	4
Alfie	6/2/67	6/16/67	31	4
The Windows Of The World	9/8/67	9/22/67	27	3
(Theme From) Valley Of The Dolls	1/29/68	3/4/68	1	8
/I Say A Little Prayer	11/3/67	12/8/67	11	8
Do You Know The Way To San Jose	4/15/68	5/27/68	10	8
(There's) Always Something There To Remind Me	9/2/68	9/9/68	28	3
/Who Is Gonna Love Me	9/23/68	9/30/68	28	2
Promises, Promises	11/11/68	12/9/68	24	5
This Girl's In Love With You	2/10/69	3/17/69	6	7
The April Fools	5/26/69	6/9/69	29	3
You've Lost That Lovin' Feeling	10/13/69	11/3/69	21	5
I'll Never Fall In Love Again	12/22/69	2/2/70	6	10
Washington, Baby				
That's How Heartaches Are Made	5/3/63	5/17/63	18	3
Washington, Dinah				
Love Walked In	10/15/60	11/5/60	19	4
Our Love Is Here To Stay	5/27/61	6/3/61	28	4
September In The Rain	11/18/61	11/25/61	27	2
Where Are You	6/16/62	6/16/62	35	1
Watts 103rd St. Rhythm Band				
Do Your Thing	3/3/69	4/7/69	7	9
Till You Get Enough	8/4/69	8/11/69	31	3

Artist / Title	Debut	Peak	Pos	Wks
We Five				
You Were On My Mind	8/6/65	9/24/65	2	11
Let's Get Together	12/10/65	12/24/65	28	3
Welch, Lenny				
Since I Fell For You	12/13/63	1/10/64	15	7
Welk, Lawrence				
Calcutta	1/7/61	2/11/61	1	12
Theme From The Brothers Grimm	6/30/62	7/7/62	32	2
Zero-Zero	12/15/62	1/12/63	20	6
Breakwater	8/9/63	9/6/63	16	5
Fiesta	11/1/63	11/15/63	19	4
Apples And Bananas	2/26/65	3/26/65	11	7
Wells, Mary				
Bye Bye Baby	4/22/61	4/29/61	35	2
I Don't Want To Take A Chance	8/26/61	8/26/61	37	1
The One Who Really Loves You	3/17/62	4/21/62	10	8
You Beat Me To The Punch	8/25/62	9/15/62	23	4
Two Lovers	12/15/62	1/12/63	18	5
Your Old Stand By	6/7/63	6/14/63	28	3
You Lost The Sweetest Boy	10/25/63	10/25/63	28	2
/What's Easy For Two Is So Hard For One	12/13/63	1/24/64	5	7
My Guy	4/10/64	5/22/64	15	8
Never, Never Leave Me	3/26/65	4/16/65	25	4
also see Gaye, Marvin & Mary Wells				
Whitcomb, Ian & Bluesville				
You Turn Me On (Turn On Song)	6/4/65	7/2/65	13	7
White, Tony Joe				
Polk Salad Annie	6/30/69	8/4/69	5	10
Roosevelt And Ira Lee (Night Of The Mossacin)	10/13/69	11/10/69	16	6
Whiteside, Bobby				
Say It Softly	4/16/65	5/14/65	11	7
Whiting, Margaret				
The Wheel Of Hurt	11/18/66	11/25/66	31	3
Who				
I Can See For Miles	11/10/67	12/8/67	5	6
Call Me Lightning	4/8/68	5/13/68	20	6
Magic Bus	8/19/68	9/9/68	5	7
Pinball Wizard	3/31/69	5/12/69	5	10
Wilcox, Harlow & the Oakies				
Groovy Grubworm	10/27/69	11/24/69	19	7

Artist / Title	Debut	Peak	Pos	Wks
Williams, Andy				
You Don't Want My Love	11/26/60	12/17/60	16	7
The Bilbao Song	6/3/61	6/17/61	18	4
Danny Boy	12/9/61	12/16/61	27	2
Stranger On The Shore	6/16/62	6/23/62	34	2
Don't You Believe It	10/27/62	11/10/62	15	8
Twilight Time	12/22/62	12/22/62	40	1
Can't Get Used To Losing You	3/15/63	4/12/63	4	11
Hopeless	7/19/63	8/9/63	22	4
A Fool Never Learns	1/10/64	2/21/64	13	11
On The Street Where You Live	10/2/64	10/2/64	29	1
Dear Heart	12/18/64	12/25/64	21	2
And Roses And Roses	4/23/65	4/23/65	27	1
Ain't It True	9/24/65	9/24/65	35	1
Music To Watch Girls By	4/14/67	5/5/67	20	6
Battle Hymn Of The Republic	10/14/68	11/4/68	14	6
Williams, Danny				
White On White	3/27/64	5/1/64	3	7
Williams Jr., Hank				
Long Gone Lonesome Blues	2/7/64	2/28/64	23	6
Williams, Mason				
Classical Gas	7/1/68	8/12/68	2	9
Williams, Maurice & the Zodiacs				
Stay	10/14/60	10/15/60	1	7
Williams, Roger				
Maria	12/16/61	12/30/61	32	3
Lara's Theme From "Dr. Zhivago"	3/25/66	4/8/66	23	5
Born Free	9/23/66	9/30/66	37	3
Williams, Smiley				
The Cure	8/11/62	8/18/62	37	2
Wils, Hal				
The Lumberjack	10/30/64	10/30/64	27	2
Wilson, Al				
The Snake	9/2/68	10/7/68	17	8
Wilson, Brian				
Caroline, No	3/11/66	3/25/66	17	6
also see the Beach Boys				
Wilson, J. Frank & the Cavaliers				
Last Kiss	8/28/64	9/18/64	3	11

Artist	Title	Debut	Peak	Pos	Wks

Wilson, Jackie
- Alone At Last — 10/29/60 — 11/5/60 — 30 — 3
- My Empty Arms — 2/11/61 — 2/18/61 — 30 — 2
- Please Tell Me Why — 4/8/61 — 4/8/61 — 37 — 1
- I'm Coming On Back To You — 7/29/61 — 8/5/61 — 33 — 2
- Baby Workout — 3/29/63 — 4/12/63 — 21 — 4
- (Your Love Keeps Lifting Me) Higher And Higher — 9/15/67 — 9/29/67 — 20 — 5

Wilson, Nancy
- (You Don't Know) How Glad I Am — 7/17/64 — 8/7/64 — 27 — 3
- Face It Girl, It's Over — 6/17/68 — 7/22/68 — 19 — 8

Wilson, Robin
- Nervous Auctioneer — 11/12/60 — 11/12/60 — 38 — 1

Wind
- Make Believe — 9/15/69 — 10/27/69 — 13 — 8

Winding, Kai
- Baby Elephant Walk — 7/28/62 — 8/4/62 — 33 — 2
- More — 7/26/63 — 9/6/63 — 10 — 9

Winstons
- Color Him Father — 6/2/69 — 7/7/69 — 6 — 8
- Love Of The Common People — 9/15/69 — 9/22/69 — 34 — 2

Wonder, Stevie
- Fingertips—Pt. 2 — 7/19/63 — 8/2/63 — 6 — 5
- Hey Harmonica Man — 7/3/64 — 7/3/64 — 38 — 2
- High Heel Sneakers — 10/1/65 — 10/1/65 — 35 — 1
- Uptight (Everything's Alright) — 1/7/66 — 1/28/66 — 24 — 7
- Travlin' Man — 4/14/67 — 4/21/67 — 33 — 2
- I Was Made To Love Her — 7/7/67 — 8/11/67 — 7 — 7
- I'm Wondering — 10/13/67 — 11/10/67 — 27 — 5
- Shoo-Be-Doo-Be-Doo-Da-Day — 4/8/68 — 5/20/68 — 7 — 8
- For Once In My Life — 10/28/68 — 12/9/68 — 2 — 12
- My Cherie Amour — 6/23/69 — 7/21/69 — 6 — 9
- Yester-Me, Yester-You, Yesterday — 11/3/69 — 12/15/69 — 4 — 11

Rednow, Eivets
- Alfie — 10/7/68 — 10/14/68 — 32 — 3

Wood, Bobby
- If I'm A Fool For Loving You — 7/3/64 — 7/24/64 — 22 — 8

Wood, Brenton
- The Oogum Boogum Song — 5/5/67 — 5/19/67 — 26 — 5
- Gimme Little Sign — 8/25/67 — 10/13/67 — 8 — 10
- Baby You Got It — 11/17/67 — 12/8/67 — 24 — 4

Artist / Title	Debut	Peak	Pos	Wks
Wooley, Sheb				
That's My Pa	2/3/62	2/17/62	13	5
also see Colder, Ben				
Wynette, Tammy				
Stand By Your Man	12/16/68	1/27/69	22	7
Singing My Song	4/14/69	4/28/69	33	3
Yarbrough, Glenn				
Baby The Rain Must Fall	5/14/65	5/21/65	16	5
Yardbirds				
For Your Love	5/28/65	7/2/65	7	8
Heart Full Of Soul	8/13/65	9/10/65	8	8
I'm A Man	11/26/65	12/31/65	10	6
Shapes Of Things	3/11/66	4/15/66	4	11
Over Under Sideways Down	7/1/66	7/29/66	16	9
Little Games	5/19/67	5/19/67	28	2
Ha Ha Said The Clown	8/18/67	9/8/67	27	4
Yellow Balloon				
Yellow Balloon	5/5/67	5/19/67	14	6
Young, Barry				
One Has My Name (The Other Has My Heart)	11/12/65	12/10/65	8	6
Young, Faron				
Hello Walls	4/22/61	5/13/61	8	6
Backtrack	10/28/61	11/25/61	19	5
The Comeback	7/7/62	7/7/62	40	1
Yellow Bandana	3/8/63	3/15/63	28	2
Young, Kathy & the Innocents				
A Thousand Stars	11/5/60	11/19/60	1	12
Happy Birthday Blues	3/4/61	3/25/61	14	6
Magic Is The Night	9/2/61	9/30/61	12	5
also see the Innocents				
Youngbloods				
Grizzly Bear	12/2/66	12/30/66	13	7
Get Together	7/28/69	9/15/69	4	11
Young-Holt Trio				
Wack Wack	1/6/67	1/13/67	32	3
Young-Holt Unlimited				
Soulful Strut	12/2/68	1/20/69	3	11
also see Lewis, Ramsey				
Young Rascals				
I Ain't Gonna Eat Out My Heart Anymore	12/24/65	1/14/66	21	5

Artist	Title	Debut	Peak	Pos	Wks
	Good Lovin'	3/25/66	4/22/66	3	10
	You Better Run	6/10/66	7/1/66	21	6
	I've Been Lonely Too Long	2/10/67	2/24/67	24	6
	Groovin'	5/5/67	6/16/67	3	9
	A Girl Like You	7/21/67	8/25/67	11	8
	How Can I Be Sure	9/15/67	10/13/67	3	9
	It's Wonderful	12/1/67	12/29/67	12	8

Rascals
	A Beautiful Morning	4/1/68	5/13/68	3	11
	People Got To Be Free	7/8/68	8/19/68	1	13
	A Ray Of Hope	12/9/68	12/23/68	22	4
	Heaven	2/3/69	2/24/69	26	5
	See	5/19/69	6/16/69	12	8
	Carry Me Back	9/1/69	10/6/69	17	7

Yuro, Timi
	Hurt	7/29/61	8/12/61	10	6
	Smile	12/9/61	12/9/61	37	1
	What's A Matter Baby (Is It Hurting You)	7/28/62	8/11/62	18	4
	The Love Of A Boy	12/1/62	12/8/62	37	2
	Make The World Go Away	7/5/63	9/13/63	17	7

Zager & Evans
	In The Year 2525 (Exordium & Terminus)	6/23/69	7/14/69	1	10

Zill, Pat
	Pick Me Up On Your Way Down	5/13/61	5/20/61	34	2

Zombies
	She's Not There	10/23/64	12/4/64	1	12
	Tell Her No	1/22/65	2/19/65	7	8
	She's Coming Home	5/7/65	5/14/65	24	4
	Whenever You're Ready	9/24/65	10/8/65	29	3
	Indication	8/5/66	8/12/66	27	3
	Time Of The Season	1/27/69	3/10/69	2	12

ALPHABETICAL LISTING BY TITLE

Debut	Peak	Title	Artist	Pos	Wks
9/15/67	9/29/67	A Banda	Herb Alpert & the Tijuana Brass	29	3
5/13/66	5/13/66	"A" Team, The	S/Sgt. Barry Sadler	34	1
7/14/69	8/11/69	Abergavenny	Shannon	20	5
1/31/64	2/28/64	Abigail Beecher	Freddy Cannon	17	6
7/26/63	9/6/63	Abilene	George Hamilton IV	5	10
11/4/68	12/2/68	Abraham, Martin And John	Dion	1	11
8/27/65	9/24/65	Action	Freddy Cannon	4	7
11/29/63	12/6/63	Adios (My Secret Love)	Donald Jenkins	36	2
11/10/62	11/10/62	Again	Lettermen	39	1
3/18/61	3/18/61	Age For Love, The	Jimmy Charles	38	1
9/10/65	9/17/65	Agent Double-O-Soul	Edwin Starr	29	3
7/14/62	7/28/62	Ahab, The Arab	Ray Stevens	6	5
1/12/63	1/12/63	Ain't Gonna Kiss Ya	Ribbons	39	2
9/9/66	10/21/66	Ain't Gonna Lie	Keith	14	8
3/20/64	4/10/64	Ain't Gonna Tell Anybody	Jimmy Gilmer	19	6
6/11/65	6/18/65	Ain't It A Shame	Major Lance	34	2
9/24/65	9/24/65	Ain't It True	Andy Williams	35	1
6/30/67	7/14/67	Ain't No Mountain High Enough	Marvin Gaye & Tammi Terrell	25	5
4/8/68	4/29/68	Ain't No Way	Aretha Franklin	14	5
4/29/68	6/3/68	Ain't Nothing Like The Real Thing	Marvin Gaye & Tammi Terrell	16	6
8/14/64	8/14/64	Ain't She Sweet	Beatles	39	1
4/19/63	4/26/63	Ain't That A Shame	Four Seasons	28	4
7/1/66	7/1/66	Ain't Too Proud To Beg	Temptations	36	2
7/21/62	7/21/62	Air Travel	Ray & Bob	40	1
6/16/67	6/16/67	Airplane Song (My Airplane)	Royal Guardsmen	36	1
7/17/64	7/24/64	Al-Di-La	Ray Charles Singers	29	3
6/16/62	7/7/62	Al Di La	Emilio Pericoli	3	7
7/29/66	8/26/66	Alfie	Cilla Black	19	6
10/7/68	10/14/68	Alfie	Eivets Rednow	32	3
6/2/67	6/16/67	Alfie	Dionne Warwick	31	4
2/8/63	3/1/63	Alice In Wonderland	Neil Sedaka	19	4
7/15/68	8/26/68	Alice Long (You're Still My Favorite Girlfriend)	Tommy Boyce & Bobby Hart	6	8
12/16/66	1/20/67	All	James Darren	19	7

Debut	Peak	Title	Artist	Pos	Wks
10/20/62	12/1/62	All Alone Am I	Brenda Lee	4	9
10/7/68	10/28/68	All Along The Watchtower	Jimi Hendrix Experience	25	4
1/15/65	2/19/65	All Day And All Of The Night	Kinks	3	8
3/1/63	3/15/63	All I Have To Do Is Dream	Richard Chamberlain	17	5
6/2/67	6/23/67	All I Need	Temptations	33	4
6/25/65	7/23/65	All I Really Want To Do	Byrds	11	7
9/23/66	10/7/66	All I See Is You	Dusty Springfield	28	4
1/21/61	2/11/61	All In My Mind	Teri Anders	29	4
3/20/64	4/17/64	All My Loving	Jimmy Griffin	14	6
7/14/62	7/21/62	All Night Long	Sandy Nelson	33	2
3/11/61	3/18/61	All Of Everything	Frankie Avalon	29	2
4/9/65	4/16/65	All Of My Life	Lesley Gore	35	2
3/24/62	3/24/62	All Of This For Sally	Mark Dinning	40	1
7/21/67	8/11/67	All You Need Is Love	Beatles	8	9
8/11/62	9/15/62	Alley Cat	Bent Fabric	6	10
7/24/64	7/24/64	Alone	Four Seasons	39	2
10/29/60	11/5/60	Alone At Last	Jackie Wilson	30	3
6/16/69	7/21/69	Along Came Jones	Ray Stevens	16	6
3/3/62	3/10/62	Along Came Linda	Tommy Boyce	27	3
6/10/66	7/15/66	Along Comes Mary	Association	12	8
10/14/60	10/14/60	Alvin For President	Chipmunks	31	1
3/10/62	3/17/62	Alvin Twist, The	Chipmunks	28	2
9/2/68	9/9/68	(There's) Always Something There To Remind Me	Dionne Warwick	28	3
11/4/68	11/18/68	Always Together	Dells	34	3
8/28/64	8/28/64	Always Together	Al Martino	38	1
12/24/60	12/24/60	Am I Losing You	Jim Reeves	37	2
12/15/67	1/15/68	Am I That Easy To Forget	Engelbert Humperdinck	14	7
1/8/65	1/15/65	Amen	Impressions	34	2
8/26/61	9/16/61	Amor	Ben E. King	18	5
4/26/63	4/26/63	Amy	Paul Petersen	39	1
8/7/64	8/14/64	And I Love Her	Beatles	21	3
5/7/65	5/7/65	And I Love Him	Esther Phillips	39	1
4/23/65	4/23/65	And Roses And Roses	Andy Williams	27	1
10/20/69	11/17/69	And When I Die	Blood, Sweat & Tears	4	10
1/14/66	2/4/66	Andrea	Sunrays	12	6
2/12/65	2/26/65	Angel	Johnny Tillotson	34	3
12/17/60	1/7/61	Angel Baby	Rosie & the Originals	4	9
2/25/61	2/25/61	Angel Hands	Billie Jean Norton	37	1
5/20/68	6/17/68	Angel Of The Morning	Merrilee Rush & the Turnabouts	2	9
1/21/61	3/4/61	Angel On My Shoulder	Shelby Flint	8	9
8/21/64	8/21/64	Angelito	Rene & Rene	40	1
4/5/63	4/26/63	Ann-Marie	Belmonts	16	4
11/18/61	12/2/61	Annabelle Lee	Coeds	23	3

Ron Smith • 131

Debut	Peak	Title	Artist	Pos	Wks
3/24/62	3/31/62	Annie Get Your Yo-Yo	Little Junior Parker	33	2
6/26/64	7/3/64	Annie Is Back	Little Richard	36	2
5/5/67	5/19/67	Another Day, Another Heartache	Fifth Dimension	23	4
8/2/63	8/16/63	Another Fool Like Me	Ned Miller	23	3
4/26/63	5/3/63	Another Saturday Night	Sam Cooke	34	2
7/8/66	7/8/66	Answer Lies Within, The	Neil Sedaka	40	1
1/21/66	2/25/66	Answer To My Prayer, The	Neil Sedaka	19	7
4/28/62	5/12/62	Any Day Now (My Wild Beautiful Bird)	Chuck Jackson	31	3
6/19/64	6/19/64	Any Old Time Of The Day	Dionne Warwick	37	1
10/6/69	10/27/69	Any Way That You Want Me	Evie Sands	23	5
11/27/64	1/1/65	Any Way You Want It	Dave Clark Five	4	10
10/14/60	10/14/60	Anymore	Teresa Brewer	30	1
11/29/63	11/29/63	Anyone Else	Gene McDaniels	39	1
5/13/68	5/20/68	Anyone For Tennis	Cream	38	3
1/10/64	1/31/64	Anyone Who Had A Heart	Dionne Warwick	23	6
9/8/67	9/29/67	Anything Goes	Harpers Bizarre	18	5
3/10/62	3/17/62	Anything That's Part Of You	Elvis Presley	13	2
1/28/61	2/25/61	Apache	Jorgen Ingmann	1	10
2/26/65	2/26/65	Apache '65	Arrows featuring Davie Allan	37	2
12/3/65	12/3/65	Apple Of My Eye	Roy Head	38	2
2/26/65	3/26/65	Apples And Bananas	Lawrence Welk	11	7
8/25/67	9/29/67	Apples, Peaches, Pumpkin Pie	Jay & the Techniques	8	8
5/26/69	6/9/69	April Fools, The	Dionne Warwick	29	3
3/10/69	3/24/69	Aquarius/Let The Sunshine In	Fifth Dimension	1	13
4/5/63	4/5/63	Arabia	Delcoes	40	1
1/13/62	1/13/62	Archie's Melody	Byliners	38	1
9/10/65	9/24/65	Are You A Boy Or Are You A Girl	Barbarians	18	4
11/19/60	12/3/60	Are You Lonesome To-Night	Elvis Presley	1	12
2/24/67	3/10/67	Are You The Kind	Flock	23	4
10/20/69	11/17/69	Aren't We The Lucky Ones	Vic Dana	28	6
9/9/61	9/23/61	As If I Didn't Know	Adam Wade	26	3
11/20/64	12/18/64	As Tears Go By	Marianne Faithfull	11	6
12/24/65	1/14/66	As Tears Go By	Rolling Stones	16	4
1/10/64	1/31/64	As Usual	Brenda Lee	15	6
3/11/61	4/8/61	Asia Minor	Kokomo	3	9
11/6/64	11/27/64	Ask Me	Elvis Presley	5	8

Debut	Peak	Title	Artist	Pos	Wks
2/19/65	2/19/65	Ask The Lonely	Four Tops	29	4
8/26/61	9/23/61	Astronaut, The (Part 1)	Jose Jimenez	5	6
2/11/61	3/4/61	At Last	Etta James	28	4
2/5/65	2/5/65	At The Club	Drifters	35	2
1/28/66	2/25/66	At The Scene	Dave Clark Five	13	7
8/2/63	8/9/63	At The Shore	Johnny Caswell	17	3
3/24/67	4/14/67	At The Zoo	Simon & Garfunkel	16	8
4/28/69	5/19/69	Atlantis	Donovan	11	6
1/7/66	1/14/66	Attack	Toys	24	2
10/14/61	10/14/61	Autumn In Cheyenne	Al Caiola	34	1
6/24/68	8/5/68	Autumn Of My Life	Bobby Goldsboro	11	8
1/6/69	3/10/69	Baby, Baby Don't Cry	Smokey Robinson & the Miracles	6	12
9/25/64	10/16/64	Baby Be Mine	Jelly Beans	15	6
4/8/61	5/20/61	Baby Blue	Echoes	4	10
9/16/68	10/28/68	Baby, Come Back	Equals	15	7
9/10/65	9/17/65	Baby Don't Go	Sonny & Cher	24	2
2/28/64	3/6/64	Baby, Don't You Cry	Ray Charles	33	2
7/28/62	8/4/62	Baby Elephant Walk	Kai Winding	33	2
12/8/62	12/15/62	Baby Has Gone Bye Bye	George Maharis	26	4
11/29/63	11/29/63	Baby I Do Love You	Galens	35	1
7/21/67	8/25/67	Baby I Love You	Aretha Franklin	16	8
6/9/69	7/21/69	Baby, I Love You	Andy Kim	4	12
1/10/64	1/17/64	Baby, I Love You	Ronettes	20	4
2/3/67	3/10/67	Baby I Need Your Lovin'	Johnny Rivers	5	10
8/28/64	10/2/64	Baby I Need Your Loving	Four Tops	13	7
10/27/69	12/1/69	Baby, I'm For Real	Originals	6	10
7/2/65	8/6/65	Baby, I'm Yours	Barbara Lewis	4	7
1/13/62	2/24/62	Baby It's You	Shirelles	5	9
9/22/69	11/10/69	Baby It's You	Smith	3	12
1/6/69	2/3/69	Baby Let's Wait	Royal Guardsmen	17	6
10/16/64	11/20/64	Baby Love	Supremes	6	9
1/8/68	2/19/68	Baby, Now That I've Found You	Foundations	5	9
12/3/60	12/17/60	Baby Oh Baby	Shells	33	3
2/18/66	2/25/66	Baby Scratch My Back	Slim Harpo	20	4
6/9/62	6/23/62	Baby Sittin' Boogie	Ralph Bendix	8	5
2/11/61	3/11/61	Baby Sittin' Boogie	Buzz Clifford	3	8
5/14/65	5/21/65	Baby The Rain Must Fall	Glenn Yarbrough	16	5
3/29/63	4/12/63	Baby Workout	Jackie Wilson	21	4
11/17/67	12/8/67	Baby You Got It	Brenton Wood	24	4
6/3/61	6/3/61	Bacardi	Ralph Marterie	36	1
1/25/63	2/8/63	Bachelor Man	Johnny Cymbal	19	3

Debut	Peak	Title	Artist	Pos	Wks
9/9/61	9/23/61	Back Beat No. 1	Rondels	9	5
2/24/69	3/10/69	Back Door Man	Derek	29	3
5/27/68	6/3/68	Back In Love Again	Buckinghams	32	3
5/7/65	6/4/65	Back In My Arms Again	Supremes	5	8
3/18/68	3/25/68	Back On My Feet Again	Foundations	32	2
11/3/69	11/24/69	Backfield In Motion	Mel & Tim	13	7
4/15/66	5/6/66	Backstage	Gene Pitney	10	7
10/28/61	11/25/61	Backtrack	Faron Young	19	5
8/26/66	9/9/66	Bad Little Woman	Shadows Of Knight	19	6
5/12/69	6/9/69	Bad Moon Rising	Creedence Clearwater Revival	1	11
5/22/64	6/19/64	Bad To Me	Billy J. Kramer & the Dakotas	1	5
6/23/62	7/21/62	Balboa Blue	Marketts	11	6
9/22/69	10/20/69	Ball Of Fire	Tommy James & the Shondells	9	9
2/26/68	4/1/68	Ballad Of Bonnie And Clyde, The	Georgie Fame	9	9
12/29/62	1/12/63	Ballad Of Jed Clampett, The	Lester Flatt & Earl Scruggs	17	5
10/29/60	11/5/60	Ballad Of The Alamo	Bud & Travis	18	5
2/4/66	3/11/66	Ballad Of The Green Berets	S/Sgt. Barry Sadler	2	8
8/25/67	9/15/67	Ballad Of You & Me & Pooneil	Jefferson Airplane	28	4
4/29/66	6/3/66	Band Of Gold	Mel Carter	21	7
9/9/61	9/23/61	Band Of Gold	Roommates	24	3
10/21/66	10/28/66	"Bang" "Bang"	Joe Cuba Sextet	31	3
3/11/66	4/15/66	Bang Bang (My Baby Shot Me Down)	Cher	3	10
10/21/68	11/18/68	Bang-Shang-A-Lang	Archies	11	7
1/7/66	1/28/66	Barbara Ann	Beach Boys	2	8
5/20/61	6/10/61	Barbara-Ann	Regents	3	8
12/8/69	1/12/70	Barbara, I Love You	New Colony Six	13	8
5/27/66	5/27/66	Barefootin'	Robert Parker	37	1
4/9/65	4/16/65	Barracuda, The	Alvin Cash & the Crawlers	28	3
2/11/66	2/25/66	Batman	Jan & Dean	25	3
5/6/66	5/27/66	Batman And His Grandmother	Dickie Goodman	9	4
2/11/66	3/4/66	Batman Theme	Neil Hefti	29	4
1/28/66	2/25/66	Batman Theme	Marketts	17	6
10/14/68	11/4/68	Battle Hymn Of The Republic	Andy Williams	14	6
5/22/64	5/22/64	Be Anything (But Be Mine)	Connie Francis	21	4
6/28/63	7/19/63	Be Careful Of Stones That You Throw	Dion	19	5
12/13/63	12/13/63	Be Mad Little Girl	Bobby Darin	34	2

Debut	Peak	Title	Artist	Pos	Wks
8/30/63	9/20/63	Be My Baby	Ronettes	2	8
5/6/61	5/20/61	Be My Boy	Paris Sisters	7	7
11/15/63	12/6/63	Be True To Your School	Beach Boys	7	8
6/28/63	7/19/63	Be True To Yourself	Bobby Vee	12	5
8/4/62	8/4/62	Beach Party	King Curtis & the Noble Knights	35	2
5/29/64	6/5/64	Beans In My Ears	Serendipity Singers	32	5
1/27/67	3/3/67	Beat Goes On, The	Sonny & Cher	5	8
3/27/64	4/17/64	Beatle Time	Livers	28	4
4/1/68	5/13/68	Beautiful Morning, A	Rascals	3	11
11/10/67	12/8/67	Beautiful People	Bobby Vee	6	8
5/5/67	5/5/67	Beautiful Story, A	Sonny & Cher	38	2
9/9/66	9/23/66	Beauty Is Only Skin Deep	Temptations	18	5
8/7/64	9/4/64	Because	Dave Clark Five	2	8
8/27/65	8/27/65	Because You're Mine	James Darren	34	1
9/1/62	9/15/62	Beechwood 4-5789	Marvelettes	28	4
5/21/65	6/18/65	Before And After	Chad & Jeremy	17	6
11/10/67	11/10/67	Beg, Borrow And Steal	Ohio Express	31	2
3/17/67	4/21/67	Beggin'	Four Seasons	23	7
12/16/68	1/20/69	Bella Linda	Grass Roots	12	7
6/19/64	7/3/64	Belshazah	Johnny Cash	34	3
5/5/62	6/2/62	Ben Casey, Theme From	Valjean	11	6
7/7/62	7/21/62	Ben Crazy	Dickie Goodman	25	3
11/17/67	1/15/68	Bend Me, Shape Me	American Breed	1	13
9/30/61	10/7/61	Berlin Melody	Billy Vaughn	33	2
2/17/62	2/17/62	Bermuda	Linda Scott	38	1
3/17/67	4/21/67	Bernadette	Four Tops	20	7
10/4/63	10/4/63	Betty In Bermudas	Dovells	40	1
10/7/61	10/28/61	Big Bad John	Jimmy Dean	2	11
11/3/67	11/3/67	Big Boss Man	Elvis Presley	36	1
12/13/63	12/13/63	Big Boss Man	Charlie Rich	38	1
1/7/66	1/28/66	Big Bright Eyes	Danny Hutton	17	7
9/23/61	10/7/61	Big Cold Wind	Pat Boone	27	4
4/7/62	4/14/62	Big Draft, The	Four Preps	31	2
10/13/62	10/27/62	Big Girls Don't Cry	Four Seasons	1	9
10/21/61	10/28/61	Big John	Shirelles	34	1
12/11/64	12/11/64	Big Man In Town	Four Seasons	22	1
2/1/63	2/15/63	Big Wide World	Teddy Randazzo	15	4
6/3/61	6/17/61	Bilbao Song, The	Andy Williams	18	4
7/15/66	8/5/66	Billy And Sue	B. J. Thomas	31	5
2/14/64	3/13/64	Bird Dance Beat	Trashmen	14	6
8/11/62	8/11/62	Bird Man, The	Highwaymen	33	2
1/12/63	2/8/63	Bird, The	Dutones	21	5
11/24/62	12/8/62	(The Bossa Nova) Bird	Dells	19	3

Debut	Peak	Title	Artist	Pos	Wks
5/17/63	5/24/63	Birdland	Chubby Checker	28	2
1/29/65	3/12/65	Birds And The Bees, The	Jewel Akens	7	10
4/12/63	4/26/63	Bird's The Word, The	Rivingtons	31	3
7/7/69	8/11/69	Birthday	Underground Sunshine	2	9
9/13/63	10/4/63	Birthday Party	Pixies Three	8	6
9/6/63	9/13/63	Bit Of Soul, A	McKinley Mitchell	32	2
4/3/64	5/1/64	Bits And Pieces	Dave Clark Five	5	6
8/26/66	9/30/66	Black Is Black	Los Bravos	4	9
7/15/61	7/29/61	Black Land Farmer	Frankie Miller	13	6
5/26/69	7/7/69	Black Pearl	Sonny Charles & the Checkmates, Ltd.	13	8
2/15/63	3/22/63	Blame It On The Bossa Nova	Eydie Gorme	4	9
12/27/63	1/10/64	Bless 'Em All	Jane Morgan	24	5
9/16/61	10/7/61	Bless You	Tony Orlando	11	5
9/10/65	9/17/65	Blowin' In The Wind	Steve Alaimo	36	2
7/5/63	8/30/63	Blowin' In The Wind	Peter, Paul & Mary	4	10
3/8/63	4/5/63	Blue	Jack Reno	20	5
10/15/60	11/19/60	Blue Angel	Roy Orbison	11	7
9/27/63	10/18/63	Blue Bayou	Roy Orbison	4	7
10/11/63	10/18/63	Blue Guitar	Richard Chamberlain	34	2
3/25/61	4/1/61	Blue Moon	Marcels	1	9
5/31/63	6/21/63	Blue On Blue	Bobby Vinton	4	9
12/31/60	1/14/61	Blue Tango	Bill Black	27	3
10/15/60	10/15/60	Blue Velvet	Statues	37	1
8/30/63	9/13/63	Blue Velvet	Bobby Vinton	1	9
3/20/64	3/20/64	Blue Winter	Connie Francis	27	3
7/7/67	8/11/67	Blue's Theme	Davie Allan & the Arrows	4	7
10/6/62	11/17/62	Bluebirds Over The Mountain	Echoes	15	7
5/19/62	5/26/62	Blues (Stay Away From Me)	Ace Cannon	34	2
11/18/61	11/25/61	Bo Diddley	Bo Diddley	32	2
6/17/61	7/15/61	Bobby	Neil Scott	8	7
2/18/61	3/4/61	Bobby Layne	Phil Gary	30	4
10/20/62	11/17/62	Bobby's Girl	Marcie Blane	1	13
6/10/61	7/8/61	Boll Weevil Song, The	Brook Benton	15	6
4/8/61	5/13/61	Bonanza	Al Caiola	4	8
1/27/62	1/27/62	Bonecracker, The	Johnny & the Debonaires	38	2
6/16/62	7/7/62	Bongo Stomp	Little Joey & the Flips	17	5
1/4/63	1/25/63	Bonnie Do	Johnny Cooper	19	5
3/22/63	3/22/63	Bony Moronie	Appalachians	36	2
11/17/67	1/8/68	Boogaloo Down Broadway	Fantastic Johnny C	6	10
2/17/62	3/10/62	Boogie Twist	Paul Gallis	31	4

Debut	Peak	Title	Artist	Pos	Wks
7/8/61	7/29/61	Boogie Woogie	B. Bumble & the Stingers	18	5
3/20/64	3/20/64	Book Of Love	Raindrops	29	2
12/25/64	1/8/65	Boom Boom	Animals	18	3
5/5/62	5/19/62	Boom Boom	John Lee Hooker	23	3
7/1/66	8/19/66	Born A Woman	Sandy Posey	14	12
9/23/66	9/30/66	Born Free	Roger Williams	37	3
7/8/68	8/12/68	Born To Be Wild	Steppenwolf	1	11
2/8/63	2/22/63	Boss Guitar	Duane Eddy	26	3
10/18/63	11/15/63	Bossa Nova Baby	Elvis Presley	13	9
11/4/68	12/9/68	Both Sides Now	Judy Collins	9	10
5/24/63	5/31/63	Bounce, The	Olympics	19	4
6/9/67	6/16/67	Bowling Green	Everly Brothers	34	3
3/31/69	5/5/69	Boxer, The	Simon & Garfunkel	1	11
1/15/65	2/5/65	Boy From New York City, The	Ad Libs	14	7
5/3/63	5/17/63	(Today I Met) The Boy I'm Gonna Marry	Darlene Love	19	4
7/14/69	8/11/69	Boy Named Sue, A	Johnny Cash	7	10
11/1/63	11/29/63	Boy Next Door, The	Secrets	8	7
11/17/62	12/8/62	Boy Trouble	Revlons	27	5
1/10/64	1/17/64	Boy You Ought To See Her Now	Kevin & Greg	37	2
10/22/65	10/29/65	Boys	Beatles	18	5
8/11/62	8/11/62	Boys' Night Out, The	Patti Page	35	1
11/10/69	12/15/69	Brand New Me, A	Dusty Springfield	19	8
8/28/64	10/2/64	Bread And Butter	Newbeats	5	7
7/7/69	7/28/69	Break Away	Beach Boys	27	4
1/22/65	2/5/65	Break Away (From That Boy)	Newbeats	23	4
1/20/62	2/10/62	Break It To Me Gently	Brenda Lee	14	6
6/17/66	6/17/66	Break Out	Mitch Ryder & the Detroit Wheels	35	1
5/6/61	5/27/61	Breakin' In A Brand New Broken Heart	Connie Francis	6	7
1/21/66	1/28/66	Breakin' Up Is Breakin' My Heart	Roy Orbison	35	2
4/3/64	4/24/64	(The Best Part Of) Breakin' Up	Ronettes	23	4
7/14/62	8/4/62	Breaking Up Is Hard To Do	Neil Sedaka	1	9
8/9/63	9/6/63	Breakwater	Lawrence Welk	16	5
6/21/63	7/5/63	Brenda	Cupids	27	4
5/28/65	6/18/65	Bring It On Home To Me	Animals	21	6
10/28/68	11/18/68	Bring It On Home To Me	Eddie Floyd	24	5
3/5/65	3/12/65	Bring Your Love To Me	Righteous Brothers	34	2
9/23/61	10/28/61	Bristol Stomp	Dovells	4	9

Debut	Peak	Title	Artist	Pos	Wks
6/2/62	6/30/62	Bristol Twistin' Annie	Dovells	10	6
8/18/62	8/18/62	Broken Heart	Fiestas	39	1
5/6/68	6/3/68	Brooklyn Roads	Neil Diamond	22	5
3/3/69	4/21/69	Brother Love's Travelling Salvation Show	Neil Diamond	7	10
6/30/62	7/7/62	Brothers Grimm, Theme From The	Lawrence Welk	32	2
8/18/67	10/6/67	Brown Eyed Girl	Van Morrison	4	11
1/13/69	2/17/69	Build Me Up Buttercup	Foundations	3	9
12/3/60	12/31/60	Bumble Bee	LaVern Baker	25	6
4/2/65	4/2/65	Bumble Bee	Searchers	30	2
3/25/61	4/15/61	Bumble Boogie	B. Bumble & the Stingers	8	9
10/13/62	10/27/62	Burning Of Atlanta, The	Claude King	26	3
1/22/68	1/29/68	Burning Spear	Soulful Strings	32	3
7/8/66	8/12/66	Bus Stop	Hollies	1	11
8/9/63	9/13/63	Bust Out	Busters	12	7
9/13/63	10/25/63	Busted	Ray Charles	17	7
3/25/61	5/6/61	(I Don't Know Why) But I Do	Clarence "Frogman" Henry	5	9
5/26/69	6/9/69	But It's Alright	J.J. Jackson	24	5
7/14/62	7/14/62	But Not For Me	Ketty Lester	27	1
1/20/69	3/3/69	But You Know I Love You	First Edition	13	8
10/8/65	10/29/65	But You're Mine	Sonny & Cher	23	5
2/8/63	2/22/63	Butterfly Baby	Bobby Rydell	17	5
4/14/67	5/12/67	Buy For Me The Rain	Nitty Gritty Dirt Band	21	7
6/3/61	6/3/61	Buzz Buzz A-Diddle-It	Freddy Cannon	32	2
2/24/62	3/10/62	B'wa Nina (Pretty Girl)	Tokens	23	4
12/1/67	12/15/67	By The Time I Get To Phoenix	Glen Campbell	32	3
4/22/61	4/29/61	Bye Bye Baby	Mary Wells	35	2
1/22/65	2/12/65	Bye, Bye, Baby (Baby Goodbye)	Four Seasons	10	6
2/21/64	2/21/64	Bye Bye Barbara	Johnny Mathis	29	2
7/1/66	7/22/66	Cadillac	New Colony Six	27	5
1/7/61	2/11/61	Calcutta	Lawrence Welk	1	12
1/28/61	2/11/61	Calendar Girl	Neil Sedaka	11	4
1/14/66	3/4/66	California Dreamin'	Mamas & the Papas	1	14
7/9/65	8/13/65	California Girls	Beach Boys	3	7
3/10/67	4/28/67	California Nights	Lesley Gore	8	9
12/30/68	1/20/69	California Soul	Fifth Dimension	18	6
12/20/63	1/24/64	California Sun	Rivieras	3	10
2/18/66	3/11/66	Call Me	Chris Montez	17	5
3/4/61	3/18/61	Call Me Anytime	Frankie Avalon	29	3
4/8/68	5/13/68	Call Me Lightning	Who	20	6
7/28/62	8/18/62	Call Me Mr. In-Between	Burl Ives	16	5
2/1/63	2/1/63	Call On Me	Bobby Bland	40	1

Debut	Peak	Title	Artist	Pos	Wks
1/6/69	2/3/69	Can I Change My Mind	Tyrone Davis	10	7
12/13/63	12/20/63	Can I Get A Witness	Marvin Gaye	33	3
5/8/64	5/8/64	Can You Do It	Contours	38	1
3/20/64	4/10/64	Can't Buy Me Love	Beatles	3	8
3/15/63	4/12/63	Can't Get Used To Losing You	Andy Williams	4	11
10/6/67	10/20/67	Can't Happen Without You	Power Plant	33	3
12/23/61	2/3/62	Can't Help Falling In Love	Elvis Presley	4	8
4/7/67	5/19/67	Can't Seem To Make You Mine	Seeds	9	8
6/2/67	7/14/67	Can't Take My Eyes Off You	Frankie Valli	1	13
8/5/68	8/5/68	Can't You Find Another Way (Of Doing It)	Sam & Dave	38	2
1/29/65	3/12/65	Can't You Hear My Heartbeat	Herman's Hermits	3	10
12/16/66	1/20/67	Can't You See I Still Love You	Flock	22	7
6/3/68	7/8/68	Can't You See Me Cry	New Colony Six	10	8
6/19/64	7/10/64	Can't You See That She's Mine	Dave Clark Five	2	7
11/12/60	11/26/60	Canadian Sunset	Cameos	30	3
8/13/65	8/20/65	Candy	Astors	28	2
7/5/63	8/2/63	Candy Girl	Four Seasons	3	10
9/9/61	9/23/61	Candy Man	Roy Orbison	4	4
8/14/64	9/11/64	Car Hop	Exports	9	7
9/10/65	9/24/65	Cara-Lin	Strangeloves	28	5
6/18/65	7/16/65	Cara, Mia	Jay & the Americans	3	8
1/29/68	2/5/68	Carmen	Herb Alpert & the Tijuana Brass	34	2
3/11/66	3/25/66	Caroline, No	Brian Wilson	17	6
2/19/68	3/11/68	Carpet Man	Fifth Dimension	31	4
7/14/67	8/18/67	Carrie-Anne	Hollies	4	9
9/1/69	10/6/69	Carry Me Back	Rascals	17	7
5/5/67	6/2/67	Casino Royale	Herb Alpert & the Tijuana Brass	15	6
1/4/63	2/8/63	Cast Your Fate To The Wind	Vince Guaraldi Trio	3	8
4/9/65	4/16/65	Cast Your Fate To The Wind	Sounds Orchestral	27	2
3/15/63	3/15/63	Castaway	Hayley Mills	31	1
9/8/67	9/8/67	Cat In The Window (The Bird In The Sky)	Petula Clark	28	3
6/4/65	6/18/65	Catch The Wind	Donovan	20	5
7/23/65	9/3/65	Catch Us If You Can	Dave Clark Five	3	9
4/21/62	5/19/62	Caterina	Perry Como	9	7
1/14/61	1/14/61	C'est Si Bon (It's So Good)	Conway Twitty	38	1

Debut	Peak	Title	Artist	Pos	Wks
10/13/62	11/3/62	Cha-Cha-Cha, The	Bobby Rydell	18	5
10/14/60	10/14/60	Chain Gang	Sam Cooke	17	2
12/1/67	1/22/68	Chain Of Fools	Aretha Franklin	5	10
9/16/68	10/7/68	Chained	Marvin Gaye	32	4
12/1/62	1/4/63	Chains	Cookies	17	6
9/23/66	10/14/66	Changes	Crispian St. Peters	25	5
6/11/65	7/2/65	Chantilly Lace	Rene & Rene	19	5
5/8/64	5/29/64	Chapel Of Love	Dixie Cups	3	8
2/18/61	3/11/61	Charlena	Sevilles	24	4
6/17/61	7/1/61	Charleston, The	Ernie Fields	12	7
5/20/61	5/27/61	Charlie Wasn't There	Barbara Evans	29	2
4/5/63	5/10/63	Charms	Bobby Vee	11	7
2/10/62	2/17/62	Chattanooga Choo Choo	Floyd Cramer	32	3
3/11/66	3/18/66	Cheater, The	Bob Kuban & the In-Men	28	2
12/6/63	12/6/63	Cheer Leader, The	Paul Petersen	40	1
8/19/66	9/2/66	Cherish	Association	1	10
9/9/66	10/21/66	Cherry, Cherry	Neil Diamond	2	9
11/3/69	11/3/69	Cherry Hill Park	Billy Joe Royal	35	1
2/18/61	2/25/61	Cherry Pink And Apple Blossom White	Jerry Murad's Harmonicats	32	2
10/21/68	11/25/68	Chewy Chewy	Ohio Express	3	10
9/22/67	11/3/67	Child Of Clay	Jimmie Rodgers	17	7
10/22/65	11/12/65	Child Of Our Times	Barry McGuire	25	5
12/17/60	1/14/61	Chills And Fever	Ronnie Love	5	9
8/16/63	9/13/63	China Nights (Shina No Yoru)	Kyu Sakamoto	21	5
2/3/62	2/24/62	Chip Chip	Gene McDaniels	21	4
3/24/69	5/12/69	Chokin' Kind, The	Joe Simon	10	10
5/27/68	6/10/68	Choo Choo Train	Box Tops	23	4
9/11/64	10/9/64	Chug-A-Lug	Roger Miller	5	7
4/14/62	4/14/62	Cinderella	Jack Ross	34	1
5/12/62	6/9/62	Cindy's Birthday	Johnny Crawford	5	8
11/4/68	11/25/68	Cinnamon	Derek	4	12
12/29/62	1/12/63	Cinnamon Cinder (It's A Very Nice Dance)	Pastel Six	18	6
3/26/65	4/9/65	Clapping Song (Clap Pat Clap Slap), The	Shirley Ellis	27	3
7/1/68	8/12/68	Classical Gas	Mason Williams	2	9
7/21/69	7/28/69	Clean Up Your Own Backyard	Elvis Presley	34	3
11/12/65	11/12/65	Cleo's Back	Jr. Walker & the All-Stars	38	1
6/11/65	6/11/65	Climb, The	Kingsmen	38	1
8/28/64	9/25/64	Clinging Vine	Bobby Vinton	13	7
9/29/62	10/27/62	Close To Cathy	Mike Clifford	5	6

Debut	Peak	Title	Artist	Pos	Wks
4/14/67	5/12/67	Close Your Eyes	Peaches & Herb	28	6
2/8/63	3/1/63	Closer To Heaven	Nick Noble	23	4
12/2/68	1/6/69	Cloud Nine	Temptations	11	9
7/31/64	8/28/64	C'mon And Swim (Part 2)	Bobby Freeman	8	7
6/9/67	7/21/67	C'mon Marianne	Four Seasons	8	10
8/4/67	8/25/67	Cold Sweat—Part 2	James Brown	30	4
6/2/69	7/7/69	Color Him Father	Winstons	6	8
1/6/67	2/3/67	Color My World	Petula Clark	19	6
9/25/64	10/23/64	Come A Little Bit Closer	Jay & the Americans	3	10
4/5/63	5/3/63	Come And Get These Memories	Martha & the Vandellas	11	5
3/26/65	4/16/65	Come And Stay With Me	Marianne Faithfull	19	5
10/11/63	10/18/63	Come Back	Johnny Mathis	32	2
1/12/63	2/8/63	Come Back Little Girl	Ronnie Rice	20	6
3/10/62	3/31/62	Come Back Silly Girl	Lettermen	15	5
8/4/67	9/8/67	Come Back When You Grow Up	Bobby Vee	2	11
6/14/63	7/5/63	Come Go With Me	Dion	11	5
2/19/65	3/19/65	Come Home	Dave Clark Five	7	7
10/14/60	10/14/60	Come Home, Come Home	Shepherds	22	1
1/31/64	2/14/64	Come On	Tommy Roe	28	3
7/28/62	7/28/62	Come On Baby	Bruce Channel	34	1
5/26/67	7/21/67	Come On Down To My Boat	Every Mothers' Son	2	14
5/20/66	6/17/66	Come On Let's Go	McCoys	11	6
7/7/62	8/11/62	Come On Little Angel	Belmonts	4	8
11/20/64	1/1/65	Come See About Me	Supremes	2	10
1/15/68	1/22/68	Come See About Me	Jr. Walker & the All-Stars	36	2
4/8/61	4/8/61	Come Softly To Me	Raymond Lefevre	38	1
10/6/69	11/3/69	Come Together	Beatles	1	16
3/19/65	3/19/65	Come Tomorrow	Manfred Mann	38	3
7/7/62	7/7/62	Comeback, The	Faron Young	40	1
11/10/62	11/24/62	Comin' Home Baby	Mel Torme	32	3
1/10/64	1/10/64	Comin' In The Back Door	Baja Marimba Band	34	1
12/23/66	1/20/67	Coming Home Soldier	Bobby Vinton	17	6
11/4/66	12/2/66	Coming On Strong	Brenda Lee	15	6
12/9/66	12/16/66	Communication Breakdown	Roy Orbison	25	3
4/7/69	5/5/69	Composer, The	Diana Ross & the Supremes	21	5
1/20/62	2/10/62	Concerto For The X-15	Elliott Evans	20	4
5/14/65	5/28/65	Concrete And Clay	Eddie Rambeau	16	5
5/21/65	5/28/65	Concrete And Clay	Unit 4+2	16	3
12/16/68	1/13/69	Condition Red	Goodees	15	5

Debut	Peak	Title	Artist	Pos	Wks
1/4/63	1/4/63	Coney Island Baby	Excellents	31	1
12/10/60	12/24/60	Confidential	Fleetwoods	26	3
4/10/64	4/24/64	Congratulations	Rick Nelson	32	3
4/28/62	5/19/62	Conscience	James Darren	18	4
4/22/61	4/29/61	Continental Walk, The	Rollers	33	3
3/24/62	4/14/62	Cookin'	Al Casey Combo	13	5
9/15/62	10/13/62	Cool Breeze	Daylighters	17	4
5/13/66	6/10/66	Cool Jerk	Capitols	8	7
12/17/60	1/7/61	Corinna, Corinna	Ray Peterson	6	8
5/8/64	5/29/64	Cotton Candy	Al Hirt	19	4
1/27/62	2/24/62	Cotton Fields	Highwaymen	3	7
5/19/62	6/2/62	Count Every Star	Linda Scott	21	3
4/9/65	5/7/65	Count Me In	Gary Lewis & the Playboys	4	8
2/26/68	3/4/68	Country Girl—City Man	Billy Vera & Judy Clay	26	4
10/21/68	10/28/68	Court Of Love	Unifics	27	3
4/8/68	5/20/68	Cowboys To Girls	Intruders	8	8
11/25/61	12/16/61	Crazy	Patsy Cline	23	4
5/5/67	5/19/67	Creeque Alley	Mamas & the Papas	15	4
12/9/68	1/13/69	Crimson And Clover	Tommy James & the Shondells	1	12
9/27/63	10/18/63	Cross Fire	Orlons	23	4
11/8/63	11/29/63	Crossfire Time	Dee Clark	26	5
2/3/69	3/3/69	Crossroads	Cream	15	6
6/23/62	7/14/62	Crowd, The	Roy Orbison	16	4
1/8/65	2/5/65	Crusher, The	Novas	6	6
11/25/66	12/9/66	Cry	Ronnie Dove	16	7
9/20/63	9/27/63	Cry Baby	Garnet Mimms	36	3
3/31/62	4/7/62	Cry Baby Cry	Angels	37	2
3/4/68	4/22/68	Cry Like A Baby	Box Tops	2	11
8/18/67	8/25/67	Cry Softly Lonely One	Roy Orbison	27	3
2/10/62	2/24/62	Cry To Me	Solomon Burke	28	3
5/27/66	5/27/66	Crying	Jay & the Americans	26	3
9/16/61	10/7/61	Crying	Roy Orbison	3	7
5/21/65	6/25/65	Crying In The Chapel	Elvis Presley	7	9
1/27/62	3/3/62	Crying In The Rain	Everly Brothers	5	9
1/7/66	1/21/66	Crying Time	Ray Charles	33	5
6/9/69	7/7/69	Crystal Blue Persuasion	Tommy James & the Shondells	1	12
7/22/61	8/5/61	Cupid	Sam Cooke	28	4
12/22/69	12/29/69	Cupid	Johnny Nash	35	3
8/11/62	8/18/62	Cure, The	Smiley Williams	37	2
10/21/68	11/25/68	Cycles	Frank Sinatra	13	8

Debut	Peak	Title	Artist	Pos	Wks
4/26/63	5/17/63	Da Doo Ron Ron (When He Walked Me Home)	Crystals	3	8
1/28/61	2/4/61	Daddy Cool	Daddy Cool	36	3
1/27/69	2/17/69	Daddy Sang Bass	Johnny Cash	31	4
5/6/61	5/27/61	Daddy's Home	Shep & the Limelites	10	6
2/17/67	2/24/67	Daddy's Little Girl	Al Martino	34	4
8/18/69	9/22/69	Daddy's Little Man	O. C. Smith	17	8
12/13/63	1/17/64	Daisy Petal Pickln'	Jimmy Gilmer & the Fireballs	9	8
12/24/60	1/28/61	Dance By The Light Of The Moon	Olympics	9	9
11/13/64	12/11/64	Dance Dance Dance	Beach Boys	10	6
7/19/63	7/26/63	Dance Dance Dance	Joey Dee	33	2
9/8/62	9/15/62	Dance Is Over, The	Little Billy	33	2
6/3/61	7/15/61	Dance On Little Girl	Paul Anka	13	8
5/13/61	5/20/61	Dance The Mess Around	Chubby Checker	32	2
2/19/68	3/18/68	Dance To The Music	Sly & the Family Stone	11	8
10/15/65	11/5/65	Dance With Me	Mojo Men	27	4
7/14/62	8/4/62	Dancin' Party	Chubby Checker	23	4
6/16/62	6/16/62	Dancin' The Strand	Maureen Gray	34	1
12/9/66	1/13/67	Dancing In The Street	Mamas & the Papas	5	8
9/11/64	10/9/64	Dancing In The Street	Martha & the Vandellas	6	8
9/15/67	10/13/67	Dandelion	Rolling Stones	16	6
9/30/66	10/28/66	Dandy	Herman's Hermits	6	8
6/5/64	7/17/64	Dang Me	Roger Miller	11	9
8/12/66	8/26/66	Dangling Conversation, The	Simon & Garfunkel	24	3
7/19/63	8/16/63	Danke Schoen	Wayne Newton	17	5
12/9/61	12/16/61	Danny Boy	Andy Williams	27	2
10/15/60	10/15/60	Dark At The Top Of The Stairs, Theme From The	Ernie Freeman	35	1
12/15/62	1/4/63	Darkest Street In Town	Jimmy Clanton	15	4
1/29/68	2/5/68	Darlin'	Beach Boys	27	3
2/10/67	3/10/67	Darling Be Home Soon	Lovin' Spoonful	18	7
8/7/64	8/21/64	Dartell Stomp, The	Mustangs	13	6
6/21/63	7/12/63	Daughter	Blenders	12	5
9/27/63	11/1/63	Dawn	David Rockingham Trio	16	6
1/31/64	2/7/64	Dawn (Go Away)	Four Seasons	2	7
8/12/68	8/19/68	Day By Day	Tom Jones	36	2
5/27/66	6/10/66	Day For Decision	Johnny Sea	9	3
5/5/69	6/2/69	Day Is Done	Peter, Paul & Mary	11	7
9/13/63	10/4/63	Day The Sawmill Closed Down, The	Dickey Lee	19	4
12/24/65	12/24/65	Day Tripper	Beatles	1	9
3/4/66	4/1/66	Daydream	Lovin' Spoonful	3	6

Debut	Peak	Title	Artist	Pos	Wks
11/3/67	11/24/67	Daydream Believer	Monkees	1	13
11/24/62	11/24/62	Daydreamin'	Cory Wade	36	1
7/29/61	8/19/61	Daydreams	Johnny Crawford	17	6
6/16/69	6/30/69	Days Of Sand And Shovels, The	Bobby Vinton	31	5
3/27/64	5/8/64	Dead Man's Curve	Jan & Dean	1	13
12/1/67	12/1/67	Dear Eloise	Hollies	38	1
12/18/64	12/25/64	Dear Heart	Andy Williams	21	2
12/3/60	12/10/60	Dear John	Pat Boone	36	2
1/20/62	2/17/62	Dear Lady Twist	Gary U.S. Bonds	12	8
11/24/62	12/1/62	Dear Lonely Hearts	Nat "King" Cole	27	2
2/17/62	3/10/62	Dear One	Larry Finnegan	4	7
7/29/61	8/5/61	Dedicated (To The Songs I Love)	Three Friends	27	2
2/24/67	3/31/67	Dedicated To The One I Love	Mamas & the Papas	3	8
3/4/61	4/8/61	Dedicated To The One I Love	Shirelles	4	7
2/25/66	2/25/66	Dedication Song, The	Freddy Cannon	33	1
10/4/63	11/8/63	Deep Purple	Nino Tempo & April Stevens	1	8
4/1/68	5/6/68	Delilah	Tom Jones	24	6
7/19/63	8/9/63	Denise	Randy & the Rainbows	6	8
10/13/62	10/27/62	Desafinado	Stan Getz & Charlie Byrd	21	5
8/2/63	8/16/63	Desert Pete	Kingston Trio	25	3
7/19/63	8/9/63	Detroit City	Bobby Bare	3	7
3/10/67	3/31/67	Detroit City	Tom Jones	26	6
7/5/63	8/2/63	(You're The) Devil In Disguise	Elvis Presley	5	6
10/14/60	10/29/60	Devil Or Angel	Bobby Vee	12	4
10/21/66	12/9/66	Devil With A Blue Dress On & Good Golly Miss Molly	Mitch Ryder & the Detroit Wheels	4	14
8/18/62	9/1/62	Devil Woman	Marty Robbins	19	4
11/15/63	12/6/63	Devil's A'waitin'	Glencoves	24	4
10/14/60	10/14/60	Diamonds And Pearls	Paradons	36	1
2/26/65	2/26/65	Diana	Bobby Rydell	38	1
5/8/64	5/29/64	Diane	Bachelors	8	7
4/29/66	6/3/66	Did You Ever Have To Make Up Your Mind	Lovin' Spoonful	3	8
8/4/69	9/1/69	Did You See Her Eyes	Illusion	10	7
12/22/62	12/22/62	Diddle-Dee-Dum (What Happens When Your Love Has Gone)	Belmonts	39	1
12/15/67	2/12/68	Different Drum	Stone Poneys	4	11

Debut	Peak	Title	Artist	Pos	Wks
1/14/66	1/14/66	Dig You Baby	Lorraine Ellison	36	1
5/19/67	6/16/67	Ding Dong! The Witch Is Dead	Fifth Estate	13	6
4/22/66	6/24/66	Dirty Water	Standells	6	13
2/17/67	2/24/67	Dis-Advantages Of You, The	Brass Ring	36	3
5/27/66	5/27/66	Distant Drums	Jim Reeves	31	1
7/15/66	8/12/66	Distant Shores	Chad & Jeremy	21	6
4/15/61	5/6/61	Dixie, Theme From	Duane Eddy	17	5
2/10/69	3/3/69	Dizzy	Tommy Roe	1	11
7/31/64	8/21/64	Do I Love You	Ronettes	23	4
7/29/68	9/16/68	Do It Again	Beach Boys	2	11
6/2/67	7/7/67	Do It Again A Little Bit Slower	Jon & Robin & the In Crowd	7	8
5/10/63	5/24/63	Do It—Rat Now	Bill Black's Combo	20	3
1/13/62	2/10/62	Do-Re-Mi	Lee Dorsey	22	5
10/7/68	11/11/68	Do Something To Me	Tommy James & the Shondells	19	6
3/8/63	3/15/63	Do The Bird	Dee Dee Sharp	26	3
9/30/68	10/14/68	Do The Choo Choo	Archie Bell & the Drells	25	3
3/12/65	3/19/65	Do The Clam	Elvis Presley	32	4
5/7/65	5/21/65	Do The Freddie	Freddie & the Dreamers	9	6
3/3/62	3/10/62	Do The New Continental	Dovells	25	3
12/11/64	1/1/65	Do-Wacka-Do	Roger Miller	17	5
9/11/64	9/25/64	Do Wah Diddy Diddy	Manfred Mann	2	10
1/8/65	1/15/65	Do What You Do Well	Ned Miller	26	2
8/5/68	8/19/68	Do What You Gotta Do	Bobby Vee	37	3
8/27/65	9/10/65	Do You Believe In Magic	Lovin' Spoonful	12	7
4/15/68	5/27/68	Do You Know The Way To San Jose	Dionne Warwick	10	8
5/8/64	6/12/64	Do You Love Me	Dave Clark Five	6	8
8/25/62	9/22/62	Do You Love Me	Contours	5	9
3/26/65	4/23/65	Do You Wanna Dance	Beach Boys	5	6
3/27/64	3/27/64	Do You Want To Dance	Classmen	33	1
4/17/64	4/24/64	Do You Want To Know A Secret	Beatles	7	6
3/3/69	4/7/69	Do Your Thing	Watts 103rd St. Rhythm Band	7	9
1/29/68	3/11/68	(Sittin' On The) Dock Of The Bay	Otis Redding	2	11
4/21/62	5/12/62	Doctor Feel-Good	Dr. Feelgood & the Interns	15	5
8/26/61	9/16/61	Does Your Chewing Gum Lose Its Flavor	Lonnie Donegan	4	6
4/29/68	5/20/68	Does Your Mama Know About Me	Bobby Taylor & the Vancouvers	22	4
12/10/60	1/14/61	Doll House	Donnie Brooks	19	7
11/8/63	11/15/63	Dominique	Singing Nun (Soeur Sourire)	1	9
5/20/61	6/10/61	Don't Be Afraid	Bobby Rydell	11	6
3/15/63	4/5/63	Don't Be Afraid, Little Darlin'	Steve Lawrence	13	5

Debut	Peak	Title	Artist	Pos	Wks
10/14/60	10/29/60	Don't Be Cruel	Bill Black's Combo	15	5
10/14/61	11/4/61	Don't Blame Me	Everly Brothers	17	4
2/24/62	3/17/62	Don't Break The Heart That Loves You	Connie Francis	5	7
5/6/66	6/10/66	Don't Bring Me Down	Animals	7	7
7/21/62	7/21/62	Don't Cry Baby	Aretha Franklin	37	1
11/24/69	1/12/70	Don't Cry Daddy	Elvis Presley	4	11
11/27/64	11/27/64	Don't Ever Leave Me	Connie Francis	28	1
11/12/65	11/12/65	Don't Fool With Fu Manchu	Ramrods	37	1
12/18/64	1/29/65	Don't Forget I Still Love You	Bobbi Martin	14	7
11/4/61	11/4/61	Don't Get Around Much Anymore	Belmonts	32	1
3/17/69	4/14/69	Don't Give In To Him	Gary Puckett & the Union Gap	6	9
7/8/68	8/5/68	Don't Give Up	Petula Clark	31	6
11/17/62	12/8/62	Don't Go Near The Eskimos	Ben Colder	33	3
10/13/62	10/27/62	Don't Go Near The Indians	Rex Allen	27	3
6/16/67	6/30/67	Don't Go Out Into The Rain (You're Going To Melt)	Herman's Hermits	22	6
1/7/61	1/21/61	Don't Go To Strangers	Etta James	27	3
10/27/62	11/17/62	Don't Hang Up	Orlons	12	7
10/23/64	12/4/64	Don't It Make You Feel Good	Overlanders	7	7
8/25/69	9/29/69	Don't It Make You Want To Go Home	Joe South	15	8
6/25/65	8/13/65	Don't Just Stand There	Patty Duke	7	9
12/1/69	12/22/69	Don't Let Love Hang You Up	Jerry Butler	29	5
2/26/65	3/12/65	Don't Let Me Be Misunderstood	Animals	17	5
6/12/64	7/17/64	Don't Let The Sun Catch You Crying	Gerry & the Pacemakers	6	9
3/13/64	4/17/64	Don't Let The Rain Come Down (Crooked Little Man)	Serendipity Singers	1	10
8/4/67	8/11/67	Don't Let The Rain Fall On Me	Critters	29	2
12/22/62	1/12/63	Don't Make Me Over	Dionne Warwick	25	5
6/7/63	6/7/63	Don't Make My Baby Blue	Frankie Laine	27	1
3/1/63	3/29/63	Don't Mention My Name	Shepherd Sisters	7	6
1/28/66	1/28/66	Don't Mess With Bill	Marvelettes	30	2
5/26/62	6/16/62	Don't Play That Song (You Lied)	Ben E. King	25	4

Debut	Peak	Title	Artist	Pos	Wks
3/4/66	3/25/66	Don't Push Me	Hedgehoppers Anonymous	34	5
6/21/63	6/28/63	Don't Say Goodnight And Mean Goodbye	Shirelles	27	5
3/8/63	4/19/63	Don't Say Nothin' Bad	Cookies	5	8
3/8/63	3/8/63	Don't Set Me Free	Ray Charles	30	1
6/2/67	7/7/67	Don't Sleep In The Subway	Petula Clark	15	6
6/10/68	7/29/68	Don't Take It So Hard	Paul Revere & the Raiders	11	9
10/4/63	10/18/63	Don't Think Twice, It's All Right	Peter, Paul & Mary	16	4
11/26/65	12/17/65	Don't Think Twice, It's All Right	Wonder Who?	8	6
6/26/64	7/24/64	Don't Throw Your Love Away	Searchers	6	6
6/21/63	6/21/63	Don't Try To Fight It, Baby	Eydie Gorme	25	3
10/25/63	10/25/63	Don't Wait Too Long	Tony Bennett	31	2
3/1/63	3/15/63	Don't Wanna Think About Paula	Dickey Lee	16	4
2/18/61	3/18/61	Don't Worry	Marty Robbins	1	9
10/27/62	11/10/62	Don't You Believe It	Andy Williams	15	8
3/24/67	4/28/67	Don't You Care	Buckinghams	1	10
10/14/60	10/14/60	Don't You Just Know It	Fendermen	39	1
3/4/66	4/15/66	Don't You Know	Keith Everette	8	9
9/13/63	10/4/63	Donna The Prima Donna	Dion	3	7
10/16/64	11/6/64	Door Is Still Open To My Heart, The	Dean Martin	7	5
4/29/61	4/29/61	Door Is Still Open To My Heart, The	Skyliners	39	1
11/25/61	12/2/61	Door To Paradise	Bobby Rydell	14	3
8/28/64	8/28/64	Double Mirror Around Shades	Andy & the Manhattans	40	1
8/12/68	9/16/68	Down At Lulu's	Ohio Express	3	8
7/9/65	8/27/65	Down In The Boondocks	Billy Joe Royal	5	8
11/10/69	12/8/69	Down On The Corner	Creedence Clearwater Revival	3	10
12/25/64	1/15/65	Downtown	Petula Clark	1	11
6/16/62	7/14/62	Dr. Kildare, Theme From (Three Stars Will Shine Tonight)	Richard Chamberlain	13	6
11/29/63	1/10/64	Drag City	Jan & Dean	1	10
7/1/61	7/1/61	Dream	Etta James	37	1
7/15/68	8/19/68	Dream A Little Dream Of Me	Mama Cass Elliot	12	8
3/10/62	3/31/62	Dream Baby (How Long Must I Dream)	Roy Orbison	10	6
3/18/61	3/18/61	Dream Boy	Annette with the Afterbeats	36	1
4/16/65	5/7/65	Dream On Little Dreamer	Perry Como	15	5
9/30/61	10/21/61	(He's My) Dreamboat	Connie Francis	19	5
7/8/68	7/15/68	Dreams Of The Everyday Housewife	Glen Campbell	28	4

Debut	Peak	Title	Artist	Pos	Wks
6/24/68	6/24/68	Dreams Of The Everyday Housewife	Wayne Newton	37	2
2/3/62	3/3/62	Dreamy Eyes	Johnny Tillotson	8	7
11/8/63	11/29/63	Drip Drop	Dion	3	8
8/30/63	9/13/63	Drownin' My Sorrows	Connie Francis	27	3
5/26/62	6/9/62	Drummin' Up A Storm	Sandy Nelson	25	3
8/20/65	8/27/65	Drums A Go-Go	Persuaders	21	2
2/10/62	3/3/62	Drums Are My Beat	Sandy Nelson	21	5
4/14/67	4/14/67	Dry Your Eyes	Brenda & the Tabulations	38	2
4/7/62	4/7/62	Duchess Of Earl	Pearlettes	39	1
12/24/65	12/24/65	Duck, The	Jackie Lee	40	1
1/27/62	2/10/62	Duke Of Earl	Gene Chandler	1	9
11/11/61	11/11/61	Duke's Place	Duke Ellington & Louis Armstrong	35	1
5/27/66	5/27/66	Dum-De-Da	Bobby Vinton	36	1
7/8/61	8/5/61	Dum Dum	Brenda Lee	16	7
11/22/63	1/3/64	Dumb Head	Ginny Arnell	3	10
6/3/68	6/3/68	D. W. Washburn	Monkees	31	1
11/17/69	12/15/69	Early In The Morning	Vanity Fare	16	9
4/7/69	5/5/69	Earth Angel (Will You Be Mine)	Vogues	18	5
5/31/63	6/21/63	Easier Said Than Done	Essex	1	10
12/2/66	12/23/66	East West	Herman's Hermits	7	7
6/25/65	7/2/65	(Such An) Easy Question	Elvis Presley	24	3
8/4/69	9/22/69	Easy To Be Hard	Three Dog Night	1	12
12/10/65	12/24/65	Ebb Tide	Righteous Brothers	18	5
10/18/63	10/18/63	Eefin Alvin	Chipmunks	40	1
2/12/65	2/26/65	Eight Days A Week	Beatles	1	9
4/8/66	4/29/66	Eight Miles High	Byrds	15	6
5/10/63	6/7/63	18 Yellow Roses	Bobby Darin	11	6
3/3/62	3/3/62	El Cid	Billy Storm	35	1
5/3/63	5/17/63	El Watusi	Ray Barretto	13	4
8/12/66	9/2/66	Eleanor Rigby	Beatles	3	8
11/10/69	11/24/69	Eleanor Rigby	Aretha Franklin	23	5
9/30/68	11/4/68	Elenore	Turtles	2	9
8/30/63	9/13/63	(Native Girl) Elephant Walk	Donald Jenkins	22	4
10/20/69	11/17/69	Eli's Coming	Three Dog Night	3	9
2/11/66	3/11/66	Elusive Butterfly	Bob Lind	5	8
1/28/61	2/11/61	Emotions	Brenda Lee	28	4
9/20/63	10/11/63	Enamorado	Keith Colley	16	4

Debut	Peak	Title	Artist	Pos	Wks
1/14/61	1/28/61	Enchantment	Melody Mates	14	4
2/26/68	3/11/68	End Of Our Road, The	Gladys Knight & the Pips	25	3
2/8/63	3/8/63	End Of The World, The	Skeeter Davis	1	11
5/7/65	5/21/65	Engine Engine #9	Roger Miller	6	5
11/12/65	12/3/65	England Swings	Roger Miller	15	7
4/9/65	4/16/65	Entertainer, The	Tony Clarke	36	3
2/3/67	2/24/67	Epistle To Dippy	Donovan	21	7
11/3/62	12/1/62	Eso Beso (That Kiss!)	Paul Anka	12	6
12/2/61	12/9/61	Ev'rybody's Cryin'	Jimmie Beaumont	27	2
10/27/67	11/10/67	Even The Bad Times Are Good	Tremeloes	28	3
10/20/67	11/17/67	Everlasting Love	Robert Knight	6	7
10/7/61	11/11/61	Everlovin'	Rick Nelson	7	7
6/10/61	6/24/61	Every Beat Of My Heart	Gladys Knight & the Pips	28	3
7/22/61	7/29/61	Every Breath I Take	Gene Pitney	30	2
8/26/66	9/30/66	Every Day And Every Night	Trolls	10	7
7/3/64	7/3/64	Every Little Bit Hurts	Brenda Holloway	32	2
9/15/62	9/29/62	Every Night (Without You)	Paul Anka	22	3
6/21/63	7/19/63	Every Step Of The Way	Johnny Mathis	25	6
9/27/63	10/18/63	Everybody	Tommy Roe	3	6
10/11/63	10/11/63	Everybody Go Home	Eydie Gorme	22	2
2/4/61	2/11/61	Everybody Knew	La Rolls	37	2
12/15/67	1/15/68	Everybody Knows	Dave Clark Five	19	6
4/3/64	4/3/64	Everybody Knows	Drew-Vels	35	2
10/9/64	11/6/64	Everybody Knows (I Still Love You)	Dave Clark Five	15	5
10/8/65	10/29/65	Everybody Loves A Clown	Gary Lewis & the Playboys	5	7
12/8/62	12/29/62	Everybody Loves A Lover	Shirelles	36	4
4/14/62	5/12/62	Everybody Loves Me But You	Brenda Lee	17	5
7/17/64	8/14/64	Everybody Loves Somebody	Dean Martin	1	9
9/13/63	9/13/63	Everybody Monkey	Freddy Cannon	37	1
11/4/61	11/11/61	Everybody's Gotta Pay Some Dues	Miracles	26	2
9/1/69	10/6/69	Everybody's Talkin'	Nilsson	5	8
1/8/65	1/22/65	Everyday	Rogues	22	3
12/30/68	2/10/69	Everyday People	Sly & the Family Stone	1	12
5/12/69	6/23/69	Everyday With You Girl	Classics IV featuring Dennis Yost	14	9
9/24/65	11/5/65	Everyone's Gone To The Moon	Jonathan King	10	7
1/29/68	3/4/68	Everything That Touches You	Association	6	8

Debut	Peak	Title	Artist	Pos	Wks
11/20/64	12/18/64	Everything's Alright	Newbeats	13	5
11/10/69	12/22/69	Evil Woman Don't Play Your Games With Me	Crow	6	11
4/22/66	5/27/66	Evol-Not Love	Five Americans	8	6
11/12/60	11/19/60	Excuse Me	Nick Noble	35	3
11/26/60	12/24/60	Exodus	Ferrante & Teicher	1	15
5/6/61	5/20/61	Exodus	Eddie Harris	8	7
12/8/67	1/22/68	Explosion In Your Soul	Soul Survivors	23	7
9/22/67	11/17/67	Expressway To Your Heart	Soul Survivors	9	10
8/5/68	9/16/68	Eyes Of A New York Woman, The	B. J. Thomas	19	7
6/17/68	7/22/68	Face It Girl, It's Over	Nancy Wilson	19	8
10/13/67	11/17/67	Face The Autumn	Family	12	7
8/4/67	8/18/67	Fakin' It	Simon & Garfunkel	23	4
12/11/64	1/1/65	Fall Away	Eddie Albert	10	5
6/7/63	7/5/63	Falling	Roy Orbison	6	7
10/21/61	10/21/61	Faraway Star	Chordettes	34	1
6/19/64	7/10/64	Farmer John	Premiers	22	4
6/19/64	7/10/64	Father Sebastian	Ramblers	10	6
1/13/69	1/20/69	Feelin' So Good (S.k.o.o.b.y-D.o.o)	Archies	37	2
11/10/67	11/17/67	Felicidad	Sally Field	33	3
2/19/65	3/12/65	Ferry Cross The Mersey	Gerry & the Pacemakers	1	7
11/25/61	12/2/61	Fever	Pete Bennett	25	2
11/12/65	12/10/65	Fever	McCoys	16	6
11/1/63	11/15/63	Fiesta	Lawrence Welk	19	4
2/24/67	3/31/67	59th Street Bridge Song (Feelin' Groovy)	Harpers Bizarre	18	8
4/1/61	4/1/61	Find Another Girl	Jerry Butler	35	1
1/15/65	1/29/65	Finders Keepers, Losers Weepers	Nella Dodds	34	3
10/11/63	11/1/63	Fine Fine Boy, A	Darlene Love	18	5
7/19/63	8/2/63	Fingertips—Pt. 2	Stevie Wonder	6	5
9/2/68	9/23/68	Fire	Crazy World Of Arthur Brown	1	10
9/30/68	11/4/68	Fire	Five By Five	5	9
10/11/63	10/25/63	Fireball Mail	Jim & Joe	15	4
6/19/64	7/3/64	First Night Of The Full Moon	Jack Jones	11	8
4/7/69	4/14/69	First Of May	Bee Gees	32	3
5/31/63	5/31/63	First Quarrel	Paul & Paula	37	3

Debut	Peak	Title	Artist	Pos	Wks
7/29/61	8/5/61	Fish, The	Bobby Rydell	18	4
10/11/63	11/8/63	500 Miles Away From Home	Bobby Bare	15	6
11/19/65	12/17/65	Five O'Clock World	Vogues	1	10
9/9/66	9/30/66	Flamingo	Herb Alpert & the Tijuana Brass	33	5
1/7/61	1/21/61	Flamingo Express	Royaltones	5	8
12/3/65	12/24/65	Flowers On The Wall	Statler Brothers	20	5
1/25/63	2/8/63	Fly Me To The Moon-Bossa Nova	Joe Harnell	12	6
10/14/61	11/18/61	Fly, The	Chubby Checker	15	6
12/23/61	1/20/62	Flying Circle	Frank Slay	13	7
5/19/62	6/2/62	Follow That Dream	Elvis Presley	16	4
3/29/63	4/12/63	Follow The Boys	Connie Francis	26	4
10/7/68	10/28/68	Fool For You	Impressions	31	4
10/15/60	11/5/60	Fool In Love, A	Ike & Tina Turner	27	5
1/10/64	2/21/64	Fool Never Learns, A	Andy Williams	13	11
10/7/61	11/18/61	Fool #1	Brenda Lee	7	10
8/12/68	9/30/68	Fool On The Hill, The	Sergio Mendes & Brasil '66	9	9
4/19/63	5/24/63	Foolish Little Girl	Shirelles	5	8
2/17/62	2/17/62	Fools Hall Of Fame, The	Paul Anka	36	1
11/1/63	11/29/63	Fools Rush In	Rick Nelson	13	7
12/24/60	12/31/60	Fools Rush In (Where Angels Fear To Tread)	Brook Benton	27	4
8/26/61	9/23/61	Foot Stomping—Part 1	Flares	13	8
2/5/65	2/12/65	For Lovin' Me	Peter, Paul & Mary	34	3
10/28/61	11/11/61	For Me And My Gal	Freddy Cannon	24	3
10/28/68	12/9/68	For Once In My Life	Stevie Wonder	2	12
2/10/67	3/24/67	For What It's Worth (Stop, Hey What's That Sound)	Buffalo Springfield	4	11
1/10/64	2/14/64	For You	Rick Nelson	8	7
5/28/65	7/2/65	For Your Love	Yardbirds	7	8
6/30/67	7/7/67	For Your Precious Love	Oscar Toney Jr.	36	3
3/13/64	4/24/64	Forever	Pete Drake	8	10
3/18/68	4/22/68	Forever Came Today	Diana Ross & the Supremes	19	7
11/29/63	2/7/64	Forget Him	Bobby Rydell	5	12

Debut	Peak	Title	Artist	Pos	Wks
9/1/62	9/1/62	Forgive Me	Babs Tino	36	1
10/27/69	12/8/69	Fortunate Son	Creedence Clearwater Revival	3	12
6/9/62	7/7/62	Fortuneteller	Bobby Curtola	6	8
9/29/62	9/29/62	409	Beach Boys	5	7
9/13/63	9/20/63	Four Strong Winds	Ian & Sylvia	33	2
9/23/61	9/30/61	Frankie And Johnny	Brook Benton	21	3
8/16/63	8/16/63	Frankie And Johnny	Sam Cooke	34	3
3/25/66	4/8/66	Frankie And Johnny	Elvis Presley	27	5
10/28/66	11/11/66	Free Again	Barbra Streisand	24	4
1/20/62	1/20/62	Free Me	Johnny Preston	37	1
12/31/60	1/21/61	Freeway	Fugitives	16	6
3/19/65	3/19/65	Freeway Flyer	Jan & Dean	30	3
6/19/64	6/26/64	French Riviera, The	Webb Pierce	37	2
6/26/64	7/3/64	French Song, The	Lucille Starr	31	2
5/12/67	5/19/67	Friday On My Mind	Easybeats	25	3
7/1/66	7/1/66	Friday's Child	Nancy Sinatra	34	3
4/15/68	4/22/68	Friends	Beach Boys	37	2
5/27/61	6/3/61	Frogg	Brothers Four	29	3
12/22/62	1/25/63	From A Jack To A King	Ned Miller	7	7
9/11/64	10/9/64	From A Window	Billy J. Kramer & the Dakotas	4	8
6/21/63	7/12/63	From Me To You	Del Shannon	15	6
12/8/62	12/22/62	From The Bottom Of My Heart	Dean Martin	11	6
5/8/64	5/15/64	Fugitive	Jan Davis	20	3
2/14/64	3/13/64	Fun, Fun, Fun	Beach Boys	3	10
6/10/61	6/17/61	(There Was A) Fungus Among Us	Hugh Barrett	14	6
8/18/67	9/22/67	Funky Broadway	Wilson Pickett	7	8
3/25/68	5/13/68	Funky Street	Arthur Conley	8	9
5/6/61	5/6/61	Funny	Maxine Brown	38	1
9/4/64	9/4/64	Funny	Joe Hinton	19	2
6/16/67	6/30/67	Funny Familiar Forgotten Feelings	Tom Jones	33	4
1/20/62	2/3/62	Funny How Time Slips Away	Jimmy Elledge	23	3
10/25/63	10/25/63	Funny How Time Slips Away	Johnny Tillotson	35	1
4/21/62	5/19/62	Funny Way Of Laughin'	Burl Ives	19	5
10/9/64	10/30/64	Gale Winds	Egyptian Combo	16	5
12/16/66	12/23/66	Gallant Men	Senator Everett McKinley Dirksen	24	4
3/10/69	4/7/69	Galveston	Glen Campbell	5	8
3/12/65	4/2/65	Game Of Love	Wayne Fontana & the Mindbenders	2	8
1/20/69	2/17/69	Games People Play	Joe South	8	8
12/24/65	1/7/66	Gamma Goochee	Kingsmen	38	3
10/2/64	10/16/64	Garden In The Rain	Vic Dana	25	3

Debut	Peak	Title	Artist	Pos	Wks
11/18/61	12/16/61	Garden Of Eden	Bobby Comstock	10	6
5/24/63	5/31/63	Gee Little Girl	Nick Noble	22	4
11/19/60	12/31/60	Gee Whiz	Innocents	18	7
2/11/61	2/25/61	Gee Whiz (Look At His Eyes)	Carla Thomas	19	3
10/7/68	10/14/68	Gentle On My Mind	Glen Campbell	26	2
10/14/60	10/14/60	Georgia On My Mind	Ray Charles	14	6
7/22/66	7/29/66	Georgia Rose	Tony Bennett	38	2
1/14/66	2/25/66	Georgiana	Princetons	10	7
12/23/66	2/3/67	Georgy Girl	Seekers	2	11
9/9/66	9/30/66	Get Away	Georgie Fame	21	5
4/28/69	5/12/69	Get Back	Beatles	1	11
5/5/67	5/5/67	Get Me To The World On Time	Electric Prunes	28	2
10/8/65	10/29/65	Get Off Of My Cloud	Rolling Stones	1	9
9/22/67	9/29/67	Get On Up	Esquires	24	3
1/22/68	2/19/68	Get Out Now	Tommy James & the Shondells	27	5
11/3/69	11/24/69	Get Rhythm	Johnny Cash	18	6
7/28/69	9/15/69	Get Together	Youngbloods	4	11
8/18/67	9/8/67	Gettin' Together	Tommy James & the Shondells	13	6
7/14/62	7/14/62	Gimme A Little Kiss	Michael Landon	34	1
12/23/61	12/23/61	Gimme A Little Kiss	Originals	39	1
3/17/69	4/28/69	Gimme Gimme Good Lovin'	Crazy Elephant	5	10
8/25/67	10/13/67	Gimme Little Sign	Brenton Wood	8	10
1/6/67	2/10/67	Gimme Some Lovin'	Spencer Davis Group	8	7
9/22/62	11/3/62	Gina	Johnny Mathis	3	10
3/24/62	4/14/62	Ginny Come Lately	Brian Hyland	17	5
5/5/67	5/12/67	Girl	Pride & Joy	27	4
6/25/65	7/2/65	Girl Come Running	Four Seasons	36	2
4/16/65	4/16/65	Girl Don't Come	Sandie Shaw	39	1
6/12/64	6/26/64	Girl From Ipanema, The	Stan Getz & Astrud Gilberto	6	7
5/13/66	6/17/66	Girl In Love	Outsiders	10	7
7/21/67	8/25/67	Girl Like You, A	Young Rascals	11	8
3/25/61	4/15/61	Girl Of My Best Friend	Ral Donner	2	8
9/9/66	10/21/66	Girl On A Swing	Gerry & the Pacemakers	13	7
4/9/65	4/23/65	Girl On The Billboard	Del Reeves	17	4
9/2/68	10/7/68	Girl Watcher	O'Kaysions	7	9
11/5/65	11/12/65	Girl With Red Hair	Nick Noble	34	2
10/14/60	10/14/60	Girl With The Story In Her Eyes	Safaris	32	1

Debut	Peak	Title	Artist	Pos	Wks
4/7/67	4/28/67	Girl, You'll Be A Woman Soon	Neil Diamond	9	7
12/27/63	1/17/64	Girls Grow Up Faster Than Boys	Cookies	31	5
5/19/67	6/2/67	Girls In Love	Gary Lewis & the Playboys	21	5
8/21/64	8/21/64	Girl's Alright With Me, The	Temptations	36	1
4/7/69	5/5/69	Gitarzan	Ray Stevens	2	8
8/13/65	9/3/65	Give All Your Love To Me	Gerry & the Pacemakers	12	4
1/8/65	1/29/65	Give Him A Great Big Kiss	Shangri-Las	10	5
7/21/69	8/4/69	Give Peace A Chance	Plastic Ono Band	17	6
5/21/65	6/11/65	Give Us Your Blessings	Shangri-Las	9	7
2/14/64	3/27/64	Glad All Over	Dave Clark Five	2	11
10/20/67	11/17/67	Glad To Be Unhappy	Mamas & the Papas	17	5
2/1/63	3/1/63	Globetrottin'	Tornadoes	10	5
2/18/66	4/1/66	Gloria	Shadows Of Knight	1	12
4/15/61	4/15/61	Glory Of Love	Roommates	38	1
10/7/66	10/21/66	Go Away Little Girl	Happenings	15	4
12/1/62	12/22/62	Go Away Little Girl	Steve Lawrence	1	10
3/5/65	4/9/65	Go Now!	Moody Blues	4	10
2/10/67	3/10/67	Go Where You Wanna Go	Fifth Dimension	14	8
11/18/61	11/18/61	God, Country And My Baby	Johnny Burnette	36	2
1/8/68	1/29/68	Goin' Out Of My Head/Can't Take My Eyes Off You	Lettermen	5	8
1/21/66	1/28/66	Going To A Go-Go	Miracles	25	4
1/12/63	1/19/63	Going To Boston	Little Sisters	36	2
10/15/60	10/15/60	Going To Memphis	Johnny Cash	27	1
12/9/68	1/13/69	Going Up The Country	Canned Heat	6	9
2/19/65	3/26/65	Goldfinger	John Barry	4	10
4/9/65	4/16/65	Goldfinger	Shirley Bassey	14	3
11/13/64	12/4/64	Gone, Gone, Gone	Everly Brothers	13	5
5/15/64	5/29/64	Gonna Get Along Without You Now	Tracy Dee	32	3
2/14/64	2/14/64	Gonna Send You Back To Georgia (A City Slick)	Timmy Shaw	31	1
5/8/64	5/29/64	Good Golly Miss Molly	Swinging Blue Jeans	21	4
5/31/63	5/31/63	Good Life, The	Tony Bennett	35	1
3/25/66	4/22/66	Good Lovin'	Young Rascals	3	10
2/3/69	2/17/69	Good Lovin' Ain't Easy To Come By	Marvin Gaye & Tammi Terrell	22	4
3/10/62	3/31/62	Good Luck Charm	Elvis Presley	2	7

Debut	Peak	Title	Artist	Pos	Wks
5/26/69	6/16/69	Good Morning Starshine	Oliver	3	12
2/14/64	2/21/64	Good News	Sam Cooke	33	3
6/30/69	7/28/69	Good Old Rock 'N Roll	Cat Mother & the All Night News Boys	16	6
3/18/68	5/13/68	Good, The Bad And The Ugly, The	Hugo Montenegro	4	11
12/9/66	1/6/67	Good Thing	Paul Revere & the Raiders	4	7
2/4/61	3/4/61	Good Time Baby	Bobby Rydell	9	7
7/3/64	7/17/64	Good Times	Sam Cooke	34	3
10/21/66	11/11/66	Good Vibrations	Beach Boys	1	11
5/5/69	6/2/69	Goodbye	Mary Hopkin	16	6
7/1/61	7/1/61	Goodbye Again, Theme From	Ferrante & Teicher	36	1
4/15/68	5/6/68	Goodbye Baby (I Don't Want To See You Cry)	Tommy Boyce & Bobby Hart	28	4
10/14/61	11/18/61	Goodbye Cruel World	James Darren	1	12
6/30/62	7/21/62	Goodbye Dad	Castle Sisters	18	4
4/21/67	4/21/67	Goodbye To All You Women	Bobby Goldsboro	40	1
2/5/65	3/12/65	Goodnight	Roy Orbison	18	6
6/30/62	6/30/62	Goodnight Irene	Jerry Reed	32	1
12/16/68	2/3/69	Goodnight My Love	Paul Anka	13	9
5/31/63	7/5/63	Goodnight My Love	Fleetwoods	15	7
10/28/68	12/9/68	Goody Goody Gumdrops	1910 Fruitgum Co.	15	10
12/18/64	12/25/64	Google Eye	Nashville Teens	25	2
12/20/63	1/17/64	Gorilla, The	Ideals	19	6
9/11/64	9/11/64	Got My Hands On Some Lovin'	Artistics	38	1
4/8/66	4/22/66	Got My Mojo Working (Part 1)	Jimmy Smith	32	4
5/3/63	5/17/63	Got You On My Mind	Cookie & his Cupcakes	34	3
6/17/61	7/1/61	Graduation Song...Pomp And Circumstance, The	Adrian Kimberly	21	3
10/25/63	11/1/63	Grass Is Greener, The	Brenda Lee	28	2
6/23/62	6/23/62	Gravy (For My Mashed Potatoes)	Dee Dee Sharp	37	1
4/7/69	6/9/69	Grazing In The Grass	Friends Of Distinction	6	13
6/17/68	7/22/68	Grazing In The Grass	Hugh Masakela	3	10
9/30/66	10/28/66	Great Airplane Strike, The	Paul Revere & the Raiders	9	6
9/30/61	10/28/61	(He's The) Great Impostor	Fleetwoods	15	5
1/20/67	1/27/67	Great Train Robbery, The	Little Boy Blues	33	3
8/11/69	8/25/69	Green Fields	Vogues	27	3
5/6/66	5/20/66	Green Grass	Gary Lewis & the Playboys	11	7
3/11/61	3/18/61	Green Grass Of Texas	Texans	23	3

Debut	Peak	Title	Artist	Pos	Wks
7/19/63	8/2/63	Green, Green	New Christy Minstrels	10	5
1/13/67	2/17/67	Green, Green Grass Of Home	Tom Jones	11	8
7/14/62	7/14/62	Green Leaves Of Summer, The	Kenny Ball & his Jazzmen	37	1
2/26/68	3/18/68	Green Light	American Breed	21	4
8/25/62	9/22/62	Green Onions	Booker T. & the MG's	12	6
7/28/69	9/1/69	Green River	Creedence Clearwater Revival	4	10
12/1/67	1/29/68	Green Tambourine	Lemon Pipers	2	12
1/25/63	2/15/63	Greenback Dollar	Kingston Trio	12	5
9/16/68	10/14/68	Greenberg, Glickstein, Charles, David Smith And Jones	Cryan' Shames	11	6
3/25/61	4/15/61	Greener Pastures	Stonewall Jackson	13	6
6/10/66	7/1/66	Grim Reaper Of Love	Turtles	26	4
12/2/66	12/30/66	Grizzly Bear	Youngbloods	13	7
9/8/67	9/8/67	Groovin'	Booker T. & the MG's	40	1
5/5/67	6/16/67	Groovin'	Young Rascals	3	9
10/27/69	11/24/69	Groovy Grubworm	Harlow Wilcox & the Oakies	19	7
4/8/66	5/20/66	Groovy Kind Of Love, A	Mindbenders	2	10
7/10/64	7/10/64	Growin' Up Too Fast	Diane Renay	32	1
8/28/64	9/18/64	G.T.O.	Ronny & the Daytonas	13	5
8/12/66	9/23/66	Guantanamera	Sandpipers	7	8
3/10/62	3/31/62	Guitar Boogie Shuffle Twist	Virtues	21	4
10/6/62	11/10/62	(Dance With The) Guitar Man	Duane Eddy	6	8
3/3/62	3/3/62	Gunga Didn't	Lord Didd	36	1
1/28/61	2/11/61	Gunslinger	Bo Diddley	30	3
12/2/61	12/2/61	Gypsy Rover, The	Highwaymen	32	1
10/21/61	12/2/61	Gypsy Woman	Impressions	11	5
5/24/63	6/28/63	Gypsy Woman	Rick Nelson	6	8
8/18/67	9/8/67	Ha Ha Said The Clown	Yardbirds	27	4
3/10/69	4/28/69	Hair	Cowsills	1	12
10/21/66	11/18/66	Hair On My Chinny Chin Chin	Sam the Sham & the Pharaohs	18	7
2/22/63	2/22/63	Half A Man	Willie Nelson	39	1
12/15/62	1/12/63	Half Heaven-Half Heartache	Gene Pitney	10	6
6/3/61	6/3/61	Halfway To Paradise	Tony Orlando	37	1
7/8/68	8/12/68	Halfway To Paradise	Bobby Vinton	15	7
7/10/64	8/14/64	Handy Man	Del Shannon	7	9
11/18/68	1/13/69	Hang 'Em High	Booker T. & the MG's	7	13
11/19/65	12/3/65	Hang On Sloopy	Ramsey Lewis Trio	19	5
8/20/65	9/24/65	Hang On Sloopy	McCoys	1	10
6/3/66	6/17/66	Hanky Panky	Tommy James & the Shondells	1	9
7/14/67	7/28/67	Happening, The	Herb Alpert & the Tijuana Brass	33	3
4/7/67	4/28/67	Happening, The	Supremes	7	6

Debut	Peak	Title	Artist	Pos	Wks
7/7/67	7/7/67	Happy	Blades Of Grass	39	2
10/1/65	10/15/65	Happy Birthday Baby	Dolly Parton	29	3
3/4/61	3/25/61	Happy Birthday Blues	Kathy Young	14	6
12/23/66	12/23/66	Happy Birthday Sweet Jesus	Patti Page	39	1
11/11/61	12/16/61	Happy Birthday, Sweet Sixteen	Neil Sedaka	5	10
4/22/61	5/13/61	Happy Ending	Teddy Randazzo	26	4
1/13/62	1/20/62	Happy Jose (Ching, Ching)	Jack Ross	25	2
4/29/68	5/13/68	Happy Song (Dum-Dum), The	Otis Redding	26	4
6/24/66	7/1/66	Happy Summer Days	Ronnie Dove	38	2
2/10/67	3/31/67	Happy Together	Turtles	1	12
7/10/64	8/7/64	Hard Day's Night, A	Beatles	1	10
1/28/66	2/4/66	Hard Day's Night, A	Ramsey Lewis Trio	30	2
12/3/65	12/24/65	Harlem Nocturne	Viscounts	11	4
2/7/64	2/7/64	Harlem Shuffle	Bob & Earl	33	2
10/14/60	10/14/60	Harmony	Billy Bland	37	1
8/19/68	9/2/68	Harper Valley P.T.A.	Jeannie C. Riley	1	6
7/5/63	7/12/63	Harry The Hairy Ape	Ray Stevens	34	2
7/8/61	7/22/61	Hats Off To Larry	Del Shannon	2	9
8/7/64	9/25/64	Haunted House	"Jumpin'" Gene Simmons	12	8
6/30/62	7/14/62	Have A Good Time	Sue Thompson	21	4
9/25/64	10/23/64	Have I The Right	Honeycombs	1	10
11/22/63	12/13/63	Have You Heard	Duprees	25	4
1/15/65	1/29/65	Have You Looked Into Your Heart	Jerry Vale	8	6
9/30/66	10/21/66	Have You Seen Your Mother, Baby, Standing In The Shadow	Rolling Stones	8	5
6/23/62	7/7/62	Havin' A Party	Sam Cooke	27	3
3/11/61	3/25/61	Havin' Fun	Dion	27	3
3/31/69	5/5/69	Hawaii Five-O	Ventures	16	6
12/18/64	1/1/65	Hawaii Tattoo	Waikakis	12	5
11/4/66	12/2/66	Hazy Shade Of Winter, A	Simon & Garfunkel	14	6
6/10/66	6/17/66	He	Righteous Brothers	29	3
4/1/66	4/8/66	He Cried	Shangri-Las	34	3
1/27/62	2/10/62	He Knows I Love Him Too Much	Paris Sisters	16	7
2/21/64	2/28/64	He Says The Same Things To Me	Skeeter Davis	29	4
11/12/60	11/19/60	He Will Break Your Heart	Jerry Butler	16	10
9/29/62	10/27/62	He's A Rebel	Crystals	2	11
4/5/63	4/5/63	He's Got The Power	Exciters	35	1
9/27/63	10/4/63	He's Mine (I Love Him, I Love Him, I Love Him)	Alice Wonder Land	22	3
3/8/63	3/22/63	He's So Fine	Chiffons	1	10

Debut	Peak	Title	Artist	Pos	Wks
1/12/63	2/8/63	He's Sure The Boy I Love	Crystals	7	7
6/17/61	7/15/61	Heart And Soul	Cleftones	4	7
8/26/61	9/16/61	Heart And Soul	Jan & Dean	6	6
10/27/62	11/17/62	Heart Breaker	Dean Christie	17	4
8/13/65	9/10/65	Heart Full Of Soul	Yardbirds	8	8
7/28/62	8/11/62	Heart In Hand	Brenda Lee	19	3
1/29/65	2/5/65	Heart Of Stone	Rolling Stones	11	5
10/21/61	11/18/61	Heartaches	Marcels	11	7
2/8/63	2/8/63	Heartaches And Happiness	X. Lincoln	40	1
3/25/61	4/1/61	Hearts Of Stone	Bill Black's Combo	29	4
8/16/63	9/13/63	Heat Wave	Martha & the Vandellas	20	8
2/3/69	2/24/69	Heaven	Rascals	26	5
11/17/69	12/15/69	Heaven Knows	Grass Roots	22	8
6/17/61	6/24/61	Heaven Needed An Angel	Al Alberts	33	2
3/20/64	5/15/64	Hello, Dolly!	Louis Armstrong	3	12
12/15/62	12/15/62	Hello Faithless	Dora Hall	39	1
11/24/67	12/15/67	Hello Goodbye	Beatles	1	9
9/27/63	9/27/63	Hello Heartache, Goodbye Love	Little Peggy March	31	2
1/20/67	1/20/67	Hello Hello	Sopwith Camel	28	2
7/1/68	7/29/68	Hello, I Love You	Doors	1	11
1/27/69	2/3/69	Hello It's Me	Nazz	36	2
5/13/61	5/27/61	Hello Mary Lou	Ricky Nelson	1	10
8/2/63	8/16/63	Hello Mudduh Hello Fadduh (A Letter From Camp)	Allan Sherman	2	6
8/25/62	9/15/62	Hello Out There	Nick Noble	15	5
2/12/65	2/12/65	Hello Pretty Girl	Ronnie Dove	37	1
5/17/63	6/14/63	Hello Stranger	Barbara Lewis	3	6
4/22/61	5/13/61	Hello Walls	Faron Young	8	6
7/30/65	9/10/65	Help!	Beatles	1	12
11/4/66	12/2/66	Help Me Girl	Outsiders	19	6
5/7/65	5/28/65	Help Me Rhonda	Beach Boys	2	9
9/9/68	10/14/68	Help Yourself	Tom Jones	27	6
2/24/62	3/17/62	Her Royal Majesty	James Darren	6	6
4/7/67	5/12/67	Here Comes My Baby	Tremeloes	3	9
6/3/68	6/24/68	Here Comes The Judge	Shorty Long	11	5
4/26/63	5/24/63	Here I Stand	Rip Chords	16	5
11/26/65	11/26/65	Here It Comes Again	Fortunes	31	1
6/2/67	7/7/67	Here We Go Again	Ray Charles	18	9
7/28/67	8/25/67	Heroes And Villians	Beach Boys	13	7

Debut	Peak	Title	Artist	Pos	Wks
11/5/65	11/19/65	Hey Baby	Five Emprees	24	4
2/10/62	3/3/62	Hey! Baby	Bruce Channel	1	10
9/8/67	10/13/67	Hey Baby (They're Playing Our Song)	Buckinghams	5	9
3/20/64	3/20/64	Hey, Bobba Needle	Chubby Checker	28	3
2/28/64	3/6/64	Hey Jean, Hey Dean	Dean & Jean	38	2
8/9/63	9/20/63	Hey Girl	Freddie Scott	12	7
7/3/64	7/3/64	Hey Harmonica Man	Stevie Wonder	38	2
8/27/65	8/27/65	Hey Ho	Guess Who	39	1
5/20/66	7/1/66	Hey Joe	Leaves	11	8
9/2/68	9/16/68	Hey Jude	Beatles	1	11
12/23/68	1/27/69	Hey Jude	Wilson Pickett	21	6
1/20/67	2/3/67	Hey, Leroy, Your Mama's Callin' You	Jimmy Castor	31	4
3/10/62	3/10/62	Hey, Let's Twist	Joey Dee & the Starliters	34	2
12/27/63	1/31/64	Hey Little Cobra	Rip Chords	4	9
11/8/63	11/8/63	Hey Little Girl	Major Lance	20	4
12/9/61	1/6/62	Hey! Little Girl	Del Shannon	19	5
10/4/63	10/25/63	Hey Lover	Debbie Dovale	11	7
4/10/64	4/17/64	Hey, Mr. Sax Man	Boots Randolph	36	3
12/29/62	1/25/63	Hey Paula	Paul & Paula	1	11
12/29/69	2/2/70	Hey There Lonely Girl	Eddie Holman	3	13
9/30/68	10/28/68	Hey, Western Union Man	Jerry Butler	17	6
6/12/64	7/17/64	Hickory, Dick And Doc	Bobby Vee	18	6
10/6/62	10/6/62	Hide & Go Seek, Part 1	Bunker Hill	33	1
2/4/66	2/11/66	Hide & Seek	Sheep	38	2
4/14/62	4/14/62	Hide 'Nor Hair	Ray Charles	40	1
10/1/65	10/1/65	High Heel Sneakers	Stevie Wonder	35	1
9/15/67	9/29/67	(Your Love Keeps Lifting Me) Higher And Higher	Jackie Wilson	20	5
10/7/68	11/4/68	Hi-Heel Sneakers	Jose Feliciano	20	6
1/31/64	2/21/64	Hi-Heel Sneakers	Tommy Tucker	12	6
4/21/67	5/26/67	Him Or Me- What's It Gonna Be	Paul Revere & the Raiders	4	9
3/10/67	4/7/67	Hippy Dippy Weatherman	George Carlin	17	7
3/6/64	3/27/64	Hippy Hippy Shake	Swinging Blue Jeans	13	5
4/15/66	4/15/66	History Repeats Itself	Buddy Starcher	18	5
6/2/62	6/9/62	Hit Record	Brook Benton	33	2
9/16/61	10/21/61	Hit The Road Jack	Ray Charles	4	8
2/22/63	3/1/63	Hitch Hike	Marvin Gaye	36	2
7/8/68	7/29/68	Hitch It To The Horse	Fantastic Johnny C	32	4
7/23/65	8/27/65	Hold Me, Thrill Me, Kiss Me	Mel Carter	4	9
10/14/68	11/18/68	Hold Me Tight	Johnny Nash	5	8

Debut	Peak	Title	Artist	Pos	Wks
6/16/67	7/7/67	Hold On	Mauds	15	8
1/22/65	1/29/65	Hold What You've Got	Joe Tex	33	2
11/5/65	11/12/65	Hole In The Wall	Packers	36	2
10/27/67	10/27/67	Holiday	Bee Gees	36	1
10/13/69	11/17/69	Holly Holy	Neil Diamond	2	14
10/15/65	10/15/65	Home Of The Brave	Jody Miller	37	1
2/4/66	2/25/66	Homeward Bound	Simon & Garfunkel	8	7
3/18/68	4/8/68	Honey	Bobby Goldsboro	1	10
12/1/67	12/29/67	Honey Chile	Martha & the Vandellas	20	5
7/14/69	7/28/69	Honky Tonk Women	Rolling Stones	1	11
9/20/63	10/4/63	Honolulu Lulu	Jan & Dean	6	6
1/14/61	1/28/61	Hoochi Coochi Coo, The	Hank Ballard & the Midnighters	23	3
12/2/68	1/20/69	Hooked On A Feeling	B. J. Thomas	5	12
9/23/66	10/28/66	Hooray For Hazel	Tommy Roe	4	9
6/14/63	7/12/63	Hootenanny	Glencoves	14	7
7/19/63	8/9/63	Hopeless	Andy Williams	22	4
5/27/68	7/1/68	Horse, The	Cliff Nobles & Co.	4	10
9/8/69	10/20/69	Hot Fun In The Summertime	Sly & the Family Stone	3	10
4/26/63	5/17/63	Hot Pastrami	Dartells	10	5
10/14/60	10/14/60	Hot Rod Lincoln	Johnny Bond	7	1
2/17/69	3/24/69	Hot Smoke & Sasafrass	Bubble Puppy	6	8
12/1/62	12/1/62	Hotel Happiness	Brook Benton	35	1
8/28/64	8/28/64	House Is Not A Home, A	Dionne Warwick	39	3
8/14/64	9/11/64	House Of The Rising Sun, The	Animals	1	9
8/12/68	8/26/68	House That Jack Built, The	Aretha Franklin	16	5
8/27/65	8/27/65	Houston	Dean Martin	40	1
9/15/67	10/13/67	How Can I Be Sure	Young Rascals	3	9
3/1/63	3/15/63	How Can I Forget	Jimmy Holiday	21	4
1/20/67	2/10/67	How Do You Catch A Girl	Sam the Sham & the Pharaohs	21	5
7/17/64	8/21/64	How Do You Do It	Gerry & the Pacemakers	6	8
4/15/66	5/13/66	How Does That Grab You, Darlin'	Nancy Sinatra	11	6
7/17/64	8/7/64	(You Don't Know) How Glad I Am	Nancy Wilson	27	3
5/26/62	5/26/62	How Is Julie	Lettermen	31	2
7/19/63	8/9/63	How Many Teardrops	Lou Christie	19	4
6/24/61	6/24/61	How Many Tears	Bobby Vee	31	4
1/12/63	1/12/63	How Much Is That Doggie In The Window	Patti Page	40	1
1/1/65	1/1/65	How Sweet It Is (To Be Loved By You)	Marvin Gaye	18	3

Debut	Peak	Title	Artist	Pos	Wks
7/22/68	7/22/68	How Sweet It Is, Montage From	Love Generation	39	2
12/10/60	12/10/60	How To Handle A Woman	Johnny Mathis	39	1
5/6/68	6/24/68	How'd We Ever Get This Way	Andy Kim	3	10
10/29/60	11/19/60	Hucklebuck, The	Chubby Checker	6	9
9/8/62	9/29/62	Hully Gully Baby	Dovells	10	5
3/31/62	4/28/62	Hully Gully Callin' Time	Jive Five	27	4
12/17/60	12/31/60	Hully Gully Twist, (Let's Do) The	Bill Doggett	31	5
4/8/61	5/6/61	Hundred Pounds Of Clay, A	Gene McDaniels	10	9
7/16/65	7/23/65	Hung On You	Righteous Brothers	31	2
6/17/66	7/22/66	Hungry	Paul Revere & the Raiders	3	11
10/8/65	10/15/65	Hungry For Love	Sam Remo	20	3
2/24/67	3/3/67	Hunter Gets Captured By The Game, The	Marvelettes	29	3
7/1/68	7/29/68	Hurdy Gurdy Man	Donovan	6	8
10/29/60	11/19/60	Hurricane	Dave "Baby" Cortez	18	5
7/29/61	8/12/61	Hurt	Timi Yuro	10	6
7/14/69	8/18/69	Hurt So Bad	Lettermen	2	13
3/5/65	3/12/65	Hurt So Bad	Little Anthony & the Imperials	26	5
2/25/66	2/25/66	Husbands And Wives	Roger Miller	31	2
8/26/68	9/23/68	Hush	Deep Purple	5	8
9/22/67	11/10/67	Hush	Billy Joe Royal	5	9
5/28/65	6/11/65	Hush, Hush, Sweet Charlotte	Patti Page	13	7
6/23/69	6/30/69	Hushabye	Jay & the Americans	38	3
11/5/60	11/12/60	Hushabye Little Guitar	Paul Evans	23	2
8/2/63	8/2/63	I (Who Have Nothing)	Ben E. King	32	2
10/11/63	11/8/63	I Adore Him	Angels	8	7
12/24/65	1/14/66	I Ain't Gonna Eat Out My Heart Anymore	Young Rascals	21	5
4/29/66	6/10/66	I Am A Rock	Simon & Garfunkel	3	9
7/10/64	7/31/64	I Believe	Bachelors	15	4
6/3/66	7/1/66	I Call Your Name	Buckinghams	14	6
3/17/69	4/21/69	I Can Hear Music	Beach Boys	11	9
9/23/66	11/11/66	I Can Make It With You	Pozo-Seco Singers	17	9
11/12/65	12/3/65	I Can Never Go Home Anymore	Shangri-Las	6	6
11/10/67	12/8/67	I Can See For Miles	Who	5	6
6/9/69	6/23/69	I Can Sing A Rainbow/Love Is Blue	Dells	28	3

Debut	Peak	Title	Artist	Pos	Wks
12/29/67	2/12/68	I Can Take Or Leave Your Loving	Herman's Hermits	22	7
3/20/64	3/20/64	I Can't Dance	Allan Sherman	39	1
8/18/69	10/6/69	I Can't Get Next To You	Temptations	2	14
4/15/68	4/15/68	I Can't Get You Out Of My Mind	Paul Anka	37	1
4/1/66	4/1/66	I Can't Grow Peaches On A Cherry Tree	Just Us	36	1
10/20/62	11/17/62	I Can't Help It (If I'm Still In Love With You)	Johnny Tillotson	20	4
5/21/65	6/25/65	I Can't Help Myself	Four Tops	1	11
3/4/66	4/15/66	I Can't Let Go	Hollies	11	8
5/20/68	5/27/68	I Can't Make It Alone	Bill Medley	37	2
3/27/64	3/27/64	I Can't Stand It	Soul Sisters	32	1
9/27/63	10/25/63	I Can't Stay Mad At You	Skeeter Davis	5	9
8/5/68	8/26/68	I Can't Stop Dancing	Archie Bell & the Drells	11	6
5/12/62	5/26/62	I Can't Stop Loving You	Ray Charles	1	10
1/10/64	1/17/64	I Can't Stop Talking About You	Steve Lawrence & Eydie Gorme	26	2
5/7/65	5/7/65	I Can't Stop Thinking Of You	Bobbi Martin	36	1
11/25/68	12/23/68	I Can't Turn You Loose	Chambers Brothers	16	6
12/17/65	2/4/66	I Confess	New Colony Six	2	10
4/28/69	5/26/69	I Could Never Lie To You	New Colony Six	7	8
5/6/68	6/24/68	I Could Never Love Another (After Loving You)	Temptations	13	8
7/22/66	8/12/66	I Couldn't Live Without Your Love	Petula Clark	3	6
1/14/61	2/4/61	I Count The Tears	Drifters	14	5
8/18/67	9/29/67	I Dig Rock And Roll Music	Peter, Paul & Mary	14	7
5/7/65	5/7/65	I Do Love You	Billy Stewart	35	2
7/17/64	7/24/64	I Don't Believe It	Angello's Angels	33	2
9/18/64	10/2/64	I Don't Care (Just As Long As You Love Me)	Buck Owens	28	2
12/9/61	12/30/61	I Don't Know Why	Linda Scott	7	7
5/29/64	6/5/64	I Don't Wanna Be A Loser	Lesley Gore	35	3
3/18/61	3/25/61	I Don't Want To Cry	Chuck Jackson	28	3
4/24/64	5/8/64	I Don't Want To Be Hurt Anymore	Nat "King" Cole	28	3
8/6/65	8/20/65	I Don't Want To Lose You Baby	Chad & Jeremy	27	3
2/26/68	3/4/68	I Don't Want To Love You	Barry Lee Show	28	4
10/2/64	11/6/64	I Don't Want To See You Again	Peter & Gordon	18	5

Debut	Peak	Title	Artist	Pos	Wks
2/12/65	2/26/65	I Don't Want To Spoil The Party	Beatles	1	9
8/26/61	8/26/61	I Don't Want To Take A Chance	Mary Wells	37	1
6/24/61	7/15/61	I Dreamed Of A Hill-Billy Heaven	Tex Ritter	7	7
8/5/61	9/2/61	I Fall To Pieces	Patsy Cline	17	5
11/27/64	12/18/64	I Feel Fine	Beatles	1	9
5/27/61	6/10/61	I Feel So Bad	Elvis Presley	15	4
1/7/66	2/11/66	I Fought The Law	Bobby Fuller Four	4	9
11/12/65	12/3/65	I Found A Girl	Jan & Dean	9	7
5/29/64	7/3/64	I Get Around	Beach Boys	1	11
1/15/65	2/12/65	I Go To Pieces	Peter & Gordon	5	8
1/20/69	2/24/69	I Got A Line On You	Spirit	7	8
11/22/63	11/29/63	I Got A Woman	Freddie Scott	23	3
2/22/63	3/8/63	I Got Burned	Ral Donner	17	4
4/28/67	5/19/67	I Got Rhythm	Happenings	2	9
3/18/68	4/29/68	I Got The Feelin'	James Brown	6	8
11/4/66	12/9/66	I Got The Feelin' (Oh No No)	Neil Diamond	19	8
3/22/63	3/29/63	I Got What I Wanted	Brook Benton	34	2
11/19/65	12/24/65	I Got You (I Feel Good)	James Brown	21	6
7/23/65	8/13/65	I Got You Babe	Sonny & Cher	1	12
8/18/67	9/8/67	I Had A Dream	Paul Revere & the Raiders	8	6
12/16/66	2/10/67	I Had Too Much To Dream (Last Night)	Electric Prunes	6	11
12/20/63	1/10/64	I Have A Boyfriend	Chiffons	21	6
10/29/65	11/26/65	I Hear A Symphony	Supremes	3	8
4/1/66	4/29/66	I Hear Trumpets Blow	Tokens	20	6
12/23/61	1/6/62	I Hear You Knocking	Fats Domino	34	3
11/18/68	12/9/68	I Heard It Through The Grapevine	Marvin Gaye	1	13
11/24/67	12/29/67	I Heard It Through The Grapevine	Gladys Knight & the Pips	9	8
12/4/64	12/11/64	I Just Can't Say Goodbye	Bobby Rydell	25	2
9/25/64	10/2/64	I Just Don't Understand	Tommy Adderly	21	4
8/5/61	9/2/61	I Just Don't Understand	Ann-Margret	12	6
9/15/62	9/15/62	I Keep Forgettin'	Chuck Jackson	37	1
10/1/65	10/22/65	I Knew You When	Billy Joe Royal	20	5
7/26/63	8/2/63	I Know	Ronnie Rice	36	2
12/2/61	1/27/62	I Know (You Don't Love Me No More)	Barbara George	9	10
3/26/65	4/16/65	I Know A Place	Petula Clark	2	8
4/29/66	5/13/66	I Know You Better Than That	Bobby Goldsboro	28	4

164 • Chicago Top 40 Charts 1960-1969

Debut	Peak	Title	Artist	Pos	Wks
3/25/66	4/8/66	I Lie Awake	New Colony Six	20	7
10/9/64	10/9/64	I Like It	Gerry & the Pacemakers	22	2
7/2/65	7/23/65	I Like It Like That	Dave Clark Five	7	8
8/7/64	8/21/64	I Like It Like That	Miracles	32	4
6/24/61	7/29/61	I Like It Like That, Part 1	Chris Kenner	8	8
6/16/67	7/14/67	I Like The Way	Tommy James & the Shondells	13	8
8/27/65	9/10/65	I Live For The Sun	Sunrays	28	4
11/10/62	11/24/62	I Lost My Baby	Joey Dee	28	3
9/30/61	11/18/61	I Love How You Love Me	Paris Sisters	2	9
11/4/68	12/16/68	I Love How You Love Me	Bobby Vinton	2	13
7/1/66	7/22/66	I Love Onions	Susan Christie	30	5
5/20/68	7/1/68	I Love You	People	2	9
5/12/62	6/9/62	I Love You	Volumes	7	6
4/19/63	5/17/63	I Love You Because	Al Martino	5	6
10/14/60	10/14/60	I Love You In The Same Old Way	Paul Anka	28	1
2/7/64	2/28/64	I Love You More And More Every Day	Al Martino	8	8
7/28/62	8/18/62	I Love You The Way You Are	Bobby Vinton	3	8
8/25/67	9/29/67	I Make A Fool Of Myself	Frankie Valli	10	8
12/1/62	12/8/62	I May Not Live To See Tomorrow	Brian Hyland	32	2
9/2/68	9/30/68	I Met Her In Church	Box Tops	23	5
10/15/65	10/22/65	I Miss You So	Little Anthony & the Imperials	29	4
3/5/65	3/5/65	I Must Be Seeing Things	Gene Pitney	25	3
11/26/60	12/3/60	I Need A Change	Miracles	30	2
5/27/68	7/8/68	I Need Love	Third Booth	2	10
12/9/66	12/23/66	I Need Somebody	? & the Mysterians	33	3
10/29/60	10/29/60	I Need You	Patti Page	17	2
7/7/62	7/28/62	I Need Your Loving	Don Gardner & Dee Dee Ford	27	5
5/8/64	5/15/64	I Only Have Eyes For You	Cliff Richard	19	4
3/25/61	3/25/61	I Pity The Fool	Bobby Bland	35	1
9/9/66	9/30/66	I Really Don't Want To Know	Ronnie Dove	24	4
9/16/61	10/7/61	I Really Love You So	Stories	17	6
8/25/62	9/15/62	I Remember You	Frank Ifield	8	6
5/22/64	6/19/64	I Rise, I Fall	Johnny Tillotson	22	5
6/24/66	7/29/66	I Saw Her Again	Mamas & the Papas	3	8
2/21/64	3/6/64	I Saw Her Standing There	Beatles	4	7
12/15/62	1/4/63	I Saw Linda Yesterday	Dickey Lee	6	8
8/12/68	9/16/68	I Say A Little Prayer	Aretha Franklin	8	8

Debut	Peak	Title	Artist	Pos	Wks
11/3/67	12/8/67	I Say A Little Prayer	Dionne Warwick	11	8
11/10/67	12/15/67	I Second That Emotion	Smokey Robinson & the Miracles	8	10
1/7/66	2/11/66	I See The Light	Five Americans	16	7
7/10/64	7/31/64	I Should Have Known Better	Beatles	1	6
4/28/62	5/26/62	I Sold My Heart To The Junkman	Blue-Belles	8	6
12/23/68	2/3/69	I Started A Joke	Bee Gees	6	10
12/29/69	1/5/70	I Started Loving You Again	Al Martino	38	2
9/10/65	9/24/65	I Still Love You	Vejtables	23	3
7/21/67	8/4/67	I Take It Back	Sandy Posey	23	4
7/28/67	8/25/67	I Thank The Lord For The Night Time	Neil Diamond	6	8
1/22/68	3/11/68	I Thank You	Sam & Dave	14	8
2/3/67	2/24/67	I Think We're Alone Now	Tommy James & the Shondells	1	10
6/16/69	6/30/69	I Turned You On	Isley Brothers	35	3
4/9/65	4/16/65	I Understand (Just How You Feel)	Freddie & the Dreamers	24	3
10/21/61	12/2/61	I Understand (Just How You Feel)	G-Clefs	4	10
5/15/64	6/5/64	I Understand Them	Patty Cakes	14	5
9/23/61	9/23/61	I Wake Up Crying	Chuck Jackson	37	1
1/19/63	2/15/63	I Wanna Be Around	Tony Bennett	14	7
4/22/68	6/3/68	I Wanna Live	Glen Campbell	19	7
6/26/64	8/7/64	I Wanna Love Him So Bad	Jelly Beans	6	8
10/21/66	12/2/66	I Wanna Meet You	Cryan' Shames	6	8
11/11/61	12/2/61	I Wanna Thank You	Bobby Rydell	14	5
6/4/65	7/2/65	I Want Candy	Strangeloves	4	8
10/14/60	10/29/60	I Want To Be Wanted	Brenda Lee	7	8
2/18/66	3/4/66	I Want To Go With You	Eddy Arnold	35	3
1/17/64	1/31/64	I Want To Hold Your Hand	Beatles	1	12
3/31/62	4/14/62	I Want To Love You	Renee Roberts	19	4
8/18/67	8/25/67	I Want To Love You For What You Are	Ronnie Dove	32	2
9/6/63	10/11/63	I Want To Stay Here	Steve Lawrence & Eydie Gorme	18	6
6/24/66	7/1/66	I Want You	Bob Dylan	22	4
11/17/69	12/15/69	I Want You Back	Jackson 5	2	12
8/11/69	9/22/69	I Want You To Know	New Colony Six	11	9
4/21/67	5/19/67	I Was Kaiser Bill's Batman	Whistling Jack Smith	13	6
7/7/67	8/11/67	I Was Made To Love Her	Stevie Wonder	7	7
10/20/62	11/3/62	I Was Such A Fool (To Fall In Love With You)	Connie Francis	34	3
4/21/62	4/28/62	I Will	Vic Dana	31	2

Debut	Peak	Title	Artist	Pos	Wks
2/12/68	3/25/68	I Will Always Think About You	New Colony Six	1	11
4/5/63	4/26/63	I Will Follow Him	Little Peggy March	1	7
6/21/63	6/21/63	I Wish I Were A Princess	Little Peggy March	27	1
1/15/68	2/19/68	I Wish It Would Rain	Temptations	2	8
3/24/62	4/14/62	I Wish That We Were Married	Ronnie & the Hi-Lites	7	6
11/29/63	12/20/63	I Wish You Love	Gloria Lynne	10	7
10/28/61	11/18/61	I Wonder (If Your Love Will Ever Belong To Me)	Pentagons	18	5
12/15/67	2/5/68	I Wonder What She's Doing Tonite	Tommy Boyce & Bobby Hart	2	11
7/28/69	9/8/69	I'd Wait A Million Years	Grass Roots	5	11
7/16/65	7/23/65	I'll Always Love You	Spinners	29	4
4/16/65	5/21/65	I'll Be Doggone	Marvin Gaye	29	7
1/8/65	1/15/65	I'll Be There	Gerry & the Pacemakers	25	3
6/18/65	6/18/65	I'll Be With You In Apple Blossom Time	Wayne Newton	37	1
8/30/63	9/13/63	I'll Believe It When I See It	Sierras	23	3
7/24/64	8/21/64	I'll Cry Instead	Beatles	19	5
6/25/65	7/2/65	I'll Feel A Whole Lot Better	Byrds	30	2
3/25/66	5/6/66	I'll Go Crazy	Buckinghams	19	8
11/24/69	12/8/69	I'll Hold Out My Hand	Clique	28	4
4/1/61	5/6/61	I'll Just Have A Cup Of Coffee (Then I'll Go)	Claude Gray	18	7
7/24/64	8/7/64	I'll Keep You Satisfied	Billy J. Kramer & the Dakotas	16	5
5/27/66	5/27/66	I'll Love You Forever	Holidays	35	1
8/27/65	9/10/65	I'll Make All Your Dreams Come True	Ronnie Dove	22	6
2/28/64	3/20/64	I'll Make You Mine	Bobby Vee	15	6
6/16/62	7/21/62	I'll Never Dance Again	Bobby Rydell	7	8
7/21/69	9/1/69	I'll Never Fall In Love Again	Tom Jones	8	11
12/22/69	2/2/70	I'll Never Fall In Love Again	Dionne Warwick	6	10
3/12/65	4/23/65	I'll Never Find Another You	Seekers	9	11
8/12/61	8/26/61	I'll Never Smile Again	Platters	28	4
11/11/61	11/25/61	I'll Never Stop Wanting You	Brian Hyland	25	4
9/15/62	10/6/62	I'll Remember Carol	Tommy Boyce	9	5
11/12/60	11/19/60	I'll Save The Last Dance For You	Damita Jo	17	4
2/10/62	2/24/62	I'll See You In My Dreams	Pat Boone	26	3
2/24/67	3/10/67	I'll Take Care Of Your Cares	Frankie Laine	31	5

Debut	Peak	Title	Artist	Pos	Wks
4/14/62	5/5/62	I'll Take You Home	Corsairs	16	5
9/20/63	10/4/63	I'll Take You Home	Drifters	26	3
8/13/65	8/27/65	I'll Take You Where The Music's Playing	Drifters	19	3
6/12/64	7/3/64	I'll Touch A Star	Terry Stafford	17	5
6/30/62	6/30/62	I'll Try Something New	Miracles	37	2
3/17/69	3/31/69	I'll Try Something New	Diana Ross & the Supremes & the Temptations	23	3
12/9/66	12/30/66	I'm A Believer	Monkees	1	12
7/9/65	7/30/65	I'm A Fool	Dino, Desi & Billy	4	7
5/6/61	5/27/61	I'm A Fool To Care	Joe Barry	18	5
8/6/65	8/27/65	I'm A Happy Man	Jive Five	15	4
3/24/67	4/28/67	I'm A Man	Spencer Davis Group	22	7
11/26/65	12/31/65	I'm A Man	Yardbirds	10	6
6/24/68	7/29/68	I'm A Midnight Mover	Wilson Pickett	17	6
9/2/61	9/16/61	I'm A Telling You	Jerry Butler	29	4
7/12/63	8/16/63	I'm Afraid To Go Home	Brian Hyland	7	6
8/13/65	8/27/65	I'm Alive	Hollies	28	3
2/17/62	2/17/62	I'm Blue (The Gong-Gong Song)	Ikettes	37	1
4/8/66	4/8/66	I'm Comin' Home, Cindy	Trini Lopez	26	3
10/18/63	10/25/63	I'm Coming Back To You	Julie London	34	2
7/29/61	8/5/61	I'm Coming On Back To You	Jackie Wilson	33	2
10/9/64	10/30/64	I'm Crying	Animals	9	5
11/13/64	12/25/64	I'm Gonna Be Strong	Gene Pitney	17	7
1/4/63	1/12/63	I'm Gonna Be Warm This Winter	Connie Francis	28	3
7/15/61	8/19/61	I'm Gonna Knock On Your Door	Eddie Hodges	6	7
2/12/68	2/26/68	I'm Gonna Make You Love Me	Madeline Bell	36	3
12/2/68	1/6/69	I'm Gonna Make You Love Me	Diana Ross & the Supremes & the Temptations	1	12
8/25/69	9/29/69	I'm Gonna Make You Mine	Lou Christie	2	10
11/11/66	11/25/66	I'm Gonna Make You Mine	Shadows Of Knight	25	4
7/24/64	8/7/64	I'm Happy Just To Dance With You	Beatles	20	3
6/25/65	7/16/65	I'm Henry VIII, I Am	Herman's Hermits	2	6
10/6/62	10/20/62	I'm Here To Get My Baby Out Of Jail	Everly Brothers	31	3
10/14/68	11/11/68	I'm In A Different World	Four Tops	26	5
12/15/67	12/29/67	I'm In Love	Wilson Pickett	18	4

Debut	Peak	Title	Artist	Pos	Wks
2/8/63	3/8/63	I'm In Love Again	Rick Nelson	22	4
4/29/61	5/13/61	I'm In The Mood For Love	Chimes	27	4
12/9/68	1/6/69	I'm Into Lookin' For Someone	Bobby Vee	31	5
10/23/64	11/20/64	I'm Into Something Good	Herman's Hermits	1	12
6/23/67	7/21/67	I'm Just Waiting Anticipating For Her To Show Up	New Colony Six	14	8
9/27/63	10/11/63	I'm Leaving It Up To You	Dale & Grace	2	8
1/13/69	2/10/69	I'm Livin' In Shame	Diana Ross & the Supremes	11	8
12/16/66	12/23/66	(I Know) I'm Losing You	Temptations	20	2
5/24/63	6/21/63	I'm Movin' On	Matt Lucas	10	6
5/26/62	5/26/62	I'm No Fool Anymore	Flamingos	37	2
4/28/62	5/5/62	I'm On My Way	Highwaymen	18	3
10/28/66	11/25/66	I'm Ready For Love	Martha & the Vandellas	19	8
5/10/63	5/17/63	I'm Saving My Love	Skeeter Davis	23	3
2/25/66	4/8/66	I'm So Lonesome I Could Cry	B. J. Thomas	10	10
7/10/64	7/10/64	I'm Sorry	Pete Drake	26	3
3/12/65	4/2/65	I'm Telling You Now	Freddie & the Dreamers	1	8
9/9/61	9/16/61	I'm Thankful	Steve Alaimo	36	2
5/21/65	5/21/65	I'm The One Who Loves You	Dean Martin	40	1
11/25/66	11/25/66	(Come 'Round Here) I'm The One You Need	Miracles	37	2
8/18/62	8/18/62	I'm Tossin' & Turnin' Again	Bobby Lewis	38	1
10/13/67	11/10/67	I'm Wondering	Stevie Wonder	27	5
10/7/66	10/21/66	I'm Your Puppet	James & Bobby Purify	26	4
9/10/65	9/24/65	I'm Yours	Elvis Presley	15	4
4/14/69	5/19/69	I've Been Hurt	Bill Deal & the Rhondels	9	9
2/10/67	2/24/67	I've Been Lonely Too Long	Young Rascals	24	6
6/18/65	6/18/65	I've Been Loving You Too Long (To Stop Now)	Otis Redding	35	1
8/19/66	9/23/66	I've Been Wrong	Buckinghams	13	7
1/22/65	2/5/65	I've Got A Tiger By The Tail	Buck Owens	20	5
10/13/62	10/13/62	I've Got A Woman Part 1	Jimmy McGriff	38	2
3/10/62	3/24/62	I've Got Bonnie	Bobby Rydell	17	5
12/24/65	12/24/65	I've Got To Be Somebody	Billy Joe Royal	35	1

Debut	Peak	Title	Artist	Pos	Wks
1/6/67	1/20/67	I've Got To Have A Reason	Dave Clark Five	23	5
9/23/66	10/7/66	I've Got You Under My Skin	Four Seasons	22	5
1/20/69	2/24/69	I've Gotta Be Me	Sammy Davis, Jr.	4	10
9/9/68	10/21/68	I've Gotta Get A Message To You	Bee Gees	3	10
6/19/64	7/10/64	I've Had It	Crestones	21	4
8/26/68	9/2/68	I've Never Found A Girl (To Love Me Like You Do)	Eddie Floyd	38	2
1/13/67	1/27/67	I've Passed This Way Before	Jimmy Ruffin	31	4
4/1/61	5/13/61	I've Told Every Little Star	Linda Scott	2	9
9/16/68	9/23/68	Ice In The Sun	Status Quo	34	2
9/29/62	10/13/62	If A Man Answers	Bobby Darin	25	3
12/16/66	12/16/66	If Every Day Was Like Christmas	Elvis Presley	33	2
12/9/68	2/3/69	If I Can Dream	Elvis Presley	7	11
12/1/67	1/15/68	If I Could Build My Whole World Around You	Marvin Gaye & Tammi Terrell	11	9
4/21/62	5/5/62	If I Cried Every Time You Hurt Me	Wanda Jackson	26	3
1/21/61	1/28/61	If I Didn't Care	Platters	30	3
8/9/63	9/13/63	If I Had A Hammer	Trini Lopez	7	8
8/11/62	9/8/62	If I Had A Hammer (The Hammer Song)	Peter, Paul & Mary	2	8
2/19/65	3/12/65	If I Loved You	Chad & Jeremy	16	5
12/15/62	12/15/62	If I Never Get To Heaven	Kathy Dee	34	3
12/15/69	2/9/70	If I Never Knew Your Name	Vic Dana	7	13
2/26/65	3/26/65	If I Ruled The World	Tony Bennett	17	6
10/14/66	11/11/66	If I Were A Carpenter	Bobby Darin	16	8
5/6/68	6/10/68	If I Were A Carpenter	Four Tops	7	8
7/3/64	7/24/64	If I'm A Fool For Loving You	Bobby Wood	22	8
8/19/68	8/26/68	If Love Is In Your Heart	Friend & Lover	36	2
5/17/63	6/28/63	If My Pillow Could Talk	Connie Francis	28	4
3/4/68	4/8/68	If You Can Want	Smokey Robinson & the Miracles	16	6
12/16/66	12/23/66	If You Go Away	Damita Jo	34	2
12/30/61	1/13/62	If You Gotta Make A Fool Of Somebody	James Ray	30	3
6/18/65	7/2/65	If You Really Want Me To, I'll Go	Ron-Dels	21	4
8/27/65	8/27/65	If You Wait For Love	Bobby Goldsboro	38	1

Debut	Peak	Title	Artist	Pos	Wks
4/12/63	5/3/63	If You Wanna Be Happy	Jimmy Soul	2	9
4/2/65	5/7/65	Iko Iko	Dixie Cups	9	7
12/3/65	12/24/65	Il Silenzio	Nini Rosso	8	5
12/2/61	12/2/61	Image—Part 1	Hank Levine	37	1
12/6/63	12/13/63	Impossible Happened, The	Little Peggy March	35	3
9/16/68	10/7/68	In-A-Gadda-Da-Vida	Iron Butterfly	22	4
11/10/67	12/8/67	In And Out Of Love	Diana Ross & the Supremes	13	6
12/1/62	12/22/62	In Between Years, The	James MacArthur	9	6
1/15/65	1/29/65	'In' Crowd, The	Dobie Gray	20	6
8/6/65	9/17/65	'In' Crowd, The	Ramsey Lewis Trio	2	10
3/1/63	3/15/63	In Dreams	Roy Orbison	14	6
5/15/64	5/15/64	In My Lonely Room	Martha & the Vandellas	35	1
11/15/63	12/6/63	In My Room	Beach Boys	7	7
3/25/68	4/1/68	In Need Of A Friend	Cowsills	27	3
7/28/67	7/28/67	In The Chapel In The Moonlight	Dean Martin	40	1
5/12/69	6/2/69	In The Ghetto	Elvis Presley	4	8
11/4/61	11/25/61	In The Middle Of A Heartache	Wanda Jackson	21	5
3/31/67	5/19/67	In The Midnight Hour	Michael & the Messengers	5	10
3/11/68	3/11/68	In The Midnight Hour	Mirettes	39	1
9/10/65	9/17/65	In The Midnight Hour	Wilson Pickett	33	2
7/17/64	8/14/64	In The Misty Moonlight	Jerry Wallace	11	7
2/24/69	3/10/69	In The Still Of The Night	Paul Anka	31	5
1/10/64	1/17/64	In The Still Of The Night	Reflections	16	4
6/23/69	7/14/69	In The Year 2525 (Exordium & Terminus)	Zager & Evans	1	10
8/5/61	8/5/61	In Time	Steve Lawrence	29	1
9/29/67	11/10/67	Incense And Peppermints	Strawberry Alarm Clock	2	11
2/3/67	2/17/67	Indescribably Blue	Elvis Presley	25	4
1/27/69	3/10/69	Indian Giver	1910 Fruitgum Co.	5	10
6/3/68	7/15/68	Indian Lake	Cowsills	5	11
8/19/68	9/23/68	(The Lament Of The Cherokee) Indian Reservation	Don Fardon	6	8
8/5/66	8/12/66	Indication	Zombies	27	3
10/8/65	10/22/65	Inky Dinky Spider (The Spider Song)	Kids Next Door	28	3
3/11/68	3/25/68	Inner Light, The	Beatles	2	3
3/25/66	3/25/66	Inside- Looking Out	Animals	26	3
9/11/64	9/11/64	Invasion, The	Buchanan & Greenfield	22	1
4/3/64	4/10/64	Invisible Tears	Ned Miller	32	3
1/6/62	1/27/62	Irresistible You	Bobby Darin	12	6
9/29/69	10/20/69	Is That All There Is	Peggy Lee	16	6
3/29/63	4/19/63	Island Of Dreams	Springfields	14	4

Debut	Peak	Title	Artist	Pos	Wks
5/19/69	6/30/69	Israelites	Desmond Dekker & the Aces	4	10
8/6/65	9/10/65	It Ain't Me, Babe	Turtles	6	10
7/7/67	8/4/67	It Could Be We're In Love	Cryan' Shames	1	12
11/25/61	11/25/61	It Do Me So Good	Ann-Margret	34	1
6/18/65	7/23/65	It Feels So Right	Elvis Presley	22	5
8/28/64	9/25/64	It Hurts To Be In Love	Gene Pitney	6	9
9/13/63	9/13/63	It Hurts To Be Sixteen	Andrea Carroll	39	1
7/16/65	7/16/65	It Just Happened That Way	Roger Miller	31	4
6/24/61	7/8/61	It Keeps Rainin'	Fats Domino	16	5
5/12/62	6/16/62	It Keeps Right On A-Hurtin'	Johnny Tillotson	10	8
9/1/62	9/22/62	It Might As Well Rain Until September	Carole King	13	5
9/22/67	11/10/67	It Must Be Him	Vikki Carr	6	10
1/14/66	2/11/66	It Was A Very Good Year	Frank Sinatra	22	5
12/30/61	2/17/62	It Will Stand	Showmen	6	9
9/10/65	9/17/65	It's A Man Down There	G.L. Crockett	34	2
2/7/64	3/27/64	It's All In The Game	Cliff Richard	7	10
8/21/64	9/11/64	It's All Over Now	Rolling Stones	16	6
9/27/63	11/8/63	It's All Right	Impressions	17	7
1/29/65	2/12/65	It's Alright	Adam Faith	11	6
6/16/67	6/30/67	It's Cold Outside	Choir	25	5
4/16/65	5/7/65	It's Gonna Be Alright	Gerry & the Pacemakers	7	5
8/20/65	9/3/65	It's Gonna Take A Miracle	Royalettes	15	3
8/26/61	9/9/61	It's Gonna Work Out Fine	Ike & Tina Turner	30	3
12/10/65	1/14/66	It's Good News Week	Hedgehoppers Anonymous	3	7
5/7/65	5/7/65	It's Got The Whole World Shakin'	Sam Cooke	38	1
2/5/65	2/12/65	It's Gotta Last Forever	Billy J. Kramer & the Dakotas	35	2
5/7/65	5/7/65	It's Growing	Temptations	32	2
10/7/61	10/7/61	It's Just A House Without You	Brook Benton	23	1
6/25/65	7/23/65	It's Just A Little Bit Too Late	Wayne Fontana & the Mindbenders	20	5
11/26/65	1/7/66	It's My Life	Animals	10	9
5/3/63	5/24/63	It's My Party	Lesley Gore	1	8
6/3/68	6/24/68	It's Nice To Be With You	Monkees	21	4
5/7/65	5/28/65	It's Not Unusual	Tom Jones	3	8
10/14/60	10/14/60	It's Now Or Never	Elvis Presley	5	2
12/23/66	1/27/67	It's Now Winter's Day	Tommy Roe	14	9
10/28/66	11/25/66	It's Only Love	Tommy James & the Shondells	11	8
4/14/69	4/21/69	It's Only Love	B. J. Thomas	29	4
4/24/64	5/29/64	It's Over	Roy Orbison	9	8
5/6/66	5/27/66	It's Over	Jimmie Rodgers	24	6

Debut	Peak	Title	Artist	Pos	Wks
7/28/67	7/28/67	It's The Little Things	Sonny & Cher	39	1
7/23/65	8/6/65	It's The Same Old Song	Four Tops	6	5
2/25/66	3/18/66	It's Too Late	Bobby Goldsboro	37	4
12/22/62	1/12/63	It's Up To You	Rick Nelson	12	7
12/1/67	12/29/67	It's Wonderful	Young Rascals	12	8
10/6/67	10/27/67	(Loneliness Made Me Realize) It's You That I Need	Temptations	28	5
3/10/69	4/14/69	It's Your Thing	Isley Brothers	1	11
10/14/61	11/11/61	It's Your World	Marty Robbins	11	6
1/15/68	2/12/68	Itchycoo Park	Small Faces	11	6
5/5/62	5/19/62	Itty Bitty Pieces	James Ray	32	3
9/22/69	10/20/69	Jack And Jill	Tommy Roe	24	5
6/23/67	7/7/67	Jackson	Nancy Sinatra & Lee Hazelwood	26	6
11/19/60	11/19/80	Jaguar And Thunderbird	Chuck Berry	39	1
11/17/69	1/5/70	Jam Up And Jelly Tight	Tommy Roe	5	13
3/31/62	4/21/62	Jam, The—Part 1	Bobby Gregg & his Friends	26	4
12/9/61	12/9/61	Jambalaya (On The Bayou)	Fats Domino	38	1
10/13/62	10/27/62	James (Hold The Ladder Steady)	Sue Thompson	29	3
10/2/64	10/23/64	James Bond Theme, The	Billy Strange	11	5
1/27/62	2/24/62	Jamie	Eddie Holland	24	5
5/5/62	5/26/62	Jane, Jane, Jane	Kingston Trio	25	4
1/25/63	2/22/63	Java	Floyd Cramer	22	5
1/10/64	1/17/64	Java	Al Hirt	10	7
2/12/68	2/26/68	Jealous Love	Wilson Pickett	25	3
8/25/69	10/13/69	Jean	Oliver	3	12
5/13/68	6/3/68	Jelly Jungle (Of Orange Marmalade)	Lemon Pipers	29	4
4/15/68	5/6/68	Jennifer Eccles	Hollies	15	6
3/11/68	4/15/68	Jennifer Juniper	Donovan	13	8
1/7/66	2/4/66	Jenny Take A Ride!	Mitch Ryder & the Detroit Wheels	18	7
9/30/61	9/30/61	Jeremiah Peabody's Poly Unsaturated Green And Purple Pills	Ray Stevens	36	2
6/4/65	6/18/65	Jerk It	Gypsies	33	3
1/8/65	1/15/65	Jerk, The	Larks	33	2
9/15/69	10/13/69	Jesus Is A Soul Man	Lawrence Reynolds	11	7
8/11/67	8/11/67	Jill	Gary Lewis & the Playboys	37	1

Debut	Peak	Title	Artist	Pos	Wks
6/24/61	7/22/61	Jimmy Love	Cathy Carroll	11	7
3/24/67	4/28/67	Jimmy Mack	Martha & the Vandellas	11	7
2/11/61	3/11/61	Jimmy's Girl	Johnny Tillotson	4	8
12/1/69	1/5/70	Jingle Jangle	Archies	8	9
7/28/62	8/11/62	Jivin' Around	Al Casey Combo	20	4
3/10/62	3/24/62	Johnny Angel	Shelley Fabares	1	10
6/23/62	7/28/62	Johnny Get Angry	Joanie Sommers	3	8
3/17/62	4/14/62	Johnny Jingo	Hayley Mills	18	5
6/30/62	7/21/62	Johnny Loves Me	Shelley Fabares	16	4
3/10/69	3/31/69	Johnny One Time	Brenda Lee	31	4
12/23/61	1/20/62	Johnny Will	Pat Boone	21	5
9/9/61	10/7/61	Johnny Willow	Fred Darian	14	5
8/19/66	9/16/66	Joker Went Wild, The	Brian Hyland	8	9
6/2/67	6/2/67	Jokers, The	Peter & Gordon	37	2
6/5/64	6/5/64	Jose He Say	Linda Laurie	26	2
7/15/68	8/26/68	Journey To The Center Of The Mind	Amboy Dukes	5	8
7/23/65	7/23/65	Ju Ju Hand	Sam the Sham & the Pharaohs	37	2
11/24/67	12/22/67	Judy In Disguise (With Glasses)	John Fred & his Playboy Band	1	12
7/19/63	8/16/63	Judy's Turn To Cry	Lesley Gore	6	7
8/26/66	9/16/66	Jug Band Music	Mugwumps	20	5
9/30/61	9/30/61	Juke Box Saturday Night	Nino & the Ebb Tides	38	1
6/17/68	7/1/68	Jumpin' Jack Flash	Rolling Stones	1	11
6/3/61	6/17/61	Jura (I Swear I Love You)	Les Paul & Mary Ford	28	3
5/7/65	6/11/65	Just A Little	Beau Brummels	6	8
11/26/65	12/3/65	Just A Little Bit	Roy Head	31	2
9/17/65	10/22/65	Just A Little Bit Better	Herman's Hermits	2	9
12/22/67	1/22/68	Just As Much As Ever	Bobby Vinton	13	7
7/3/64	7/17/64	Just Be True	Gene Chandler	24	5
11/11/61	11/11/61	Just Because	McGuire Sisters	39	1
2/5/68	3/11/68	Just Dropped In (To See What Condition My Condition Was In)	First Edition	4	8
4/1/61	5/13/61	Just For Old Time's Sake	McGuire Sisters	10	8
9/9/66	9/16/66	Just Like A Woman	Bob Dylan	37	3
11/26/65	12/24/65	Just Like Me	Paul Revere & the Raiders	9	9
4/23/65	6/4/65	Just Once In My Life	Righteous Brothers	11	8
6/28/63	7/12/63	Just One Look	Doris Troy	26	3
12/2/66	1/6/67	Just One Smile	Gene Pitney	10	7
10/21/61	12/2/61	Just Out Of Reach (Of My Two Open Arms)	Solomon Burke	6	9
8/20/65	9/17/65	Just You	Sonny & Cher	19	7
12/20/63	1/10/64	Kansas City	Trini Lopez	31	4
9/10/65	9/24/65	Kansas City Star	Roger Miller	36	3
8/4/69	9/1/69	Keem-O-Sabe	Electric Indian	13	7
11/15/63	11/15/63	Keep An Eye On Her	Jaynetts	35	2

Debut	Peak	Title	Artist	Pos	Wks
10/8/65	11/12/65	Keep On Dancing	Gentrys	1	11
10/14/68	10/21/68	Keep On Lovin' Me Honey	Marvin Gaye & Tammi Terrell	34	3
7/24/64	8/7/64	Keep On Pushing	Impressions	31	3
12/25/64	1/22/65	Keep Searchin' (We'll Follow The Sun)	Del Shannon	4	7
12/1/67	12/1/67	Keep The Ball Rollin'	Jay & the Techniques	26	2
8/19/68	8/26/68	Keep The One You Got	Joe Tex	37	2
11/10/62	11/17/62	Keep Your Hands Off My Baby	Little Eva	30	2
5/31/63	6/28/63	Kentucky	Bob Moore	14	6
11/17/62	12/8/62	Kentucky Means Paradise	Glen Campbell	16	5
11/18/68	12/16/68	Kentucky Woman	Deep Purple	25	5
10/13/67	11/17/67	Kentucky Woman	Neil Diamond	16	6
7/12/63	7/12/63	Key To My Heart, The	Taffys	39	1
3/11/66	4/8/66	Kicks	Paul Revere & the Raiders	1	13
4/22/66	5/20/66	Killer Joe	Kingsmen	20	7
5/3/63	5/24/63	Killer Joe	Rocky Fellers	22	4
11/18/66	12/16/66	Kind Of A Drag	Buckinghams	2	12
8/9/63	9/6/63	Kind Of Boy You Can't Forget, The	Raindrops	4	7
2/5/65	3/5/65	King Of The Road	Roger Miller	3	10
9/22/62	10/6/62	King Of The Whole Wide World	Elvis Presley	23	3
12/25/64	1/29/65	Kiss And Run	Bobby Skel	6	8
11/5/65	11/26/65	Kiss Away	Ronnie Dove	18	5
2/12/68	3/11/68	Kiss Me Goodbye	Petula Clark	7	9
4/10/64	4/24/64	Kiss Me Sailor	Diane Renay	18	3
3/6/64	3/20/64	Kissin' Cousins	Elvis Presley	20	5
9/2/61	9/23/61	Kissin' On The Phone	Paul Anka	20	5
12/23/66	1/20/67	Knight In Rusty Armor	Peter & Gordon	16	6
10/14/60	10/14/60	Kookie Little Paradise, A	Jo Ann Campbell	20	1
11/24/69	1/12/70	La La La (If I Had You)	Bobby Sherman	10	10
2/19/68	3/25/68	La- La- Means I Love You	Delfonics	6	9
3/10/67	4/7/67	Lady	Jack Jones	33	5
11/17/67	11/24/67	Lady Bird	Nancy Sinatra & Lee Hazelwood	39	2
11/4/66	11/25/66	Lady Godiva	Peter & Gordon	5	7
3/11/68	4/1/68	Lady Madonna	Beatles	1	9
6/10/68	7/15/68	Lady Willpower	Gary Puckett & the Union Gap	4	10
3/12/65	4/9/65	Land Of 1000 Dances	Cannibal & the Headhunters	5	7

Debut	Peak	Title	Artist	Pos	Wks
6/14/63	7/12/63	Land Of 1000 Dances	Chris Kenner	22	5
8/5/66	8/19/66	Land Of 1000 Dances	Wilson Pickett	19	5
5/27/66	7/8/66	Land Of Milk & Honey, The	Vogues	18	8
3/25/66	4/8/66	Lara's Theme From "Dr. Zhivago"	Roger Williams	23	5
5/21/65	6/4/65	Last Chance To Turn Around	Gene Pitney	28	3
11/26/60	12/24/60	Last Date	Floyd Cramer	10	9
8/28/64	9/18/64	Last Kiss	J. Frank Wilson & the Cavaliers	3	11
4/19/63	5/17/63	Last Leaf, The	Cascades	14	5
7/22/61	8/5/61	Last Night	Mar-Keys	14	6
10/14/60	10/14/60	Last One To Know, The	Fleetwoods	19	1
6/24/66	7/15/66	Last Time Around	Del-Vetts	26	6
4/9/65	5/14/65	Last Time, The	Rolling Stones	4	9
9/16/66	10/21/66	Last Train To Clarksville	Monkees	1	11
9/29/67	10/20/67	Last Waltz, The	Engelbert Humperdinck	18	6
3/3/67	3/10/67	Laudy Miss Clawdy	Buckinghams	27	5
8/27/65	9/17/65	Laugh At Me	Sonny	12	6
1/29/65	2/26/65	Laugh Laugh	Beau Brummels	4	9
7/7/69	8/11/69	Laughing	Guess Who	12	8
6/11/65	7/16/65	Laurie (Strange Things Happen)	Dickey Lee	8	7
5/22/64	6/5/64	Lavender Sax	Clifford Scott	32	3
2/22/63	3/8/63	Lawrence Of Arabia, Theme From	Ferrante & Teicher	27	3
8/4/69	8/18/69	Lay Lady Lay	Bob Dylan	4	9
11/17/67	12/1/67	Lazy Day	Spanky & Our Gang	33	3
7/3/64	7/17/64	Lazy Elsie Molly	Chubby Checker	33	3
2/25/61	3/25/61	Lazy River	Bobby Darin	9	8
12/11/64	12/25/64	Leader Of The Laundromat	Detergents	7	3
10/16/64	11/6/64	Leader Of The Pack	Shangri-Las	1	8
4/8/66	5/6/66	Leaning On The Lamp Post	Herman's Hermits	9	7
10/13/69	12/1/69	Leaving On A Jet Plane	Peter, Paul & Mary	4	15
1/29/65	2/12/65	Lemon Tree	Trini Lopez	27	4
6/2/62	6/23/62	Lemon Tree	Peter, Paul & Mary	17	4
1/29/65	1/29/65	Leroy	Norma Tracy	35	2
11/25/68	12/2/68	Les Bicyclettes De Belsize	Engelbert Humperdinck	31	2
9/11/64	9/18/64	Let It Be Me	Jerry Butler & Betty Everett	27	2
9/15/67	10/20/67	Let It Out (Let It All Hang Out)	Hombres	2	10
5/12/69	6/16/69	Let Me	Paul Revere & the Raiders	4	11
11/19/65	12/3/65	Let Me Be	Turtles	33	3

Debut	Peak	Title	Artist	Pos	Wks
7/29/61	8/19/61	Let Me Belong To You	Brian Hyland	2	9
1/25/63	2/8/63	Let Me Go The Right Way	Supremes	23	3
1/27/62	3/10/62	Let Me In	Sensations	6	9
8/12/61	9/16/61	Let The Four Winds Blow	Fats Domino	14	7
8/11/67	8/11/67	Let The Good Times Roll & Feel So Good	Bunny Sigler	35	1
12/8/67	12/22/67	Let The Heartaches Begin	Long John Baldry	27	3
7/8/61	7/22/61	Let The Sunshine In	Teddy Randazzo	28	3
11/4/61	12/2/61	Let There Be Drums	Sandy Nelson	1	13
10/14/61	10/21/61	Let True Love Begin	Nat "King" Cole	30	2
6/17/68	7/8/68	Let Yourself Go	Elvis Presley	24	4
8/12/66	9/9/66	Let's Call It A Day Girl	Razor's Edge	21	7
9/1/62	9/29/62	Let's Dance	Chris Montez	1	9
9/23/61	10/14/61	Let's Get Together	Hayley Mills	1	9
12/10/65	12/24/65	Let's Get Together	We Five	28	3
6/7/63	6/14/63	Let's Go	Roy Hamilton	39	2
10/13/62	11/10/62	Let's Go (Pony)	Routers	7	8
10/15/60	11/12/60	Let's Go, Let's Go, Let's Go	Hank Ballard & the Midnighters	19	6
5/10/63	5/24/63	Let's Go Steady Again	Neil Sedaka	26	3
4/16/65	4/23/65	Let's Go To Hawaii	Rivieras	25	2
12/2/61	12/30/61	Let's Go Trippin'	Dick Dale & the Del-Tones	19	5
10/22/65	12/3/65	Let's Hang On	Four Seasons	1	13
4/17/64	6/5/64	Let's Have A Party	Rivieras	4	9
2/15/63	3/1/63	Let's Limbo Some More	Chubby Checker	25	3
5/19/67	6/30/67	Let's Live For Today	Grass Roots	4	11
1/8/65	1/29/65	Let's Lock The Door (And Throw Away The Key)	Jay & the Americans	4	9
4/15/66	5/13/66	Let's Start All Over Again	Ronnie Dove	29	5
10/14/60	10/15/60	Let's Think About Living	Bob Luman	9	4
2/8/63	2/22/63	Let's Turkey Trot	Little Eva	35	3
7/15/61	8/12/61	Let's Twist Again	Chubby Checker	2	8
12/27/63	2/14/64	Letter From Sherry	Dale Ward	7	9
1/13/62	2/10/62	Letter Full Of Tears	Gladys Knight & the Pips	21	6
3/27/64	3/27/64	Letter To The Beatles, A	Four Preps	35	1
2/24/69	4/7/69	Letter, The	Arbors	21	9
8/18/67	9/22/67	Letter, The	Box Tops	1	13
6/17/66	8/12/66	Lil' Red Riding Hood	Sam the Sham & the Pharaohs	4	12
9/24/65	10/22/65	Liar Liar	Castaways	7	9
5/19/62	6/2/62	(The Man Who Shot) Liberty Valence	Gene Pitney	3	8

Debut	Peak	Title	Artist	Pos	Wks
5/20/68	7/1/68	Licking Stick—Licking Stick (Part 1)	James Brown	15	7
9/8/62	9/22/62	Lie To Me	Brook Benton	31	3
1/7/66	2/4/66	Lies	Knickerbockers	6	7
7/15/61	7/22/61	Life Is But A Dream	Earls	33	2
6/23/67	8/18/67	Light My Fire	Doors	2	14
7/22/68	8/19/68	Light My Fire	Jose Feliciano	4	10
1/7/66	2/4/66	Lightnin' Strikes	Lou Christie	1	9
10/13/67	10/20/67	Lightning's Girl	Nancy Sinatra	25	3
1/14/66	1/14/66	Like A Baby	Len Barry	35	1
2/12/65	2/12/65	Like A Child	Julie Rogers	38	2
8/6/65	8/27/65	Like A Rolling Stone	Bob Dylan	7	6
4/1/61	4/15/61	Like, Long Hair	Paul Revere & the Raiders	9	6
11/26/60	12/10/60	Like Strangers	Everly Brothers	16	4
5/13/68	6/10/68	Like To Get To Know You	Spanky & Our Gang	9	6
4/21/62	6/2/62	Limbo Rock	Champs	5	9
10/6/62	11/3/62	Limbo Rock	Chubby Checker	23	5
2/15/63	3/8/63	Linda	Jan & Dean	9	7
11/25/61	12/23/61	Lion Sleeps Tonight, The	Tokens	1	11
5/28/65	6/18/65	Lipstick Traces (On A Cigarette)	O'Jays	25	4
4/21/62	5/26/62	Lipstick Traces (On A Cigarette)	Benny Spellman	10	6
6/9/62	6/16/62	Lisa	Ferrante & Teicher	28	2
8/26/68	9/2/68	Listen Here	Eddie Harris	34	2
1/21/66	2/18/66	Listen People	Herman's Hermits	3	8
11/25/61	12/16/61	Little Altar Boy	Vic Dana	19	4
11/4/68	12/9/68	Little Arrows	Leapy Lee	18	6
3/22/63	4/26/63	Little Band Of Gold	James Gilreath	9	7
1/8/65	1/15/65	Little Bell	Dixie Cups	25	3
4/5/63	4/5/63	Little Bird	Pete Jolly Trio	38	2
3/24/67	4/14/67	Little Bit Me, A Little Bit You	Monkees	1	8
8/11/67	8/11/67	Little Bit Now, A	Dave Clark Five	38	1
5/12/67	7/7/67	Little Bit O' Soul	Music Explosion	1	13
6/11/65	7/2/65	Little Bit Of Heaven, A	Ronnie Dove	16	6
8/26/61	9/16/61	Little Bit Of Soap, A	Jarmels	20	4
7/14/62	7/21/62	Little Bitty Pretty One	Clyde McPhatter	34	2
1/27/62	2/10/62	Little Bitty Tear, A	Burl Ives	7	6
9/29/62	10/20/62	Little Black Book	Jimmy Dean	18	5
6/5/64	6/12/64	Little Blue River	Melrose Elementary Band	33	2

Debut	Peak	Title	Artist	Pos	Wks
2/21/64	3/20/64	Little Boxes	Pete Seeger	25	5
1/31/64	1/31/64	Little Boy	Crystals	32	2
1/17/64	1/31/64	Little Boy, The	Tony Bennett	16	5
1/14/66	1/14/66	Little Boy (In Grown Up Clothes)	Four Seasons	37	1
3/4/61	3/18/61	Little Boy Sad	Johnny Burnette	27	3
5/8/64	6/19/64	Little Children	Billy J. Kramer & the Dakotas	1	11
9/20/63	10/4/63	Little Deuce Coupe	Beach Boys	7	5
5/27/61	6/10/61	Little Devil	Neil Sedaka	12	6
7/21/62	8/18/62	Little Diane	Dion	5	7
4/10/64	6/5/64	Little Donna	Rivieras	4	8
6/17/61	6/17/61	Little Egypt (Ying-Yang)	Coasters	37	1
5/19/67	5/19/67	Little Games	Yardbirds	28	2
6/10/66	7/1/66	Little Girl	Syndicate Of Sound	28	4
12/3/65	12/10/65	Little Girl I Once Knew, The	Beach Boys	24	4
3/25/61	4/8/61	Little Girl, Little Boy	Al Martino	27	3
3/4/68	3/4/68	Little Green Apples	Roger Miller	34	1
9/23/68	10/21/68	Little Green Apples	O. C. Smith	4	9
9/11/64	10/9/64	Little Honda	Hondells	13	7
4/2/65	5/7/65	Little Latin Lupe Lu	Chancellors	14	7
5/31/63	5/31/63	Little Latin Lupe Lu	Righteous Brothers	32	1
3/18/66	3/25/66	Little Latin Lupe Lu	Mitch Ryder & the Detroit Wheels	28	2
6/18/65	7/9/65	Little Lonely One	Tom Jones	34	4
10/7/66	10/21/66	Little Man	Sonny & Cher	19	4
7/23/65	8/27/65	Little Miss Sad	Five Emprees	3	8
3/18/61	4/8/61	Little Miss Stuck-Up	Playmates	5	7
11/18/61	12/9/61	Little Miss U.S.A.	Barry Mann	19	4
7/3/64	7/24/64	Little Old Lady (From Pasadena)	Jan & Dean	5	9
9/8/67	9/29/67	Little Ole Man (Uptight-Everything's Alright)	Bill Cosby	3	8
3/25/61	3/25/61	Little Pedro	Olympics	26	1
6/30/62	8/4/62	Little Red Rented Rowboat	Joe Dowell	20	6
11/1/63	11/8/63	Little Red Rooster	Sam Cooke	29	4
9/9/61	9/30/61	Little Sister	Elvis Presley	6	6
3/18/61	3/18/61	Little Star	Chuck Berry	37	1
3/15/63	3/15/63	Little Star	Bobby Callender	39	1
11/19/60	12/10/60	Little Tear	Gary Stites	25	4
2/5/65	3/12/65	Little Things	Bobby Goldsboro	6	8
1/12/63	2/15/63	Little Town Flirt	Del Shannon	5	9
9/1/69	9/29/69	Little Woman	Bobby Sherman	1	10
8/13/65	8/20/65	Little You, A	Freddie & the Dreamers	30	2
2/28/64	3/6/64	Live Wire	Martha & the Vandellas	37	2
2/28/64	3/13/64	Liverpool	Viceroys	24	4
11/22/63	11/29/63	Living A Lie	Al Martino	25	2
3/17/62	3/24/62	Lizzie Borden	Chad Mitchell Trio	25	2

Debut	Peak	Title	Artist	Pos	Wks
12/2/68	1/20/69	Lo Mucho Que Te Quiero (The More I Love You)	Rene & Rene	19	8
7/21/62	8/25/62	Loco-Motion, The	Little Eva	2	9
11/22/63	12/13/63	Loddy Lo	Chubby Checker	14	6
5/5/62	5/5/62	Lolita, Theme From	Orchestra Del Oro	40	1
4/7/62	4/14/62	Lollipops And Roses	Jack Jones	26	2
9/15/62	9/22/62	Lollipops And Roses	Paul Petersen	26	4
5/8/64	5/8/64	Loneliest Night, The	Dale & Grace	35	3
5/21/65	6/4/65	L-O-N-E-L-Y	Bobby Vinton	26	4
10/27/62	12/8/62	Lonely Bull, The	Herb Alpert & the Tijuana Brass	5	10
7/7/67	8/25/67	Lonely Drifter	Pieces Of Eight	18	10
12/3/60	12/3/60	Lonely Girl	Jackie DeShannon	37	1
11/5/60	12/3/60	Lonely Teenager	Dion	3	12
9/22/62	10/6/62	Long As The Rose Is Red	Florraine Darlin	25	3
2/7/64	2/28/64	Long Gone Lonesome Blues	Hank Williams Jr.	23	6
2/10/69	3/17/69	Long Green	Fireballs	10	7
6/2/67	6/2/67	Long Legged Girl (With The Short Dress On)	Elvis Presley	35	2
1/21/66	2/11/66	Long Live Our Love	Shangri-Las	29	5
3/12/65	4/16/65	Long Lonely Nights	Bobby Vinton	18	6
11/29/63	1/17/64	Long Tall Texan	Murry Kellum	15	9
10/27/62	11/17/62	Longest Day, The	Mitch Miller	19	4
9/16/61	10/21/61	Look In My Eyes	Chantels	12	7
1/8/65	1/29/65	Look Of Love	Lesley Gore	25	4
5/20/68	6/24/68	Look Of Love, The	Sergio Mendes & Brasil '66	9	7
10/13/67	11/10/67	Look Of Love, The	Dusty Springfield	9	7
10/8/65	11/12/65	Look Through Any Window	Hollies	3	9
10/14/66	10/21/66	Look Through My Window	Mamas & the Papas	22	3
4/15/68	5/13/68	Look To Your Soul	Johnny Rivers	21	5
1/6/67	1/13/67	Look What You've Done	Pozo-Seco Singers	35	3
2/19/68	2/26/68	Looking For A Fox	Clarence Carter	37	2
8/14/64	8/21/64	Looking For Love	Connie Francis	37	2
7/30/65	8/20/65	Looking Through The Eyes Of Love	Gene Pitney	21	4
12/29/62	1/19/63	Loop De Loop	Johnny Thunder	13	6
7/16/65	7/16/65	Loser, The	Skyliners	39	1
3/24/67	3/31/67	Loser (With A Broken Heart), The	Gary Lewis & the Playboys	25	3
4/19/63	5/31/63	Losing You	Brenda Lee	9	7
2/11/61	2/18/61	Lost Love	H. B. Barnum	36	2
2/3/62	2/17/62	Lost Someone	James Brown	26	3

Debut	Peak	Title	Artist	Pos	Wks
11/8/63	12/13/63	Louie Louie	Kingsmen	2	9
10/21/66	11/18/66	Louie, Louie	Sandpipers	21	7
4/29/61	4/29/61	Louisiana Mama	Gene Pitney	40	1
5/13/61	6/10/61	Louisiana Man	Rusty & Doug	6	9
4/21/69	5/19/69	Love (Can Make You Happy)	Mercy	2	10
1/7/66	1/7/66	Love Bug	Jack Jones	31	1
9/8/67	9/8/67	Love Bug Leave My Heart Alone	Martha & the Vandellas	31	3
11/24/62	12/15/62	Love Came To Me	Dion	3	7
4/28/62	4/28/62	Love Can't Wait	Marty Robbins	40	1
10/14/68	11/11/68	Love Child	Diana Ross & the Supremes	1	14
3/31/67	4/14/67	Love Eyes	Nancy Sinatra	23	5
2/15/63	3/8/63	Love For Sale	Arthur Lyman Group	23	5
10/14/66	10/21/66	Love Is A Hurtin' Thing	Lou Rawls	32	5
6/21/63	6/28/63	Love Is A Once In A Lifetime Thing	Dick & DeeDee	39	2
2/12/68	3/25/68	Love Is All Around	Troggs	23	7
7/17/64	7/24/64	Love Is All We Need	Vic Dana	19	5
2/12/68	2/19/68	Love Is Blue	Al Martino	38	2
1/15/68	2/5/68	Love Is Blue	Paul Mauriat	1	11
1/27/67	2/10/67	Love Is Here And Now You're Gone	Supremes	9	8
4/29/66	5/6/66	Love Is Like An Itching In My Heart	Supremes	25	4
10/13/67	11/17/67	Love Is Strange	Peaches & Herb	11	7
2/24/62	3/3/62	Love Is The Sweetest Thing	Saverio Saridis	18	4
2/4/61	2/11/61	Love Keeps Calling	Sammy Turner	38	2
3/17/62	4/7/62	Love Letters	Ketty Lester	13	5
7/8/66	7/8/66	Love Letters	Elvis Presley	22	7
8/12/68	9/9/68	Love Makes A Woman	Barbara Acklin	19	5
2/11/66	3/11/66	Love Makes The World Go Round	Deon Jackson	21	6
8/25/62	9/8/62	Love Me As I Love You	George Maharis	21	3
4/24/64	5/15/64	Love Me Do	Beatles	1	10
5/19/69	6/30/69	Love Me Tonight	Tom Jones	9	11
3/17/62	3/24/62	Love Me Warm And Tender	Paul Anka	20	5
4/29/66	5/6/66	Love Me With All Of Your Heart	Bachelors	31	4
5/8/64	5/22/64	Love Me With All Your Heart	Ray Charles Singers	6	8
1/7/61	1/21/61	Love Music	George Greeley	30	3
1/21/61	2/11/61	(I Wanna) Love My Life Away	Gene Pitney	8	7

Debut	Peak	Title	Artist	Pos	Wks
12/1/62	12/8/62	Love Of A Boy, The	Timi Yuro	37	2
5/24/63	5/24/63	Love Of My Man, The	Theola Kilgore	33	1
5/27/61	6/3/61	Love Of My Own, A	Carla Thomas	33	2
9/15/69	9/22/69	Love Of The Common People	Winstons	34	2
12/18/64	1/8/65	Love Potion Number Nine	Searchers	1	10
5/3/63	5/10/63	Love She Can Count On, A	Miracles	33	3
10/4/63	10/11/63	Love So Fine, A	Chiffons	25	2
10/15/60	11/5/60	Love Walked In	Dinah Washington	19	4
10/13/69	11/24/69	Love Will Find A Way	Jackie DeShannon	14	9
12/16/61	12/16/61	Love You	Bob Conrad	35	3
12/16/66	1/27/67	Love You So Much	New Colony Six	2	10
4/8/66	4/15/66	Love's Made A Fool Of You	Bobby Fuller Four	20	3
12/9/61	12/9/61	Loveland	Paul Anka	35	1
5/26/62	6/9/62	Loveless Life	Ral Donner	28	3
3/10/62	3/31/62	Lover Please	Clyde McPhatter	13	6
9/24/65	11/5/65	Lover's Concerto, A	Toys	2	10
4/15/66	4/15/66	Lover's Concerto, A	Sarah Vaughan	40	1
6/17/68	7/22/68	Lover's Holiday	Peggy Scott & Jo Jo Benson	23	7
8/5/61	9/9/61	Lover's Island	Blue Jays	12	8
9/29/62	11/10/62	Lovers By Night, Strangers By Day	Fleetwoods	6	9
5/5/62	6/2/62	Lovers Who Wander	Dion	6	8
1/4/63	1/4/63	Lovesick Blues	Frank Ifield	33	1
1/21/61	2/18/61	Lovey Dovey	Buddy Knox	16	6
2/3/69	2/24/69	Lovin' Things	Grass Roots	25	5
1/20/67	2/3/67	Lovin' You	Bobby Darin	23	4
6/3/61	7/1/61	Lullaby Of Love	Frank Gari	26	5
3/18/66	3/18/66	Lullaby Of Love	Poppies	34	1
10/30/64	10/30/64	Lumberjack, The	Hal Wils	27	2
8/18/69	8/18/69	Luna Trip	Dickie Goodman	34	2
5/6/68	6/3/68	MacArthur Park	Richard Harris	5	8
6/30/62	7/21/62	(Girls, Girls, Girls) Made To Love	Eddie Hodges	12	6
8/19/68	9/9/68	Magic Bus	Who	5	7
10/14/68	11/11/68	Magic Carpet Ride	Steppenwolf	2	8
9/2/61	9/30/61	Magic Is The Night	Kathy Young	12	5
9/2/61	9/23/61	Magic Moon (Clair De Lune)	Rays	21	4
2/11/66	3/18/66	Magic Town	Vogues	11	7
5/7/65	5/7/65	Magic Trumpet	University Orchestra	33	1

Debut	Peak	Title	Artist	Pos	Wks
11/12/60	1/14/61	Magnificent Seven, The	Al Caiola	3	12
9/1/69	9/15/69	Mah-Na-Mah-Na	Pete Howard	34	3
2/17/67	3/10/67	Mairzy Doats	Innocence	21	5
12/16/61	1/27/62	Majestic, The	Dion	10	7
9/15/69	10/27/69	Make Believe	Wind	13	8
8/11/62	8/11/62	Make It Easy On Yourself	Jerry Butler	28	2
10/22/65	11/19/65	Make It Easy On Yourself	Walker Brothers	23	8
4/17/64	4/17/64	Make Me Forget	Bobby Rydell	30	2
10/1/65	10/29/65	Make Me Your Baby	Barbara Lewis	14	6
12/10/65	12/10/65	Make The World Go Away	Eddy Arnold	34	1
7/5/63	9/13/63	Make The World Go Away	Timi Yuro	17	7
11/3/69	11/24/69	Make Your Own Kind Of Music	Mama Cass Elliot	20	5
1/15/65	1/22/65	Makin' Whoopee	Ray Charles	36	3
5/20/66	5/27/66	Mama	B.J. Thomas	29	2
12/29/62	1/12/63	Mama Didn't Lie	Jan Bradley	30	4
7/19/63	8/2/63	Mama Don't Allow	Rooftop Singers	18	4
2/8/63	2/15/63	Mama-Oom-Mow-Mow	Rivingtons	37	2
5/13/61	6/3/61	Mama Said	Shirelles	10	6
10/6/62	10/27/62	Mama Sang A Song	Stan Kenton	11	6
11/18/66	11/25/66	Mame	Herb Alpert & the Tijuana Brass	20	5
5/13/61	5/27/61	Man In Orbit	Spacemen	25	3
4/29/68	6/3/68	Man Without Love, A	Engelbert Humperdinck	21	7
8/16/63	8/16/63	Man's Temptation	Gene Chandler	37	3
5/24/63	6/21/63	Manhattan Spiritual	Santo & Johnny	20	5
3/4/61	3/18/61	Manhunt	Richard Maltby	28	3
11/26/60	12/17/60	Many Tears Ago	Connie Francis	14	6
7/14/69	8/11/69	Marrakesh Express	Crosby, Stills & Nash	15	6
12/16/61	12/30/61	Maria	Roger Williams	32	3
10/18/63	11/15/63	Maria Elena	Los Indios Tabajaras	2	9
7/9/65	7/30/65	Marie	Bachelors	23	4
8/30/63	8/30/63	Marlena	Four Seasons	17	2
8/16/63	9/6/63	Martian Hop	Ran-Dells	2	8
12/20/63	12/27/63	Marvelous Toy, The	Chad Mitchell Trio	26	2
6/9/67	6/16/67	Mary In The Morning	Al Martino	28	3

Debut	Peak	Title	Artist	Pos	Wks
8/4/62	8/4/62	Mary's Little Lamb	James Darren	39	1
3/3/62	4/14/62	Mashed Potato Time	Dee Dee Sharp	2	12
11/24/67	12/8/67	(The Lights Went Out In) Massachusetts	Bee Gees	21	4
4/22/68	5/27/68	Master Jack	Four Jacks & A Jill	5	8
11/15/63	11/29/63	Matador, The	Johnny Cash	17	3
4/17/64	4/17/64	Matador, The	Major Lance	39	1
9/11/64	10/16/64	Match Box	Beatles	13	7
2/1/63	2/1/63	Mathilda	Roosevelt Nettles	39	1
2/10/69	3/17/69	May I	Bill Deal & the Rhondels	8	8
10/22/65	11/12/65	May The Bird Of Paradise Fly Up Your Nose	Little Jimmy Dickens	32	4
8/7/64	8/28/64	Maybe I Know	Lesley Gore	21	6
6/30/62	7/7/62	Maybe It's Because I Love You	Ronnie Rice	33	2
2/5/68	2/26/68	Maybe Just Today	Bobby Vee	19	5
2/24/69	2/24/69	Maybe Tomorrow	Iveys	37	1
8/14/64	9/18/64	Maybelline	Johnny Rivers	12	6
8/7/64	8/28/64	Me Japanese Boy I Love You	Bobby Goldsboro	26	4
4/1/68	4/1/68	Me, The Peaceful Heart	Lulu	35	2
9/13/63	10/18/63	Mean Woman Blues	Roy Orbison	4	11
3/22/63	4/19/63	Mecca	Gene Pitney	6	6
1/20/67	2/10/67	Mechanical Man, The	Ben Bolt	23	5
5/5/69	6/16/69	Medicine Man (Part I)	Buchanan Brothers	5	10
5/5/67	5/5/67	Melancholy Music Man	Righteous Brothers	29	2
11/11/66	12/9/66	Mellow Yellow	Donovan	2	10
3/24/69	4/14/69	Memories	Elvis Presley	21	5
10/14/61	10/14/61	Memories Of Oldies But Goodies	Little Caesar & the Romans	39	1
4/5/63	4/26/63	Memory Lane	Hippies	29	4
5/31/63	6/28/63	Memphis	Lonnie Mack	11	7
5/29/64	6/26/64	Memphis	Johnny Rivers	3	9
2/19/68	3/4/68	Men Are Gettin' Scarce	Joe Tex	24	4
12/24/65	1/21/66	Men In My Little Girl's Life, The	Mike Douglas	12	6
2/17/69	3/24/69	Mendocino	Sir Douglas Quintet	11	7
3/24/69	4/28/69	Mercy	Ohio Express	9	9
2/10/67	2/24/67	Mercy, Mercy, Mercy	Cannonball Adderley	25	4
6/16/67	7/28/67	Mercy, Mercy, Mercy	Buckinghams	4	9
4/22/66	5/13/66	Message To Michael	Dionne Warwick	25	5
10/28/61	11/11/61	Mexican Joe	David Carroll	29	3
3/24/67	3/31/67	Mexican Road Race	Herb Alpert & the Tijuana Brass	39	3
8/7/64	8/14/64	Mexican Shuffle, The	Herb Alpert & the Tijuana Brass	15	4

Debut	Peak	Title	Artist	Pos	Wks
8/26/61	10/7/61	Mexico	Bob Moore	1	10
7/8/61	7/29/61	Michael	Highwaymen	1	11
8/28/64	8/28/64	Michael	Trini Lopez	30	3
9/6/63	9/13/63	Michael—Pt. 1	Steve Alaimo	33	2
1/7/66	1/28/66	Michelle	David & Jonathan	23	4
8/16/63	9/13/63	Mickey's Monkey	Miracles	16	6
3/13/64	3/20/64	Midnight	David Rockingham Trio	19	4
9/2/68	10/7/68	Midnight Confessions	Grass Roots	2	11
11/17/69	1/12/70	Midnight Cowboy	Ferrante & Teicher	6	12
2/24/62	3/10/62	Midnight In Moscow	Kenny Ball & his Jazzmen	2	8
11/15/63	1/3/64	Midnight Mary	Joey Powers	4	9
2/5/65	2/19/65	Midnight Special	Johnny Rivers	23	4
2/26/68	4/15/68	Mighty Quinn (Quinn The Eskimo)	Manfred Mann	7	9
9/8/62	9/8/62	Mile And A Quarter, A	Sonny James	38	1
9/10/65	9/24/65	Millions Of Roses	Steve Lawrence	27	3
6/5/64	6/19/64	Milord	Bobby Darin	28	3
10/20/69	11/17/69	Mind, Body & Soul	Flaming Ember	22	6
10/27/62	11/10/62	Mind Over Matter	Nolan Strong	16	3
4/14/69	4/21/69	Mini-Skirt Minnie	Wilson Pickett	33	2
6/16/69	6/30/69	Minotaur, The	Dick Hyman & his Electric Eclectics	32	3
11/24/62	11/24/62	Minstrel And Queen	Impressions	34	1
4/21/67	5/19/67	Mirage	Tommy James & the Shondells	1	8
1/21/61	1/28/61	Misfits, The	Don Costa	36	2
9/23/61	10/7/61	Missing You	Ray Peterson	9	5
2/5/68	2/19/68	Mission-Impossible	Lalo Schifrin	31	3
7/15/66	7/29/66	Misty	Richard "Groove" Holmes	34	5
10/25/63	11/8/63	Misty	Lloyd Price	31	4
7/3/64	7/24/64	Mixed-Up, Shook-Up Girl	Patty & the Emblems	16	5
8/9/63	8/16/63	Mockingbird	Inez Foxx	27	4
3/4/61	3/18/61	Model Girl	Johnny Maestro	32	3
8/20/65	8/27/65	Mohair Sam	Charlie Rich	22	2
12/29/62	1/19/63	Molly	Bobby Goldsboro	22	5
6/9/69	7/7/69	Moments To Remember	Vogues	21	5
1/13/62	1/27/62	Mommy And Daddy Were Twistin'	Susan Summers	21	4
4/8/66	5/6/66	Monday, Monday	Mamas & the Papas	1	9
4/10/64	4/10/64	Money	Kingsmen	35	1
10/18/63	10/18/63	Monkey-Shine	Bill Black's Combo	36	1
8/9/63	8/16/63	Monkey Time, The	Major Lance	24	4
9/8/62	10/20/62	Monster Mash	Bobby "Boris" Pickett	1	9
12/8/62	12/22/62	Monsters' Holiday	Bobby "Boris" Pickett	8	4
4/1/68	5/6/68	Mony Mony	Tommy James & the Shondells	1	12
5/27/61	7/1/61	Moody River	Pat Boone	2	8
5/26/69	6/16/69	Moody Woman	Jerry Butler	21	5

Debut	Peak	Title	Artist	Pos	Wks
8/6/65	8/27/65	Moon Over Naples	Bert Kaempfert	16	4
11/4/61	11/4/61	Moon River	Jerry Butler	35	1
12/9/61	12/30/61	Moon River	Henry Mancini	3	15
8/6/65	8/13/65	Moonglow And Theme From 'Picnic'	Esther Phillips	32	2
8/27/65	8/27/65	Moonlight And Roses (Bring Mem'ries Of You)	Vic Dana	36	1
9/6/63	9/13/63	More	Vic Dana	14	5
7/26/63	9/6/63	More	Kai Winding	10	9
5/27/66	7/8/66	More I See You, The	Chris Montez	10	8
8/19/61	9/9/61	More Money For You And Me	Four Preps	7	7
5/5/69	5/12/69	More Today Than Yesterday	Spiral Starecase	34	3
4/28/69	6/2/69	Morning Girl	Neon Philharmonic	2	8
2/17/67	3/10/67	Morningtown Ride	Seekers	29	6
4/28/62	4/28/62	Most People Get Married	Patti Page	24	2
4/1/61	5/13/61	Mother-In-Law	Ernie K-Doe	3	9
6/23/69	7/21/69	Mother Popcorn (You Got To Have A Mother For Me) Part 1	James Brown	15	6
7/8/66	7/29/66	Mother's Little Helper	Rolling Stones	12	5
1/20/62	1/20/62	Motorcycle	Tico & the Triumphs	36	1
2/18/66	2/25/66	Moulty	Barbarians	23	4
6/17/68	7/15/68	Mountain Of Love	Ronnie Dove	27	5
11/8/63	11/8/63	Mountain Of Love	David Houston	40	1
11/13/64	12/25/64	Mountain Of Love	Johnny Rivers	5	9
8/19/61	9/16/61	Mountain's High, The	Dick & DeeDee	1	8
10/14/60	10/14/60	(You've Got To) Move Two Mountains	Marv Johnson	34	1
11/4/61	11/11/61	Movin'	Bill Black's Combo	27	2
3/8/63	4/5/63	Mr. Bass Man	Johnny Cymbal	16	6
10/14/60	10/14/60	Mr. Custer	Larry Verne	2	3
8/26/66	9/30/66	Mr. Dieingly Sad	Critters	13	8
10/20/62	11/10/62	Mr. Lonely	Buddy Grace	17	5
11/13/64	12/11/64	Mr. Lonely	Bobby Vinton	2	11
6/16/67	6/30/67	Mr. Pleasant	Kinks	28	4
10/7/66	10/14/66	Mr. Spaceman	Byrds	27	3
2/24/69	4/14/69	Mr. Sun, Mr. Moon	Paul Revere & the Raiders	5	11
5/28/65	6/18/65	Mr. Tambourine Man	Byrds	1	9
3/10/67	4/14/67	Mr. Unreliable	Cryan' Shames	7	8
4/2/65	4/23/65	Mrs. Brown You've Got A Lovely Daughter	Herman's Hermits	1	10

Debut	Peak	Title	Artist	Pos	Wks
6/9/69	7/7/69	Mrs. Robinson	Booker T. & the MG's	25	6
4/29/68	5/27/68	Mrs. Robinson	Simon & Garfunkel	2	11
7/1/66	7/8/66	(I Washed My Hands In) Muddy Water	Johnny Rivers	21	5
8/18/67	8/25/67	Museum	Herman's Hermits	28	2
8/12/61	8/12/61	Music, Music, Music	Sensations	30	1
1/6/67	2/10/67	Music To Watch Girls By	Bob Crewe Generation	12	6
4/14/67	5/5/67	Music To Watch Girls By	Andy Williams	20	6
3/4/61	3/4/61	Muskrat Ramble	Freddy Cannon	34	1
12/17/65	1/21/66	Must To Avoid, A	Herman's Hermits	5	7
5/12/67	5/19/67	My Babe	Ronnie Dove	31	3
10/25/63	10/25/63	My Babe	Righteous Brothers	39	1
11/19/65	11/26/65	My Baby	Temptations	29	2
2/4/66	2/4/66	My Baby Loves Me	Martha & the Vandellas	40	1
7/5/63	7/19/63	My Block	Four Pennies	33	3
9/30/61	9/30/61	My Blue Heaven	Duane Eddy	40	1
2/17/62	3/3/62	My Boomerang Won't Come Back	Charlie Drake	17	5
5/29/64	6/26/64	My Boy Lollipop	Millie Small	5	7
8/2/63	8/9/63	My Boyfriend's Back	Angels	1	9
6/23/69	7/21/69	My Cherie Amour	Stevie Wonder	6	9
12/15/62	1/12/63	My Coloring Book	Kitty Kallen	8	6
2/17/67	3/24/67	My Cup Runneth Over	Ed Ames	11	7
12/8/62	1/4/63	My Dad	Paul Petersen	4	8
2/11/61	2/18/61	My Empty Arms	Jackie Wilson	30	2
12/23/68	12/23/68	My Favorite Things	Herb Alpert & the Tijuana Brass	35	3
1/29/65	3/5/65	My Girl	Temptations	19	7
4/1/68	5/6/68	My Girl/Hey Girl	Bobby Vee	6	10
11/5/60	12/10/60	My Girl Josephine	Fats Domino	20	7
5/5/67	5/19/67	My Girl Josephine	Jerry Jaye	16	5
4/17/64	5/15/64	My Girl Sloopy	Vibrations	28	5
4/10/64	5/22/64	My Guy	Mary Wells	15	8
3/6/64	4/3/64	My Heart Belongs To Only You	Bobby Vinton	4	9
5/12/62	5/26/62	My Heart Comes Running Back	Nick Noble	33	3
10/14/60	10/14/60	My Heart Has A Mind Of Its Own	Connie Francis	3	2
6/19/64	7/3/64	My Heart Skips A Beat	Buck Owens	24	4
1/29/65	2/5/65	My Heart Would Know	Al Martino	28	3
8/5/66	8/12/66	My Heart's Symphony	Gary Lewis & the Playboys	20	3
12/29/69	1/26/70	My Honey And Me	Luther Ingram	19	6
7/8/61	8/5/61	My Kind Of Girl	Matt Monro	24	6
8/2/63	8/2/63	My Laura	Harry Charles	39	1
5/20/66	7/1/66	My Little Red Book	Love	18	8
1/7/66	2/4/66	My Love	Petula Clark	8	9
7/14/67	8/4/67	My Mammy	Happenings	16	5

Debut	Peak	Title	Artist	Pos	Wks
2/17/62	2/24/62	My Melancholy Baby	Marcels	34	2
11/10/62	12/8/62	My Own True Love	Duprees	12	7
6/9/69	7/14/69	My Pledge Of Love	Joe Jeffrey Group	11	9
2/4/66	2/11/66	My Ship Is Comin' In	Walker Brothers	36	2
8/26/68	9/30/68	My Special Angel	Vogues	4	10
5/24/63	5/31/63	My Summer Love	Ruby & the Romantics	21	2
4/22/61	5/20/61	My Three Sons	Bob Moore	20	6
9/24/65	9/24/65	My Town, My Guy And Me	Lesley Gore	33	1
2/28/64	2/28/64	My True Carrie, Love	Nat "King" Cole	37	1
6/28/63	6/28/63	My True Confession	Brook Benton	26	1
9/16/61	10/7/61	My True Story	Jive Five	18	5
3/31/69	4/14/69	My Way	Frank Sinatra	28	3
2/17/69	3/17/69	My Whole World Ended (The Moment You Left Me)	David Ruffin	15	5
12/1/62	12/15/62	My Wife Can't Cook	Lonnie Russ	36	3
6/30/67	7/14/67	My World Fell Down	Sagittarius	19	6
1/21/66	2/4/66	My World Is Empty Without You	Supremes	17	7
11/19/65	11/26/65	Mystic Eyes	Them	23	2
10/27/69	12/1/69	Na Na Hey Hey Kiss Him Goodbye	Steam	1	13
5/19/62	5/19/62	Na Ne Noe	Troy Shondell	37	1
3/6/64	3/6/64	Nadine (Is It You)	Chuck Berry	24	3
9/16/61	9/16/61	"Nag"	Halos	37	1
12/25/64	1/15/65	Name Game, The	Shirley Ellis	8	7
4/10/64	4/10/64	Naomi	Floyd Cramer	37	1
12/9/66	1/6/67	Nashville Cats	Lovin' Spoonful	14	6
9/29/67	10/20/67	Natural Woman (You Make Me Feel Like), A	Aretha Franklin	23	6
2/7/64	3/6/64	Navy Blue	Diane Renay	5	6
2/28/64	4/3/64	Needles And Pins	Searchers	15	6
11/10/67	12/1/67	Neon Rainbow	Box Tops	9	6
11/12/60	11/12/60	Nervous Auctioneer	Robin Wilson	38	1
5/3/63	5/10/63	Never	Earls	26	2
6/10/68	6/17/68	Never Give You Up	Jerry Butler	29	2
7/14/62	7/21/62	Never In A Million Years	Linda Scott	38	2
8/18/67	9/29/67	Never My Love	Association	2	12
3/26/65	4/16/65	Never Never Leave Me	Mary Wells	25	4
7/29/61	8/5/61	Never On Sunday	Chordettes	31	4
10/14/60	10/14/60	Never On Sunday	Don Costa	6	2
7/17/64	8/14/64	New Girl	Accents	28	5
3/27/64	5/8/64	New Girl In School, The	Jan & Dean	1	11
12/23/61	1/6/62	New Kind Of Love	Willie Harper	20	5
10/4/63	10/11/63	New Mexican Rose	Four Seasons	20	2

Debut	Peak	Title	Artist	Pos	Wks
10/15/60	11/19/60	New Orleans	Gary U.S. Bonds	3	10
12/29/67	1/22/68	New Orleans	Neil Diamond	27	5
7/9/65	8/13/65	New Orleans	Eddie Hodges	8	6
8/19/61	8/19/61	New Orleans Medley	Earl Palmer	34	1
5/19/67	6/16/67	New York Mining Disaster, 1941	Bee Gees	22	7
2/26/65	3/19/65	New York's A Lonely Town	Trade Winds	22	4
10/6/62	10/27/62	Next Door To An Angel	Neil Sedaka	8	6
10/6/67	12/29/67	Next Plane To London	Rose Garden	26	7
12/15/62	1/4/63	Night Has A Thousand Eyes, The	Bobby Vee	2	9
10/25/63	11/8/63	Night Life	Rusty Draper	23	3
8/27/65	8/27/65	Night People	Leaders	33	1
10/15/60	10/29/60	Night Theme	Mark II	29	4
2/4/66	2/4/66	Night Time	Strangeloves	37	1
5/12/62	5/12/62	Night Train	James Brown	30	1
1/14/61	2/4/61	Night With Daddy G, A	Church Street Five	7	6
10/28/66	12/2/66	Nineteen Days	Dave Clark Five	21	7
2/18/66	3/25/66	19th Nervous Breakdown	Rolling Stones	3	8
12/9/66	1/27/67	98.6	Keith	10	10
9/9/66	10/14/66	96 Tears	? & the Mysterians	1	11
12/23/61	1/13/62	Nite Owl	Dukays	18	5
9/23/68	10/7/68	Nitty Gritty	Ricardo Ray	36	3
11/29/63	11/29/63	Nitty Gritty, The	Shirley Ellis	36	1
7/21/69	9/1/69	Nitty Gritty, The	Gladys Knight & the Pips	20	8
1/22/65	2/19/65	No Arms Can Ever Hold You	Bachelors	16	6
2/3/67	3/3/67	No Fair At All	Association	19	7
12/17/65	1/21/66	No Matter What Shape (Your Stomach's In)	T-Bones	6	10
5/26/69	6/23/69	No Matter What Sign You Are	Diana Ross & the Supremes	20	5
2/3/69	3/17/69	No, Not Much	Vogues	4	10
6/21/63	6/28/63	No One	Ray Charles	35	2
8/4/62	8/11/62	No One Will Ever Know	Jimmie Rodgers	31	4
6/19/64	7/3/64	No Particular Place To Go	Chuck Berry	18	4
11/11/68	11/25/68	Nobody	Three Dog Night	34	3
1/8/68	2/19/68	Nobody But Me	Human Beinz	6	9
9/1/69	9/22/69	Nobody But You Babe	Clarence Reid	23	4
7/3/64	7/17/64	Nobody I Know	Peter & Gordon	4	7
10/14/66	10/21/66	Nobody's Baby Again	Dean Martin	39	2
1/13/62	2/3/62	Norman	Sue Thompson	3	7

Debut	Peak	Title	Artist	Pos	Wks
11/26/60	12/24/60	North To Alaska	Johnny Horton	7	8
4/17/64	5/22/64	Not Fade Away	Rolling Stones	19	7
5/31/63	7/19/63	Not Me	Orlons	22	7
10/1/65	10/15/65	Not The Lovin' Kind	Dino, Desi & Billy	24	5
3/5/65	4/2/65	Not Too Long Ago	Uniques	24	5
12/23/66	2/3/67	(We Ain't Got) Nothin' Yet	Blues Magoos	5	9
4/28/69	5/19/69	Nothing But A Heartache	Flirtations	17	5
//30/65	8/27/65	Nothing But Heartaches	Supremes	10	5
10/20/62	11/3/62	Nothing Can Change This Love	Sam Cooke	27	3
5/7/65	5/21/65	Nothing Can Stop Me	Gene Chandler	35	3
3/26/65	4/23/65	Now That You've Gone	Connie Stevens	6	5
2/25/66	3/11/66	Nowhere Man	Beatles	7	7
3/19/65	4/16/65	Nowhere To Run	Martha & the Vandellas	20	6
4/21/62	5/19/62	Number One Man	Bruce Channel	25	5
3/3/62	3/17/62	Nut Rocker	B. Bumble & the Stingers	3	7
10/21/61	10/28/61	Oasis (Part 2)	Majestics	28	2
1/13/69	1/20/69	Ob-La-Di, Ob-La-Da	Arthur Conley	38	2
8/4/67	9/1/67	Ode To Billie Joe	Bobbie Gentry	1	11
9/29/67	10/20/67	Ode To Billie Joe	Kingpins	29	4
1/20/62	1/20/62	Oh Cindy	Vibrations	38	1
4/21/69	5/26/69	Oh Happy Day	Edwin Hawkins Singers	5	9
6/10/66	6/24/66	Oh How Happy	Shades Of Blue	17	3
5/5/62	5/19/62	Oh My Angel	Bertha Tillman	24	3
8/28/64	9/18/64	Oh, Pretty Woman	Roy Orbison	1	13
3/31/67	3/31/67	Oh That's Good, No That's Bad	Sam the Sham & the Pharaohs	31	2
8/25/69	9/15/69	Oh, What A Night	Dells	31	5
8/11/62	8/18/62	Oh! What It Seemed To Be	Castells	32	2
5/20/66	6/3/66	Oh Yeah	Shadows Of Knight	13	6
1/20/67	2/3/67	Oh Yeah!	Joe Cuba Sextet	34	4
11/19/60	12/3/60	Ol' MacDonald	Frank Sinatra	18	6
4/7/62	5/12/62	Old Rivers	Walter Brennan	3	8
5/31/63	5/31/63	Old Smokey Locomotion	Little Eva	26	1
7/8/61	7/15/61	Ole Buttermilk Sky	Bill Black's Combo	33	2
11/5/60	11/5/60	Oliver Cool	Oliver Cool	33	1
3/3/67	4/28/67	On A Carousel	Hollies	2	11
3/8/63	4/12/63	On Broadway	Drifters	12	7
4/8/61	4/29/61	On The Rebound	Floyd Cramer	19	5
8/26/68	9/30/68	On The Road Again	Canned Heat	8	8
10/2/64	10/2/64	On The Street Where You Live	Andy Williams	29	1
1/28/61	2/25/61	Once In Awhile	Chimes	6	8
5/22/64	6/5/64	Once Upon A Time	Marvin Gaye & Mary Wells	25	5
3/25/61	4/8/61	Once Upon A Time	Rochell & the Candles	26	3
5/19/69	6/23/69	One	Three Dog Night	1	11

Debut	Peak	Title	Artist	Pos	Wks
5/3/63	5/3/63	One Boy Too Late	Mike Clifford	35	1
2/22/63	3/8/63	One Broken Heart For Sale	Elvis Presley	18	4
7/2/65	7/9/65	One Dyin' And A Buryin'	Roger Miller	28	4
4/22/61	4/22/61	One Eyed Jacks, Love Theme From	Ferrante & Teicher	31	2
5/24/63	6/14/63	One Fine Day	Chiffons	5	7
10/7/61	10/7/61	One Grain Of Sand	Eddy Arnold	39	1
11/12/65	12/10/65	One Has My Name (The Other Has My Heart)	Barry Young	8	6
3/19/65	4/9/65	One Kiss For Old Times' Sake	Ronnie Dove	10	7
4/22/61	4/22/61	One Little Kiss	Holidays	38	1
4/1/61	4/22/61	One Mint Julep	Ray Charles	24	5
3/10/67	3/24/67	One More Mountain To Climb	Ronnie Dove	36	4
12/18/64	12/25/64	One More Time	Ray Charles Singers	16	2
11/25/61	11/25/61	One More Time	Johnny Holiday	40	1
11/5/60	11/5/60	One Of The Lucky Ones	Anita Bryant	31	1
3/11/66	3/11/66	One On The Right Is On The Left, The	Johnny Cash	36	2
3/25/66	3/25/66	One Track Mind	Knickerbockers	27	3
9/30/61	10/7/61	One Track Mind	Bobby Lewis	21	3
10/22/65	11/26/65	1-2-3	Len Barry	1	9
7/15/68	8/26/68	1,2,3, Red Light	1910 Fruitgum Co.	2	11
6/5/64	6/5/64	One Way Love	Drifters	37	1
3/17/62	4/21/62	One Who Really Loves You, The	Mary Wells	10	8
9/8/62	9/8/62	Only Forever	Jamie Norton	39	1
9/6/63	10/11/63	Only In America	Jay & the Americans	9	7
9/15/62	10/20/62	Only Love Can Break A Heart	Gene Pitney	2	9
3/3/69	4/7/69	Only The Strong Survive	Jerry Butler	8	11
2/10/69	3/24/69	Only You (And You Alone)	Bobby Hatfield	12	9
5/5/67	5/19/67	Oogum Boogum Song, The	Brenton Wood	26	5
5/7/65	5/21/65	Ooo Baby Baby	Miracles	27	4
11/3/67	12/1/67	Open Letter To My Teenage Son, An	Victor Lundberg	6	6
5/20/66	6/17/66	Opus 17 (Don't You Worry 'Bout Me)	Four Seasons	25	5
3/5/65	3/12/65	Orange Blossom Special	Johnny Cash	23	4
8/2/63	8/2/63	Organ Shout	Dave "Baby" Cortez	30	2
12/1/67	12/22/67	Other Man's Grass Is Always Greener	Petula Clark	22	5
12/11/64	12/11/64	Other Ringo, The	Larry Finnegan	28	1

Debut	Peak	Title	Artist	Pos	Wks
2/8/63	3/8/63	Our Day Will Come	Ruby & the Romantics	7	5
6/9/62	6/16/62	Our Favorite Melodies	Gary Criss	31	3
5/27/61	6/3/61	Our Love Is Here To Stay	Dinah Washington	28	4
3/1/63	3/29/63	Our Winter Love	Bill Pursell	3	7
11/26/65	12/3/65	Our World	Johnny Tillotson	36	2
7/21/67	8/4/67	Out And About	Tommy Boyce & Bobby Hart	32	3
4/16/65	4/16/65	Out In The Streets	Shangri-Las	37	2
1/24/64	2/28/64	Out Of Limits	Marketts	3	8
3/1/63	3/15/63	Out Of My Mind	Johnny Tillotson	15	3
7/28/69	9/8/69	Out Of Sight, Out Of Mind	Little Anthony & the Imperials	15	8
10/20/67	11/17/67	Out Of The Blue	Tommy James & the Shondells	14	6
3/4/66	4/15/66	Outside The Gates Of Heaven	Lou Christie	17	8
11/12/65	12/10/65	Over And Over	Dave Clark Five	2	9
2/25/61	3/4/61	Over Someone's Shoulder	Nick Noble	32	2
12/2/61	1/13/62	Over The Mountain (Across The Sea)	Ronnie Rice	27	6
3/29/63	4/26/63	Over The Mountain (Across The Sea)	Bobby Vinton	19	5
7/1/66	7/29/66	Over Under Sideways Down	Yardbirds	16	9
10/14/60	10/14/60	Over You	Aaron Neville	27	1
9/9/68	10/14/68	Over You	Gary Puckett & the Union Gap	1	11
11/13/64	11/27/64	Over You	Paul Revere & the Raiders	22	3
5/13/66	5/27/66	Paint It, Black	Rolling Stones	1	7
10/7/66	10/28/66	(You Don't Have To) Paint Me A Picture	Gary Lewis & the Playboys	14	5
8/2/63	9/13/63	Painted, Tainted Rose	Al Martino	15	8
5/26/62	6/9/62	Palisades Park	Freddy Cannon	2	8
9/20/63	10/11/63	(Down At) Papa Joe's	Dixiebelles	13	5
8/11/62	9/1/62	Papa-Oom-Mow-Mow	Rivingtons	28	4
12/16/68	1/6/69	Papa's Got A Brand New Bag	Otis Redding	25	4
7/23/65	8/13/65	Papa's Got A Brand New Bag Part I	James Brown	19	5
10/27/67	11/24/67	Paper Cup	Fifth Dimension	26	5
1/22/65	2/19/65	Paper Tiger	Sue Thompson	11	6
6/3/66	6/24/66	Paperback Writer	Beatles	2	8
9/27/63	9/27/63	Part Time Love	Little Johnny Taylor	39	1
5/22/64	6/26/64	Party Girl	Bernadette Carroll	8	8
6/30/62	8/11/62	Party Lights	Claudine Clark	10	7

Debut	Peak	Title	Artist	Pos	Wks
7/1/66	7/1/66	Past, Present And Future	Shangri-Las	37	1
9/22/62	10/13/62	Patches	Dickey Lee	1	7
3/17/62	4/7/62	Patricia—Twist	Perez Prado	26	4
10/15/60	10/29/60	Patsy	Jack Scott	35	2
1/27/62	3/10/62	Patti Ann	Johnny Crawford	9	8
5/31/63	5/31/63	Patty Baby	Freddy Cannon	30	2
5/26/67	6/23/67	Pay You Back With Interest	Hollies	9	6
11/10/67	12/1/67	Peace Of Mind	Paul Revere & the Raiders	22	4
4/9/65	4/16/65	Peaches 'N' Cream	Ikettes	26	3
5/20/61	6/17/61	Peanut Butter	Marathons	19	5
7/1/61	7/22/61	Peanuts	Rick & the Keens	3	8
6/11/65	6/18/65	Peanuts (La Cacahuata)	Sunglows	26	2
10/30/64	11/13/64	Pearly Shells	Burl Ives	18	4
1/24/64	2/21/64	Penetration	Pyramids	4	8
2/24/67	3/10/67	Penny Lane	Beatles	4	8
5/8/64	5/22/64	People	Barbra Streisand	16	8
9/15/67	10/13/67	People Are Strange	Doors	18	6
7/8/68	8/19/68	People Got To Be Free	Rascals	1	13
7/17/64	8/14/64	People Say	Dixie Cups	10	6
6/24/68	7/8/68	People Sure Act Funny	Arthur Conley	31	3
1/14/61	1/28/61	"Pepe"	Duane Eddy	12	4
11/17/62	12/8/62	Pepino The Italian Mouse	Lou Monte	7	8
3/29/63	3/29/63	Pepino's Friend Pasqual (The Italian Pussy-Cat)	Lou Monte	38	1
12/16/61	1/6/62	Peppermint Twist—Part I	Joey Dee & the Starliters	2	9
2/10/62	3/3/62	Percolator (Twist)	Billy Joe & the Checkmates	25	4
11/5/60	12/3/60	Perfidia	Ventures	11	9
10/15/60	11/5/60	Peter Gunn	Duane Eddy	10	9
2/11/66	3/18/66	Phoenix Love Theme, The	Brass Ring	20	6
5/13/61	5/20/61	Pick Me Up On Your Way Down	Pat Zill	34	2
11/18/68	12/9/68	Pickin' Wild Mountain Berries	Peggy Scott & Jo Jo Benson	29	4
6/3/68	7/8/68	Pictures Of Matchstick Men	Status Quo	3	10
9/30/68	11/4/68	Piece Of My Heart	Big Brother & the Holding Company	16	6
6/10/66	7/22/66	Pied Piper, The	Crispian St. Peters	2	9
3/15/63	3/15/63	Pin A Medal On Joey	James Darren	36	1
4/29/66	4/29/66	Pin The Tail On The Donkey	Paul Peek	40	1
3/31/69	5/12/69	Pinball Wizard	Who	5	10
10/14/60	10/14/60	Pineapple Princess	Annette with the Afterbeats	16	3
1/31/64	2/7/64	Pink Dominos	Crescents	28	4

Debut	Peak	Title	Artist	Pos	Wks
3/15/63	4/19/63	Pipeline	Chantays	1	9
10/14/66	10/28/66	Pipeline	Chantays	20	4
7/1/61	7/1/61	Place Called Happiness, A	Anita Bryant	40	1
1/27/62	2/3/62	Play The Thing	Marlowe Morris Quintet	38	2
4/12/63	4/12/63	Play Those Oldies, Mr. D.J.	Anthony & the Sophomores	36	1
3/4/68	3/25/68	Playboy	Gene & Debbe	28	5
5/12/62	5/26/62	Playboy	Marvelettes	17	6
11/11/61	11/11/61	Playboy	Bob Vegas	36	1
7/14/67	7/28/67	Pleasant Valley Sunday	Monkees	2	10
3/17/62	3/31/62	Please Don't Ask About Barbara	Bobby Vee	28	3
11/18/66	12/2/66	Please Don't Ever Leave Me	Cyrkle	28	4
12/24/65	12/24/65	Please Don't Fight It	Dino, Desi & Billy	31	1
10/7/61	11/4/61	Please Don't Go	Ral Donner	15	6
8/30/63	8/30/63	Please Don't Talk To The Lifeguard	Diane Ray	30	1
6/2/62	6/9/62	Please Help	Dukays	27	2
3/18/61	4/15/61	Please Love Me Forever	Cathy Jean & the Roommates	4	7
10/13/67	11/17/67	Please Love Me Forever	Bobby Vinton	5	9
10/14/61	12/16/61	Please Mr. Postman	Marvelettes	9	11
11/5/65	11/12/65	Please Mr. Sullivan	Warner Brothers	35	2
3/8/63	3/15/63	Please Please Me	Beatles	35	2
2/21/64	3/20/64	Please Please Me	Beatles	2	7
8/5/68	8/19/68	Please Return Your Love To Me	Temptations	29	5
3/25/61	3/25/61	Please Say You Want Me	Little Anthony & the Imperials	32	1
6/24/61	7/22/61	Please Stay	Drifters	23	5
6/10/66	6/17/66	Please Tell Me Why	Dave Clark Five	28	3
4/8/61	4/8/61	Please Tell Me Why	Jackie Wilson	37	1
12/23/61	1/27/62	Pocketful Of Miracles	Frank Sinatra	20	6
10/15/60	11/12/60	Poetry In Motion	Johnny Tillotson	1	11
9/1/62	9/29/62	Point Of No Return	Gene McDaniels	21	5
6/30/69	8/4/69	Polk Salad Annie	Tony Joe White	5	10
2/18/61	3/11/61	Pony Time	Chubby Checker	10	7
9/9/68	9/30/68	Poor Baby	Cowsills	31	4
12/23/61	1/20/62	Poor Fool	Ike & Tina Turner	26	5
5/24/63	5/31/63	Poor Little Rich Girl	Steve Lawrence	18	3
3/19/65	4/2/65	Poor Man's Son	Reflections	25	3
9/23/66	11/18/66	Poor Side Of Town	Johnny Rivers	4	13

Debut	Peak	Title	Artist	Pos	Wks
3/24/62	3/31/62	Pop-Eye	Huey (Piano) Smith	32	2
12/16/61	12/30/61	Pop Goes The Weasel	Anthony Newley	27	3
9/22/62	10/27/62	Pop Pop Pop-Pie	Sherrys	6	7
1/19/63	1/25/63	Popeye Waddle, The	Don Covay	30	2
5/27/66	7/1/66	Popsicle	Jan & Dean	20	7
12/13/63	1/10/64	Popsicles And Icicles	Murmaids	4	9
3/3/62	3/3/62	Portrait Of A Fool	Conway Twitty	32	1
2/18/61	4/1/61	Portrait Of My Love	Steve Lawrence	6	9
10/1/65	10/22/65	Positively 4th Street	Bob Dylan	9	6
3/22/63	3/29/63	Preacherman	Charlie Russo	36	2
4/21/67	4/21/67	Precious Memories	Romeos	37	1
1/27/67	2/17/67	Pretty Ballerina	Left Banke	16	4
6/24/66	7/8/66	Pretty Flamingo	Manfred Mann	15	6
8/5/61	9/2/61	Pretty Little Angel Eyes	Curtis Lee	7	7
8/6/65	8/27/65	Pretty Little Baby	Marvin Gaye	17	4
12/13/63	12/20/63	Pretty Paper	Roy Orbison	16	3
6/16/62	6/23/62	Pretty Suzy Sunshine	Larry Finnegan	36	2
7/26/63	8/2/63	Pride And Joy	Marvin Gaye	28	3
8/26/61	9/9/61	Princess	Frank Gari	27	3
12/10/65	12/17/65	Princess In Rags	Gene Pitney	36	2
3/3/62	3/3/62	Priscilla	Gus Backus	37	1
5/17/63	5/24/63	Prisoner Of Love	James Brown	27	3
1/8/65	1/15/65	Promised Land	Chuck Berry	32	2
11/11/68	12/9/68	Promises, Promises	Dionne Warwick	24	5
1/12/63	2/8/63	Proud	Johnny Crawford	18	5
5/5/69	5/19/69	Proud Mary	Solomon Burke	26	3
1/27/69	3/10/69	Proud Mary	Creedence Clearwater Revival	3	10
5/1/64	5/15/64	P.S. I Love You	Beatles	1	9
9/9/66	10/28/66	Psychotic Reaction	Count Five	8	10
4/14/62	5/5/62	P.T. 109	Jimmy Dean	10	5
1/4/63	2/1/63	Puddin N' Tain (Ask Me Again, I'll Tell You The Same)	Alley Cats	13	5
3/15/63	4/12/63	Puff The Magic Dragon	Peter, Paul & Mary	6	8
9/22/62	10/13/62	Punish Her	Bobby Vee	16	5
11/26/65	12/24/65	Puppet On A String	Elvis Presley	27	5
12/17/60	1/21/61	Puppet Song, The	Frankie Avalon	14	7
2/21/64	3/27/64	Puppy Love	Barbara Lewis	16	7
9/22/67	11/10/67	Purple Haze	Jimi Hendrix Experience	7	9
11/10/62	11/17/62	Push And Kick, The	Mark Valentino	29	4
1/6/67	2/17/67	Pushin' Too Hard	Seeds	1	9
4/26/63	5/10/63	Pushover	Etta James	28	4

Debut	Peak	Title	Artist	Pos	Wks
6/23/69	8/4/69	Put A Little Love In Your Heart	Jackie DeShannon	3	12
24/62	3/10/62	Quarter To Four Stomp	Stompers	22	3
6/17/61	6/24/61	Quarter To Three	Gary U.S. Bonds	1	10
6/30/62	7/7/62	Queen Of My Heart	Rene & Ray	35	2
5/7/65	5/14/65	Queen Of The House	Jody Miller	16	4
6/23/69	7/21/69	Quentin's Theme	Charles Randolph Grean Sounde	3	9
2/5/68	3/11/68	Question Of Temperature, A	Balloon Farm	13	7
11/25/66	12/2/66	Questions And Answers	In Crowd	29	3
10/7/68	11/11/68	Quick Joey Small (Run Joey Run)	Kasenetz-Katz Singing Orchestral Circus	14	9
12/6/63	12/20/63	Quicksand	Martha & the Vandellas	22	4
3/12/65	4/2/65	Race Is On, The	Jack Jones	17	5
6/10/66	7/1/66	Race With The Wind	Robbs	16	5
6/26/64	7/17/64	Rag Doll	Four Seasons	1	10
12/6/63	12/20/63	Rags To Riches	Sunny & the Sunliners	32	3
6/10/66	6/24/66	Rain	Beatles	2	7
10/14/66	11/18/66	Rain On The Roof	Lovin' Spoonful	9	7
9/22/62	10/6/62	Rain Rain Go Away	Bobby Vinton	19	4
9/29/67	11/17/67	Rain, The Park & Other Things, The	Cowsills	2	13
11/10/62	11/24/62	Rainbow At Midnight	Jimmie Rodgers	15	4
5/20/61	7/8/61	Raindrops	Dee Clark	2	9
11/17/69	12/22/69	Raindrops Keep Fallin' On My Head	B. J. Thomas	2	13
5/27/61	6/17/61	Rainin' In My Heart	Slim Harpo	15	5
3/10/62	3/17/62	Rains Came, The	Big Sambo & the House Wreckers	34	2
4/15/66	5/13/66	Rainy Day Women #12 & 35	Bob Dylan	3	7
5/27/61	6/17/61	Rama Lama Ding Dong	Edsels	9	6
1/20/69	3/3/69	Ramblin' Gamblin' Man	Bob Seger System	2	9
8/11/62	9/15/62	Ramblin' Rose	Nat "King" Cole	3	9
6/14/63	6/28/63	Rat Race	Drifters	33	3
11/12/60	12/3/60	Rat Race, The	Richard Maltby	8	10
12/9/68	12/23/68	Ray Of Hope, A	Rascals	22	4
11/27/64	11/27/64	Reach Out For Me	Dionne Warwick	29	1
9/23/66	11/4/66	Reach Out I'll Be There	Four Tops	2	10
5/6/68	5/27/68	Reach Out Of The Darkness	Friend & Lover	3	8
6/30/69	8/4/69	Reconsider Me	Johnny Adams	21	7
1/7/66	1/14/66	Recovery	Fontella Bass	25	4
3/12/65	4/9/65	Red Roses For A Blue Lady	Vic Dana	15	5

Debut	Peak	Title	Artist	Pos	Wks
2/26/65	3/12/65	Red Roses For A Blue Lady	Bert Kaempfert	12	4
3/5/65	4/9/65	Red Roses For A Blue Lady	Wayne Newton	15	6
5/27/66	7/8/66	Red Rubber Ball	Cyrkle	4	10
4/17/64	5/8/64	Red Ryder	Murry Kellum	25	5
4/23/65	5/21/65	Reelin' & Rockin'	Dave Clark Five	11	7
8/11/67	9/29/67	Reflections	Diana Ross & the Supremes	4	9
11/3/62	12/1/62	Release Me	Esther Phillips	18	6
5/5/67	5/26/67	Release Me (And Let Me Love Again)	Engelbert Humperdinck	8	6
8/28/64	9/11/64	Remember (Walkin' In The Sand)	Shangri-Las	2	6
4/12/63	4/19/63	Remember Diana	Paul Anka	32	3
6/26/64	7/3/64	Remember Me	Rita Pavone	23	4
11/17/62	12/22/62	Remember Then	Earls	14	6
10/15/65	10/29/65	Rescue Me	Fontella Bass	27	6
5/5/67	6/2/67	Respect	Aretha Franklin	10	8
8/5/66	8/19/66	Respectable	Outsiders	5	4
2/24/67	3/10/67	Return Of The Red Baron, The	Royal Guardsmen	20	5
10/20/62	12/15/62	Return To Sender	Elvis Presley	2	12
9/15/69	10/20/69	Reuben James	Kenny Rogers & the First Edition	10	9
8/16/63	9/20/63	Rev Up	Manuel & the Renegades	5	7
1/6/62	1/6/62	Revenge	Brook Benton	33	1
4/5/63	5/3/63	Reverend Mr. Black	Kingston Trio	6	6
9/2/68	9/30/68	Revolution	Beatles	2	8
1/25/63	2/22/63	Rhythm Of The Rain	Cascades	2	10
11/3/62	11/24/62	Ride!	Dee Dee Sharp	20	4
9/10/65	10/1/65	Ride Away	Roy Orbison	20	4
10/16/64	11/6/64	Ride The Wild Surf	Jan & Dean	17	4
7/30/65	7/30/65	Ride Your Pony	Lee Dorsey	28	1
2/4/61	2/25/61	(Ghost) Riders In The Sky	Ramrods	18	6
11/6/64	11/20/64	Right Or Wrong	Ronnie Dove	13	6
8/19/61	9/2/61	Right Or Wrong	Wanda Jackson	19	4
11/25/68	12/2/68	Right Relations	Johnny Rivers	36	3
8/11/62	8/18/62	Right String But The Wrong Yo-Yo	Dr. Feelgood & the Interns	12	7
10/1/65	10/22/65	Ring Dang Doo	Sam the Sham & the Pharaohs	18	5
6/21/63	7/12/63	Ring Of Fire	Johnny Cash	10	7
10/30/64	12/4/64	Ringo	Lorne Greene	2	8
7/7/62	8/18/62	Rinky Dink	Dave "Baby" Cortez	12	7
2/21/64	3/13/64	Rip Van Winkle	Devotions	12	4

Debut	Peak	Title	Artist	Pos	Wks
1/6/62	1/6/62	Rivalry	Johnny Cooper	38	1
10/14/61	10/28/61	Roach, The	Gene & Wendell	24	3
9/24/65	10/29/65	Road Runner	Gants	10	8
6/10/66	6/10/66	(I'm A) Road Runner	Jr. Walker & the All-Stars	38	1
6/26/64	6/26/64	(We're Gonna) Rock Around The Clock	Bill Haley & his Comets	35	1
10/14/61	10/14/61	Rock Island Line	Lonnie Donegan	37	1
2/17/69	4/7/69	Rock Me	Steppenwolf	6	11
7/5/63	7/19/63	Rock Me In The Cradle Of Love	Dee Dee Sharp	32	4
11/11/61	11/18/61	Rock-A-Bye Your Baby With A Dixie Melody	Aretha Franklin	30	2
12/23/61	1/6/62	Rock-A-Hula Baby	Elvis Presley	10	4
8/7/64	8/21/64	Rockin' Robin	Rivieras	8	5
3/20/64	3/20/64	Roll Over Beethoven	Princeton Five	37	1
8/19/61	8/26/61	Roll Over Beethoven	Velaires	29	2
8/26/66	9/16/66	Roller Coaster	Ides Of March	19	6
6/23/67	7/14/67	(Just Like) Romeo And Juliet	Michael & the Messengers	12	8
4/3/64	5/22/64	(Just Like) Romeo & Juliet	Reflections	13	9
5/19/69	6/16/69	Romeo & Juliet, Love Theme From	Henry Mancini	1	11
4/10/64	5/15/64	Ronnie	Four Seasons	10	7
5/27/61	6/3/61	Ronnie	Joe Marcy	31	3
5/3/63	5/17/63	Ronnie, Call Me When You Get A Chance	Shelley Fabares	26	3
1/6/62	1/13/62	Room Full Of Tears	Drifters	31	2
10/13/69	11/10/69	Roosevelt And Ira Lee (Night Of The Mossacin)	Tony Joe White	16	6
9/17/65	10/22/65	Roses And Rainbows	Danny Hutton	10	7
6/9/62	6/30/62	Roses Are Red (My Love)	Bobby Vinton	1	10
5/19/67	6/2/67	Round Round	Jonathan King	23	4
7/14/62	7/28/62	Route 66 Theme	Nelson Riddle	26	3
6/30/67	7/7/67	Royal Blue Summer Sunshine Day	Bystanders	35	2
12/24/60	1/21/61	Rubber Ball	Bobby Vee	6	9
12/24/60	12/31/60	Ruby	Ray Charles	35	3
12/8/62	12/15/62	Ruby Ann	Marty Robbins	13	3
1/12/63	2/15/63	Ruby Baby	Dion	2	11
6/16/69	7/14/69	Ruby, Don't Take Your Love To Town	Kenny Rogers & the First Edition	5	9
10/15/60	10/29/60	Ruby Duby Du	Tobin Mathews & Co.	1	8

Debut	Peak	Title	Artist	Pos	Wks
1/20/67	2/24/67	Ruby Tuesday	Rolling Stones	2	9
11/10/62	12/1/62	Rumors	Johnny Crawford	9	5
3/3/69	3/31/69	Run Away Child, Running Wild	Temptations	7	7
11/12/65	12/17/65	Run, Baby Run (Back Into My Arms)	Newbeats	12	7
7/8/61	7/15/61	Run, Run, Run	Ronny Douglas	29	3
8/4/67	8/25/67	Run, Run, Run	Third Rail	19	6
11/25/61	12/9/61	Run To Him	Bobby Vee	2	10
9/23/68	11/11/68	Run To Me	Montanas	8	11
8/12/61	8/12/61	Runaround	Regents	37	1
10/7/61	10/21/61	Runaround Sue	Dion	1	11
4/8/61	4/29/61	Runaway	Del Shannon	1	10
5/13/61	6/3/61	Running Scared	Roy Orbison	2	9
6/24/61	7/22/61	Sacred	Castells	6	9
9/30/61	11/4/61	Sad Movies (Make Me Cry)	Sue Thompson	6	8
5/24/63	5/31/63	Sad, Sad Girl And Boy	Impressions	25	3
1/31/64	3/13/64	Saginaw, Michigan	Lefty Frizzell	25	5
10/29/60	11/12/60	Sailor (Your Home Is The Sea)	Lolita	5	10
1/4/63	1/4/63	Sailor Boy	Cathy Carr	36	1
9/16/61	9/23/61	Sailor Man	Bobby Bare	35	2
8/30/63	9/27/63	Sally, Go 'Round The Roses	Jaynetts	2	6
8/4/62	8/4/62	Sally Was A Good Old Girl	Hank Cochran	38	1
10/25/63	11/8/63	Saltwater Taffy	Morty Jay & the Surferin' Cats	26	4
7/22/61	8/5/61	San Antonio Rose	Floyd Cramer	11	6
6/2/67	7/14/67	San Francisco (Be Sure To Wear Flowers In Your Hair)	Scott McKenzie	5	11
3/15/63	4/12/63	Sandy	Dion	9	6
12/24/65	1/28/66	Sandy	Ronny & the Daytonas	9	9
12/15/62	12/22/62	Santa Claus Is Watching You	Ray Stevens	19	2
12/24/65	1/14/66	Satin Pillows	Bobby Vinton	32	5
6/18/65	7/9/65	(I Can't Get No) Satisfaction	Rolling Stones	1	10
8/12/66	9/2/66	Satisfied With You	Dave Clark Five	29	6
11/1/63	11/1/63	Saturday Night	New Christy Minstrels	40	1
12/4/64	12/25/64	Saturday Night At The Movies	Drifters	18	4
8/9/63	8/9/63	Saturday Sunshine	Burt Bacharach	39	1
6/10/68	6/17/68	Saturday's Father	Four Seasons	31	2
9/11/64	10/2/64	Save It For Me	Four Seasons	16	4
10/14/60	10/15/60	Save The Last Dance For Me	Drifters	2	7

Debut	Peak	Title	Artist	Pos	Wks
7/2/65	7/30/65	Save Your Heart For Me	Gary Lewis & the Playboys	3	7
4/22/61	5/6/61	Saved	LaVern Baker	30	3
3/8/63	3/22/63	Sax Fifth Avenue	Johnny Beecher	22	5
7/29/66	8/26/66	Say I Am (What I Am)	Tommy James & the Shondells	2	6
4/16/65	5/14/65	Say It Softly	Bobby Whiteside	11	7
10/29/65	10/29/65	Say Something Funny	Patty Duke	39	1
9/11/64	9/25/64	Say You	Ronnie Dove	22	3
11/18/68	12/16/68	Scarborough Fair	Sergio Mendes & Brasil '66	19	7
3/11/68	4/1/68	Scarborough Fair/Canticle	Simon & Garfunkel	19	4
11/4/61	11/25/61	School Is In	Gary U.S. Bonds	17	4
8/12/61	8/26/61	School Is Out	Gary U.S. Bonds	3	5
10/15/60	10/29/60	Scoop Scoobie Doobie	Jessie Hill	31	2
10/28/61	10/28/61	Scratchin'	Twilighters	36	1
11/13/64	11/27/64	Scratchy	Travis Wammack	12	6
10/22/65	10/29/65	Sea Cruise	Hondells	32	2
1/25/63	2/8/63	Seagrams	Viceroys	27	5
6/23/62	7/21/62	Sealed With A Kiss	Brian Hyland	1	9
7/1/68	8/5/68	Sealed With A Kiss	Gary Lewis & the Playboys	5	9
5/5/67	5/19/67	Searchin'	Mugwumps	33	4
11/25/61	12/2/61	Searching	Jack Eubanks	17	2
7/29/66	8/5/66	Searching For My Love	Bobby Moore	25	5
4/21/69	6/2/69	Seattle	Perry Como	27	7
5/26/62	6/9/62	Second Hand Love	Connie Francis	26	3
1/7/66	2/4/66	Second Hand Rose	Barbra Streisand	20	6
3/18/66	4/15/66	Secret Agent Man	Johnny Rivers	2	10
10/14/66	11/4/66	Secret Love	Billy Stewart	26	5
3/25/68	3/25/68	Security	Etta James	34	2
5/19/69	6/16/69	See	Rascals	12	8
11/25/68	12/16/68	See Saw	Aretha Franklin	12	6
12/15/62	12/29/62	See See Rider	LaVern Baker	33	3
10/7/66	11/11/66	See See Rider	Eric Burdon & the Animals	13	7
1/10/64	2/28/64	See The Funny Little Clown	Bobby Goldsboro	4	10
7/22/66	8/19/66	See You In September	Happenings	4	10
8/14/64	8/28/64	Selfish One	Jackie Ross	33	3
2/15/63	2/22/63	Send Me Some Lovin'	Sam Cooke	36	2
12/17/60	12/31/60	Send Me The Pillow You Dream On	Browns	29	4

Debut	Peak	Title	Artist	Pos	Wks
2/26/65	3/19/65	Send Me The Pillow You Dream On	Dean Martin	21	4
8/25/62	9/8/62	Send Me The Pillow You Dream On	Johnny Tillotson	23	3
9/10/65	9/24/65	September In The Rain	Chad & Jeremy	26	3
11/18/61	11/25/61	September In The Rain	Dinah Washington	27	2
6/25/65	7/9/65	Set Me Free	Kinks	26	4
2/1/63	2/15/63	Settle Down (Goin' Down That Highway)	Peter, Paul & Mary	20	3
8/19/66	9/9/66	7 And 7 Is	Love	28	5
7/28/62	8/4/62	Seven Day Weekend	Gary U.S. Bonds	32	2
6/2/67	6/16/67	7 Rooms Of Gloom	Four Tops	27	4
6/4/65	7/2/65	Seventh Son	Johnny Rivers	11	7
12/4/64	1/15/65	Sha La La	Manfred Mann	11	8
2/3/62	2/3/62	Shadrack	Brook Benton	37	1
1/22/65	1/22/65	Shake	Sam Cooke	28	5
11/18/68	12/9/68	Shake	Shadows Of Knight	12	6
4/5/63	4/19/63	Shake A Tail Feather	Five Du-Tones	31	4
4/14/67	4/21/67	Shake Hands And Walk Away Cryin'	Lou Christie	30	4
2/25/66	3/11/66	Shake Me, Wake Me (When It's Over)	Four Tops	27	3
6/30/67	6/30/67	Shake, Rattle & Roll	Arthur Conley	37	2
2/1/63	2/1/63	Shake Sherry	Contours	34	2
4/2/65	4/16/65	Shakin' All Over	Guess Who	12	8
8/25/62	9/22/62	Shame On Me	Bobby Bare	15	5
10/14/68	11/25/68	Shame, Shame	Magic Lanterns	5	10
5/8/64	6/5/64	Shangri-La	Vic Dana	9	7
11/3/69	11/10/69	Shangri-La	Lettermen	36	2
9/16/68	10/14/68	Shape Of Things To Come	Max Frost & the Troopers	4	7
3/11/66	4/15/66	Shapes Of Things	Yardbirds	4	11
8/11/69	8/18/69	Share Your Love With Me	Aretha Franklin	33	2
6/9/62	6/23/62	Sharing You	Bobby Vee	25	3
12/8/69	12/29/69	She	Tommy James & the Shondells	23	6
3/31/62	5/12/62	She Can't Find Her Keys	Paul Petersen	8	8
11/11/66	11/18/66	(When She Needs Good Lovin') She Comes To Me	Chicago Loop	30	4
3/24/62	4/21/62	She Cried	Jay & the Americans	1	9
10/27/67	11/17/67	She Is Still A Mystery	Lovin' Spoonful	18	5
1/31/64	2/28/64	She Loves You	Beatles	1	10
2/28/64	2/28/64	She Rides With Me	Paul Petersen	33	1
11/13/64	12/11/64	She Understands Me	Johnny Tillotson	13	6

Debut	Peak	Title	Artist	Pos	Wks
5/19/67	6/9/67	She'd Rather Be With Me	Turtles	4	8
4/3/64	5/1/64	She's A Bad Motorcycle	Crestones	11	5
10/4/63	11/8/63	She's A Fool	Lesley Gore	2	10
5/20/68	6/24/68	She's A Heartbreaker	Gene Pitney	7	9
11/10/62	11/24/62	She's A Troublemaker	Majors	13	4
11/27/64	12/18/64	She's A Woman	Beatles	1	9
4/23/65	6/4/65	She's About A Mover	Sir Douglas Quintet	14	8
5/7/65	5/14/65	She's Coming Home	Zombies	24	4
12/16/61	1/27/62	She's Everything (I Wanted You To Be)	Ral Donner	7	9
11/15/63	11/29/63	She's Got Everything	Essex	22	4
3/3/62	3/10/62	She's Got You	Patsy Cline	18	4
12/10/65	1/28/66	She's Just My Style	Gary Lewis & the Playboys	7	9
4/1/68	5/20/68	She's Lookin' Good	Wilson Pickett	11	9
11/17/67	11/24/67	She's My Girl	Turtles	13	7
10/23/64	12/4/64	She's Not There	Zombies	1	12
8/11/62	9/8/62	She's Not You	Elvis Presley	13	5
6/26/64	7/31/64	She's The One	Chartbusters	9	7
7/21/62	8/25/62	Sheila	Tommy Roe	1	9
2/14/64	3/20/64	Shelter Of Your Arms, The	Sammy Davis, Jr.	8	9
8/18/62	9/1/62	Sherry	Four Seasons	1	8
4/15/68	4/29/68	Sherry Don't Go	Lettermen	33	3
10/14/60	10/29/60	Shimmy Like Kate	Olympics	14	6
2/21/64	2/21/64	Shimmy Shimmy	Orlons	39	1
2/10/62	2/24/62	Shimmy Shimmy Walk, Part 1	Megatons	31	3
4/8/68	5/20/68	Shoo-Be-Doo-Be-Doo-Da-Day	Stevie Wonder	7	8
3/20/64	3/27/64	Shoop Shoop Song (It's In His Kiss), The	Betty Everett	31	2
12/31/60	1/28/61	Shop Around	Miracles	2	9
10/15/60	10/29/60	Shoppin' For Clothes	Coasters	27	2
10/14/60	10/14/60	Shortnin' Bread	Paul Chaplain & his Emeralds	1	4
3/5/65	4/9/65	Shotgun	Jr. Walker & the All-Stars	16	8
7/29/61	8/5/61	Should I Wait	Johnny Mathis	26	2
7/24/64	8/21/64	Shout	Lulu & the Luvers	31	5
3/24/62	4/14/62	Shout—Part 1	Joey Dee & the Starliters	3	6
7/28/62	8/4/62	Shout And Shimmy	James Brown	31	2
4/7/62	5/12/62	Shout! Shout! (Knock Yourself Out)	Ernie Maresca	4	7
5/6/61	5/13/61	Shu Rah	Fats Domino	34	2
5/31/63	6/21/63	Shut Down	Beach Boys	3	9
12/1/62	12/15/62	Shutters And Boards	Jerry Wallace	15	7

Debut	Peak	Title	Artist	Pos	Wks
11/1/63	11/29/63	Shy Guy	Radiants	19	6
11/20/64	11/27/64	Sidewalk Surfin'	Jan & Dean	20	4
6/5/64	6/19/64	Sie Liebt Dich (She Loves You)	Beatles	17	4
3/25/66	4/8/66	Sign Of The Times, A	Petula Clark	25	4
6/30/67	8/25/67	Silence Is Golden	Tremeloes	9	11
4/23/65	5/21/65	Silhouettes	Herman's Hermits	1	10
8/21/64	8/21/64	Silly Ol' Summertime	New Christy Minstrels	39	1
12/16/61	12/30/61	Silver Dollar	Barry Darvell	25	3
8/11/62	9/15/62	Silver Threads And Golden Needles	Springfields	7	7
1/29/68	3/11/68	Simon Says	1910 Fruitgum Co.	2	11
2/28/64	2/28/64	(It's No) Sin	Duprees	38	2
12/13/63	1/10/64	Since I Fell For You	Lenny Welch	15	7
8/6/65	8/13/65	Since I Lost My Baby	Temptations	25	2
2/19/68	3/25/68	(Sweet Sweet Baby) Since You've Been Gone	Aretha Franklin	5	9
2/17/69	2/17/69	Sing A Simple Song	Sly & the Family Stone	1	2
4/14/69	4/28/69	Singing My Song	Tammy Wynette	33	3
11/25/66	12/23/66	Single Girl	Sandy Posey	13	5
10/15/65	11/26/65	Sinner Man	Trini Lopez	14	4
7/12/63	7/19/63	Six Days On The Road	Dave Dudley	14	5
4/28/67	5/12/67	Six O'Clock	Lovin' Spoonful	17	7
4/1/66	4/8/66	634-5789 (Soulsville U.S.A.)	Wilson Pickett	35	2
12/22/69	12/29/69	Six White Horses	Tommy Cash	37	3
10/27/67	12/8/67	Skinny Legs And All	Joe Tex	10	8
12/8/67	1/15/68	Skip A Rope	Henson Cargill	7	8
5/3/63	5/17/63	Skip To M' Limbo	Ventures	25	3
7/8/68	8/5/68	Sky Pilot (Part One)	Eric Burdon & the Animals	19	5
10/14/60	10/29/60	Sleep	Little Willie John	4	6
11/22/63	11/22/63	Sleep Walk	Nick Noble	33	1
7/15/68	8/26/68	Slip Away	Clarence Carter	13	7
12/6/63	1/3/64	Slippin' & Slidin'	Jim & Monica	12	9
4/1/66	4/15/66	Sloop John B	Beach Boys	12	6
9/11/64	10/2/64	Slow Down	Beatles	14	5
3/17/62	4/21/62	Slow Twistin'	Chubby Checker	8	7
12/9/61	12/30/61	Small Sad Sam	Phil McLean	14	5
12/9/61	12/9/61	Smile	Timi Yuro	37	1

Debut	Peak	Title	Artist	Pos	Wks
10/13/69	12/1/69	Smile A Little Smile For Me	Flying Machine	8	12
12/2/61	1/6/62	Smokey Places	Corsairs	7	10
9/2/68	10/7/68	Snake, The	Al Wilson	17	8
6/2/62	6/16/62	Snap Your Fingers	Joe Henderson	23	4
3/31/69	3/31/69	Snatching It Back	Clarence Carter	36	2
6/10/68	6/10/68	Snoopy For President	Royal Guardsmen	36	1
12/9/66	12/30/66	Snoopy Vs. The Red Baron	Royal Guardsmen	2	9
11/24/67	12/15/67	Snoopy's Christmas	Royal Guardsmen	5	6
12/20/63	12/27/63	Snowman Snowman	Jaynetts	37	2
10/20/69	11/10/69	So Good Together	Andy Kim	24	4
7/22/66	7/29/66	(You Make Me Feel) So Good	McCoys	35	3
10/7/61	11/11/61	So Long Baby	Del Shannon	14	7
6/7/63	7/19/63	So Much In Love	Tymes	3	10
10/14/60	10/15/60	So Sad (To Watch Good Love Go Bad)	Everly Brothers	3	3
4/15/61	4/15/61	So Sick	Lucky Clark	40	1
4/28/62	6/2/62	So This Is Love	Castells	9	7
9/22/62	10/6/62	So What	Bill Black's Combo	32	3
2/3/67	2/24/67	So You Want To Be A Rock 'N' Roll Star	Byrds	20	5
2/10/67	3/3/67	Sock It To Me-Baby!	Mitch Ryder & the Detroit Wheels	10	7
9/11/64	10/2/64	Softly, As I Leave You	Frank Sinatra	23	4
3/31/62	5/5/62	Soldier Boy	Shirelles	1	9
7/24/64	8/7/64	Sole Sole Sole	Siw Malmkvist & Umberto Marcato	21	3
9/2/61	9/9/61	Solitaire	Embers	36	2
9/3/65	9/24/65	Some Enchanted Evening	Jay & the Americans	3	6
4/8/61	5/13/61	Some Kind Of Wonderful	Drifters	9	6
11/17/62	12/15/62	Some Kinda Fun	Chris Montez	9	7
6/3/68	7/8/68	Some Things You Never Get Used To	Diana Ross & the Supremes	18	6
7/1/68	8/5/68	Somebody Cares	Tommy James & the Shondells	14	7
7/7/67	8/4/67	Somebody Help Me	Spencer Davis Group	21	6
9/10/65	9/17/65	Somebody New	Rivieras	32	2
10/14/60	10/14/60	Somebody To Love	Bobby Darin	40	1
4/7/67	5/26/67	Somebody To Love	Jefferson Airplane	1	11
11/10/69	12/8/69	Someday We'll Be Together	Diana Ross & the Supremes	1	14
9/11/64	10/2/64	Some Day We're Gonna Love Again	Searchers	19	5
12/3/60	12/31/60	Someday You'll Want Me To Want You	Brook Benton	27	6
3/17/67	4/21/67	Somethin' Stupid	Nancy & Frank Sinatra	2	10

Debut	Peak	Title	Artist	Pos	Wks
10/6/69	11/3/69	Something	Beatles	1	16
11/19/65	11/19/65	Something About You	Four Tops	25	3
9/6/63	9/6/63	Something Old, Something New	Paul & Paula	39	1
3/24/62	3/31/62	Something's Got A Hold On Me	Etta James	30	2
8/19/61	8/19/61	Sometime	Gene Thomas	39	1
8/26/66	9/9/66	Sometimes Good Guys Don't Wear White	Standells	39	3
1/8/65	1/15/65	Sometimes I Wonder	Major Lance	37	2
1/10/64	1/17/64	Somewhere	Tymes	34	3
7/1/66	8/12/66	Somewhere My Love	Ray Conniff	18	8
9/29/69	10/6/69	Son Of A Lovin' Man	Buchanan Brothers	35	3
11/25/68	1/13/69	Son-Of-A Preacher Man	Dusty Springfield	4	11
10/28/61	11/25/61	Soothe Me	Sims Twins	12	7
3/11/66	5/6/66	(You're My) Soul And Inspiration	Righteous Brothers	8	11
7/14/69	8/18/69	Soul Deep	Box Tops	3	10
9/9/68	9/30/68	Soul Drippin'	Mauds	12	5
6/30/67	7/7/67	Soul Finger	Bar-Kays	30	3
7/22/68	9/2/68	Soul-Limbo	Booker T. & the MG's	13	8
9/22/67	11/3/67	Soul Man	Sam & Dave	13	8
3/25/68	5/13/68	Soul Serenade	Willie Mitchell	19	8
3/17/62	4/7/62	Soul Twist	King Curtis & the Noble Knights	28	4
12/2/68	1/20/69	Soulful Strut	Young-Holt Unlimited	3	11
1/27/69	2/17/69	Soulshake	Peggy Scott & Jo Jo Benson	20	4
3/4/68	4/1/68	Sound Asleep	Turtles	23	5
5/19/67	6/23/67	Sound Of Love	Five Americans	15	7
2/25/61	2/25/61	Sound-Off	Titus Turner	38	1
12/10/65	1/14/66	Sounds Of Silence, The	Simon & Garfunkel	1	10
2/15/63	3/8/63	South Street	Orlons	6	7
2/7/64	2/14/64	Southtown, U.S.A.	Dixiebelles	22	3
12/10/65	12/31/65	Spanish Eyes	Al Martino	17	6
2/18/61	3/25/61	Spanish Harlem	Ben E. King	3	8
11/24/62	12/1/62	Spanish Lace	Gene McDaniels	33	2
11/25/66	12/2/66	Spanish Nights And You	Connie Francis	18	5
5/20/61	5/20/61	Sparkle And Shine	Four Couquettes	38	1
8/2/63	8/16/63	S.P.C.L.G.	Society Girls	32	3
5/12/69	6/16/69	Special Delivery	1910 Fruitgum Co.	11	9
9/2/68	9/9/68	Special Occasion	Smokey Robinson & the Miracles	34	2
6/23/62	7/28/62	Speedy Gonzales	Pat Boone	9	7
6/2/69	7/7/69	Spinning Wheel	Blood, Sweat & Tears	2	10
10/7/66	10/21/66	Spinout	Elvis Presley	23	4
12/29/67	2/12/68	Spooky	Classics IV	3	11
4/10/64	4/10/64	Spring Cleaning	Angello's Angels	30	3

Debut	Peak	Title	Artist	Pos	Wks
5/17/63	5/17/63	Spring In Manhattan	Tony Bennett	37	1
8/2/63	8/2/63	St. Louis Blues	Joe Burton	37	1
10/20/67	11/17/67	Stag-O-Lee	Wilson Pickett	15	6
6/10/61	6/24/61	Stand By Me	Ben E. King	29	3
2/10/67	2/24/67	Stand By Me	Spyder Turner	31	4
12/16/68	1/27/69	Stand By Your Man	Tammy Wynette	22	7
12/16/66	1/20/67	Standing In The Shadows Of Love	Four Tops	10	8
3/6/64	3/6/64	Stardust	Nino Tempo & April Stevens	28	3
8/5/61	9/9/61	Starlight, Starbright	Linda Scott	4	8
3/20/64	5/1/64	Stay	Four Seasons	13	7
10/14/60	10/15/60	Stay	Maurice Williams & the Zodiacs	1	7
4/17/64	4/17/64	Stay Awhile	Dusty Springfield	37	2
7/1/68	8/5/68	Stay In My Corner	Dells	9	9
1/10/64	1/31/64	Stay With Me	Nick Noble	18	5
10/29/60	10/29/60	Stay With Me	Ed Townsend	40	1
3/4/61	3/25/61	Stayin' In	Bobby Vee	18	6
7/24/64	8/21/64	Steal Away	Jimmy Hughes	28	5
6/16/62	6/16/62	Steel Guitar And A Glass Of Wine, A	Paul Anka	30	1
2/18/61	2/25/61	Steel Guitar Rag	Tobin Mathews & Co.	30	2
3/10/62	3/17/62	Step By Step	Anita Bryant	31	2
5/26/67	6/30/67	Step Out Of Your Mind	American Breed	9	8
10/1/65	10/22/65	Steppin' Out	Paul Revere & the Raiders	17	6
12/9/66	12/30/66	(I'm Not Your) Steppin' Stone	Monkees	1	12
12/13/63	12/13/63	Stewball	Peter, Paul & Mary	36	1
8/12/61	9/2/61	Stick Shift	Duals	15	5
5/24/63	6/14/63	Still	Bill Anderson	6	7
12/22/67	1/8/68	Still Burning	Drifters	29	3
5/10/63	6/7/63	Sting Ray	Routers	6	7
6/24/68	7/29/68	Stoned Soul Picnic	Fifth Dimension	7	9
1/24/64	2/7/64	Stop And Think It Over	Dale & Grace	13	8
3/18/66	3/25/66	Stop Her On Sight (S.O.S.)	Edwin Starr	35	2
2/19/65	3/19/65	Stop! In The Name Of Love	Supremes	2	9
10/21/66	11/25/66	Stop Stop Stop	Hollies	8	8
10/6/62	10/13/62	Stop The Music	Shirelles	31	2
8/11/62	8/11/62	Stop The Wedding	Etta James	34	3
11/4/68	12/23/68	Stormy	Classics IV featuring Dennis Yost	4	11
4/5/63	4/26/63	Stormy	Corsairs	21	4
4/7/62	4/28/62	Story Of My Life, The	Big Al Downing	15	5

Debut	Peak	Title	Artist	Pos	Wks
2/11/61	2/18/61	Story Of My Love, The	Paul Anka	29	2
6/10/68	7/1/68	Story Of Rock And Roll, The	Turtles	33	4
10/11/63	10/25/63	Story Untold, A	Emotions	25	4
11/11/68	12/2/68	Straight Life, The	Bobby Goldsboro	27	5
7/8/61	7/15/61	Stranded In The Jungle	Vibrations	32	2
1/4/63	1/12/63	Strange I Know	Marvelettes	32	4
10/15/60	11/5/60	Stranger From Durango	Richie Allen	14	6
3/5/65	3/5/65	Stranger In Town	Del Shannon	34	3
4/7/62	5/12/62	Stranger On The Shore	Mr. Acker Bilk	1	12
6/16/62	6/23/62	Stranger On The Shore	Andy Williams	34	2
5/13/66	6/10/66	Strangers In The Night	Frank Sinatra	2	10
11/19/60	12/10/60	Strawberry Blonde	Frank D'rone	27	4
2/24/67	3/10/67	Strawberry Fields Forever	Beatles	4	7
5/31/63	6/14/63	String Along	Rick Nelson	12	3
6/2/62	6/16/62	Stripper, The	David Rose	1	10
11/3/62	11/3/62	Stubborn Kind Of Fellow	Marvin Gaye	38	1
4/16/65	4/23/65	Subterranean Homesick Blues	Bob Dylan	34	4
5/26/62	6/16/62	Such A Night	Vince Everett	16	5
8/21/64	8/21/64	Such A Night	Elvis Presley	38	1
3/4/68	3/25/68	Suddenly You Love Me	Tremeloes	29	4
10/25/63	11/8/63	Sue's Gotta Be Mine	Del Shannon	16	4
7/1/66	7/29/66	Sugar And Spice	Cryan' Shames	4	8
8/6/65	8/6/65	Sugar Dumpling	Sam Cooke	39	1
7/10/64	7/17/64	Sugar Lips	Al Hirt	27	4
9/22/69	10/27/69	Sugar On Sunday	Clique	16	6
4/24/64	5/22/64	Sugar Over You	Carol Vega	31	5
9/13/63	10/4/63	Sugar Shack	Jimmy Gilmer & the Fireballs	1	11
8/4/69	9/1/69	Sugar, Sugar	Archies	1	13
11/11/66	12/30/66	Sugar Town	Nancy Sinatra	5	10
9/22/69	11/3/69	Suite: Judy Blue Eyes	Crosby, Stills & Nash	3	11
5/24/63	5/31/63	Sukiyaki	Kyu Sakamoto	1	9
7/8/66	7/29/66	Summer In The City	Lovin' Spoonful	1	9
9/10/65	10/15/65	Summer Nights	Marianne Faithfull	10	7
6/18/65	7/2/65	Summer Place, Theme From A	Lettermen	25	5
6/9/62	6/23/62	Summer Place, Theme From A	Dick Roman	9	5
12/1/67	1/15/68	Summer Rain	Johnny Rivers	8	9
9/9/66	9/23/66	Summer Samba (So Nice)	Walter Wanderley	20	6
8/28/64	9/18/64	Summer Song, A	Chad & Jeremy	6	7
9/9/66	9/30/66	Summer Wind	Frank Sinatra	27	5

Debut	Peak	Title	Artist	Pos	Wks
6/7/63	6/21/63	Summer's Comin'	Kirby St. Romain	19	4
11/5/60	11/5/60	Summer's Gone	Paul Anka	32	1
5/27/61	6/17/61	Summertime	Marcels	8	5
8/5/66	8/19/66	Summertime	Billy Stewart	18	4
3/11/68	4/15/68	Summertime Blues	Blue Cheer	5	8
6/9/62	7/7/62	Summertime, Summertime	Jamies	5	6
4/22/66	5/13/66	Sun Ain't Gonna Shine (Anymore), The	Walker Brothers	19	5
3/1/63	3/29/63	Sun Arise	Rolf Harris	6	5
11/19/65	12/10/65	Sunday And Me	Jay & the Americans	10	5
3/31/67	4/14/67	Sunday For Tea	Peter & Gordon	26	4
12/15/69	12/22/69	Sunday Mornin'	Oliver	37	2
6/2/67	7/7/67	Sunday Will Never Be The Same	Spanky & Our Gang	12	8
10/29/60	11/5/60	Sundowners, Theme From The	Felix Slatkin	29	3
7/15/66	8/19/66	Sunny	Bobby Hebb	8	11
8/5/66	9/9/66	Sunny Afternoon	Kinks	12	7
5/12/67	5/19/67	Sunshine Girl	Parade	39	3
6/11/65	7/23/65	Sunshine, Lollipops And Rainbows	Lesley Gore	13	7
12/22/67	2/5/68	Sunshine Of Your Love	Cream	8	9
7/22/68	8/26/68	Sunshine Of Your Love	Cream	7	7
8/5/66	8/26/66	Sunshine Superman	Donovan	1	10
3/4/66	3/25/66	Sure Gonna Miss Her	Gary Lewis & the Playboys	12	5
6/14/63	7/12/63	Surf City	Jan & Dean	1	10
8/30/63	10/4/63	Surfer Girl	Beach Boys	7	8
10/25/63	11/8/63	Surfer Street	Allisons	32	3
2/10/62	2/24/62	Surfer's Stomp	Marketts	33	3
12/20/63	1/10/64	Surfin' Bird	Trashmen	3	8
6/28/63	7/26/63	Surfin' Hootenanny	Al Casey	27	5
9/15/62	9/29/62	Surfin' Safari	Beach Boys	5	9
4/12/63	5/10/63	Surfin' U.S.A.	Beach Boys	6	8
2/18/61	3/11/61	Surrender	Elvis Presley	5	8
11/24/67	1/15/68	Susan	Buckinghams	5	11
10/6/62	10/27/62	Susie Darlin'	Tommy Roe	22	4
9/9/68	10/14/68	Susie Q (Part One)	Creedence Clearwater Revival	6	9
3/13/64	4/10/64	Suspicion	Terry Stafford	1	10
9/22/69	10/13/69	Suspicious Minds	Elvis Presley	1	11
11/19/60	12/10/60	Sway	Bobby Rydell	8	6
8/25/62	9/1/62	Sweet And Lovely	Nino Tempo & April Stevens	35	2
10/21/68	11/18/68	Sweet Blindness	Fifth Dimension	19	5
6/30/69	8/4/69	Sweet Caroline (Good Times Never Seemed So Good)	Neil Diamond	8	11

Debut	Peak	Title	Artist	Pos	Wks
3/17/69	4/21/69	Sweet Cherry Wine	Tommy James & the Shondells	4	11
7/15/66	7/29/66	Sweet Dreams	Tommy McLain	9	5
3/11/68	4/1/68	Sweet Inspiration	Sweet Inspirations	13	7
6/10/66	8/5/66	Sweet Pea	Tommy Roe	9	9
4/14/67	6/2/67	Sweet Soul Music	Arthur Conley	7	9
5/6/66	6/17/66	Sweet Talkin' Guy	Chiffons	18	8
8/14/64	8/28/64	Sweet William	Millie Small	32	3
9/30/61	10/21/61	Sweets For My Sweet	Drifters	9	6
3/24/67	4/21/67	Sweets For My Sweet	Riddles	19	6
6/23/62	6/23/62	Swingin' Gently	Earl Grant	38	1
7/21/62	8/18/62	Swingin' Safari, A	Billy Vaughn	7	6
7/5/63	7/5/63	Swinging On A Star	Big Dee Irwin	38	1
9/22/62	9/22/62	Swiss Maid, The	Del Shannon	35	2
5/26/62	6/9/62	Ta Ta Tee Ta Ta	Barbara English	34	3
7/22/61	7/29/61	Take A Fool's Advice	Nat "King" Cole	31	2
10/29/65	11/19/65	Take A Heart	Sorrows	16	6
10/6/69	11/24/69	Take A Letter Maria	R.B. Greaves	6	11
6/24/61	7/1/61	Take Five	Dave Brubeck Quartet	32	2
4/1/61	4/22/61	Take Good Care Of Her	Adam Wade	12	6
8/26/61	9/23/61	Take Good Care Of My Baby	Bobby Vee	1	9
4/1/68	5/6/68	Take Good Care Of My Baby	Bobby Vinton	8	7
7/14/67	8/25/67	Take Me Back	Flock	12	9
7/16/65	7/23/65	Take Me Back	Little Anthony & the Imperials	25	3
10/28/68	11/4/68	Take Me For A Little While	Vanilla Fudge	38	2
4/12/63	4/26/63	Take These Chains From My Heart	Ray Charles	18	4
3/18/68	4/29/68	Take Time To Know Her	Percy Sledge	24	7
11/22/63	11/29/63	Talk Back Trembling Lips	Johnny Tillotson	12	6
11/11/66	12/2/66	Talk Talk	Music Machine	8	6
9/20/63	10/18/63	Talk To Me	Sunny & the Sunglows	13	5
12/3/60	12/3/60	Talk To Me Baby	Annette with the Afterbeats	32	2
1/24/64	1/31/64	Talking About My Baby	Impressions	36	4
4/10/64	5/8/64	Tall Cool One	Wailers	4	9
5/10/63	5/31/63	Tamoure	Bill Justis	7	6
3/4/68	3/25/68	Tapioca Tundra	Monkees	1	4
10/29/65	12/3/65	Taste Of Honey	Herb Alpert & the Tijuana Brass	3	11
9/15/62	9/22/62	Taste Of Honey, A	Martin Denny	32	3

Debut	Peak	Title	Artist	Pos	Wks
4/28/62	5/5/62	Teach Me To Twist	Bobby Rydell & Chubby Checker	32	2
5/19/62	6/2/62	Teach Me Tonight	George Maharis	18	3
10/6/62	10/13/62	Tear For Tear	Gene Chandler	34	2
8/5/61	8/5/61	Tear, A	Gene McDaniels	37	1
11/12/65	12/3/65	Tears	Ken Dodd	23	6
5/29/64	6/19/64	Tears And Roses	Al Martino	25	5
8/12/61	8/12/61	Tears On My Pillow	McGuire Sisters	35	1
8/18/62	9/22/62	Teen Age Idol	Rick Nelson	16	7
10/23/64	11/27/64	Teen Beat '65	Sandy Nelson	15	5
10/11/63	10/25/63	Teenage Cleopatra	Tracy Dee	32	3
12/31/60	1/28/61	Teenage Vows Of Love	Dreamers	11	6
1/22/65	2/19/65	Tell Her No	Zombies	7	8
12/13/63	1/17/64	Tell Him	Drew-Vels	21	6
11/24/62	12/22/62	Tell Him	Exciters	15	7
3/8/63	3/15/63	Tell Him I'm Not Home	Chuck Jackson	25	4
12/16/66	1/20/67	Tell It Like It Is	Aaron Neville	11	7
4/3/64	4/10/64	Tell It On The Mountain	Peter, Paul & Mary	29	2
4/7/67	4/21/67	Tell It To My Face	Keith	28	3
12/23/66	1/27/67	Tell It To The Rain	Four Seasons	21	8
12/8/67	1/8/68	Tell Mama	Etta James	19	6
4/21/62	5/26/62	Tell Me	Dick & Deedee	5	7
7/1/61	7/1/61	Tell Me Why	Belmonts	38	1
11/4/61	11/4/61	Tell Me Why	Nate Nelson	40	1
12/24/65	1/7/66	Tell Me Why	Elvis Presley	23	3
5/22/64	6/26/64	Tell Me Why	Bobby Vinton	17	7
10/27/62	12/1/62	Telstar	Tornadoes	1	11
6/10/61	7/15/61	Temptation	Everly Brothers	2	8
10/13/69	11/24/69	Ten Commandments Of Love, The	Little Anthony & the Imperials	28	7
6/14/63	7/12/63	Ten Commandments Of Love, The	James MacArthur	18	5
12/8/62	12/29/62	Ten Little Indians	Beach Boys	25	4
6/30/62	7/14/62	Tennessee	Jan & Dean	20	4
5/19/69	6/2/69	Testify (I Wonna)	Johnnie Taylor	32	3
10/11/63	10/25/63	Thank You And Goodnight	Angels	13	3
3/27/64	4/10/64	Thank You Girl	Beatles	7	9
11/29/63	12/13/63	That Boy John	Raindrops	21	5
1/24/64	2/7/64	That Girl Belongs To Yesterday	Gene Pitney	31	4
12/20/63	12/20/63	That Lucky Old Sun	Ray Charles	29	2
5/20/61	6/10/61	That Old Black Magic	Bobby Rydell	11	6
10/27/62	11/17/62	That Stranger Used To Be My Girl	Trade Martin	14	5

Debut	Peak	Title	Artist	Pos	Wks
10/4/63	11/1/63	That Sunday, That Summer	Nat "King" Cole	12	8
3/1/63	3/8/63	That's All	Rick Nelson	22	2
3/25/61	3/25/61	That's All I Want From You	Barbara McNair	33	1
6/9/62	6/30/62	That's For Me To Know	Tommy Manno	26	4
5/3/63	5/17/63	That's How Heartaches Are Made	Baby Washington	18	3
10/15/60	10/15/60	That's How Much	Brian Hyland	36	1
11/25/66	12/23/66	That's Life	Frank Sinatra	18	7
2/3/62	2/17/62	That's My Pa	Sheb Wooley	13	5
5/26/62	6/9/62	That's Old Fashioned (That's The Way Love Should Be)	Everly Brothers	8	7
1/13/67	1/20/67	That's The Tune	Vogues	30	3
3/27/64	4/24/64	That's The Way Boys Are	Lesley Gore	13	8
2/22/63	3/1/63	That's The Way Love Is	Bobby Bland	33	2
9/1/69	10/6/69	That's The Way Love Is	Marvin Gaye	6	9
4/15/61	4/15/61	That's The Way We Love	Paramours	37	1
4/29/61	5/20/61	That's The Way With Love	Piero Soffici	5	6
8/5/61	8/5/61	That's What Girls Are Made For	Spinners	38	2
2/25/61	3/11/61	Them That Got	Ray Charles	27	3
8/16/63	8/30/63	Then He Kissed Me	Crystals	5	7
6/18/65	6/25/65	Then I'll Count Again	Johnny Tillotson	24	2
1/13/67	3/10/67	Then You Can Tell Me Goodbye	Casinos	8	11
7/14/67	7/14/67	There Goes My Everything	Engelbert Humperdinck	28	3
5/31/63	6/14/63	There Goes My Heart Again	Fats Domino	35	3
11/29/63	1/3/64	There! I've Said It Again	Bobby Vinton	1	11
12/22/67	2/12/68	There Is	Dells	10	9
8/18/67	9/8/67	There Is A Mountain	Donovan	22	5
9/8/62	9/15/62	There Is No Greater Love	Wanderers	35	2
12/24/60	1/21/61	There She Goes	Jerry Wallace	22	6
1/15/68	2/19/68	There Was A Time	James Brown	8	7
8/12/66	9/9/66	There Will Never Be Another You	Chris Montez	24	6
2/17/69	2/17/69	There'll Come A Time	Betty Everett	36	2
2/3/67	3/3/67	There's A Kind Of Hush	Herman's Hermits	2	10
3/27/64	4/10/64	There's A Meetin' Tonight	Jo & Eddie	34	3
1/28/61	2/18/61	There's A Moon Out Tonight	Capris	7	7

Debut	Peak	Title	Artist	Pos	Wks
5/17/63	5/17/63	There's Another Place I Can't Go	Charlie Rich	40	1
1/6/69	2/3/69	There's Gonna Be A Showdown	Archie Bell & the Drells	20	6
11/25/66	12/30/66	There's Got To Be A Word	Innocence	18	7
12/16/61	12/30/61	There's No Other (Like My Baby)	Crystals	23	5
1/28/66	2/11/66	These Boots Are Made For Walkin'	Nancy Sinatra	2	10
4/14/69	5/19/69	These Eyes	Guess Who	3	10
12/8/69	12/22/69	These Eyes	Jr. Walker & the All-Stars	28	4
5/13/61	5/27/61	They Call Me The Fool	Nick Noble	27	3
4/15/61	4/15/61	They'll Never Take Her Love	Johnny Horton	30	1
7/15/66	7/22/66	They're Coming To Take Me Away, Ha-Haaa!	Napoleon XIV	6	2
12/2/61	12/2/61	They're Playing Our Song	Jamie Norton	34	1
7/21/62	8/18/62	Things	Bobby Darin	10	5
12/3/60	12/10/60	Things I Didn't Say	Jordan Brothers	33	2
9/15/67	9/15/67	Things I Should Have Said	Grass Roots	34	1
11/11/68	12/30/68	Things I'd Like To Say	New Colony Six	2	13
10/16/64	11/6/64	Things In This House, The	Bobby Darin	22	3
5/13/68	6/10/68	Think	Aretha Franklin	11	8
2/21/64	2/28/64	Think Nothing About It	Gene Chandler	32	2
5/7/65	5/7/65	Think Of The Good Times	Jay & the Americans	34	2
3/11/61	3/18/61	Think Twice	Brook Benton	20	3
11/15/63	11/15/63	31 Flavors	Shirelles	38	2
1/15/65	2/5/65	This Diamond Ring	Gary Lewis & the Playboys	1	10
7/1/66	7/22/66	This Door Swings Both Ways	Herman's Hermits	9	6
4/5/63	4/12/63	This Empty Place	Dionne Warwick	32	2
8/18/69	9/15/69	This Girl Is A Woman Now	Gary Puckett & the Union Gap	3	11
2/10/69	3/17/69	This Girl's In Love With You	Dionne Warwick	6	7
2/25/66	2/25/66	This Golden Ring	Fortunes	38	1
5/13/68	6/10/68	This Guy's In Love With You	Herb Alpert	1	11
8/16/63	8/30/63	This Is All I Ask	Tony Bennett	18	4
10/4/63	10/4/63	This Is My Prayer	Theola Kilgore	39	1
3/3/67	3/24/67	This Is My Song	Petula Clark	9	7

Debut	Peak	Title	Artist	Pos	Wks
4/19/63	5/10/63	This Little Girl	Dion	19	5
1/6/69	2/17/69	This Magic Moment	Jay & the Americans	6	9
3/18/66	3/18/66	This Old Heart Of Mine (Is Weak For You)	Isley Brothers	29	3
8/19/61	9/9/61	This Time	Troy Shondell	1	8
3/25/61	4/1/61	This World We Love In	Mina	12	6
5/17/63	6/7/63	Those Lazy-Hazy-Crazy Days Of Summer	Nat "King" Cole	17	4
6/3/61	7/1/61	Those Oldies But Goodies (Remind Me Of You)	Little Caesar & the Romans	9	6
9/30/68	10/28/68	Those Were The Days	Mary Hopkin	1	12
1/1/65	1/22/65	Thou Shalt Not Steal	Dick & Deedee	6	5
11/5/60	11/19/60	Thousand Stars, A	Kathy Young	1	12
10/14/60	10/14/60	Three Nights A Week	Fats Domino	23	2
5/15/64	6/19/64	Three Window Coupe	Rip Chords	10	8
4/16/65	5/7/65	Ticket To Ride	Beatles	2	8
6/28/63	7/19/63	Tie Me Kangaroo Down, Sport	Rolf Harris	4	6
6/16/62	6/23/62	Tiger Twist	Armando	31	2
3/25/68	5/13/68	Tighten Up	Archie Bell & the Drells	2	10
9/15/62	9/22/62	Tijuana Border	El Clod	27	2
11/11/61	12/30/61	'Til	Angels	17	5
11/11/68	12/16/68	Till	Vogues	11	8
8/4/62	8/25/62	Till Death Do Us Part	Bob Braun	13	5
3/25/66	4/15/66	Till The End Of The Day	Kinks	24	5
6/14/63	7/19/63	Till Then	Classics	5	7
9/8/62	9/8/62	Till There Was You	Valjean	34	1
8/4/69	8/11/69	Till You Get Enough	Watts 103rd St. Rhythm Band	31	3
5/20/61	5/20/61	Time	Jerry Jackson	39	1
11/4/66	12/2/66	Time After Time	Chris Montez	17	6
5/13/68	6/3/68	Time For Livin'	Association	25	5
9/16/68	10/7/68	Time Has Come Today	Chambers Brothers	13	6
11/6/64	11/27/64	Time Is On My Side	Rolling Stones	7	7
3/24/69	5/5/69	Time Is Tight	Booker T. & the MG's	10	9
1/27/69	3/10/69	Time Of The Season	Zombies	2	12
8/12/61	8/26/61	Time Was	Flamingos	31	3
3/25/66	4/22/66	Time Won't Let Me	Outsiders	4	8
11/4/66	12/2/66	Tiny Bubbles	Don Ho & the Aliis	24	6
8/5/66	8/12/66	Tip Of My Fingers, The	Eddy Arnold	31	3
5/27/68	6/10/68	Tip-Toe Thru The Tulips With Me	Tiny Tim	14	3
3/26/65	4/30/65	Tired Of Waiting For You	Kinks	2	8
2/10/62	3/3/62	To A Sleeping Beauty	Jimmy Dean	7	6
4/1/61	4/15/61	To Be Loved (Forever)	Pentagons	16	4

Debut	Peak	Title	Artist	Pos	Wks
10/29/60	12/3/60	To Each His Own	Platters	12	8
12/22/67	1/22/68	To Give (The Reason I Live)	Frankie Valli	7	8
7/9/65	7/16/65	To Know You Is To Love You	Peter & Gordon	33	4
4/7/69	4/28/69	To Know You Is To Love You	Bobby Vinton	24	5
11/24/62	12/15/62	To Love	Ral Donner	16	5
8/4/67	8/11/67	To Love Somebody	Bee Gees	31	3
3/17/62	4/7/62	(What A Sad Way) To Love Someone	Ral Donner	8	5
9/15/67	11/3/67	To Sir With Love	Lulu	1	13
9/9/68	9/9/68	To Wait For Love	Herb Alpert	36	1
9/25/64	10/23/64	Tobacco Road	Nashville Teens	4	8
5/8/64	5/22/64	Today	New Christy Minstrels	14	5
5/19/62	5/19/62	Today's Teardrops	Col. Joye & the Joy Boys	39	1
1/17/64	1/24/64	Today's Teardrops	Rick Nelson	33	2
7/15/61	8/19/61	Together	Connie Francis	8	7
4/8/66	4/15/66	Together Again	Ray Charles	36	3
3/29/63	5/3/63	Tom Cat	Rooftop Singers	13	7
5/14/65	6/4/65	Tommy	Reparata & the Delrons	22	5
8/30/63	9/20/63	Tommy Makes Girls Cry	Kelly Garrett	23	4
12/22/67	2/19/68	Tomorrow	Strawberry Alarm Clock	13	9
6/2/69	6/9/69	Tomorrow Tomorrow	Bee Gees	36	2
10/28/61	11/25/61	Tonight	Ferrante & Teicher	9	8
7/1/61	7/22/61	Tonight (Could Be The Night)	Velvets	12	6
4/15/61	5/20/61	Tonight I Fell In Love	Tokens	3	8
4/8/61	5/5/61	Tonight My Love, Tonight	Paul Anka	12	6
10/14/60	10/14/60	Tonight's The Night	Chiffons	24	1
4/28/69	6/16/69	Too Busy Thinking About My Baby	Marvin Gaye	7	12
5/5/67	5/5/67	Too Many Fish In The Sea & Three Little Fishes	Mitch Ryder & the Detroit Wheels	33	2
2/5/68	3/11/68	Too Much Talk	Paul Revere & the Raiders	8	8
12/9/68	1/13/69	Too Weak To Fight	Clarence Carter	17	7
3/4/61	3/25/61	Top Forty, News, Weather & Sports	Mark Dinning	13	5
9/15/62	9/29/62	Torture	Kris Jensen	23	3
7/1/61	7/29/61	Tossin' And Turnin'	Bobby Lewis	3	8
12/30/68	2/3/69	Touch Me	Doors	1	10
2/18/61	3/4/61	Touchables, The	Dickie Goodman	1	7
5/6/61	5/20/61	Touchables In Brooklyn, The	Dickie Goodman	16	4

Debut	Peak	Title	Artist	Pos	Wks
10/21/61	11/11/61	Tower Of Strength	Gene McDaniels	10	6
3/10/62	3/10/62	Town I Live In, The	McKinley Mitchell	36	2
12/30/61	1/20/62	Town Without Pity	Gene Pitney	1	9
10/11/63	10/25/63	Tra La La La Suzy	Dean & Jean	12	5
2/17/69	3/17/69	Traces	Classics IV featuring Dennis Yost	3	9
7/30/65	7/30/65	Tracker, The	Sir Douglas Quintet	26	1
7/23/65	7/30/65	Tracks Of My Tears, The	Miracles	37	2
6/2/67	7/7/67	Tracks Of My Tears, The	Johnny Rivers	9	8
9/8/69	10/27/69	Tracy	Cuff Links	2	11
4/22/61	5/27/61	Tragedy	Fleetwoods	4	7
8/11/69	9/22/69	Train, The	1910 Fruitgum Co.	9	10
7/15/66	7/29/66	Trains And Boats And Planes	Dionne Warwick	28	4
7/22/61	8/19/61	Transistor Sister	Freddy Cannon	18	6
4/14/67	4/21/67	Travlin' Man	Stevie Wonder	33	2
9/29/67	11/3/67	Treat Her Groovy	New Colony Six	12	7
9/3/65	10/15/65	Treat Her Right	Roy Head	14	8
9/13/63	10/4/63	Treat My Baby Good	Bobby Darin	20	4
5/13/61	6/3/61	Triangle	Janie Grant	5	9
1/12/63	1/19/63	Trouble In Mind	Aretha Franklin	24	3
1/12/63	1/12/63	Trouble Is My Middle Name	Bobby Vinton	27	2
8/20/65	9/24/65	Trouble With A Woman	Kip & Ken	9	8
7/21/69	8/11/69	True Grit	Glen Campbell	25	4
1/17/64	2/28/64	True Love Goes On And On	Burl Ives	21	7
7/19/63	8/9/63	True Love Never Runs Smooth	Gene Pitney	11	7
5/7/65	5/21/65	True Love Ways	Peter & Gordon	18	6
4/15/61	4/15/61	Trust In Me	Etta James	32	1
10/6/69	11/3/69	Try A Little Kindness	Glen Campbell	8	8
10/8/65	10/22/65	Try To Remember	Brothers Four	22	7
3/25/66	4/15/66	Try Too Hard	Dave Clark Five	16	7
8/5/68	9/9/68	Tuesday Afternoon (Forever Afternoon)	Moody Blues	12	8
1/27/62	2/24/62	Tuff	Ace Cannon	18	7
11/22/63	12/20/63	Turn Around	Dick & Deedee	12	6
10/28/61	12/2/61	Turn Around, Look At Me	Glen Campbell	13	7
6/17/68	7/22/68	Turn Around, Look At Me	Vogues	2	11
8/26/66	9/16/66	Turn-Down Day	Cyrkle	15	7
10/20/69	11/10/69	Turn On A Dream	Box Tops	23	5
12/23/61	1/6/62	Turn On Your Love Light	Bobby Bland	29	3
10/29/65	12/10/65	Turn! Turn! Turn! (To Everything There Is A Season)	Byrds	6	8
12/1/69	12/15/69	Turn! Turn! Turn!/To Everything There Is A Season	Judy Collins	32	3

Debut	Peak	Title	Artist	Pos	Wks
8/18/67	8/25/67	Twelve Thirty (Young Girls Are Coming To The Canyon)	Mamas & the Papas	23	5
11/1/63	12/6/63	Twenty Four Hours From Tulsa	Gene Pitney	2	10
3/22/63	3/29/63	Twenty Miles	Chubby Checker	33	2
3/3/69	3/31/69	Twenty-Five Miles	Edwin Starr	11	9
9/18/64	10/16/64	20-75	Willie Mitchell	20	4
12/22/62	12/22/62	Twilight Time	Andy Williams	40	1
1/1/65	1/29/65	Twine Time	Alvin Cash & the Crawlers	13	6
4/22/66	5/6/66	Twinkle Toes	Roy Orbison	23	5
12/16/61	1/20/62	Twist, The	Chubby Checker	2	11
3/6/64	3/13/64	Twist And Shout	Beatles	1	8
7/7/62	8/4/62	Twist And Shout	Isley Brothers	15	5
1/13/62	1/27/62	Twist-Her	Bill Black's Combo	25	3
4/14/62	4/28/62	Twist, Twist Senora	Gary U.S. Bonds	14	4
3/10/62	3/10/62	Twistin' At Woodchopper's Ball	Ronn Metcalfe	39	1
5/12/62	6/2/62	Twistin' Matilda	Jimmy Soul	10	6
2/24/62	2/24/62	Twistin' Postman	Marvelettes	39	1
3/3/62	3/31/62	Twistin' The Night Away	Sam Cooke	3	9
10/14/60	11/5/60	Twistin' U.S.A.	Danny & the Juniors	8	6
6/24/68	8/5/68	Two-Bit Manchild	Neil Diamond	24	7
4/19/63	5/10/63	Two Faces Have I	Lou Christie	1	9
6/16/67	6/30/67	Two In The Afternoon	Dino, Desi & Billy	29	3
4/19/63	5/10/63	Two Kinds Of Teardrops	Del Shannon	20	4
12/15/62	1/12/63	Two Lovers	Mary Wells	18	5
4/14/62	4/21/62	Two Of A Kind	Sue Thompson	29	2
1/4/63	2/8/63	2,000 Pound Bee (Part 2), The	Ventures	8	7
1/17/64	2/14/64	Um, Um, Um, Um, Um, Um	Major Lance	21	6
12/16/61	1/13/62	Unchain My Heart	Ray Charles	24	5
7/16/65	8/27/65	Unchained Melody	Righteous Brothers	13	7
11/1/63	11/15/63	Unchained Melody	Vito & the Salutations	32	3
1/10/64	1/10/64	Uncle Willie Time	Bobby Miller	36	1
7/17/64	8/28/64	Under The Boardwalk	Drifters	4	9
11/11/61	11/18/61	Under The Moon Of Love	Curtis Lee	29	2
12/24/65	1/7/66	Under Your Spell Again	Johnny Rivers	33	3
3/13/64	4/17/64	Understand Your Man	Johnny Cash	18	6
4/15/61	5/20/61	Underwater	Frogmen	2	9
3/25/68	4/29/68	Unicorn, The	Irish Rovers	7	9
11/19/65	12/3/65	Universal Coward	Jan Berry	35	3
10/15/65	10/29/65	Universal Soldier	Donovan	16	4

Debut	Peak	Title	Artist	Pos	Wks
10/23/64	11/13/64	Unless You Care	Terry Black	22	4
1/13/62	1/13/62	Unsquare Dance	Dave Brubeck Quartet	33	1
9/22/62	10/13/62	Untie Me	Tams	21	4
2/25/66	2/25/66	Up And Down	McCoys	34	1
11/10/69	12/15/69	Up On Cripple Creek	Band	11	10
2/26/68	4/1/68	Up On The Roof	Cryan' Shames	10	7
12/15/62	1/4/63	Up On The Roof	Drifters	5	8
5/26/67	6/16/67	Up-Up And Away	Fifth Dimension	5	6
2/17/67	3/17/67	Ups And Downs	Paul Revere & the Raiders	8	7
1/7/66	1/28/66	Uptight (Everything's Alright)	Stevie Wonder	24	7
3/31/62	5/12/62	Uptown	Crystals	5	9
3/25/68	5/13/68	U.S. Male	Elvis Presley	11	8
9/2/61	9/9/61	UT, The	Harry & the Marvels	37	2
1/21/61	2/11/61	Utopia	Frank Gari	14	6
8/4/62	8/18/62	Vacation	Connie Francis	27	3
2/26/68	3/25/68	Valleri	Monkees	1	8
1/29/68	3/4/68	Valley Of The Dolls, Theme From	Dionne Warwick	1	8
2/21/64	2/28/64	Vaya Con Dios	Drifters	24	3
12/1/69	1/5/70	Venus	Shocking Blue	1	12
9/1/62	9/29/62	Venus In Blue Jeans	Jimmy Clanton	2	8
4/14/62	5/19/62	Village Of Love	Nathaniel Mayer	2	9
5/26/62	6/16/62	Violetta	Ray Adams	6	6
9/15/67	9/29/67	Visit To A Sad Planet	Leonard Nimoy	22	3
11/24/62	11/24/62	Volare	Ace Cannon	38	1
10/14/60	10/14/60	Volare	Bobby Rydell	29	1
5/14/65	6/18/65	Voodoo Woman	Bobby Goldsboro	22	6
12/3/60	1/14/61	Wabash Blues	Viscounts	8	8
1/6/67	1/13/67	Wack Wack	Young-Holt Trio	32	3
8/5/66	8/12/66	Wade In The Water	Ramsey Lewis	26	3
6/23/62	7/14/62	Wah Watusi, The	Orlons	4	6
2/25/66	3/11/66	Wait A Minute	Tim Tam & the Turn-Ons	26	4
10/14/60	11/5/60	Wait For Me	Playmates	4	10
7/5/63	8/2/63	Wait Til My Bobby Gets Home	Darlene Love	13	5
12/22/69	1/26/70	Walk A Mile In My Shoes	Joe South	12	9
12/4/64	12/25/64	Walk Away	Matt Monro	19	6
2/5/68	2/26/68	Walk Away Renee	Four Tops	10	5
10/14/60	10/14/60	Walk- Don't Run	Ventures	21	1
7/31/64	8/28/64	Walk- Don't Run '64	Ventures	15	7

Debut	Peak	Title	Artist	Pos	Wks
5/21/65	6/18/65	Walk In The Black Forest, A	Horst Jankowski	5	9
1/19/63	2/15/63	Walk Like A Man	Four Seasons	1	10
11/11/61	12/16/61	Walk On By	Leroy Van Dyke	4	11
6/19/64	6/26/64	Walk On By	Dionne Warwick	22	3
6/2/62	6/2/62	Walk On The Wild Side—Part 1	Jimmy Smith	28	1
2/25/61	3/25/61	Walk Right Back	Everly Brothers	1	11
12/29/62	1/19/63	Walk Right In	Rooftop Singers	1	10
2/17/67	4/14/67	Walk Tall	Two Of Clubs	9	10
12/2/61	12/9/61	Walkin' Back To Happiness	Helen Shapiro	33	2
12/22/69	2/2/70	Walkin' In The Rain	Jay & the Americans	11	9
9/6/63	10/4/63	Walkin' Miracle, A	Essex	5	6
3/18/66	3/18/66	Walkin' My Cat Named Dog	Norma Tanega	35	2
11/6/64	11/27/64	Walking In The Rain	Ronettes	17	5
10/18/63	10/18/63	Walking Proud	Steve Lawrence	28	2
11/29/63	11/29/63	Walking The Dog	Rufus Thomas	30	2
1/6/62	2/10/62	Wanderer, The	Dion	2	10
9/15/62	10/20/62	Warmed Over Kisses (Left Over Love)	Brian Hyland	12	6
10/11/63	11/1/63	Washington Square	Village Stompers	1	9
10/20/67	11/24/67	Watch The Flowers Grow	Four Seasons	9	7
7/22/61	7/22/61	Watch Your Step	Bobby Parker	32	1
7/8/61	8/5/61	Water Boy	Don Shirley Trio	7	7
3/11/61	4/8/61	Water Was Red, The	Johnny Cymbal	12	6
4/5/63	4/26/63	Watermelon Man	Mongo Santamaria	20	5
2/4/61	2/25/61	Watusi, The	Vibrations	16	6
4/7/69	4/14/69	Way It Used To Be, The	Engelbert Humperdinck	31	3
3/13/64	3/27/64	Way You Do The Things You Do, The	Temptations	27	3
9/2/61	9/30/61	Way You Look Tonight, The	Lettermen	4	9
1/8/68	2/12/68	We Can Fly	Cowsills	18	6
12/10/65	12/24/65	We Can Work It Out	Beatles	1	11
5/12/62	6/2/62	We Girls	Jan Bradley	23	4
7/7/69	7/7/69	We Got More Soul	Dyke & the Blazers	35	2
8/27/65	10/29/65	We Gotta Get Out Of This Place	Animals	13	10
9/8/67	10/13/67	We Love You	Rolling Stones	16	7
3/6/64	3/20/64	We Love You, Beatles	Carefrees	9	5
9/11/64	10/9/64	We'll Sing In The Sunshine	Gale Garnett	7	9

Debut	Peak	Title	Artist	Pos	Wks
4/22/68	4/29/68	Wear It On Our Face	Dells	32	4
12/8/67	1/8/68	Wear Your Love Like Heaven	Donovan	23	4
9/29/69	11/3/69	Wedding Bell Blues	Fifth Dimension	2	12
11/20/64	1/1/65	Wedding, The	Julie Rogers	8	9
8/19/68	9/23/68	Weight, The	Jackie DeShannon	22	6
2/24/69	2/24/69	Weight, The	Aretha Franklin	34	2
7/21/62	7/28/62	Welcome Home Baby	Shirelles	31	2
12/2/61	12/9/61	Well, I Told You	Chantels	29	3
12/17/65	1/28/66	Well Respected Man, A	Kinks	16	7
5/19/62	6/16/62	West Of The Wall	Toni Fisher	9	7
2/17/67	3/24/67	Western Union	Five Americans	10	10
9/13/63	9/27/63	Wham!	Lonnie Mack	33	3
4/19/63	5/31/63	What A Guy	Raindrops	6	9
10/21/61	10/28/61	What A Party	Fats Domino	30	2
2/25/61	3/4/61	What A Price	Fats Domino	31	4
5/15/64	6/12/64	What A Sad Thing That Was	Jim & Monica	27	5
7/22/61	7/29/61	What A Sweet Thing That Was	Shirelles	33	2
12/2/61	12/16/61	What A Walk	Bobby Lewis	22	4
3/10/67	3/24/67	What A Woman In Love Won't Do	Sandy Posey	31	4
4/12/63	4/12/63	What Are Boys Made Of	Percells	38	1
7/23/65	8/6/65	What Are We Going To Do	Davy Jones	30	3
9/30/66	11/18/66	What Becomes Of The Brokenhearted	Jimmy Ruffin	11	9
10/15/65	10/15/65	What Color (Is A Man)	Bobby Vinton	40	1
5/7/65	5/7/65	What Do You Want With Me	Chad & Jeremy	23	3
2/8/63	3/1/63	What Does A Girl Do	Marcie Blane	12	4
6/2/69	7/21/69	What Does It Take (To Win Your Love)	Jr. Walker & the All-Stars	5	11
6/5/64	7/17/64	What Have I Got Of My Own	Trini Lopez	5	8
2/12/65	2/26/65	What Have They Done To The Rain	Searchers	29	4
9/22/62	10/6/62	What Kind Of Fool Am I	Sammy Davis, Jr.	18	4
1/31/64	1/31/64	What Kind Of Fool (Do You Think I Am)	Tams	33	3
8/18/69	9/1/69	What Kind Of Fool Do You Think I Am	Bill Deal & the Rhondels	17	7
8/25/62	9/15/62	What Kind Of Love Is This	Joey Dee & the Starliters	9	7
8/2/63	8/16/63	What Makes Little Girls Cry	Victorians	18	6
1/8/65	1/8/65	What Now	Gene Chandler	36	1

Debut	Peak	Title	Artist	Pos	Wks
3/11/66	3/11/66	What Now My Love	Herb Alpert & the Tijuana Brass	35	2
1/28/66	2/25/66	What Now My Love	Sonny & Cher	21	8
6/18/65	7/23/65	What The World Needs Now Is Love	Jackie DeShannon	4	8
12/22/62	1/19/63	What To Do With Laurie	Mike Clifford	10	6
1/25/63	2/15/63	What Will Mary Say	Johnny Mathis	9	7
12/15/69	12/22/69	What You Gave Me	Marvin Gaye & Tammi Terrell	32	2
1/27/62	2/3/62	What'd I Say	Calvin Carter	35	2
3/25/61	4/22/61	What'd I Say	Jerry Lee Lewis	13	7
5/22/64	5/29/64	What'd I Say	Elvis Presley	26	5
4/14/62	4/28/62	What'd I Say (Part 1)	Bobby Darin	26	4
7/28/62	8/11/62	What's A Matter Baby (Is It Hurting You)	Timi Yuro	18	4
12/13/63	1/24/64	What's Easy For Two Is So Hard For One	Mary Wells	5	7
6/4/65	6/4/65	What's He Doing In My World	Eddy Arnold	39	1
7/2/65	7/30/65	What's New Pussycat	Tom Jones	2	8
2/10/62	2/17/62	What's So Good About Good-By	Miracles	34	2
2/10/62	2/17/62	What's The Reason	Bobby Edwards	31	2
9/1/69	9/29/69	What's The Use Of Breaking Up	Jerry Butler	23	6
3/3/62	3/24/62	What's Your Name	Don & Juan	6	6
11/18/66	11/25/66	Wheel Of Hurt, The	Margaret Whiting	31	3
12/17/60	1/7/61	Wheels	String-A-Longs	8	9
6/28/63	7/26/63	When A Boy Falls In Love	Mel Carter	13	5
5/20/66	6/3/66	When A Man Loves A Woman	Percy Sledge	10	5
8/18/69	10/6/69	When I Die	Motherlode	15	9
12/9/61	12/16/61	When I Fall In Love	Lettermen	11	8
10/2/64	10/16/64	When I Grow Up (To Be A Man)	Beach Boys	19	3
4/9/65	4/9/65	When I'm Gone	Brenda Holloway	39	1
12/15/69	12/22/69	When Julie Comes Around	Cuff Links	34	3
2/4/66	2/25/66	When Liking Turns To Loving	Ronnie Dove	26	5
3/3/62	3/17/62	When My Little Girl Is Smiling	Drifters	29	3
12/16/61	1/20/62	When The Boy In Your Arms	Connie Francis	14	6
12/6/63	1/10/64	When The Lovelight Starts Shining Through His Eyes	Supremes	18	7
12/13/63	12/20/63	When The Wind Blows In Chicago	George McCurn	31	2

Debut	Peak	Title	Artist	Pos	Wks
11/13/64	11/13/64	When You Walk In The Room	Searchers	28	1
2/19/65	3/12/65	Whenever A Teenager Cries	Reparata & the Delrons	15	6
4/10/64	5/8/64	Whenever He Holds You	Bobby Goldsboro	9	7
9/24/65	10/8/65	Whenever You're Ready	Zombies	29	3
6/16/62	6/16/62	Where Are You	Dinah Washington	35	1
7/31/64	8/21/64	Where Did Our Love Go	Supremes	1	8
11/5/65	11/12/65	Where Do You Go	Cher	28	3
4/10/64	4/24/64	Where Does Love Go	Freddie Scott	21	3
3/3/62	3/31/62	Where Have All The Flowers Gone	Kingston Trio	8	7
10/15/65	10/29/65	Where Have All The Flowers Gone	Johnny Rivers	25	5
2/4/61	3/25/61	Where The Boys Are	Connie Francis	2	11
7/22/66	7/29/66	Where Were You When I Needed You	Grass Roots	27	3
12/23/66	2/3/67	Where Will The Words Come From	Gary Lewis & the Playboys	15	8
5/12/69	6/2/69	Where's The Playground Susie	Glen Campbell	29	4
1/10/64	1/10/64	Whispering	Nino Tempo & April Stevens	17	4
1/6/62	1/20/62	White Fang	Soupy Sales	31	3
3/27/64	5/1/64	White On White	Danny Williams	3	7
6/30/67	7/21/67	White Rabbit	Jefferson Airplane	6	7
9/23/68	10/28/68	White Room	Cream	4	10
3/17/62	3/24/62	White Rose Of Athens, The	David Carroll	29	2
7/14/67	8/4/67	Whiter Shade Of Pale, A	Procol Harum	11	6
7/16/65	8/6/65	Whittier Blvd.	Thee Midniters	20	5
10/28/66	11/11/66	Who Am I	Petula Clark	27	4
9/23/68	9/30/68	Who Is Gonna Love Me	Dionne Warwick	28	2
8/12/61	8/26/61	Who Put The Bomp (In The Bomp, Bomp, Bomp)	Barry Mann	4	6
1/25/63	2/8/63	Who Stole The Keeshka	Matys Brothers	17	5
12/8/67	1/8/68	Who Will Answer	Ed Ames	9	7
8/6/65	8/27/65	Who'll Be The Next In Line	Kinks	14	4
10/28/68	11/25/68	Who's Making Love	Johnnie Taylor	8	9
11/24/69	1/5/70	Whole Lotta Love	Led Zeppelin	2	11
10/15/60	10/15/60	Whole Lotta Shakin' Goin' On	Chubby Checker	33	1
1/22/65	2/5/65	Whose Heart Are You Breaking Tonight	Connie Francis	25	6

Debut	Peak	Title	Artist	Pos	Wks
2/15/63	3/1/63	Why Do Lovers Break Each Other's Heart	Bob B. Soxx & the Blue Jeans	22	3
9/6/63	9/6/63	Why Don't You Believe Me	Duprees	37	1
11/11/68	12/9/68	Wichita Lineman	Glen Campbell	8	11
9/29/67	9/29/67	Wide Trackin'	Fabulous Pack	36	1
11/3/62	12/1/62	Wiggle Wobble	Les Cooper	20	6
10/27/67	11/3/67	Wild Honey	Beach Boys	31	2
1/6/67	1/6/67	Wild Thing	Senator Bobby	30	2
6/17/66	7/15/66	Wild Thing	Troggs	1	9
1/25/63	3/15/63	Wild Weekend	Rebels	3	10
5/10/63	5/31/63	Wildwood Days	Bobby Rydell	15	6
11/3/62	11/17/62	Wildwood Flower	Nana Mouskouri	27	3
7/26/63	8/2/63	Will Power	Cookies	34	2
3/17/69	4/28/69	Will You Be Staying After Sunday	Peppermint Rainbow	14	9
2/19/68	3/11/68	Will You Love Me Tomorrow	Four Seasons	15	6
12/31/60	2/4/61	Will You Love Me Tomorrow	Shirelles	1	12
12/18/64	1/1/65	Willow Weep For Me	Chad & Jeremy	13	6
10/28/66	12/9/66	Winchester Cathedral	New Vaudeville Band	1	12
9/8/67	9/22/67	Windows Of The World, The	Dionne Warwick	27	3
5/19/67	6/2/67	Windy	Association	1	12
1/21/61	2/11/61	Wings Of A Dove	Ferlin Husky	15	8
12/15/69	1/26/70	Winter World Of Love	Engelbert Humperdinck	13	9
7/12/63	8/2/63	Wipe Out	Surfaris	1	8
8/19/66	9/16/66	Wipe Out	Surfaris	4	9
1/6/67	1/20/67	Wish Me A Rainbow	Gunter Kallman Chorus	38	4
5/8/64	5/8/64	Wish Someone Would Care	Irma Thomas	36	2
10/7/66	10/28/66	Wish You Were Here, Buddy	Pat Boone	18	6
7/3/64	8/14/64	Wishin' And Hopin'	Dusty Springfield	2	10
5/21/65	5/21/65	Wishing It Was You	Connie Francis	31	4
10/25/63	11/15/63	Witchcraft	Elvis Presley	13	4
8/5/66	9/9/66	With A Girl Like You	Troggs	15	7
6/2/69	6/16/69	With Pen In Hand	Vikki Carr	31	3
6/17/68	7/1/68	With Pen In Hand	Billy Vera	35	4
9/10/65	9/24/65	With These Hands	Tom Jones	16	4
12/22/69	2/2/70	Without Love (There Is Nothing)	Tom Jones	7	10
9/2/61	9/23/61	Without You	Johnny Tillotson	8	6
11/4/61	11/11/61	Without Your Love	Wendy Hill	28	3
11/29/63	12/27/63	Wives And Lovers	Jack Jones	13	5

Debut	Peak	Title	Artist	Pos	Wks
10/7/61	10/7/61	Wizard Of Love	Ly-Dells	32	1
5/26/62	7/14/62	Wolverton Mountain	Claude King	7	8
8/18/62	8/25/62	(I'm The Girl On) Wolverton Mountain	Jo Ann Campbell	25	4
2/18/66	3/11/66	Woman	Peter & Gordon	16	7
10/29/60	11/5/60	Woman From Liberia	Jimmie Rodgers	16	3
12/1/67	12/29/67	Woman, Woman	Gary Puckett & the Union Gap	3	11
11/11/61	11/11/61	Wonder Like You, A	Rick Nelson	7	2
7/28/62	8/25/62	Wonderful Dream, A	Majors	6	6
11/8/63	12/6/63	Wonderful Summer	Robin Ward	1	10
9/6/63	9/27/63	Wonderful! Wonderful!	Tymes	10	5
5/28/65	6/25/65	Wonderful World	Herman's Hermits	3	7
11/24/69	1/5/70	Wonderful World, Beautiful People	Jimmy Cliff	10	10
12/3/60	12/31/60	Wonderland By Night	Bert Kaempfert	1	13
7/22/61	8/19/61	Wooden Heart	Gus Backus	4	7
4/23/65	6/11/65	Wooly Bully	Sam the Sham & the Pharaohs	1	11
7/14/67	7/28/67	Words	Monkees	2	10
12/2/66	1/13/67	Words Of Love	Mamas & the Papas	5	10
3/1/63	4/5/63	Work Out	Michael Clark	24	4
8/11/62	9/8/62	Work Song	Don Caron	26	5
6/24/66	7/1/66	Work Song, The	Herb Alpert & the Tijuana Brass	31	2
10/20/62	11/3/62	Workin' For The Man	Roy Orbison	26	3
8/5/68	9/9/68	Workin' On A Groovy Thing	Patti Drew	17	6
7/14/69	8/11/69	Workin' On A Groovy Thing	Fifth Dimension	11	9
8/19/66	9/2/66	Working In The Coal Mine	Lee Dorsey	22	7
2/11/66	3/4/66	Working My Way Back To You	Four Seasons	12	8
7/21/62	7/21/62	Workout (Part 1)	Ricky Dee	36	1
5/8/64	5/22/64	World I Used To Know, The	Jimmie Rodgers	10	6
6/18/65	7/2/65	World Of Our Own, A	Seekers	23	3
8/20/65	10/1/65	World Through A Tear, The	Neil Sedaka	4	9
5/22/64	6/12/64	World Without Love, A	Peter & Gordon	1	9
5/22/64	5/29/64	World Without Love, A	Bobby Rydell	10	5
2/28/64	2/28/64	Worried Guy	Johnny Tillotson	25	2
7/31/64	8/14/64	Worry	Johnny Tillotson	19	5
12/16/68	1/27/69	Worst That Could Happen	Brooklyn Bridge	3	11
4/29/66	5/6/66	Would You Believe	Baker Knight	34	3
8/5/66	9/9/66	Wouldn't It Be Nice	Beach Boys	7	9
1/17/64	2/14/64	Wow Wow Wee (He's The Boy For Me)	Angels	14	6

Debut	Peak	Title	Artist	Pos	Wks
6/24/61	7/1/61	Writing On The Wall, The	Adam Wade	30	2
9/23/61	10/21/61	Ya Ya	Lee Dorsey	6	7
3/1/63	3/8/63	Yakety Sax	Boots Randolph	25	2
3/5/65	3/26/65	Yeh, Yeh	Georgie Fame	16	6
5/5/67	5/19/67	Yellow Balloon	Yellow Balloon	14	6
3/8/63	3/15/63	Yellow Bandana	Faron Young	28	2
6/3/61	7/8/61	Yellow Bird	Arthur Lyman Group	3	9
8/12/66	9/23/66	Yellow Submarine	Beatles	4	6
4/23/65	5/7/65	Yes It Is	Beatles	2	7
6/25/65	7/23/65	Yes, I'm Ready	Barbara Mason	19	6
6/3/68	6/17/68	Yester Love	Smokey Robinson & the Miracles	32	3
11/3/69	12/15/69	Yester-Me Yester-You Yesterday	Stevie Wonder	4	11
9/3/65	10/15/65	Yesterday	Beatles	1	11
11/10/67	12/1/67	Yesterday	Ray Charles	24	4
11/19/65	12/10/65	Yesterday	Al DeLory	25	4
11/15/63	11/29/63	Yesterday And You (Armen's Theme)	Bobby Vee	18	5
6/30/69	7/28/69	Yesterday, When I Was Young	Roy Clark	24	5
7/15/68	7/29/68	Yesterday's Dreams	Four Tops	26	3
4/17/64	5/22/64	Yesterday's Gone	Chad & Jeremy	3	9
10/13/62	10/13/62	Yield Not To Temptation	Bobby Bland	37	1
1/22/68	1/29/68	You	Marvin Gaye	36	3
6/10/61	7/1/61	You Always Hurt The One You Love	Clarence "Frogman" Henry	11	5
3/31/62	4/21/62	You Are Mine	Frankie Avalon	18	5
11/17/62	12/1/62	You Are My Sunshine	Ray Charles	21	4
12/24/60	1/21/61	You Are The Only One	Ricky Nelson	17	6
2/18/66	4/1/66	You Baby	Turtles	5	11
8/25/62	9/15/62	You Beat Me To The Punch	Mary Wells	23	4
7/28/62	9/8/62	You Belong To Me	Duprees	4	8
3/17/62	4/7/62	You Better Move On	Arthur Alexander	21	4
6/10/66	7/1/66	You Better Run	Young Rascals	21	6
11/3/67	12/8/67	You Better Sit Down Kids	Cher	3	10
4/22/61	5/6/61	You Can Depend On Me	Brenda Lee	28	4
2/25/61	3/18/61	You Can Have Her	Roy Hamilton	18	5
8/2/63	9/6/63	You Can Never Stop Me Loving You	Johnny Tillotson	9	8
4/17/64	4/17/64	You Can't Do That	Beatles	3	4
8/12/66	9/30/66	You Can't Hurry Love	Supremes	2	10

Debut	Peak	Title	Artist	Pos	Wks
8/4/62	8/18/62	You Can't Judge A Book By Its Cover	Bo Diddley	25	4
4/26/63	5/24/63	You Can't Sit Down	Dovells	3	10
6/17/61	7/15/61	You Can't Sit Down Part 2	Phil Upchurch Combo	11	6
12/10/65	1/14/66	You Didn't Have To Be So Nice	Lovin' Spoonful	11	8
11/1/63	11/22/63	You Don't Have To Be A Baby To Cry	Caravelles	8	6
6/3/66	7/1/66	You Don't Have To Say You Love Me	Dusty Springfield	5	9
7/28/62	8/18/62	You Don't Know Me	Ray Charles	14	5
11/3/67	11/3/67	You Don't Know Me	Elvis Presley	36	1
5/27/68	6/10/68	You Don't Know What You Mean To Me	Sam & Dave	35	3
7/15/61	8/12/61	You Don't Know What You've Got (Until You Lose It)	Ral Donner	3	8
5/6/66	5/20/66	You Don't Love Me	Gary Walker	23	4
3/22/63	3/22/63	You Don't Love Me Anymore (And I Can Tell)	Rick Nelson	31	2
1/3/64	1/24/64	You Don't Own Me	Lesley Gore	1	9
11/26/60	12/17/60	You Don't Want My Love	Andy Williams	16	7
3/3/69	3/31/69	You Gave Me A Mountain	Frankie Laine	26	5
1/27/67	2/24/67	You Got To Me	Neil Diamond	16	7
3/31/67	4/21/67	You Got What It Takes	Dave Clark Five	6	7
8/25/69	9/29/69	You, I	Rugbys	8	8
10/28/66	11/25/66	You Keep Me Hangin' On	Supremes	3	8
7/29/68	9/2/68	You Keep Me Hangin' On	Vanilla Fudge	5	8
9/22/67	10/20/67	You Keep Running Away	Four Tops	28	5
8/11/67	9/29/67	You Know What I Mean	Turtles	9	9
1/21/61	1/28/61	You Know You Belong To Someone Else	Fabian	37	2
10/25/63	10/25/63	You Lost The Sweetest Boy	Mary Wells	28	2
7/7/67	7/7/67	You Made Me Feel Like Someone	Babies	33	1
10/14/60	10/14/60	You Mean Everything To Me	Neil Sedaka	9	2
6/9/67	6/23/67	You Must Have Been A Beautiful Baby	Dave Clark Five	21	4
9/16/61	9/30/61	You Must Have Been A Beautiful Baby	Bobby Darin	7	6

Debut	Peak	Title	Artist	Pos	Wks
10/16/64	11/13/64	You Really Got Me	Kinks	2	8
10/23/64	11/20/64	You Should Have Seen The Way He Looked At Me	Dixie Cups	14	5
1/6/69	2/17/69	You Showed Me	Turtles	2	11
4/24/64	4/24/64	You Take One Step	Joe Henderson	39	1
4/14/62	5/5/62	You Talk About Love	Barbara George	33	4
10/14/60	10/14/60	You Talk Too Much	Joe Jones	4	3
7/16/65	7/30/65	You Tell Me Why	Beau Brummels	19	5
6/4/65	7/2/65	You Turn Me On (Turn On Song)	Ian Whitcomb & Bluesville	13	7
10/14/60	11/5/60	You Want Love	Clyde Stacy & the Nitecaps	12	4
4/23/65	5/7/65	You Were Made For Me	Freddie & the Dreamers	22	6
8/6/65	9/24/65	You Were On My Mind	We Five	2	11
5/14/65	5/28/65	You Were Only Fooling (While I Was Falling In Love)	Vic Damone	21	4
3/10/62	3/24/62	You Win Again	Fats Domino	32	3
5/27/66	6/17/66	You Wouldn't Listen	Ides Of March	7	9
7/22/66	8/5/66	You You You	Mel Carter	33	4
7/2/65	7/30/65	You'd Better Come Home	Petula Clark	17	5
7/7/62	7/21/62	You'll Lose A Good Thing	Barbara Lynn	23	4
9/29/69	10/13/69	You'll Never Walk Alone	Brooklyn Bridge	33	4
8/5/68	9/9/68	You're All I Need To Get By	Marvin Gaye & Tammi Terrell	14	7
3/31/67	4/21/67	You're Gonna Be Mine	New Colony Six	8	5
8/11/67	9/15/67	You're My Everything	Temptations	20	6
7/30/65	8/13/65	(Say) You're My Girl	Roy Orbison	18	3
11/1/63	11/15/63	You're No Good	Betty Everett	17	4
1/8/65	1/15/65	You're Nobody Till Somebody Loves You	Dean Martin	20	3
9/9/61	9/16/61	You're On Top	Untouchables	35	2
11/19/60	12/17/60	You're Sixteen	Johnny Burnette	5	9
9/24/65	10/29/65	You're The One	Vogues	2	9
6/21/63	6/28/63	You're The Only One	Connie Francis	28	2
1/8/65	1/8/65	You're The Only World I Know	Sonny James	28	2
10/7/61	11/4/61	You're The Reason	Bobby Edwards	3	9
1/19/63	3/1/63	You're The Reason I'm Living	Bobby Darin	6	8
2/4/61	2/11/61	You've Been Torturing Me	Four Young Men	27	2
1/29/68	3/11/68	You've Got To Be Loved	Montanas	11	8
10/15/65	10/29/65	You've Got To Hide Your Love Away	Silkie	15	4

Debut	Peak	Title	Artist	Pos	Wks
9/15/67	10/6/67	You've Got To Pay The Price	Al Kent	32	4
8/20/65	10/1/65	You've Got Your Troubles	Fortunes	12	9
12/25/64	1/22/65	You've Lost That Lovin' Feelin'	Righteous Brothers	2	10
10/13/69	11/3/69	You've Lost That Lovin' Feeling	Dionne Warwick	21	5
3/10/69	4/7/69	You've Made Me So Very Happy	Blood, Sweat & Tears	3	10
1/19/63	2/8/63	You've Really Got A Hold On Me	Miracles	28	4
4/15/68	4/15/68	You've Still Got A Place In My Heart	Dean Martin	35	3
3/8/63	4/26/63	Young And In Love	Dick & Deedee	11	8
5/20/68	6/24/68	Young Birds Fly	Cryan' Shames	15	6
3/4/68	4/1/68	Young Girl	Gary Puckett & the Union Gap	2	10
4/1/66	4/8/66	Young Love	Lesley Gore	38	3
3/8/63	4/12/63	Young Lovers	Paul & Paula	7	7
10/25/63	11/15/63	Young Wings Can Fly (Higher Than You Know)	Ruby & the Romantics	24	4
3/10/62	4/7/62	Young World	Rick Nelson	7	8
9/29/67	9/29/67	Younger Generation	Janis Ian	28	2
3/4/61	3/18/61	Your Friends	Dee Clark	31	3
7/28/69	9/15/69	Your Good Thing (Is About To End)	Lou Rawls	13	11
6/10/61	7/8/61	Your Graduation Means Goodbye	Cardigans	8	6
5/31/63	6/21/63	Your Graduation Means Goodbye	Cardigans	13	5
11/18/61	12/9/61	Your Ma Said You Cried In Your Sleep Last Night	Kenny Dino	13	6
8/4/62	9/1/62	Your Nose Is Gonna Grow	Johnny Crawford	8	6
6/7/63	6/14/63	Your Old Stand By	Mary Wells	28	3
12/10/60	1/14/61	Your Other Love	Flamingos	22	6
10/25/63	11/1/63	Your Other Love	Connie Francis	33	3
10/6/67	10/20/67	Your Precious Love	Marvin Gaye & Tammi Terrell	20	5
2/8/63	2/15/63	Your Used To Be	Brenda Lee	32	2
10/2/64	10/2/64	Yours	Lucille Starr	25	1
4/22/68	5/20/68	Yummy Yummy Yummy	Ohio Express	1	11
12/29/67	1/15/68	Zabadak	Dave Dee, Dozy, Beaky, Mick & Tich	34	3
12/15/62	1/12/63	Zero-Zero	Lawrence Welk	20	6
10/29/60	10/29/60	Zing! Went The Strings Of My Heart	Demensions	39	1
11/10/62	12/8/62	Zip-A-Dee-Doo-Dah	Bob B. Soxx & the Blue Jeans	13	7
8/4/67	9/1/67	Zip Code	Five Americans	12	7
1/7/66	1/28/66	Zorba The Greek	Herb Alpert & the Tijuana Brass	10	5

YEARLY TOP 40 CHARTS

Top Hits of 1960:

Since the Silver Dollar Survey didn't start until October 14, 1960, here are the Top Ten hits from that date through the end of 1960:

1.	Wonderland By Night	Bert Kaempfert
2.	Are You Lonesome To-night	Elvis Presley
3.	Exodus	Ferrante & Teicher
4.	Poetry In Motion	Johnny Tillotson
5.	Ruby Duby Du	Tobin Mathews & Co.
6.	A Thousand Stars	Kathy Young & the Innocents
7.	Stay	Maurice Williams & the Zodiacs
8.	Shortnin' Bread	Paul Chaplain & his Emeralds
9.	Save The Last Dance For Me	Drifters
10.	Mr. Custer	Larry Verne

Top Hits of 1961:

1.	Michael	Highwaymen
2.	Quarter To Three	Gary U.S. Bonds
3.	The Lion Sleeps Tonight	Tokens
4.	Runaround Sue	Dion
5.	Runaway	Del Shannon
6.	Blue Moon	Marcels
7.	Let There Be Drums	Sandy Nelson
8.	Hello Mary Lou	Ricky Nelson
9.	Calcutta	Lawrence Welk
10.	Goodbye Cruel World	James Darren
11.	Take Good Care Of My Baby	Bobby Vee
12.	This Time	Troy Shondell
13.	The Touchables	Dickie Goodman
14.	Will You Love Me Tomorrow	Shirelles
15.	Walk Right Back	Everly Brothers
16.	Apache	Jorgen Ingmann
17.	Mexico	Bob Moore
18.	Don't Worry	Marty Robbins
19.	Let's Get Together	Hayley Mills
20.	The Mountain's High	Dick & DeeDee
21.	Big Bad John	Jimmy Dean
22.	Running Scared	Roy Orbison
23.	Hats Off To Larry	Del Shannon
24.	Let Me Belong To You	Brian Hyland
25.	Where The Boys Are	Connie Francis
26.	Run To Him	Bobby Vee
27.	Raindrops	Dee Clark
28.	Shop Around	Miracles
29.	I've Told Every Little Star	Linda Scott

30.	I Love How You Love Me	Paris Sisters
31.	Underwater	Frogmen
32.	Moody River	Pat Boone
33.	Let's Twist Again	Chubby Checker
34.	Girl Of My Best Friend	Ral Donner
35.	Temptation	Everly Brothers
36.	Moon River	Henry Mancini
37.	Yellow Bird	Arthur Lyman Group
38.	Asia Minor	Kokomo
39.	Baby Sittin' Boogie	Buzz Clifford
40.	Barbara-Ann	Regents

Top Hits of 1962:

1.	Sherry	Four Seasons
2.	I Can't Stop Loving You	Ray Charles
3.	Hey! Baby	Bruce Channel
4.	Johnny Angel	Shelley Fabares
5.	Go Away Little Girl	Steve Lawrence
6.	Telstar	Tornadoes
7.	Roses Are Red (My Love)	Bobby Vinton
8.	Big Girls Don't Cry	Four Seasons
9.	Duke Of Earl	Gene Chandler
10.	Breaking Up Is Hard To Do	Neil Sedaka
11.	Town Without Pity	Gene Pitney
12.	Bobby's Girl	Marcie Blane
13.	Stranger On The Shore	Mr. Acker Bilk
14.	Sealed With A Kiss	Brian Hyland
15.	Let's Dance	Chris Montez
16.	She Cried	Jay & the Americans
17.	The Stripper	David Rose
18.	Soldier Boy	Shirelles
19.	Monster Mash	Bobby "Boris" Pickett
20.	Sheila	Tommy Roe
21.	Patches	Dickey Lee
22.	Mashed Potato Time	Dee Dee Sharp
23.	The Twist	Chubby Checker
24.	He's A Rebel	Crystals
25.	The Wanderer	Dion
26.	The Peppermint Twist- Part I	Joey Dee & the Starliters
27.	The Loco-Motion	Little Eva
28.	Midnight In Moscow	Kenny Ball & his Jazzmen
29.	Good Luck Charm	Elvis Presley

30.	Return to Sender	Elvis Presley
31.	Only Love Can Break A Heart	Gene Pitney
32.	Village Of Love	Nathaniel Mayer
33.	Palisades Park	Freddy Cannon
34.	Venus In Blue Jeans	Jimmy Clanton
35.	If I Had A Hammer (The Hammer Song)	Peter, Paul & Mary
36.	(The Man Who Shot) Liberty Valence	Gene Pitney
37.	Twistin' The Night Away	Sam Cooke
38.	Old Rivers	Walter Brennan
39.	I Love You The Way You Are	Bobby Vinton
40.	Norman	Sue Thompson

Top Hits of 1963:

1. My Boyfriend's Back — Angels
2. Sugar Shack — Jimmy Gilmer & the Fireballs
3. He's So Fine — Chiffons
4. Walk Like A Man — Four Seasons
5. Surf City — Jan & Dean
6. Easier Said Than Done — Essex
7. Wonderful Summer — Robin Ward
8. Dominique — Singing Nun
9. Blue Velvet — Bobby Vinton
10. Sukiyaki — Kyu Sakamoto
11. Hey Paula — Paul & Paula
12. The End Of The World — Skeeter Davis
13. Walk Right In — Rooftop Singers
14. Two Faces Have I — Lou Christie
15. I Will Follow Him — Little Peggy March
16. Washington Square — Village Stompers
17. Pipeline — Chantays
18. It's My Party — Lesley Gore
19. Deep Purple — Nino Tempo & April Stevens
20. Wipe Out — Surfaris
21. Hello Muddah, Hello Faddah — Alan Sherman
22. If You Wanna Be Happy — Jimmy Soul
23. The Night Has A Thousand Eyes — Bobby Vee
24. I'm Leaving It Up To You — Dale & Grace
25. Ruby Baby — Dion
26. Rhythm Of The Rain — Cascades
27. She's A Fool — Lesley Gore
28. Twenty Four Hours From Tulsa — Gene Pitney
29. Louie Louie — Kingsmen

30.	Maria Elena	Los Indios Tabajaras
31.	Be My Baby	Ronettes
32.	Martian Hop	Ran-Dells
33.	Sally Go Round The Roses	Jaynetts
34.	Shut Down	Beach Boys
35.	So Much In Love	Tymes
36.	Wild Weekend	Rebels
37.	Candy Girl	Four Seasons
38.	You Can't Sit Down	Dovells
39.	Da Doo Ron Ron	Crystals
40.	Drip Drop	Dion

Top Hits of 1964:

1.	Oh, Pretty Woman	Roy Orbison
2.	I Want To Hold Your Hand	Beatles
3.	Love Me Do	Beatles
4.	P.S. I Love You	Beatles
5.	Twist And Shout	Beatles
6.	Suspicion	Terry Stafford
7.	I Feel Fine/She's A Woman	Beatles
8.	Where Did Our Love Go	Supremes
9.	She's Not There	Zombies
10.	I'm Into Something Good	Herman's Hermits
11.	There! I've Said It Again	Bobby Vinton
12.	I Get Around	Beach Boys
13.	Little Children/Bad To Me	Billy J. Kramer & the Dakotas
14.	A Hard Day's Night/I Should Have Known Better	Beatles
15.	Rag Doll	Four Seasons
16.	Leader Of The Pack	Shangri-Las
17.	Dead Man's Curve/New Girl In School	Jan & Dean
18.	She Loves You	Beatles
19.	Have I The Right	Honeycombs
20.	Don't Let The Rain Come Down	Serendipity Singers
21.	Drag City	Jan & Dean
22.	House Of The Rising Sun	Animals
23.	Everybody Loves Somebody	Dean Martin
24.	A World Without Love	Peter & Gordon
25.	You Don't Own Me	Lesley Gore
26.	Do Wah Diddy Diddy	Manfred Mann
27.	Mr. Lonely	Bobby Vinton
28.	Glad All Over	Dave Clark Five
29.	Wishin' And Hopin'	Dusty Springfield

30.	Ringo	Lorne Greene
31.	Because	Dave Clark Five
32.	You Really Got Me	Kinks
33.	Dawn (Go Away)	Four Seasons
34.	Please Please Me	Beatles
35.	Can't You See That She's Mine	Dave Clark Five
36.	Remember (Walkin' In The Sand)	Shangri-Las
37.	Last Kiss	J. Frank Wilson & the Cavaliers
38.	Chapel Of Love	Dixie Cups
39.	Come A Little Bit Closer	Jay & the Americans
40.	Can't Buy Me Love	Beatles

Top Hits of 1965:

1. (I Can't Get No) Satisfaction — Rolling Stones
2. I Got You Babe — Sonny & Cher
3. We Can Work It Out/Day Tripper — Beatles
4. Mrs. Brown You've Got A Lovely Daughter — Herman's Hermits
5. Eight Days a Week/I Don't Want To Spoil The Party — Beatles
6. Downtown — Petula Clark
7. This Diamond Ring — Gary Lewis & the Playboys
8. Hang on Sloopy — McCoys
9. Silhouettes — Herman's Hermits
10. I'm Telling You Now — Freddie & the Dreamers
11. Let's Hang On — Four Seasons
12. Help — Beatles
13. Yesterday — Beatles
14. Keep On Dancing — Gentrys
15. Five O'Clock World — Vogues
16. Get Off Of My Cloud — Rolling Stones
17. Mr. Tambourine Man — Byrds
18. I Can't Help Myself — Four Tops
19. Wooly Bully — Sam the Sham & the Pharaohs
20. Love Potion Number Nine — Searchers
21. 1-2-3 — Len Barry
22. Ferry Cross The Mersey — Gerry & the Pacemakers
23. You've Lost That Lovin' Feelin' — Righteous Brothers
24. Game Of Love — Wayne Fontana & the Mindbenders
25. I Know A Place — Petula Clark
26. I'm Henry VIII, I Am — Herman's Hermits
27. You Were On My Mind — We 5
28. Come See About Me — Supremes

29.	A Lover's Concerto	Toys
30.	The "In" Crowd	Ramsey Lewis Trio
31.	Stop! In The Name Of Love	Supremes
32.	Help Me, Rhonda	Beach Boys
33.	Over And Over	Dave Clark Five
34.	You're The One	Vogues
35.	Just A Little Bit Better	Herman's Hermits
36.	Ticket To Ride/Yes It Is	Beatles
37.	What's New Pussycat	Tom Jones
38.	Tired Of Waiting For You	Kinks
39.	Look Through Any Window	Hollies
40.	Cara, Mia	Jay & the Americans

Top Hits of 1966:

1.	I'm A Believer/(I'm Not Your) Steppin' Stone	Monkees
2.	Cherish	Association
3.	California Dreamin'	Mamas & the Papas
4.	Kicks	Paul Revere & the Raiders
5.	Good Vibrations	Beach Boys
6.	Hanky Panky	Tommy James & the Shondells
7.	Lightnin' Strikes	Lou Christie
8.	Winchester Cathedral	New Vaudeville Band
9.	Last Train To Clarksville	Monkees
10.	Monday, Monday	Mamas & the Papas
11.	Summer In The City	Lovin' Spoonful
12.	Paint It, Black	Rolling Stones
13.	Wild Thing	Troggs
14.	Gloria	Shadows of Knight
15.	96 Tears	? & the Mysterians
16.	Bus Stop	Hollies
17.	The Sounds Of Silence	Simon & Garfunkel
18.	Sunshine Superman	Donovan
19.	These Boots Are Made For Walkin'	Nancy Sinatra
20.	Snoopy vs. The Red Baron	Royal Guardsmen
21.	A Groovy Kind Of Love	Mindbenders
22.	Secret Agent Man	Johnny Rivers
23.	Kind Of A Drag	Buckinghams
24.	You Can't Hurry Love	Supremes
25.	Reach Out I'll Be There	Four Tops
26.	Strangers In The Night	Frank Sinatra
27.	Mellow Yellow	Donovan
28.	I Confess	New Colony Six
29.	The Pied Piper	Crispian St. Peter

30.	Cherry, Cherry	Neil Diamond
31.	The Ballad Of The Green Berets	S/Sgt. Barry Sadler
32.	Paperback Writer/Rain	Beatles
33.	Barbara Ann	Beach Boys
34.	Say I Am (What I Am)	Tommy James & the Shondells
35.	Good Lovin'	Young Rascals
36.	Eleanor Rigby	Beatles
37.	Hungry	Paul Revere & the Raiders
38.	Bang Bang (My Baby Shot Me Down)	Cher
39.	I Am A Rock	Simon & Garfunkel
40.	You Keep Me Hangin' On	Supremes

Top Hits of 1967:

1.	The Letter	Box Tops
2.	Windy	Association
3.	I Think We're Alone Now	Tommy James & the Shondells
4.	It Could Be We're In Love	Cryan' Shames
5.	To Sir With Love	Lulu
6.	Daydream Believer	Monkees
7.	Can't Take My Eyes Off You	Frankie Valli
8.	Judy In Disguise (With Glasses)	John Fred & his Playboy Band
9.	Ode To Billie Joe	Bobbie Gentry
10.	Don't You Care	Buckinghams
11.	Happy Together	Turtles
12.	A Little Bit Me, A Little Bit You	Monkees
13.	Little Bit O' Soul	Music Explosion
14.	Somebody To Love	Jefferson Airplane
15.	Hello Goodbye	Beatles
16.	Pushin' Too Hard	Seeds
17.	Mirage	Tommy James & the Shondells
18.	The Rain, The Park And Other Things	Cowsills
19.	Come On Down To My Boat	Every Mother's Son
20.	Never My Love	Association
21.	Let It Out (Let It All Hang Out)	Hombres
22.	Light My Fire	Doors
23.	Georgy Girl	Seekers
24.	Come Back When You Grow Up	Bobby Vee
25.	There's A Kind of Hush	Herman's Hermits
26.	I Got Rhythm	Happenings
27.	Incense And Peppermints	Strawberry Alarm Clock
28.	On A Carousel	Hollies

29.	Something Stupid	Frank & Nancy Sinatra
30.	Pleasant Valley Sunday/Words	Monkees
31.	Love You So Much	New Colony Six
32.	Ruby Tuesday	Rolling Stones
33.	How Can I Be Sure	Young Rascals
34.	Little Ole Man (Uptight-Everything's Alright)	Bill Cosby
35.	Woman Woman	Gary Puckett & the Union Gap
36.	You Better Sit Down Kids	Cher
37.	Groovin'	Young Rascals
38.	Here Comes My Baby	Tremeloes
39.	Dedicated To The One I Love	Mamas & the Papas
40.	For What It's Worth (Stop, Hey What's That Sound)	Buffalo Springfield

Top Hits of 1968:

1. I Heard It Through The Grapevine — Marvin Gaye
2. Love Is Blue — Paul Mauriat
3. Jumpin' Jack Flash — Rolling Stones
4. Honey — Bobby Goldsboro
5. Love Child — Diana Ross & the Supremes
6. Bend Me, Shape Me — American Breed
7. This Guy's In Love With You — Herb Alpert
8. Yummy Yummy Yummy — Ohio Express
9. Fire — Crazy World of Arthur Brown
10. People Got To Be Free — Rascals
11. Those Were The Days — Mary Hopkin
12. Mony Mony — Tommy James & the Shondells
13. Hello, I Love You — Doors
14. Over You — Gary Puckett & the Union Gap
15. Valleri/Tapioca Tundra — Monkees
16. Harper Valley P.T.A. — Jeannie C. Riley
17. Hey Jude — Beatles
18. Born To Be Wild — Steppenwolf
19. Abraham, Martin And John — Dion
20. I Will Always Think About You — New Colony Six
21. Lady Madonna — Beatles
22. (Theme From) Valley Of The Dolls — Dionne Warwick
23. 1,2,3, Red Light — 1910 Fruitgum Co.
24. Midnight Confessions — Grass Roots
25. Turn Around, Look At Me — Vogues
26. Young Girl — Gary Puckett & the Union Gap
27. I Love How You Love Me — Bobby Vinton
28. I Wonder What She's Doing Tonite — Tommy Boyce & Bobby Hart

29.	Mrs. Robinson	Simon & Garfunkel
30.	I Need Love	Third Booth
31.	Angel Of The Morning	Merrilee Rush & the Turnabouts
32.	Magic Carpet Ride	Steppenwolf
33.	Things I'd Like To Say	New Colony Six
34.	Green Tambourine	Lemon Pipers
35.	For Once In My Life	Stevie Wonder
36.	(Sittin' On) The Dock Of The Bay	Otis Redding
37.	Cry Like A Baby	Box Tops
38.	Simon Says	1910 Fruitgum Co.
39.	Do It Again	Beach Boys
40.	Tighten Up	Archie Bell & the Drells

Top Hits of 1969:

1. Honky Tonk Women — Rolling Stones
2. Come Together/Something — Beatles
3. Someday We'll Be Together — Diana Ross & the Supremes
4. Get Back — Beatles
5. Aquarius/Let The Sunshine In — Fifth Dimension
6. Sugar Sugar — Archies
7. Everyday People/Sing A Simple Song — Sly & the Family Stone
8. Crimson And Clover — Tommy James & the Shondells
9. Dizzy — Tommy Roe
10. Suspicious Minds — Elvis Presley
11. It's Your Thing — Isley Brothers
12. One — Three Dog Night
13. In The Year 2525 — Zager & Evans
14. Little Woman — Bobby Sherman
15. Na Na Hey Hey Kiss Him Goodbye — Steam
16. Crystal Blue Persuasion — Tommy James & the Shondells
17. Hair — Cowsills
18. I'm Gonna Make You Love Me — Supremes & the Temptations
19. Easy To Be Hard — Three Dog Night
20. Love Theme From Romeo And Juliet — Henry Mancini
21. Bad Moon Rising — Creedence Clearwater Revival
22. The Boxer — Simon & Garfunkel
23. Touch Me — Doors
24. I Can't Get Next To You — Temptations
25. Hurt So Bad — Lettermen
26. Holly Holy — Neil Diamond
27. Wedding Bell Blues — Fifth Dimension

28.	Time Of The Season	Zombies
29.	You Showed Me	Turtles
30.	Love (Can Make You Happy)	Mercy
31.	Raindrops Keep Falling On My Head	B.J. Thomas
32.	I Want You Back	Jackson 5
33.	Tracy	Cuff Links
34.	Spinning Wheel	Blood, Sweat & Tears
35.	I'm Gonna Make You Mine	Lou Christie
36.	Ramblin' Gamblin' Man	Bob Seger System
37.	Birthday	Underground Sunshine
38.	Gitarzan	Ray Stevens
39.	Morning Girl	Neon Philharmonic
40.	Good Morning Starshine	Oliver

Top 40 Songs Of The 60's

1. I'm a Believer/(I'm Not Your) Steppin' Stone — Monkees
2. The Letter — Box Tops
3. Oh, Pretty Woman — Roy Orbison
4. Cherish — Association
5. I Want To Hold Your Hand — Beatles
6. Windy — Association
7. Honky Tonk Women — Rolling Stones
8. Michael — Highwaymen
9. (I Can't Get No) Satisfaction — Rolling Stones
10. Quarter To Three — Gary U.S. Bonds
11. I Think We're Alone Now — Tommy James & the Shondells
12. My Boyfriend's Back — Angels
13. Sherry — Four Seasons
14. Come Together/Something — Beatles
15. Someday We'll Be Together — Diana Ross & the Supremes
16. California Dreamin' — Mamas & the Papas
17. I Heard It Through The Grapevine — Marvin Gaye
18. Wonderland By Night — Bert Kaempfert
19. Kicks — Paul Revere & the Raiders
20. It Could Be We're In Love — Cryan' Shames
21. Love Is Blue — Paul Mauriat
22. Sugar Shack — Jimmy Gilmer & the Fireballs
23. Get Back — Beatles
24. The Lion Sleeps Tonight — Tokens
25. We Can Work It Out/Day Tripper — Beatles
26. I Got You Babe — Sonny & Cher
27. Runaround Sue — Dion
28. Good Vibrations — Beach Boys
29. Jumpin' Jack Flash — Rolling Stones

30.	I Can't Stop Loving You	Ray Charles
31.	Honey	Bobby Goldsboro
32.	Runaway	Del Shannon
33.	He's So Fine	Chiffons
34.	Hey! Baby	Bruce Channel
35.	Mrs. Brown You've Got A Lovely Daughter	Herman's Hermits
36.	Johnny Angel	Shelley Fabares
37.	Go Away Little Girl	Steve Lawrence
38.	Love Me Do	Beatles
39.	Blue Moon	Marcels
40.	Hanky Panky	Tommy James & the Shondells

1964 Rhythm & Blues Charts

From September 18 to December 25, 1964, a separate "R&B Music Survey" took the place of the last ten songs on the Silver Dollar Survey. Here are the Artists and songs listed during that 17-week period:

Artist	Title	Debut	Peak	Pos	Wks
Artistics	Gotta Get My Hands On Some Lovin'	9/18/64	9/18/64	10	1
Betters, Harold	Do Anything You Wanna (Part 2)	10/9/64	10/9/64	8	1
Bland, Bobby	Ain't Doing Too Bad (Part 1)	10/23/64	11/6/64	1	6
Brown, Maxine	Oh No Not My Baby	10/30/64	11/6/64	2	5
Butler, Jerry	I Stand Accused	9/18/64	9/25/64	5	3
Butler, Jerry & Betty Everett	Let It Be Me	9/25/64	10/9/64	3	4
Cash, Alvin & the Crawlers	Twine Time	12/18/64	12/18/64	1	2
Chandler, Gene	Bless Our Love	10/2/64	10/23/64	2	5
	What Now	11/20/64	12/11/64	5	6
Collier, Mitty	I Had A Talk With My Man	10/16/64	10/16/64	2	4
Cooke, Sam	That's Where It's At	11/6/64	11/6/64	10	1
Covay, Don	Mercy, Mercy	9/18/64	9/18/64	1	3
Four Tops	Baby I Need Your Loving	9/18/64	9/18/64	7	2
Franklin, Aretha	Runnin' Out Of Fools	10/9/64	10/16/64	6	2
Gaye, Marvin	Baby Don't You Do It	10/9/64	11/6/64	3	6
	How Sweet It Is To Be Loved By You	12/18/64	12/25/64	5	2
Hinton, Joe	Funny	9/18/64	9/25/64	1	4

Artist	Title	Debut	Peak	Pos	Wks
Hughes, Jimmy	Steal Away	9/18/64	9/18/64	5	2
Impressions	You Must Believe Me	9/25/64	10/2/64	1	8
	Amen	11/27/64	12/18/64	4	4
	Long, Long Winter	12/11/64	12/18/64	4	3
Jackson, Chuck	Since I Don't Have You	11/20/64	11/27/64	5	3
Jackson, Walter	It's All Over	11/6/64	12/11/64	2	5
King, B. B.	Beautician Blues	10/23/64	10/30/64	2	5
Lance, Major	Rhythm	9/18/64	9/18/64	3	7
	Sometimes I Wonder	12/11/64	12/18/64	2	2
Larks	The Jerk	12/11/64	12/25/64	2	3
Little Anthony & the Imperials	Goin' Out Of My Head	12/4/64	12/4/64	10	1
Little Milton	Sacrifice	9/18/64	9/18/64	4	1
	Blind Man	12/18/64	12/25/64	3	2
Martha & the Vandellas	Dancing In The Street	9/25/64	9/25/64	6	1
	Wild One	12/18/64	12/25/64	8	2
Marvelettes	Too Many Fish In The Sea	11/20/64	11/27/64	2	6
Miracles	That's What Love Is Made Of	10/16/64	10/30/64	3	5
Radiants	Voice Your Choice	11/27/64	12/4/64	1	5
Redding, Otis	Security	9/18/64	9/18/64	6	1
Simon, Joe	Adorable One	11/6/64	11/27/64	1	6
Smith, Jimmy	Prayer Meetin'	10/9/64	10/9/64	6	2
Temptations	Girl (Why You Wanna Make Me Blue)	9/25/64	10/2/64	3	5
Tex, Joe	Hold What You've Got	12/25/64	12/25/64	10	1
Vernon & Jewel	Lonely Lonely Nights	11/13/64	11/20/64	5	3
Warwick, Dionne	You'll Never Get To Heaven (If You Break My Heart	9/18/64	9/18/64	8	3
	Reach Out For Me	12/11/64	12/11/64	10	1
Wells, Mary	Ain't It The Truth	11/13/64	12/4/64	3	5
Wright, O.V.	That's How Strong Love Is	10/23/64	10/30/64	9	2

About the Author

Ron Smith is a 30-year veteran of oldies radio as a disk jockey, program and music director. He served for more than eight years as Music Director of WJMK-FM, Oldies 104.3 in Chicago and was Senior Music Programmer of Internet Radio for RadioWave.com in the Windy City. For over six years, he has delighted fans of 50s, 60s and 70s music with the Internet's premiere oldies Web site— www.oldiesmusic.com.

He resides in suburban Chicago with his vast music and book libraries.

Printed in the United States
40765LVS00006B/16